MEDIEVAL TOWNS

Studies in the Archaeology of Medieval Europe
Edited by: John Schofield

This series brings together new archaeological studies of medieval Europe (1100 to 1600). We want to describe life in medieval Europe and to show how archaeology does this. It is a new form of history. There will be studies of regions such as the North Sea, of subjects such as towns or castles, and of relevant areas of study such as ceramics. To what extent was Europe a cultural, economic and religious entity? Understanding leads to appreciation, and that leads to a concern for conservation of our common European past. The authors will be drawn from Britain and other European countries.

Recent and forthcoming books in the series:

Castles and Landscapes
Power, Community and Fortification in Medieval England
O.H. Creighton

Medieval Europe Around the North Sea
Brian Ayers

MEDIEVAL TOWNS

*The Archaeology of British Towns
in Their European Setting*

JOHN SCHOFIELD and ALAN VINCE

LONDON   OAKVILLE

Published by

UK: Equinox Publishing Ltd
Unit 6, The Village,
101 Amies St.,
London, SW11 2JW

US: DBBC,
28 Main Street,
Oakville, CT 06779

www.equinoxpub.com

First published in hardback by Continuum International Publishing Group Ltd in 2003.
This paperback edition with enhanced photographs published by Equinox Publishing
Ltd. in 2005 by arrangement with Continuum International Publishing Group Ltd.

British Library Cataloguing-in-Publication Data
A catalogue record for this book is available from the British Library.

ISBN 1 84553 038 1 (paperback)

Printed and bound in Great Britain by Antony Rowe, Chippenham, Wiltshire

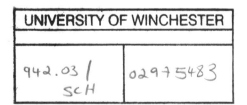

Contents

Foreword

John Schofield, series editor

This series brings together new archaeological studies of medieval Europe. We want to describe and explain life in medieval Europe between the late eleventh and seventeenth centuries, and to show how archaeology does this. It is a new form of history.

The series sets out to be a major review of recent achievements and of future directions for the subject. Each book is based on new archaeological research, often arising out of work made necessary by urban and rural redevelopment. Each volume will assess new and profitable methods of analysis, encourage debate and not avoid controversy.

The choice of subjects is deliberately wide. There will be studies of regions of Europe, such as individual countries, or areas such as the North Sea where a geographical or cultural zone will provide the scope or framework. Others will be of features of medieval life, such as towns or castles in their landscapes. A third kind will review recent work on certain classes of artefacts, to show how archaeological work is revolutionizing our view of medieval living standards, trade and religious experience. Yet others will be devoted to new and challenging methodologies rather than surveying results.

The series will address important questions: To what extent was medieval Europe a cultural, economic and religious entity? How did western Europe become a centre of civilization? How should the present countries of Europe manage and enhance their medieval heritage? Understanding leads to appreciation, and appreciation leads to a concern for conservation of our common European past. This series will constitute a formidable array of handbooks to explain why the past and its products, from artefacts to great buildings and historic landscapes, are important for enriching life in Europe today.

Figures

Acknowledgements

This book has been a joint effort: John Schofield wrote Chapters 1–3 and 6–8; Alan Vince wrote Chapters 4 and 5. For this second edition we thank especially Dave Evans for many useful suggestions.

We wish to thank the people and institutions which have helped with provision of information and illustrations for the two editions: Peter Addyman, David Andrews, Peter Armstrong, Brian Ayers, Malcolm Atkin, Jan Baart, Paul Bennett, Peter Clark and Alison Hicks (Canterbury Archaeological Trust), James Bond, Mark Brisbane, Bristol Museum and Art Gallery, Richard Bryant, Martin Carver, Andy Chopping and Maggie Cox (Museum of London Archaeology Service), Helen Clarke, Renée Colardelle, Hal Dalwood, Robin Daniels, Sue Davies (Wessex Archaeology), Anne Davis, Hubert De Witte, the École d'Architecture de Toulouse, Mike Eddy, Paul Everson, Kate Giles and her students, James Greig and Julia Wakefield, Alan Hall, Richard Hall and Patrick Ottoway (York Archaeological Trust), Carolyn Heighway, Malcolm Hurley, Jean-Ives Marin, Robina McNeil, Jean Mellor, Piera Melli, Myriame Morel-Deledalle, Julian Munby (Oxford Archaeological Unit), National Monuments Record, National Trust for Ireland, the Novgorod Archaeological Research Centre and Moscow State University, Mark Samuel, Herbert Sarfatij, Helga Seeden, Terry Slater, Barney Sloane, David Stocker, Jean Terrier, Simon Ward, John Wood, Sue Wright, and the editors of the *Archaeological Journal* and *Medieval Archaeology*.

The figures have been drawn or redrawn by Tracy Wellman, Susan Banks, Alison Hawkins and Dave Watt. Parts of the text of this second edition have been read and criticized by Brian Ayers, Anne Davis, John Giorgi, Kevin Rielly, Jane Sidell and Bill White. Where not otherwise credited, the photographs are by John Schofield.

As in the acknowledgements in the first edition of this book, we also thank those who have worked on the archaeology of British towns, particularly in the last thirty years. This book is a survey of their achievements, and is dedicated to them.

1 *Introduction*

This book is an archaeological journey through some of the towns of medieval Britain (Fig. 1.1). Its emphasis is on the discoveries by archaeological teams over the last thirty years, nearly always on sites to be developed or already under construction. Like any travel guide, this study must be selective and it will not attempt to be comprehensive in listing these discoveries. Some of our views of towns or their component parts such as castles, churches and houses will be fragmentary and fleeting, not because we are speeding by too fast, but because our knowledge is incomplete. And yet from the vast haul of information now at our disposal, after thirty years of data gathering, we can begin to ask questions of many kinds. What went on in medieval towns? How did the rich and poor live, what nourished them, what did they die of? What was the weather like, the quality of life, the restrictions or special pleasures of living in towns? All these questions, and many others, can be answered at least partially by archaeological study.

As with any good travel guide, we must start with some basic information for the traveller. In this case there are three introductory sections, dealing with the growth of medieval urban archaeology in Britain, the necessity to see medieval British towns in their European context, and a brief chronology of the period 1100–1500 as offered to us by historians and geographers. The subsequent chapters will examine the archaeological contribution to the evolving investigation of medieval towns.

For the second edition of this book, we have attempted to add more results and discussion from towns in continental Europe. This study is written by two British archaeologists, who have surveyed as much of the work of their continental colleagues as they can. It will be clear that we have not done justice, because we could not, to all the recent archaeological work in towns all over Europe. We have not been able to survey eastern Europe in detail. But this book is a contribution to the archaeological study of the western European medieval town, and we ask colleagues in other countries to write their own studies which will either complement the synthesis presented here or come to different conclusions. It is written in the belief that medieval urban archaeology should be a Europe-wide study, as is already practised in the fields of urban history and architecture. One question to be addressed along the way by archaeologists, however, is the extent to which medieval Europe was ever a cultural and economic unit, sharing its architecture, artefacts and people, as well as its problems, wars and diseases.[1]

Medieval urban archaeology in Britain and Europe

The development of medieval urban archaeology in Britain has gone through three overlapping phases: the first heroic phase of 1946–70; the Winchester experience from 1961 and establishment of archaeological units or local

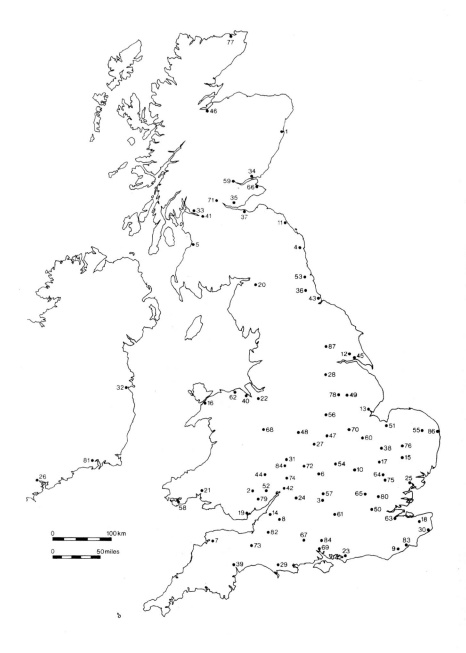

Figure 1.1 Map of Britain and Ireland, showing the sites of many of the towns discussed in this book.

Key to Figure 1.1

1	Aberdeen	45	Hull
2	Abergavenny	46	Inverness
3	Abingdon	47	Leicester
4	Alnwick	48	Lichfield
5	Ayr	49	Lincoln
6	Banbury	50	London and Westminster
7	Barnstaple	51	Lynn (Bishop's; King's)
8	Bath	52	Monmouth
9	Battle	53	Newcastle-upon-Tyne
10	Bedford	54	Northampton
11	Berwick	55	Norwich
12	Beverley	56	Nottingham
13	Boston	57	Oxford
14	Bristol	58	Pembroke
15	Bury St Edmunds	59	Perth
16	Caernarvon	60	Peterborough
17	Cambridge	61	Reading
18	Canterbury	62	Rhuddlan
19	Cardiff	63	Rochester
20	Carlisle	64	Saffron Walden
21	Carmarthen	65	St Albans
22	Chester	66	St Andrews
23	Chichester	67	Salisbury
24	Cirencester	68	Shrewsbury
25	Colchester	69	Southampton
26	Cork	70	Stamford
27	Coventry	71	Stirling
28	Doncaster	72	Stratford-upon-Avon
29	Dorchester (Dorset)	73	Taunton
30	Dover	74	Tewkesbury
31	Droitwich	75	Thaxted
32	Dublin	76	Thetford
33	Dumbarton	77	Thurso
34	Dundee	78	Torksey
35	Dunfermline	79	Usk
36	Durham	80	Waltham Abbey
37	Edinburgh	81	Waterford
38	Ely	82	Wells
39	Exeter	83	Winchelsea
40	Flint	84	Winchester
41	Glasgow	85	Worcester
42	Gloucester	86	Yarmouth
43	Hartlepool	87	York
44	Hereford		

organizations in the 1970s; and the spreading of the practice of developer funding from about 1978. A fourth stage was reached with the publication of the government's procedural note *PPG* (*Planning Policy Guidance*) *16* in 1990, and the effect of this new thinking on the conduct of archaeology in towns is beginning to become apparent ten years later.

Since the middle of the nineteenth century, archaeologists in the larger towns of Britain sought to rescue medieval finds on building sites, and sometimes recorded medieval remains in their notebooks. Urban archaeology in Britain really only began in the bomb-damaged cellars of London, Canterbury and a small number of other towns (such as Norwich or Southampton) immediately after the last war, where medieval buildings and monuments had suffered destruction along with those of more recent centuries. In Canterbury, Shepherd Frere's objectives were mainly Roman; in the City of London, W.F. Grimes conducted excavations from 1946 to 1962. Besides many spectacular Roman discoveries (such as the Cripplegate fort of the early second century), he also recorded portions of the city wall and towers in the medieval period, secular buildings, the Charterhouse and two other religious houses, three parish churches, and an investigation of a Jewish burial ground. The work in London was sufficiently innovatory that an essay by Grimes was included in a volume entitled *Recent Archaeological Excavations in Britain* in 1956, along with reports of Star Carr, the mesolithic site in Yorkshire, the Roman treasure at Snettisham, the excavation of the Sutton Hoo ship burial and other famous sites; the chapter represented 'a sustained campaign to make the most of the unique and passing opportunity offered by the clearance of bomb-damaged areas in the oldest part of London, the City'.[2] It was not fully realized at the time that towns would need consistent archaeological coverage for all future major redevelopments. Mortimer Wheeler included a short chapter on 'digging town-sites' in his seminal *Archaeology from the Earth* (1954), but it was about the excavation of tell sites in the Middle East and Pakistan. Meanwhile English historians began to produce studies of the topography of medieval towns, such as that of York by Angelo Raine (1955), which the author believed to be a 'pioneer work'; and of Canterbury by William Urry (1965). A notable precedent had been the work of H. E. Salter in reconstructing medieval Oxford (1960).

Urban excavation in Britain in the modern sense began seriously at Winchester in 1961; the research unit founded there by Martin Biddle became a prototype for many similar developments in other towns, and was especially influential in its methodology. Winchester was a good choice to reinforce Biddle's argument that all periods of a town's history were important, not just the Roman, which was the chief objective of many excavators at the time. It was also a good choice because throughout its late medieval decline and subsequent quiet centuries the core of the modern city had shrunk, leaving medieval strata intact towards the edges of the town and only now threatened with development. Thus the Lower Brook Street site, with its many medieval buildings, lanes and a small church, produced spectacular and clearly important results. Though the work in Winchester was 'research', not the extremely pressurized rescue of many towns in the 1960s and especially later decades, it provided intellectual energy and trained personnel for the new area of endeavour. Winchester introduced open-area excavation into towns. There were more or less co-ordinated efforts in Bristol, Chester, Hull, Southampton, Stamford and York. Elsewhere, such as in Cambridge or Worcester, archaeological recording during rapid redevelopment was largely a matter of local, individual initiative. But whole areas of towns were lost. At Peterborough, a large area east of the cathedral was destroyed without record in the 1960s; it probably included most of the late Saxon town and no doubt much of the medieval town.[3]

By the end of the 1960s many archaeologists were concerned about the destruction of physical evidence for Britain's history in towns. This resulted in the national survey *The Erosion of History*,[4] which drew attention to the 'crisis in urban archaeology'. It argued that the most important towns of all historical periods would be lost to archaeology in twenty years, if not before; half of the 906 historic towns remaining in mainland Britain were threatened with some sort of development, 159 of them seriously. The responsibility for this situation could be laid at several doors. Archaeologists were poorly organized and urban archaeology was a new discipline; historians did not often see the importance of other than written records. Government spokesmen continued to assert, against all experience, that existing voluntary procedures and legislation were adequate and effective (for instance, a Commons Written Answer of March 1971). Most of all, there was general ignorance about the value of the strata lying below nearly every modern town centre.

The arguments in *The Erosion of History* emphasizing the importance of a town's archaeology are worth presentation here because they formed the agenda of the subject for the next twenty years, and because the document itself was so influential in changing attitudes throughout Britain. The following paragraphs are taken verbatim, slightly condensed.

Archaeology and written records: very few towns possess more than occasional written records earlier than the thirteenth century. Yet the urban life of many of our towns has continued unbroken since the tenth or eleventh centuries, while the origins of some lie in the Roman or even pre-Roman periods. A town may have been in existence for a thousand years before there is written record of much more than its name. But the physical remains of the past, the tangible results of man's activity, are as important a source of history as written records. This physical evidence is the raw material of archaeology, whose purpose is to study the history of man through the material remains of his past activities against the setting of the natural environment in which he acted.

Archaeology is relevant to all periods of a town's history: archaeological evidence may relate to any and every period of a town's existence, from the moment of its origin. It is therefore often the only source of evidence for the beginning and early centuries of urban life. For these centuries archaeological deposits are the town's only archive. Nor does archaeological evidence lose its importance when documents begin. Until at least the nineteenth century, the evidence of archaeology and of documents is complementary. Each records aspects of the past with which the other does not deal.

Archaeology often has evidence wider than that from written sources: the original written evidence for a town's history is always selective, dealing with those matters which required written records, such as government and records of land-holding. Archaeological evidence, whether buried or above ground, may provide information on activities which have a concrete or physical component. As a result archaeological research is concerned with the environment within which human action takes place.

Archaeology has a place in determining the future form of the town: in the designation of conservation areas and the selection of features to figure prominently in these areas, archaeological considerations are essential. The preservation of a unique identity is often the crucial problem facing a town's planners today. A successful solution to this problem requires a mature comprehension of the factors that led it to take its own particular course. In this comprehension the results of archaeological enquiry are essential.

Urban archaeology is complex: the below-ground archaeological deposits resulting from the growth of a town are by nature very extensive both in area and in depth. The former reflects the absolute size of the town as the most complex of human settlements; the latter is a function of long-continued occupation on one site. Two further factors must be added: the extraordinary complexity of town sites due to frequent disturbance of the ground throughout a town's life, and the difficulty that the entire archaeological area lies below a living community with its own requirements of daily life. It is this last fact which now threatens to destroy without record the deposits of our history.

Archaeological work in towns will always be selective: not every site can be excavated, and a minimum coverage must be observation of the site during contractors' work [what came to be called 'watching briefs']. Such observations, if properly recorded and continued over years, can produce good results; but they must be accompanied by the proper investigation of selected sites by controlled excavation. The selection of priorities will vary from town to town, but questions of origin and the evolution of the street plan and defences (if any) will always be fundamental.

Though it outlined the threat to all the towns considered, the survey highlighted six representative places, in several of which some archaeological work had already begun. But large portions of towns had already been lost to development: a quarter of Gloucester (Fig. 1.2), a third of Abingdon, a third of Chester, and nearly half of Cambridge. These examples were reminders of the vulnerability of the archaeology of towns.

Archaeological enthusiasm and determination grew in towns where archaeologists (often amateurs and volunteers) already worked, and began to spread to other towns: in Southampton, Oxford (Fig. 1.3), Gloucester, Lincoln, Colchester, Leicester, York (Fig. 1.4) and Chester. At Norwich, there was an attempt to place rescue work in a historical context, and this was important in both arguing for the recording of standing buildings (then almost unknown among urban archaeologists), and for attaching documentary historians to rescue units.[5] In Scotland an important survey of 1972 drew attention to a similar threat to the town centres north of the border; projects quickly blossomed, at Aberdeen and Edinburgh in 1973, and at Perth in 1974.[6] The City of London was late in this process, and provision of a proper archaeological unit there at the end of 1973 was due to a combination of patient negotiation by the Guildhall Museum and the impending development by the Corporation of the site of the late medieval and Tudor Baynard's Castle

Figure 1.2 Gloucester largely escaped wartime damage and in 1951, as shown here, was an architecturally Victorian industrial town, with medieval plots and street pattern intact – and a good stock of medieval buildings (many hidden and unappreciated). The same view today would show a vista of roof-top car-parks, the 1970s solution to traffic problems. Development in the 1970s obliterated more than a quarter of the medieval street pattern and associated medieval plot boundaries. Archaeology in the early 1970s, though often poorly funded and desperately short of time, was highly cost-effective in terms of information, mostly about the Roman past. The 1980s, when development slowed, produced much piecemeal information from assessments and watching briefs but failed to fulfil archaeological expectations, due in part to the lack of larger area projects against which to calibrate the accumulated information. The lack of information about Gloucester's waterfront (behind the photographer), now covered with piled buildings, has been a particular failing of the last twenty years (National Monuments Record; comments by Carolyn Heighway).

on the waterfront. This site, excavated in 1972, was crucial in the development of archaeology in the capital, for it was clearly an important example of the potential damage being inflicted on our heritage, and was used by the increasingly vocal and expert pressure group Rescue (founded 1971, and still active today). The waterfront of London, and by implication waterfronts in other historic towns, was to become a major archaeological priority in the next two decades. The London arrangements had also been urged by a Rescue

Figure 1.3 Oxford Castle, 1970s: a section through the outer bailey of the castle. The Saxon occupation layers which preceded the castle are at the top of the section (Oxford Archaeological Unit).

report, *The Future of London's Past*, which summarized present knowledge with a new methodology of overlaid maps, and was so innovatory in its thinking that town archaeologists throughout Britain and over much of continental Europe bought a copy and read it.[7]

During the 1970s and early 1980s archaeologists widened the debate and scope of their activities from being purely reactive to formulating strategic plans. Several county-wide surveys of threats to towns were produced: for example, for Berkshire, Dorset, Essex, Oxfordshire, Somerset, Surrey and Sussex. There were also policy statements for individual towns such as Boston, Gloucester, Lichfield and Newcastle. As an example of this kind of survey, we can cite the case of Taunton in Somerset.[8]

Taunton's urban origins go back to the eighth century; a Saxon royal estate grew into a religious and administrative centre. By the end of the tenth century, it had a mint and probably defences. At the time of Domesday Book it had 64 burgesses, a market and mint, and three mills; it was the third largest town in Somerset after Bath and Ilchester. In the twelfth century the bishop of Winchester converted the bishop's hall into a castle, and the Saxon minster was later replaced by an Augustinian priory.

Though some excavations had recently taken place, the centre of the town was, in 1977, of 'enormous archaeological potential'. 'No excavation has ever been carried out on the large Augustinian priory site; even its exact site is unknown.

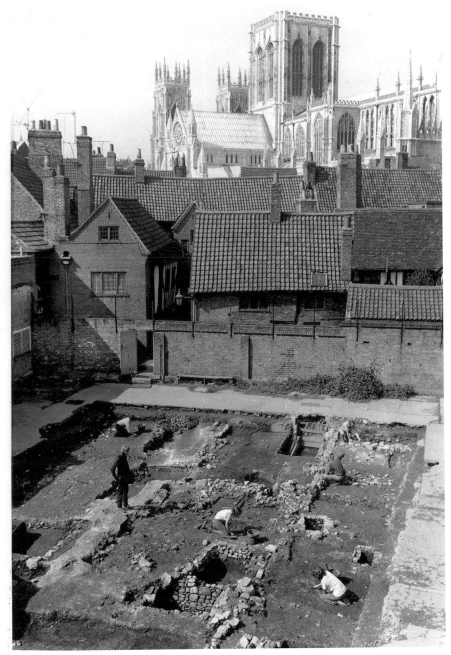

Figure 1.4 Excavation in York, 1970s: medieval and post-medieval structures being investigated at the Bedern site (York Archaeological Trust). Here excavation removed only the strata to be affected by development, leaving lower strata intact.

Little is known of the archaeology of the castle, particularly of the outer bailey area, even though the documentary evidence is good. Little is known about the town's defences and nothing about the precise dating and arrangement of the recorded town gates. The sites of various chapels, hospitals and features mentioned in documents are uncertain and details of structures and activities represented on individual tenements are usually totally unknown.' Large areas of medieval Taunton had been redeveloped since the 1930s, mostly since 1945. Redevelopment had not been preceded by adequate archaeological investigation and many more areas, although not destroyed archaeologically, had been effectively buried under permanent car parks. The town was in grave danger of trashing its own heritage permanently. In the years since 1977, archaeological work has fortunately taken place in Taunton: notably investigations of the castle, defences, and the site of the Saxon minster of St Peter and St Paul, later the medieval priory; but questions still remain, especially concerning the town's Saxon origins.[9]

The development of town and city centres in the 1970s provided the necessity, as well as the opportunity, for urban archaeology to learn its business very quickly; and the results were encouraging. Investigations of medieval strata and buildings were plentiful. In 1981 a summary of work in 146 English towns reported excavations of bridges (at Beverley, Bristol, Exeter, Pleshey), castles (in 37 towns), cathedrals (Canterbury, Durham, Exeter, Peterborough, Wells, York), cemeteries (14), churches (14), defences (26), land reclamation and waterfront structures (Bristol, London, Plymouth, Poole, Weymouth, Yarmouth), religious houses (Benedictines, friars, Knights of St John and Templars), streets (18), suburbs (Bristol, Exeter, London, Winchester, York), and domestic and industrial buildings of all kinds, both buried and still standing.[10] Urban units also developed methods which were later applied to all kinds of archaeology. A single numbering system of stratigraphic units replaced various cumbersome, ineffective and private systems, after Peter Addyman at York decided to use the neutral term 'context' on an excavation in 1972; a diagrammatic system for expressing relationships between layers, born of the complicated sites in Winchester, was devised by Edward Harris and this became the 'Harris matrix' which is now used round the world.[11]

There were archaeological pioneers too in continental towns, from immediately after World War II: for instance in Hamburg or Bruges. As in Britain, this was a reaction to the post-war redevelopment of towns, which in some countries had been widely devastated (Fig. 1.5). At first, the will to build new cities predominated and archaeology was not important. In Stuttgart and Friedsrichshafen, more archaeological strata were lost through post-war regeneration schemes than through Allied bombing, and damage in Brussels was particularly severe in the 1960s and 1970s, with no archaeological recording. In Saragossa (Spain), irreparable damage was done to strata by a policy of encouraging underground development to solve traffic problems. But the new discipline of urban archaeology grew during the 1960s, 1970s and 1980s: in Dutch towns, in France, Germany and Switzerland (Fig. 1.6), Norway and Sweden; in fact, in all European countries from Ireland to Latvia and the former Soviet Union.[12] Irish public interest in a large Viking and medieval site at Wood Quay, Dublin, in 1973–4 changed the direction of Irish

Figure 1.5 Rue Saint-Jean, Caen, immediately after Allied bombardment in 1944. The town of William the Conqueror was nothing but a field of ruins. Inset: numerous notices were however placed near historic monuments, so that clearance operations would not level them as the town recovered (Musée de Normandie, Caen, D.R.).

archaeology for ever. Some of the first large-scale excavations ever undertaken in Irish medieval towns were in Cork and Waterford in the 1970s and 1980s, partly as a result of the discoveries in Dublin.[13] Notable advances in technique were being made in Lübeck (Germany), with first the application of dendrochronology to buildings in towns and to archaeologically recovered wood in the same programme of research, and second the interpretation of standing buildings from detailed archaeological drawings. There was also a constant and public drive to relate each new finding to an evolving view of the archaeological development of the whole town site.[14] In Germany and elsewhere archaeologists were able to show that towns existed long before historians had thought; the acquisition of a town charter, an important stage in town creation for historians, proved to be of limited significance as an indicator that a settlement had become urban.[15] Because it was new territory, many of the archaeological findings surprised archaeologists themselves, such as the extensive survival of twelfth- and thirteenth-century wooden houses in Staveren, Holland, in the 1960s, or the generally spectacular survival of wooden waterfront structures in many ports, heralded by the work at Bergen (Norway) after a serious fire in 1955. In some of the largest cities the cumulative amount of new information was staggering, for instance after forty years of investigations in Amsterdam. This included a castle which was 'more or less a complete surprise'.[16]

Figure 1.6   Geneva, Rues-Basses: investigation of medieval buildings and a medieval street below the present streets of the city, in advance of drainage works, in 1986; traces of a new quarter laid out in the thirteenth century were recorded (Service cantonal d'archéologie, Geneva).

In eastern Europe, urban archaeology in the sense described in this book has had a varied history. In Poland, the town of Elbląg (Elbing), devastated in the war, had decided to rebuild its entire central area as it was before 1939. In 1980 excavations started on a large area. Nearby on the north Baltic coast, Gdańsk (Danzig) has been a leader in urban archaeology since the 1930s; but there has been virtually no work in Warsaw. In Estonia expansion of urban archaeology has been a feature of the 1970s and 1980s.[17] The collapse of the East German state in 1989 revealed a preserved urban landscape throughout the former German Democratic Republic: despite some war losses and lack of maintenance, the quantity and quality of urban fabric which remained was of a quality hardly known any more in West Germany. There has been a start in former East German towns such as Rostock, Stralsund and Wismar, which have been much redeveloped in the 1990s. Even further east, in Novgorod (Russia), there have been many excavations from the 1930s, and especially since 1951, which have recently become a project of international co-operation (Fig. 1.7).[18]

This archaeological work, impressive in extent and determination both in mainland Europe and Britain, was however often desparate and frustratingly

Figure 1.7 Excavations at the Troitsky site, Novgorod, in 1998 showing twelfth-century levels under investigation. In the foreground a timber structure is being excavated, while in the middle and centre-left two square timber houses can be clearly seen. Towards the rear is a large wooden pavement around which the buildings within this large, enclosed property were arranged. The medieval property is one of the largest so far excavated in Novgorod with almost 1400 square metres enclosed by timber fencing. Artefacts discovered on the site indicate an administrative role for occupants of the property with wooden seals used for tax collection purposes and birch-bark documents that record the payment of tribute (S. Orlov, reproduced courtesy of the Novgorod Archaeological Research Centre and Moscow State University).

insufficient; as the archaeologist for Bordeaux wrote in 1980, 'the results [in Bordeaux] are nevertheless far from being satisfactory; too-rapid excavations, destruction of the remains, accumulation of masses of material which are difficult to study, synthetic publications always pushed back because of the interruptions caused by new rescue excavations'.[19] This was the story in too many European towns, even those (unlike Bordeaux) which had a permanent archaeological unit.

In the larger British centres, the available money was not matching the growing need as the pace of redevelopment quickened. During the post-war rebuilding of British towns, developers often allowed access to sites and sometimes made a contribution towards archaeological investigation on their sites; sometimes the sympathetic and educated attitude of a developer aided the provision of archaeological coverage in the town, for everyone's future

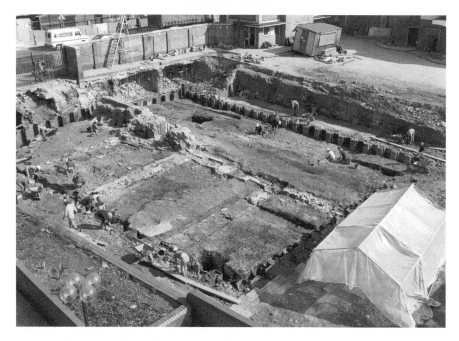

Figure 1.8 Excavation begins at Billingsgate, City of London, in 1982. A large area of medieval buildings, lasting until the Great Fire of London in 1666, is revealed. A viewing gallery for the public will be built near the street. Following the success of the Coppergate excavation in York, Billingsgate was one of several large and public archaeological urban projects in London in the early 1980s.

benefit, as in 1974 at Perth. But during the late 1970s it became clear that the existing combination of government funds and occasional sponsorship was not enough to provide an efficient service on all sites where archaeology was certain to be encountered.

In London in 1978, the Museum of London's archaeologists began suggesting to *every* developer that he or she should assume the responsibility of dealing with the archaeology on the site in an appropriate way (Fig. 1.8). A version of this policy has been pursued in most other European countries, and the expectation is now widespread, though some countries (for example, Holland, France and Belgium) continue to provide state funding for the majority of urban excavations. The principle that developers should make a financial contribution to the cost of both excavation and publication is now accepted by most governments.[20] It spreads beyond Europe; from 1992, with the support of UNESCO, an ambitious programme of excavation ahead of large-scale city centre renewal took place in Beirut (Lebanon). Here the urban history goes back nearly 5000 years; the point for this survey of medieval urban archaeology is that the work in Beirut provides a much-needed source of archaeological evidence for the Crusader period, a clash of cultures on the edge of the European world (Fig. 1.9).[21]

The purpose of this book is not to discuss the efficacy of archaeological legislation in any European country, but to outline the results of investigations

Figure 1.9 Early Fatimid (late tenth to early eleventh century) to Ottoman (sixteenth to twentieth century) pottery coming to light in excavations in the centre of Beirut in 1994 by the American University of Beirut. The pottery is local, and comprises cooking pots and tablewares in a variety of glazes and decoration. Archaeology is beginning to explore the cities of medieval Islam, to rectify a Eurocentric view of the clash of cultures known as the Crusades. Beirut has been the scene of several excavations by Lebanese and international teams, with French, Dutch and British components; urban archaeology is the same wherever it is practised.

into medieval towns. It is, however, appropriate in this brief sketch of the history of the subject from the British perspective to add a description of the fourth stage reached, after the publication of the government's *Planning Policy Guidance Note 16* of 1990, known by its initials as *PPG16*. This guideline, which took root remarkably easily because from 1990 Britain was in an economic slump (five years earlier it would have been unworkable), has had important effects. It was a national guideline to cover the archaeology of all periods from prehistory to the present in England, but it had particular consequences in medieval towns.

PPG16 states that archaeological remains should be seen as a finite and non-renewable resource, and in many cases highly fragile and vulnerable to damage and destruction. Appropriate management is therefore essential to ensure that they survive in good condition. In particular, care must be taken to ensure that archaeological remains are not needlessly or thoughtlessly destroyed. Where nationally important archaeological remains, whether scheduled or not, and their settings, are affected by a proposed development there should be a presumption in favour of their physical preservation.

When important remains are known to exist, or when archaeologists have good reason to believe that important remains exist, developers will be able to help by preparing sympathetic designs using, for example, foundations which avoid disturbing the remains altogether or minimize damage by careful siting of landscaped or open areas. There are techniques available for sealing archaeological remains underneath buildings or new landscaping, thus securing their preservation for the future even though they remain inaccessible for the time being.

If physical preservation *in situ* is not feasible, an archaeological excavation for the purposes of 'preservation by record' may be an acceptable alternative.[22] From an archaeological point of view, this should be regarded as a second best option. Agreements should also provide for the subsequent publication of the results of any excavation programme.

The effect of *PPG16* has broadly been that many more sites in towns have been tested archaeologically than in previous years, while the large excavations of archaeologically rich sites of the larger town centres in the 1970s and 1980s have become a thing of the past. The deep deposits, with all their possible information were, under pressure from the new guideline, preserved *in situ*. York is a case where the archaeologist attached to the city corporation argues this policy has been a success;[23] and to be frank, the museums which are the stores for the archaeological work of the 1970s to 1990s are straining to house and conserve all that was found in those decades, so it can be argued that all the potential new material is best left in the ground for future generations.

There have been other effects of this guideline. Some are negative. Evaluation and small-scale work opens up only part of a medieval building, whether standing or only consisting of layers in the ground. One consequence will be that most of the useful statements to be made in the future about urban structures will be based on the larger sites excavated in the 1970s and 1980s.

Other effects are positive. In the three decades up to 1990, archaeologists tried to extend their coverage to the multitude of small towns, but generally without satisfactory results; there was no productive methodology in place. This is now changing. The pace at which new archaeological information from individual small towns is produced is often quite slow, and may represent a very small and non-representative sample of an individual town. Fieldwork is however producing important baseline data for individual towns. While most of the smaller sites have not been examined to the same degree as was possible by full-scale excavations, which have become much rarer, observations of broad character have been enabled. These limited results, though frustrating to some town archaeologists, have achieved much in two areas: understanding specific localities such as suburbs and small towns by the cumulative effect of many small investigations, and fostering a sense of community involvement with archaeology.

It is only since the introduction of similar legislation into Scotland in 1994 that any significant progress has been made in urban archaeology in the highland region: in Inverness, Wick, Thurso, Tain, Nairn, Dingwall and Dornoch very little had been done, but archaeology has now taken place. Virtually no archaeological recording was carried out at Inverness when major town centre developments occurred in the 1960s; in Thurso, the medieval and possibly Norse core was extensively developed in the 1970s without any archaeological involvement. Now, in these towns and elsewhere in the region, there is a growing awareness of and interest in the town's archaeological potential; but with the development of competitive tendering for archaeological projects in Scotland, as elsewhere in Britain, urban archaeology is in a different environment from that of the 1970s.[24]

At the present time, therefore, urban archaeologists are equipped with a fairly well-developed methodology, the product of the last twenty or thirty years of common experience.[25] Especially since 1990, market forces have increasingly invaded the profession (with consequent complaint about standards from the archaeologists), and the 1970s practice of a town always being excavated by a single archaeological unit is now a thing of the past almost everywhere (though there are exceptions). Most often, sites are brought to the attention of archaeologists through planning applications.

The local planning authority decides upon ('determines') the planning application by the developer (now called 'the client' by archaeologists). The detailed methods of conservation of strata and buildings, and mitigation techniques which include preservation of strata beneath lightly piled buildings, are not discussed here; there is a growing literature on this subject.[26] Excavation is, according to the new philosophy, the third option. And any excavation or investigation will require publication, a further obligation which the developer should honour.

But sponsoring excavation and publication need not be merely a necessary duty for the developer. Archaeology and property development can coexist, with a proper recognition of each other's needs. The educational benefits are enormous; in certain towns archaeologists have made great effort to present their results to the public, notably at York, where the Jorvik Centre was established after about a million people had seen a large excavation of Viking buildings in Coppergate. As well as education, there is the image of the town to consider. In the related field of building and townscape conservation, the 1980s saw a 'rediscovery of the city as an ideal and brought a new celebration of style and variety combined with a new realisation that enterprise and image go hand in hand'.[27] A town which demonstrates care for its old buildings will attract discerning companies and workers. Now, virtually all city strategic plans contain sections both on conservation and on archaeology. This means that the archaeologist has a role to play in the conservation and presentation of medieval towns; and this theme will be touched on several times in this book.

What do archaeologists seek to study in towns? Let us start with the formation of the layers of evidence itself. Layers in towns tend to be distinctive, even colourful, by comparison with those on rural sites. Although gradual and natural accumulations do occur, the majority of urban *contexts* (the word generally used for both individual deposits and traces of past digging actions such as ditches and pits) are the stratigraphic traces of events of short duration, such as construction or demolition programmes. Urban deposits also have a high proportion of crisply definable forms such as brick and stone or waterlogged contexts containing timbers. Thus, it can be suggested, urban layers are in the main more easily defined. At the same time we must identify all the processes that created the deposits which are used as evidence, since it is a mistake to assume that they are today exactly as they were when laid down.[28]

Urban deposits are found in great variety and often in complex sequences, and they survive to varying degrees throughout the length and breadth of the town. We first need to identify the types of evidence available (organic deposits, pockets of strata preserved by terracing, surviving medieval structures) and then use them to evaluate the town as an archaeological resource (often with the use of specially prepared maps of the deposits). This has long been the approach first adopted towards a medieval town by the archaeologist.[29] In such a strategy, the town's historical monuments are listed, but there is also description of the survival, in three dimensions, of the remaining stratigraphy, which includes the monuments as standing blocks of strata.

The variety of survival in the evidence will affect the strategy of our excavations and the likely results. In the older English towns, deposits of bulky proportions, for instance, were left in Roman and Victorian times, with periods of lesser detritus between. In Prague, deposits of the twelfth and thirteenth centuries are rich and thick, but those of the fifteenth and sixteenth century are not, and this has been attributed to different rubbish disposal practices.[30] In Visby (Sweden), many excavations over recent decades have contributed to an increasingly detailed understanding about the town's deposits, their state of preservation and how they grew: for instance, large areas of dumping reflect the medieval practice of digging out the ground for cellars, and finds from fields outside the town show where rubbish was taken out and dumped at specific periods.[31] A likely conclusion will be that not all periods are available for examination everywhere, and that urban deposits are good for some things but not others. The first factor in archaeological excavation strategy must be the nature of the site (Fig. 1.10). In this matter, archaeologists should lay aside historical questions and concentrate on purely archaeological productivity; and this will tend to be highest where deposits are deep, or the survival of structures and artefacts is enhanced by ground conditions, such as along waterfronts.

During the last two decades archaeological recording has extended to standing buildings of all ages in towns (Fig. 1.11). This underlines the role of archaeologists in conservation, the management of change to historic landscapes. Buildings are just as vulnerable to invasive changes as buried archaeological deposits. They also challenge the archaeologist to lift his or her eyes from the trench, which tends to be flat and two-dimensional, to appreciate how archaeology is properly three-dimensional, from foundations to roof. Some towns are rich in secular and religious medieval buildings, furnishing reference collections of structures: Salisbury, for instance, has a well-preserved cathedral, six parish churches, several fragments of thirteenth-century houses and eighteen houses dated to the fourteenth century;[32] other towns rich in medieval buildings include Canterbury, King's Lynn and York. Fragments survive within later structures in many other towns, even those which have been redeveloped many times, such as Bristol, Norwich or Southampton. The system of medieval alleys is still preserved at Edinburgh.

Urban finds are of several kinds: ceramics (largely pottery), animal bones, human bones, buildings and loose building material, non-ceramic artefacts (in leather, wood and metals), biological and botanical evidence. Buildings and streets are types of artefact, to be analysed in the same general ways as pottery or smallfinds. The archaeologist seeks to identify economic and social groupings (including industrial, military or religious groups) in the town by purely archaeological means. Once these groups have been described and

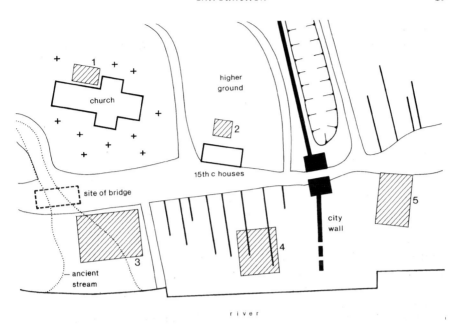

Figure 1.10 Part of a fictitious medieval town, showing some of the considerations when assessing various archaeological sites. Ditches, streams and river banks are good reservoirs of artefactual and environmental information because of their wet or damp conditions. Five sites are shown. At (1), where the church wishes to build a new parish centre, the archaeological yield will be human burials, but possibly earlier parts of the church. At (2), the site is behind standing medieval buildings, but will be less useful because it is on higher ground, with thinner deposits. At (3), the site lies in the waterfront zone and is additionally half over a buried stream; this will be expensive to excavate, but worthwhile. At (4), units of land reclamation datable by dendrochronology over several properties will be the objective. At (5), outside the city wall, the main objective will be to understand the original date and character of suburban development.

delineated, the archaeologist can move to consider the relationships between groups, both within the town – how did these military, industrial, commercial, social and religious functions fit together in the comparatively confined space of the town? – and over time, by comparing how groups rose and fell, infiltrated each other or disappeared from view. The keywords in urban archaeology are *groups*, *spaces* and *change*; though one question for medieval archaeologists to tackle is precisely what kind of change is under study. Is it short-term changes or events such as are catalogued by documents? Is it social change over longer periods? Or is it in addition broad environmental changes which require study of several centuries and even millennia? This is a question we must return to at the end of this book.

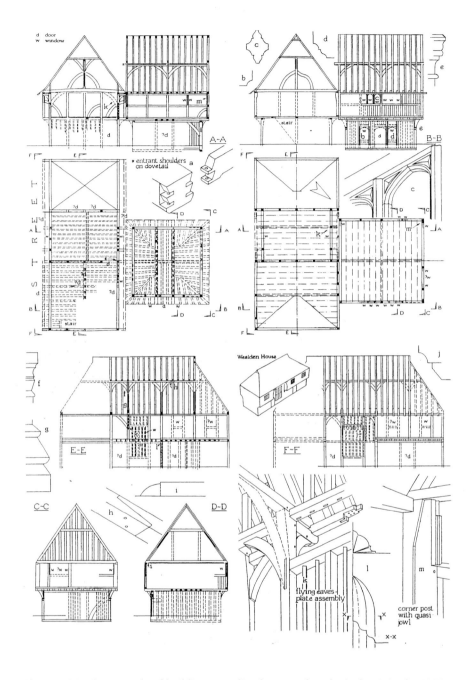

Figure 1.11 An example of building recording by an archaeological unit in the 1970s: the Maiden's Head, Wincheap, Canterbury. The drawings comprise plans, sections, details and a sketch reconstruction (John Atherton Bowen and Canterbury Archaeological Trust).

Figure 1.12 Herrmann's Inner, Middle and Outer Zones of urbanization in western Europe (1991). The towns shown are those which have relevant material for the post-Roman period up to the eleventh century. Such a map is useful for thinking about the lasting effects of Roman town topography or cultural and social values in the Middle Zone, which straddles the boundary of the Empire.

Origins of medieval towns in Europe

The development of towns in medieval Britain must be seen in a wider, European context. Herrmann (1991) has provided a useful overview. He divides Dark-Age Europe into three zones (Fig. 1.12), based on the boundaries of the former Roman empire. The inner zone comprised for our purposes southern France and Italy, centred on the Mediterranean. North of this was a middle zone, whose axes were the Rhine and the Danube (flowing north-west and south-east respectively), up to the geographical boundary of Roman power and of Roman urbanization. Beyond this, to the north and east, lay the outer zone, where Roman settlements did not exist. Roman Britain (that is, apart from most of Scotland and Ireland) lay in the middle zone, and its development should be compared with that of the Low Countries, southern Germany, Switzerland and Austria.

How did town life start again in this zone? Archaeological work in many European towns, especially since World War II, has produced much evidence demonstrating different solutions and regional variety, but some common themes are evident. The old Roman sites developed in four ways. First, there was often continuity of site without necessarily continuity of town functions such as civic order and a continuous market. In Vienna, for instance, there was certainly occupation of some kind (*Fortleben*, 'after-life') in the ruins, until after 1030 when a new town became evident within the outline of the Roman fortress. Second, there was continuity of fortifications or defences; Roman walls were renewed, in the main with more primitive techniques of construction. These rebuildings presumably indicate groups of people sheltering in the towns and using them at least periodically. An example of this is Regensburg in Bavaria, where parts of the Roman defences, including their towers, served as centres of religious and political power from which the suburbs were organized and governed. Third, some ancient towns show that settlement in them continued, but in phases which do not seem connected to each other. In Cologne, for instance, there were farms within the Roman walls. In the eighth century, new buildings and the establishment of a Frankish aristocratic centre followed, with a religious reorganization of the area. These kinds of development do not demonstrate urban continuity, but merely sporadic reuse of the site by separate groups at different times. The medieval development of Cologne began in earnest in the ninth century.[33]

The Dark Ages is a term applicable to the archaeology of this period in Britain, the Rhineland and around the Danube. From the seventh century, however, international trade began to percolate to Britain and other parts of the middle zone; even beyond, to Scandinavia. Major land routes, such as that to Kiev in the east, were used by merchants, and along them grew many of the larger eastern European towns of today; but it is an error to think that international trade was important in stimulating towns into existence. This was formerly a widely held thesis originally associated with the early twentieth-century historian Henri Pirenne, but is now discounted.[34]

There was usually a centre of secular or religious authority and therefore of local activity. In many cases, the church was the most important factor at work, and sometimes the only force which ensured survival of towns on Roman sites. In Britain, many towns owe their origins to a mother-church often called a minster, and churches are often the key to explaining the revival or emergence of towns.[35] In France, a great number of towns which were the seats of medieval bishops had a nucleus of several churches, sometimes close together on the cathedral site; churches on extramural cemeteries, sometimes of Roman origin, stimulated local growth (Fig. 1.13). A town was where religion could be found and safely practised, so some towns, like Soissons, had an impressive number of religious institutions (cathedral, churches, hospitals)

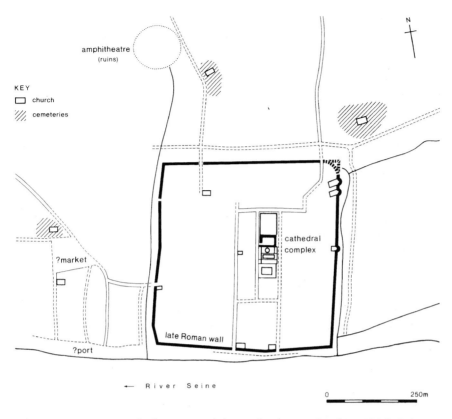

Figure 1.13 Rouen at the beginning of the ninth century (Gauthiez 1996). It is possible that the area west of the Roman walls, by the river, was one of the most southerly *wics* of Saxon Europe, to match better-known examples from Scandinavia, the Baltic and both sides of the North Sea (Hill 2001).

in the seventh and eighth centuries. Archaeology and history combine to suggest that by this time Paris had 27 ecclesiastical establishments, and possibly more. In towns in Flanders, the presence of a bishop in a town was a significant factor in the preservation or development of urban traits, as in Cambrai, Huy, Maastricht and Tournai. Throughout western Europe, many towns which became bishoprics had some kind of Roman predecessors, though not necessarily always towns.[36]

In the outer zone, where there were no Roman towns to reuse, new types of urban settlement were created; and further new towns were added to trade and communications networks within the former Roman provinces such as lowland Britain. These new settlements were of three general forms. First, independent villages might come together into a regional centre which, while defended by a princely stronghold, specialized in crafts and industry: examples of this are towns on the Danube such as Bratislava, or Novgorod. Second, there were new towns with two clear elements: a lord's castle or fortified stronghold, and a mercantile settlement often called a suburb. This type of town became common in the tenth and eleventh centuries, when the dual character of many towns is evident in all parts of the middle zone, and beyond in Denmark, Norway and Sweden. One example is Bruges, where a rich abbey was assisted by the construction of a fortification in the middle of the ninth century, perhaps as defence against the Viking raids of those times; nearby, but not yet certainly located, was a *vicus* or 'town'.[37] At the important town of Lübeck on the north coast of Germany, archaeological work has demonstrated that the documented foundation of 1143 was adjacent to an existing Slavic stronghold and its own mercantile quarter (Fig. 1.14). In Britain, however, there is no clear evidence of the use of Dark-Age royal or princely strongholds, as once thought, as nuclei of future towns.[38]

A third type of new urban settlement was the coastal trading place. These were important distribution points for foreign products and luxuries, and for that reason were assiduously controlled by local kings and princes. Some of these ports grew up at a distance from the royal centre, or flourished on the borders between kingdoms. In the eighth century London, for instance, was the port of land-locked Mercia. Places on the other side of the North Sea such as Quentovic (France) and Dorestadt (Holland) took on a great importance in international trade from the seventh century.[39] Later there were comparable sites in northern Europe, for instance Reric and Ralswiek on the north coast of Germany, Wolin (Poland) and Birka (Sweden).

These three types of town formation, characteristic of Herrmann's outer zone (that is, beyond the Rhine and Danube) but also common in the middle zone, form the background to our enquiry about medieval towns in Britain. But to generalize like this may obscure the contribution of archaeological investigations into the process of crystallization, from the late tenth century, of loosely formed places into towns, such as at Norwich or Thetford; centres with no Roman origins or a lord's stronghold. At Douai (France), the settlement was dispersed in the ninth and tenth centuries, and is only recognizable as a town by about 1200.[40]

By this date, Douai lay in one of the most urbanized areas in Europe, comprising the adjacent regions of Flanders and Liège, between the Rhine and the Somme as these two rivers flowed into the North Sea. A recent study has shown how this collection of towns developed, especially from the tenth century. International trade was significant for the larger centres, but not as important as their role as places of production, redistribution and trade on a local scale. Castles, such as those at Ghent or Antwerp, were centres for selling produce which lords stored in them; so the earliest market place was usually at the castle gate or nearby, and often called *vismarket* (fish market) or some other name which showed its local character. Towns with a religious core, such as Liège, developed economic functions and trade or industrial areas. In the twelfth and thirteenth centuries, five Flemish towns developed international fairs, annual events which attracted merchants from other countries; but in each case the town, such as Lille or Ypres, had already become a regional centre. An extra dimension, international trade, was possible when these towns began to produce luxury items in cloth and metals, suitable for export, on an industrial scale.[41]

Most of the important European cities existed before 1000, and the urban map of Europe was essentially fixed by 1200. There were new towns of the thirteenth century in almost every European country (discussed further in

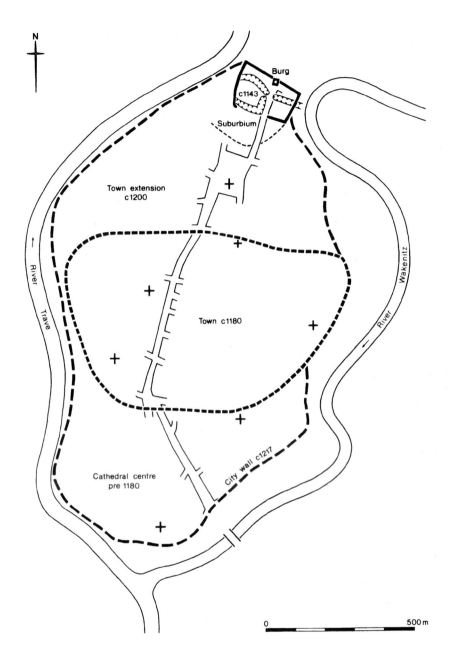

N

Burg

c1143

Suburbium

Town extension
c1200

River Trave

River Wakenitz

Town c1180

Cathedral centre
pre 1180

City wall c1217

0   500 m

Figure 1.14 Lübeck: general conclusions about the early development of the town from combining archaeological investigations with documentary references. Prior to the archaeological work, it was thought that the town was built at one instance in the middle of the twelfth century. Archaeology can trace what was there before a town received a charter, and how the town grew thereafter (Fehring 1990 and other sources).

Chapter 2), but they were generally small and remained so (at least to the end of the medieval period; their post-medieval development is not the subject of this study). The development of post-Roman towns in Britain therefore has parallels with the contemporary development of town sites in many, if not all, European countries.

An outline of the period in Britain, 1100–1500

The medieval period in the British Isles is conventionally divided into three consecutive phases: (i) the development of towns and the countryside in a period of growth, 1100–1300; (ii) the crises of the early and mid fourteenth century, including the Black Death; (iii) a long period of mixed fortunes from about 1350 to 1500, which comprised both decline for some towns and the rise of others, including in England the increasing dominance of London over a widening hinterland.

The period 1100–1300 was one of rapid population growth, in towns and in the countryside. In 1340 England's population may have been 5–6 million. Such a figure had not been reached since the third century and would not be reached again until the eighteenth century.

In the eleventh century there were already many towns in Britain, though the majority were in England, where Domesday Book records 112 places called boroughs in 1086. They were based on royal residences, or trading settlements, or the defended places of Saxons or Danes in the ninth and tenth centuries.[42] Some major centres such as Chester, Gloucester, London, Lincoln, Winchester and York had longer histories, being Roman foundations of the first century AD.

In the towns this period of comparative wealth and growth is illustrated by the range of civic and religious buildings which were constructed.[43] The great majority of urban defences in England and Wales, for instance, were built, or at least begun, before 1300. Nearly all the main bridges across rivers in England were in place before 1340, and they would dictate the form of land communications until the canal age centuries later. The Normans moved the seats of bishops to towns, which meant many new cathedrals. Hospitals were founded in and around many towns, and in the thirteenth century the friars arrived in Britain seeking populous locations. Similar expansion of towns is evident, from excavations, in Ireland.

The archaeological evidence strongly suggests a particular period of increased prosperity and urban growth after 1180. Weekly markets in the smaller towns are mentioned in the twelfth and especially in the thirteenth centuries; sometimes the grant of the market itself is recorded. The fair, on the other hand, was a kind of glorified market, usually held once a year and lasting for at least three days and sometimes for as long as six weeks. As the market was the centre for exchange within the neighbourhood, so the fair was the centre for foreign wares, brought from outside the locality. Fairs were also a major focus of trade in small towns, often attracting traders from great distances.[44]

Between 1200 and 1500 about 2800 grants of market were made by the Crown in England and Wales, over half of them in the period 1200–75.

Village markets and seasonal local fairs were augmented by weekly or bi-weekly markets held in centres of production; both existing towns and new towns. This was happening all over Europe, for instance in south-west France (the interface between the English and French kingdoms) and along the Baltic coast. Towns were valuable pieces of property, for the lord gained revenue from the court, tolls on merchandise, and from the demands of the market which benefited his own rural manors in the surrounding countryside.

In this early phase the merchants of many small British towns participated in overseas trade and London's dominance was a thing of the future. Ships still came to the river-ports of York, Lincoln, Norwich, Gloucester and Chester. Wine from the English lands in Gascony (south-west France) came to Boston in Lincolnshire; wool exports through the town rivalled those of the capital. Along the eastern and southern coasts, small and medium-sized towns fed their regions with imports, and shipped out the local produce.[45] This led to country landowners and religious houses acquiring properties in the ports, where they could trade with the surplus of their own manors and farms, and have access to the market in imported luxuries.

London, however, had been the largest and wealthiest town in England from the tenth century, and by the twelfth century was also the primary distribution centre for inland trade. Its size and wealth began to dominate south-east England. At the time of the Norman Conquest, Winchester was the centre of the Old English kingdom, but during the twelfth century Winchester's connections with the Norman kings slackened and after the loss of Normandy in 1204 the centre of the kingdom moved away from the south coast to the superior attractions of London. In 1340, London's population may have been between 80,000 and 100,000. In this respect it would bear comparison with other large cities of Europe, such as Milan, Venice, Naples, Florence and Palermo (all over 50,000 in the thirteenth century); Ghent (56,000 by about 1350); Cologne (40,000) and Bruges (35,000 in about 1340). Paris had a population variously estimated between 80,000 and 200,000; we can assume it was very big. Four towns in the Iberian peninsula were in the same league: Barcelona, Cordoba, Seville and Granada. By this time, London's pull on people and resources was affecting the whole country: only 9 per cent of immigrants came from within a radius of 10 miles or less; a large proportion (39 per cent) came from within 11–40 miles; 25 per cent from 41–80 miles; and a notable 27 per cent from over 80 miles away.[46]

In Wales, the Norman kings inherited from their Anglo-Saxon predecessors a claim to overlordship. Border raids by the Welsh in the 1060s prompted serious consideration of the Welsh question. By 1135, under successive Anglo-Norman kings, a boundary zone of castles and nascent towns had been established along the Marches from Cardiff to Chester. Towns flourished particularly in south Wales during the eleventh and twelfth centuries: places like Monmouth, Cardiff, Abergavenny, Brecon (where the first town was laid out in the castle bailey, a pattern found elsewhere in the Welsh zone), Carmarthen and Pembroke. This southern group was complemented by a second wave of fortress towns added in the north and west by Edward I's campaigns in the 1270s. By 1300, Wales had about a hundred towns, though many were small; this has led to the assertion that by this time Wales was as urbanized a country as England. So far there is little archaeological support for this, though evidence is growing.[47]

In Scotland, by the eleventh century, there were also political and economic systems which could organize and support substantial centres of population, but urban history is obscure before the widespread introduction of the 'burgh' and its privileges by King David I (1124–53) and his successors. Some towns, like Edinburgh and Stirling, grew next to citadels; while others, such as Lanark, Selkirk and Dunfermline, are on unprotected sites. In Scotland there were very few Roman sites that might be reused, so other beginnings for the medieval towns have to be sought. Some towns, such as Aberdeen, Dunfermline and St Andrews (which may have had origins in the eighth century, as suggested by recent excavation of a cemetery), were clearly in existence by the time of David I.[48] It is important (especially for English readers) to remember that Scotland was a separate kingdom. The bulk of her overseas trade was with Flanders and Artois; by the 1290s Scottish merchants had their own district in Bruges. Some of the more prominent early Scottish burgesses seem to have come from Flanders; much of the Scottish countryside was given over to sheep farming to feed the Flemish demand for wool. Spanish iron was imported at Ayr, and Spanish merchants may have bought fish at west coast ports.

In England, towards the end of the thirteenth century, there are signs of economic strain and social tensions, at least in the larger towns. The most important single industry was cloth, but in the thirteenth century, in the face of the highly urbanized Flemish industry, England became an exporter of raw materials, that is, wool. This placed England in the position of being a colony of Flanders. Flemings and Italians organized the trade, and English merchants resorted to repressive policies at home: more rigid enforcement of rules about trading (shown in the sudden increase of written records), seeking out cheaper labour in the countryside, and the development of monopolies.

The Black Death of 1348 was the *coup de grace* to a country already weakened by political problems and natural disasters.[49] England was at war with Scotland and from 1337 with France, which resulted in heavy taxes to pay for the king's campaigns. Crop failures and cattle disease caused widespread famines in 1315–25; a 50 per cent drop in production brought a 400 per cent increase in grain prices. Land prices in the middle of the City of London show that there was a decline in the fourteenth century (which lasted virtually to the middle of the sixteenth century), and it was under way well before the Black Death.[50] Though no accurate figures are available, it now seems possible that some towns in England suffered a 50 per cent loss of population from the plague: which would mean nearly 50,000 in London (as was claimed at the time or shortly after). Norwich's population fell from about 25,000 in 1333 to about 7,500 in 1377. The Black Death was a turning-point in urban history; thereafter there were great and permanent changes to the economy and social life, for instance the increased entry of women into the labour market in towns.[51]

This late medieval period, from about 1350 to 1500, has produced scores of beautiful parish churches, and many of the sturdy medieval buildings which have survived six hundred years in market towns. Rural housing improved, and there was a certain amount of conspicuous show in public and domestic building.[52] During the late fourteenth and fifteenth centuries cloth replaced wool as England's main export. By 1500 the bulk of the country's overseas trade was in English hands; so was the transformation of raw materials into finished products. The merchants had now also captured foreign markets. But many towns, some sooner than others, apparently went into decline. At Nottingham in 1376 houses were falling into decay; Bedford and Warwick similarly stagnated. At York around 1400, the textile industry was flourishing and the town's merchants engaged in overseas trade through the nearby port of Hull. Within thirty years, the textile industry had migrated to the countryside and wool exports had slumped. Hull could not compensate by more exports of cloth, for it faced Hanse opposition in the Baltic and London's interests in Flanders. Lincoln was declining more rapidly, initially from the effect of the plague and then from problems with its vital waterways, the Fosdyke to the Trent and the Witham to Boston. There was a general slump or economic depression in the middle of the fifteenth century, which adversely affected both large and small towns, particularly those dependent on exporting goods.[53] In Wales, also, towns experienced a lengthy period of decline or 'shaking out', characterized by reductions in populations and the disappearance of some small communities; but also by the growth of market centres in other places from the fifteenth century.[54] In the 1970s and 1980s there were generally sterile debates among historians about economic and demographic decline in late medieval British towns; they and geographers have now moved on and talk of change or realignment instead.[55] Many villages disappeared, but very few towns; they survived. Those in charge of towns complained, but it may be that the standard of living for ordinary people such as artisans improved.

Some towns clearly succeeded. Gloucester and Coventry switched attention from wool to cloth production. Salisbury and Norwich did likewise, and whole regions came to specialize in cloth: notably the south-west (Totnes, Castle Combe), East Anglia (Lavenham, Hadleigh) and the West Riding of Yorkshire (Halifax and Wakefield). Ports also fared better, as demonstrated by the fortunes of Bristol and London, or Hull after 1560; but not so much the southern and eastern ports such as Southampton, Boston and King's Lynn, within the increasing range of London's pull.

In the capital, whereas the earlier period had been one of urban industrial production and the growth of guild or craft power, this later period is one of decline in urban industry and the subsequent waning of the power of the guilds. At the same time London rose as the principal distributor of luxury goods (as shown in the Paston letters of the fifteenth century). Trends in this direction had started by 1300, when the pewter and brass industries were based primarily in the capital. All manufacturing trades were also stimulated by the increasing crystallization of the royal and government offices nearby at Westminster. In Scotland, Edinburgh probably had a similar dominating effect, controlling key sectors of overseas trade and contributing to the decline of many Scottish towns until 1500 or later. In general, trading zones within Britain (that is, the distribution of products) were larger in 1500 than in 1300.

We have sketched out three introductory topics: the rise and nature of medieval urban archaeology in Britain, the medieval town as a European phenomenon, and an outline of the period. The rest of this book looks at selected themes in the archaeology of the medieval town. First, two chapters form a more detailed introduction to the study of the medieval townscape: the main features in the town plan, and the domestic setting of many activities within the urban space. Then follow three chapters exploring functions against this background: crafts and industry, trade and commerce, and the role of the church (both parish churches and religious houses). To some extent military functions will be dealt with in Chapter 2 on the town plan, in brief consideration of castles and defences, but we have regretfully omitted detailed study of them, and leave that to others. Chapter 7 deals with the ecological study of medieval life in towns, its processes and their consequences. The final chapter both lists unfinished business and looks ahead to the next set of questions. It also asks what the role of the student of medieval towns is in today's society, and how archaeologists should argue for and take part in the future of medieval towns in our own century.

2 Topographical factors in the growth of towns

During the late eleventh, twelfth and thirteenth centuries urban expansion took place, to varying degrees, in all parts of Britain. For the existing Anglo-Saxon towns in England this comprised filling-out the unsettled areas within the town and spreading beyond boundaries such as defences (sometimes of Roman origin) in often carefully planned extensions. Away from the established centres, expansion took two clear forms: the foundation of new towns, and the spread of market rights and fairs which might be a catalyst to the transformation of loosely formed places into towns. Kings, lords and bishops promoted villages to boroughs, often by adding new areas of settlement. As far as general patterns can be seen in England and Wales, royal foundations were common before 1100, but seigneurial foundations (those founded by a secular or religious lord) were more conspicuous in the late twelfth and early thirteenth century. Towns were also being established in Scotland from the late eleventh century, but the mix of royal and noble founders was different and the country did not have so many new foundations in the thirteenth century as in England or Wales.[1]

The parts of a medieval town which are to be described here are common to towns all over Europe. Most of the several thousand cities and towns in medieval Europe had a market place, a church, often a castle and sometimes defences. The short analysis which follows here is necessarily of British towns, with occasional parallels from abroad. But the archaeological patterns to be observed, and the archaeological objectives, are the same for each country. Indeed, we need surveys of the topographical development of towns in other individual European countries for comparison. Only then will any regional or national differences in the history of towns, or the attitudes of people towards towns, become apparent.[2]

In this chapter, we are essentially concerned with natural and man-made boundaries (rivers, defences), definable zones inside and outside the town (trade quarters, suburbs) and major constructions or spaces in the urban landscape which were usually the focus of specific activity (castles, churches, market places, public buildings, bridges). As we review the evidence, we should keep in mind that we are seeking patterns of location or relationship – if the castle is here, the later market will probably be there – and evidence of how the principal monuments of the town affected each other by the functions they expressed. The existence of walls might cramp the limit of settlement, or the town might expand around its defences, fanning out from the gates. The expanding influence of a nodal point for public resort such as the gate of a large monastery would affect the character of its surroundings, and in particular other prominent buildings such as parish churches in its immediate vicinity. We can attempt to gauge how much architectural and artistic energy went into the construction and embellishment of public buildings and

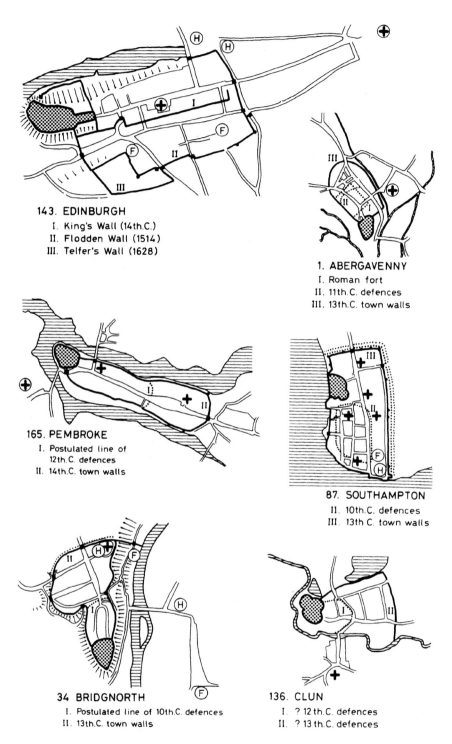

143. EDINBURGH
I. King's Wall (14th.C.)
II. Flodden Wall (1514)
III. Telfer's Wall (1628)

1. ABERGAVENNY
I. Roman fort
II. 11th.C. defences
III. 13th.C. town walls

165. PEMBROKE
I. Postulated line of
12th.C. defences
II. 14th.C. town walls

87. SOUTHAMPTON
II. 10th.C. defences
III. 13th C. town walls

34 BRIDGNORTH
I. Postulated line of 10th.C. defences
II. 13th.C. town walls

136. CLUN
I. ? 12th.C. defences
II. ? 13th.C. defences

Figure 2.1 Maps of selected medieval towns: those which enlarged their area of settlement and enclosed it with defences (Bond 1987).

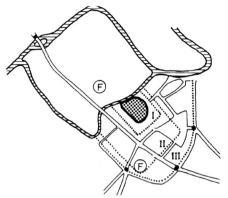

25. DONCASTER
  I. Late Roman fort, partly reutilised as outer bailey of castle
  II. Postulated line of burh defences
  III. Medieval town ditch

26. GODMANCHESTER
  I. Roman defences
  II. 9th–11th.C. defences

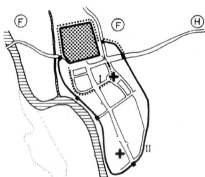

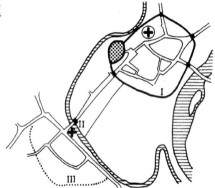

132. CARDIFF
  I. Postulated line of 12th.C. defences
  II. 14th.C. town walls

160. MONMOUTH
  I. 13th.C. town walls
  II. Monnow Gate
  III. Clawdd Du (Over Monnow)

N

 Castle
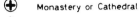 Monastery or Cathedral
 ✚ Church
 Ⓕ Friary
 Ⓗ Hospital
 ——— Town walls
 ·········· Bank / ditch defences

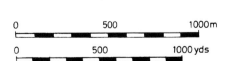

| 0 | 500 | 1000m |
| 0 | 500 | 1000 yds |

structures such as town gates or quays. Some patterns, for instance the division of towns into quarters which reflected trade specializations, wealth or local communities (clans, immigrants from specific villages or abroad, in fact any group which defined itself within the town), may be difficult to identify from archaeology alone; this particular question is dealt with in Chapters 3 and 4 below.

Contours and the form of the town: rivers and roads

First, the archaeologist should look at the way the town changed its shape and the nature of its immediate surroundings in three dimensions, usually over a long period. Deliberate man-made extensions such as reclamation into rivers is dealt with separately below; but there were other, larger and perhaps unconscious changes to the landscape as a result of the town being where it was. At Winchester, for instance, a Roman town, the walled city in its river valley had an effect like a weir in creating a silting plain upstream of the walled area. A soft, high site such as Shrewsbury, it is suggested, seems to get generally lower over time, due to constant foundation-digging.[3]

In the medieval period, many towns were moulded to contours of hills which affected the design and development of the place. Some, like Durham or Lincoln, still display the crags or steep slopes on which they were built; others, like the City of London, far less so. At Edinburgh (Fig. 2.1), the old town still clings to its narrow ridge of rock, with the High Street forming the spine for properties to either side; settlement spread below it on the south into the Cowgate valley, since the main approach roads to the citadel were from the south and east. The underlying skeleton of the town is therefore often natural features, such as hills and streams. Stream-valleys, where they either run through the town or next to it, are extremely useful reservoirs of strata, often comprised of domestic and trade rubbish from the town itself in waterlogged and therefore well-preserved condition. Wet conditions also affected the nature of buildings, as at Winchester again, where most of the documented medieval cellars were dug in the drier, higher ground on the east side of the town.[4]

The town's form can also include man-made reaction to the elements, such as sea embankments: at least 54 sea floods around England are recorded in the thirteenth century.[5] In several ports, such as Hull, the ground surface was raised throughout much of the town against future inundation. In the majority of Dutch towns which lie in the vast delta of the Rhine, Meuse and Scheldt rivers, the connections between town and landscape have greatly affected the character of archaeological research. Here the nature and movement of rivers, flooding and sedimentation are constant archaeological subjects. Because of the waterlogged conditions, finds have been numerous everywhere, and ecological research became part of Dutch urban archaeology from an early stage.[6] This relation of a town to the invading sea or a flooding river is an extension of the study of the town's waterfront.

Towns multiplied on coasts, on rivers, and along major roads. Transport by both road and water was important in the Middle Ages, but the greater traffic in goods went by water. It may have cost between twelve and eighteen times as much to transport grain by road as by water. As late as the 1770s, Adam Smith calculated that an eight-wheeled wagon travelling between London and Edinburgh could haul four tons of goods in about six weeks, but that a ship with a crew of eight travelling by sea between the two places, in about the same time, carried 200 tons; it was probably so in the medieval period.[7] The ports in particular were stimulated by an export trade in corn, minerals and wool from their hinterlands, but also by the use of the sea as a highway which linked one part of Britain to another. Nearly half of all medieval new towns in England were ports, on the coast or at estuaries; the majority of these were on the south coast, acting as shipping and landing points to and from the continent. In Wales, 24 towns occupied coastal sites. The majority were English foundations, whose garrisons could be landed and supplied by ship. Several also had profitable fishing industries during the medieval period, and the economic life of the town centred as much on the public quay as on the castle.

Rivers were crucial to the development of many towns, encouraging long-distance trade and giving commercial power to towns which were both inland and yet within reach of the sea, such as York and Cambridge, which still entertained sea-going ships in the fifteenth century. Rivers were major route-ways in Wales, and towns such as Monmouth gained importance, both strategic and economic, from being at a river-junction (Fig. 2.1). In the Thames valley the system of rivers and creeks may have been a physical factor in the creation of a geographical and economic region centred on the Thames; some Midlands counties, administrative units of Saxon origin, have rivers forming the spine of each, and the shire town lies at a central point on the system.[8] Rivers also provided lines of natural defence, sometimes making a full circuit of walls unnecessary (as at Llanidloes (Powys)). They supplied power for the town mills (as at Chipping Campden or Winchester) and water for both home and trade consumption.[9] Some towns, such as Cork in Ireland (Fig. 2.2), were surrounded by channels and in such cases there was probably more traffic on water than on routes by land. In several towns, such as Beverley between 1115 and 1130, parts of streams or rivers were canalized to improve waterborne traffic. Bristol changed the course of its river. In Flanders, Ypres grew to be the largest manufacturing centre in the county of Flanders largely because of its place on the navigable part of the river system, assisted by the digging of a canal.[10]

Rivers also had to be crossed, or made accessible by bringing roads to them for the loading and unloading of goods and people. Bridges were often instrumental in the siting of new towns, and in the development of old towns. In some cases land routes were diverted to new boroughs with new bridges, as at New Sleaford (Lincs) or Boroughbridge (N. Yorks); the names Stockbridge (Hants), Uxbridge (Mddx) and just plain Brigg (N. Lincs) emphasize the main reason for the place. New stone bridges formed natural attractions to commerce and were an essential feature of new towns, such as Midlands towns laid out by Benedictine abbeys, at Burton or Pershore. Stratford-upon-Avon only had a poor timber bridge without a causeway through marshes until the end of the fifteenth century, when it was rebuilt sumptuously in stone with fourteen arches, and country folk then flocked to the town, whereas before they had been afraid.[11] A bridge was sometimes part of a planned development of a whole new suburb or an extension of one, as at Redcliffe in Bristol in

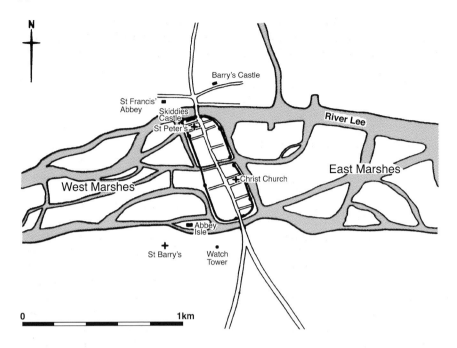

Figure 2.2   Cork in 1545, showing its position on several islands, surrounded by water (National Trust for Ireland).

the 1240s (along with quays and the Port Wall); or at Exeter, where a suburb on Exe Island was promoted by the building of St Edmund's Church and the contiguous Exe Bridge (which still partly survives) around 1200.

Once a bridge was in position, the alignment of a street might change and aim towards it, as possibly at Fishergate, Norwich. The bottleneck or limiting effect of a bridge could define different archaeological cultures: in fourteenth-century Bedford, for instance, glazed pottery from Lyveden in Northamptonshire was widespread north of the river, while the comparable ware south of the river came from Oxfordshire; this despite the existence of the stone bridge since the late twelfth century; or, the excavator suggests, perhaps because of the tolls levied upon it.[12] The effect of building a bridge at one town could be damaging to another: the construction of a bridge over the upper Thames at Abingdon in the fifteenth century was a cause of decay to nearby Wallingford, also on the river, but now placed at a severe disadvantage. The building of a bridge at Ware (Herts) was seen to damage the livelihoods of the people of Hertford. The detailed scrutiny of medieval bridges, aided by surviving building and repair accounts in municipal records, can say much about the town's understanding of its position in the hinterland, and which routes it saw as important in furthering its economic prospects.[13] On the other hand, the correlation of bridges and prosperity was not a simple linear progression: Norwich had five bridges (two more than medieval Rome), and an area as large as London's, but only one quarter of the population. Bridges were only one of many factors.

A main road running through a town was probably as important a cause of growth as any other. The Roman road system contributed to the rebirth of London after each of its periods of destruction or decline; then, as now, it was a difficult place to avoid. In England and in Wales, many medieval towns grew up on or near parts of the Roman road system. Most of the 24 medieval towns of Essex, for instance, developed on the radial roads north and east of London. Chelmsford was founded *de novo* in 1199 by the Bishop of London, who also extended the existing settlement at Braintree; both were on routeway junctions. St Osyth's priory founded Brentwood on one side of the road between London and Colchester and Ipswich in 1176, and Epping was founded by the canons of Waltham Abbey in similar fashion in the mid twelfth century.[14] Both these settlements were markets and yet occupation was for a long time confined to one side of the street only. A combination of studies of kings' itineraries round their castles and manors, and maps such as that of Matthew Paris (*c.* 1250) and the Gough map (*c.* 1340), can produce a map of medieval roads, at least in England.[15] The importance of the road itself to a settlement can be seen in the number of inns which accrued to make the village or town a stopping-place along the route, at least from the middle of the fourteenth century. It is now thought that for most inland towns, trade depended largely on the road system rather than rivers. In special situations, such as the outports of London, road connections to the capital and preferably to other parts of the country as well were vital. On the Continent, the development of roads contributed to the success in the twelfth century of the Champagne and other fairs, and throughout the Middle Ages to cities such as Nuremberg and Milan, or towns on a route between the larger centres of Cologne and Ghent.[16]

Anticipating traffic along roads or rivers may have influenced new ideas on the siting of towns. It has been suggested that in the thirteenth century in England new towns were no longer sited at the gate of a monastery or castle, but at nodes in the communication system, 'often at the boundaries of different blocks of landscape.' In this way they would be turning away from a local centre of patronage and power to the possibilities of maximizing trade in a wider locality or region.[17]

Factors in growth: planned towns and planned parts of towns

An enthusiasm for studying the plans of medieval towns has given rise to an impression (i) that they arrived as a new form of settlement in the twelfth and especially thirteenth centuries, and (ii) that they were usually fully formed and of a single period of planning. On the contrary, we now know that the tradition of planned towns can be traced back to Mercia and Wessex in the eighth and ninth centuries; and secondly, towns and villages usually contain a number of planned elements of different periods.

Medieval towns in England and Wales can be divided into two groups: those planned largely at a single instant (and sometimes also called 'planted' towns, though the metaphor may have been lost on the originators) and those of organic growth, which are usually towns with long histories. The distinction was firmly made by Maurice Beresford in his study (1967, repr. 1988) of medieval new towns, which identified 251 English and Welsh towns created

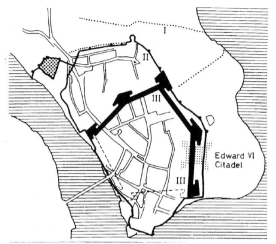

129. BERWICK-ON-TWEED

  I. Spades Mire (Early 13th.C. defences)
  II. Early 14th.C. town walls
  III. Elizabethan ramparts

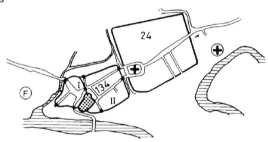

24. OLD CARMARTHEN
134. NEW CARMARTHEN
  I. Town wall (1233)
  II. Town wall (1415)

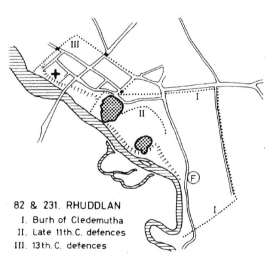

82 & 231. RHUDDLAN
  I. Burh of Cledemutha
  II. Late 11th.C. defences
  III. 13th.C. defences

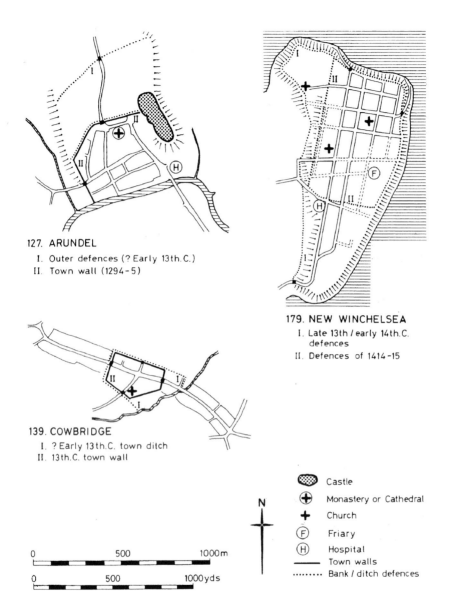

127. ARUNDEL

I. Outer defences (? Early 13th.C.)
II. Town wall (1294–5)

139. COWBRIDGE

I. ? Early 13th.C. town ditch
II. 13th.C. town wall

179. NEW WINCHELSEA

I. Late 13th / early 14th.C. defences
II. Defences of 1414–15

Castle	
Monastery or Cathedral	
Church	
Friary	
Hospital	
Town walls	
Bank / ditch defences	

0   500   1000 m
0   500   1000 yds

N

Figure 2.3 Maps of selected medieval towns: those which contracted, or radically changed, the area of settlement in the medieval period, as shown by their defences (Bond 1987).

between 1066 and 1368. Though this approach was criticized by urban historians as leading to over-simplification,[18] new towns remain a significant feature of the period.

From the modern street-plan of towns, or from maps showing their former state, we can identify certain layouts which were shared by new towns and by planned extensions to existing settlements. Three main variants have been identified. First, a small number of English towns and over thirty towns in Wales have some element of a grid pattern of streets. A chequerboard pattern formed by at least four streets and nine squares is found rarely (Salisbury; Winchelsea (Fig. 2.3)) and must always have been exceptional. A grid on a later map or evident now may however be an illusion. Ludlow, which now comprises a grid of streets, probably grew in a series of stages.[19] A second grid-plan produced a ladder-like effect with two main streets in parallel (e.g. New Shoreham, Melcombe Regis). Thirdly, particularly in the years up to 1200, an urban castle might dominate the town plan to the extent of making it circular or D-shaped, following the castle's outer defences (Barnstaple, Pleshey). Many towns comprised only one street of opposing properties, on the way to the castle; in some cases, as at Pembroke, the lie of the land dictated this.

A second group of apparently planned elements were more irregular, and concern the emphasis placed on the market, especially as defensive considerations declined during the thirteenth century. Markets might be in the main street, causing its edges to bulge into a cigar-shape, or the meeting of two or three ways might produce a triangular space; Brecon and Cardiff are built around the meeting of two streets in a T-shape. These two market-forms are very common in towns, and one might ask what, if any, deliberate policy of planning they represent, apart from the initial decision to start the market.

Ideas of what may be termed medieval town-planning are most evident in the new towns associated with Edward I. In the north at Berwick, and in Wales at Flint, Conwy and Caernarvon, he hoped both to keep the peace by establishing garrison towns but also to encourage it by promoting ports and markets; incidentally ensuring effective markets to feed the garrisons. New towns in Gascony in southern France, then held by the English crown, are called bastides; the name is related to *bâtir*, to build, and the streets, public buildings and market places of the new towns bring into clearer focus the factors at work in the design of towns. Edward I gathered together experts in the field of town-planning, as it then existed as a subject; the new towns of the years around 1300 in Wales and Gascony are the most 'planned' of all the English foundations.

Flint (1277; Fig. 2.4a) was the first of Edward's bastides in Wales, and work began simultaneously on the castle and the town. Here the land allowed regular blocks to be laid out, with space for the market inside the walls; as at Caernarvon, the castle could be defended separately and would not have to suffer the fate of the town if attacked. The town's defences, though on a large scale, were however of earth, and this despite being sited on a sandstone outcrop. It is possible that the design owed something to Edward's recent visits to Gascon towns, or the Mediterranean bastide of Aigues Mortes, which he would have seen in 1270 when departing on a crusade.[20] In turn the design of Flint may have influenced that of New Winchelsea (Sussex), the town (sub-

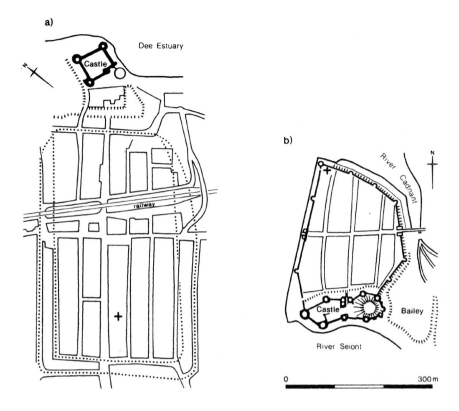

Figure 2.4 Plans of (a) Flint, (b) Caernarvon, showing main topographical elements. This also shows that Flint was from the beginning meant to be twice the size of Caernarvon.

sequently a failure) with the most rectangular grid plan in medieval England.

Caernarvon (1283; Fig. 2.4b) was to be a fortified town on the edge of the hostile kingdom of Gwynedd; in 1284, a year after work started on it, the town became the administrative and judicial capital of the principality of North Wales. Here a new castle and a new town were planned as one. There was a Welsh settlement on the site, but no concessions were made to it in the new rectangular grid of streets. Outside the remarkable castle, the small town was enclosed with stone walls, complete with towers at regular intervals and two opposed gates which marked the ends of the High Street. Other streets at right angles divided the intramural area into eight blocks; the market place lay outside the walls to the east, on the site of the previous Norman castle, next to which a large mill-pool was crossed by a stone bridge of seven arches.[21] The new town was probably meant to remind a well-travelled visitor of the Byzantine capital of Constantinople. We cannot say if the principles of order and uniformity evident in the design of streets extended to house-design, since no medieval houses survive in the town; though accounts show that unused stone from the castle was sold off cheaply to the burgesses for building. Although the Welsh bastide towns began their English period as political and

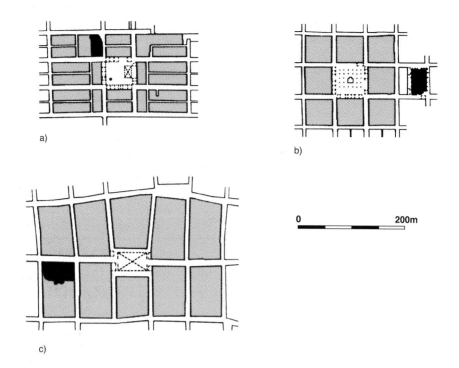

Figure 2.5 Three distinctive plans of bastide towns: (a) Monpazier (Landes); (b) Mirande (Gers); (c) Gimont (Gers) (Lauret *et al.* 1988). In each case the church is shown in black.

military centres, and all suffered during serious rebellions because they were identified with English interests, some functioned as towns in their regions just like their English counterparts. Aberystwyth was granted a market monopoly within a radius of 15 miles, and Caernarvon for 8 miles; the latter tried to prohibit trade at Bangor. Occasionally ships from Ireland, Brittany and Iberia came to Caernarvon and Cardiff.[22]

Groups of planned towns occur in most other European countries: they have been especially studied in France, Italy, Germany and Poland. To compare with the English material we look at aspects of those in Gascony, and a group in north Italy. Recent work by French scholars has emphasized the great variety of plan among the bastide towns of Gascony, but three groups sharing similar characteristics are noteworthy.[23] They are all roughly contemporary in the period 1260–1320. The first group, called the Aquitaine type, comprises 27 towns in the northern, largely English part of the region; Monpazier is the best example (Figs 2.5a, 2.7). Four large streets divide the urban space like the framework of a noughts-and-crosses board. Between them are smaller streets, and the middle blocks have transverse alleys so that the central market place (Fig. 2.6) is surrounded by thin blocks of housing. The church is most often immediately off the square, at one of the corners.

A second Gascon type comprises 15 towns largely founded by the French

Figure 2.6   The market place of Monpazier, surrounded by fourteenth- and fifteenth-century stone buildings on arcades. The walks inside the arcades, semi-public space, are usually used as extensions to the adjacent shops, today as in the medieval period. In the right foreground, the reconstructed market hall which would (and sometimes still does) hold the municipal weights and measuring implements.

king or his nobles, to the south of the first group; Mirande is the model (Figs 2.5b, 2.7). Here streets are of the same width throughout, and the blocks are square, giving a chequerboard appearance; at least eight blocks are formed around the square. The church is normally in a block to one side and outside the basic rectangle of inner blocks.

A third group of six towns, founded by French lords towards the south of the region, are named after their type-site, Gimont (Figs. 2.5c, 2.7). The Gimontois type has two or three parallel major streets crossed by smaller transverse streets so that the blocks have a rectangular shape, and the square, sometimes narrow, is placed across the axis of the main street. The church is on this axis but a block away from the square.

These are only 48 towns out of nearly 800 in the study; and quite a few bastides, like their conterparts in England and Wales, were additions to existing settlements, so that deduction from the plan alone can be hazardous. They are also different from the majority of British towns in that very few contained a castle which would distort the topography. But these three varieties show different approaches to town-planning which may reflect local or political preferences. Though some of these towns were in English territory at the time of their foundation, their squares and the arcades around the squares were features not repeated in England.

It is possible that the experiments in Gascony would be known to planners of the late thirteenth and fourteenth centuries in Florence. In northern Italy,

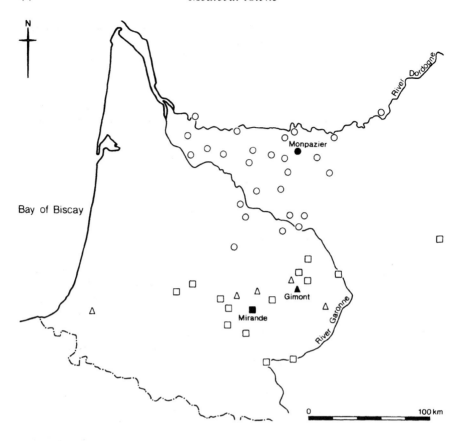

Figure 2.7 The distribution of the three types of plan in bastide towns in Gascony: circles, the Aquitaine model (like Monpazier); squares, the Gascon model (like Mirande); triangles, the Gimontois model (like Gimont) (Lauret *et al*. 1988).

towns tried more than elsewhere to establish a political and economic region or *contado* for themselves, since there was no central monarchy and wars between cities were frequent. This meant dominating the countryside, and moving villagers into new towns which had all the kit of parts at once: defences, rectilinear streets, churches and other amenities (though not usually a castle). A study has been made of several towns founded by Florence to its north and east.[24] Here, it is claimed, the streets were laid out on principles strictly derived from geometry, and the urban fabric is a work of art; the new towns mirrored their mother city in their sense of order and social composition. By insisting on straight wide streets the planners sought to destroy previous concepts of arrangement of space in Italian towns, where lords built towers and lived in straggling compounds around courtyards. They still, however, allowed that the new citizens could stay in neighbourhoods based on their original villages. But now the community was based on two sides of a street or a corner; the larger streets may have defined these quarters. At one town, San Giovanni, the street intersections were the sites of neighbourhood wells; at another, Terranuova, several major intersections had parish churches on them. Such rigour in planning is normally associated with the Renaissance in the sixteenth century; but many of the principles were being tried out before 1350.

All over Europe, however, the majority of towns were not planned at one instant, and these experiments or special cases must be seen in context. A distinction has been suggested between bastides, which were truly new towns, and 'planned' towns, which were, like Lübeck, developed on or next to previously inhabited sites;[25] but this is probably of little assistance to the archaeologist. For the majority of towns, though types of plan can be collected and analysed, a more profitable approach is to accept that many town plans were composed of a series of units of different periods. The clearest examples are those towns of great age, such as, in Britain, Abergavenny, Doncaster, Godmanchester (all shown in Fig. 2.1) and Hereford, but the apparent homogeneity of planned towns should also be regarded with caution. New towns might be laid out systematically at first, but soon spilled over and developed their own idiosyncracies. In addition, as demonstrated in many 'planned' cases, the units of new settlement were based on field boundaries and ridges, as in the twelfth century at Stratford and Lichfield (Fig. 2.8).[26] Little is known of what precedes the town of Salisbury on its site, but the alignment of some streets may have been influenced by previous drainage ditches or, more significantly, the intention to run water-channels along the middle of the streets. The completed plan there is not particularly regular; only three of the streets are parallel. Other towns were developments of villages: in 1207, a wide street was laid out from a crossing of the River Aire in Yorkshire to the outskirts of an existing village, and the town of Leeds was born.[27] There is also evidence of town extensions in England at several post-Roman periods, not just the thirteenth century: the Anglo-Saxon and Danish burhs of the ninth and tenth centuries, and Norman extensions or replanning at Northampton, Nottingham and Norwich.

The larger Scottish towns of the twelfth century show a variety of plans, including single-street designs (Elgin, Forres, Montrose), three streets converging on an important church (St Andrews), two streets at right-angles to a river or the coast (Perth, Arbroath), and triangular market places (Haddington, Dundee, Dumfries). Their apparently homogenous designs by the post-medieval period were however often the result, again, of cumulative phases of settlement from the twelfth to the fifteenth centuries and later, as suggested at Perth by analysis of street-blocks, plan units and plot widths.[28] The emphasis of wider European studies has also been on the cumulative character of town plans, often with many stages from a Dark-Age or Carolingian fortified centre, through markets, extensions and suburbs, to the fully expanded city of Renaissance times: this can still be seen by walking round Augsburg, Gdańsk, Münster or Ulm.[29]

A second conclusion, at least for Britain, is that many shrunken medieval towns still need basic fieldwork to outline their extent and component parts. At New Radnor (Powys), for instance, the town in 1335 was evidently prosperous, but is now only a village; several sections of the original grid of streets are beneath fields, some marked by hedge-lines. The shrunken port of Torksey on the River Trent is now only a small group of buildings, but was formerly of

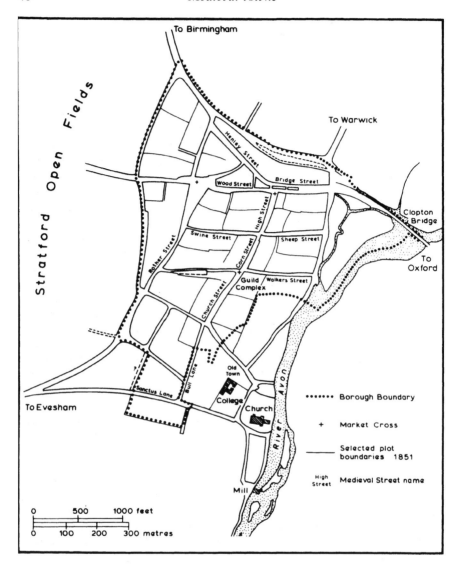

Figure 2.8 Stratford-upon-Avon: the burgages in the central area around Sheep Street and High Street, it has been argued, are based on open-field divisions of the earlier village (Slater 1980).

much more substantial urban extent, with three parish churches and two monasteries. Excavations of deserted towns, or deserted parts of towns, throw light on the tattered edges of urbanism. At the edges of medieval towns, as in many small towns today, there were farms in the same street as more urban buildings.[30]

Defences

Two clear influences on the shape, extent and rate of growth of towns were their defences and their castles. This large subject cannot be examined on a Europe-wide scale here, and only aspects of the British evidence will be discussed, to explore both the kinds of evidence they have to offer and the interleaving of their functions with others in the confined space of the town.

Defences usually signified the limits of the built-up space, and the size or the intended size of the settlement, though not necessarily the limits of the town's civil authority. Extensions to circuits might be caused by growth of population or expansion of building beyond original boundaries, as at Abergavenny, Bridgnorth and Southampton in the thirteenth century, or Cardiff and Pembroke in the fourteenth century (Fig. 2.1). Only Bristol (Figs 2.9–10), Lincoln, Norwich and York[31] developed extensions in several directions which resemble the concentric rings of defences seen in continental cities, though there may be more examples to be identified. We need to know more about towns where defences were built but the expected new housing did not follow, or where, as in Hereford and Nottingham, the enclosed spaces lapsed into cultivation or dereliction. Rebuilding the defences to define a smaller area than before, which presumably reflects urban decay or retrenchment, is rare but there are examples at New Winchelsea, where the defences in 1414–15 reduced the area of the town, and at Berwick-on-Tweed, where the Elizabethan circuit covered only two thirds of the area of the fourteenth-century town (Fig. 2.3). Alternatively, city walls might be built, or lines of defence strengthened, by joining together existing lines of the walls of stone houses and blocking up openings such as doors and windows, as is documented at Southampton in the fourteenth century, and in Edinburgh in both the fifteenth (the King's Wall, 1425–50) and the sixteenth centuries (Flodden Wall, 1513; Fig. 2.1).

Bond has distinguished seven major types of urban defences in the medieval period.[32] Roman defensive circuits were reused by medieval towns on the same sites, for instance at Canterbury, Lincoln, London and York. The walls were of masonry, and the surviving Roman gates formidable structures, so that it was usual in such towns for the majority of the medieval gates to occupy the same sites as their Roman predecessors. Any new gates, such as London's Moorgate of 1415, therefore signify new interests: in this case, reclamation of the marsh outside the walls to provide an open space for the citizens.

At other towns, a defensive circuit originally of Anglo-Saxon date was partly or wholly reused by the medieval town, as at Barnstaple, Bridgnorth (Fig. 2.1), Oxford or Totnes; this was usually of earth, though some, for instance at Hereford, Cricklade and Wallingford, had been reinforced with masonry before the Conquest. Elsewhere, Saxon circuits were superseded by expansion in the medieval town, as at Hereford, Norwich, Stamford and Worcester, and thus evidence of ramparts or ditches might lie unsuspected beneath ordinary medieval house-sites or backyards. In a further, numerically larger group of towns, the new Anglo-Saxon circuit of defences was by contrast of no post-Conquest importance (e.g. at Bedford, Maldon, Northampton, Rhuddlan (Fig. 2.3), Southampton (Fig. 2.1), Warwick and Worcester). This

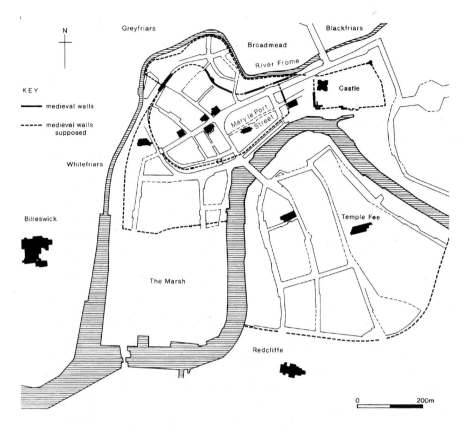

Figure 2.9 Bristol: map showing the castle and the main areas of medieval growth and their defences (City of Bristol Museum and Art Gallery). This map was produced in the 1980s, and is now subject to further revision.

presumably relates to a change of emphasis within the town after the Norman Conquest; the abandonment of older defensive concerns must mean new settlement (within the town or outside it, in another place) and changes in economic direction.

New medieval circuits or extensions were substantially of masonry in the larger towns such as Berwick (Fig. 2.3), Bristol (Fig. 2.9), Edinburgh (Fig. 2.1), London (Blackfriars), Newcastle, Norwich, Oxford (where towards the end of the thirteenth century the north-eastern side of the town was given a stretch of double walling, resembling a concentric fortification),[33] Shrewsbury, Southampton, Stirling and Worcester. Here one might look for contemporary defensive developments such as interval towers, crenellations or gunports, which appear in the later fourteenth century at the more important south coast towns such as Southampton (*c*.1360), Dover and Canterbury; on the Continent the development of artillery rendered medieval city walls useless during the following century. At Norwich in the 1390s, the city erected the surviving Cow Tower, which seems to have been a free-standing artillery tower, a remarkable development for a town. Smaller towns could also have walls

Figure 2.10 Bristol: excavation of a length of the Portwall by Temple Meads, showing the wall leaning outwards (City of Bristol Museum and Art Gallery).

Figure 2.11 The interior of the second floor of Monk Bar, York, showing the port-cullis winding mechanism and vaulting, early fourteenth century (National Monuments Record). The survival of such gates provides important parallels for use of stone and construction techniques on secular and religious sites from the twelfth century. The upper parts of gates were also lived in.

mainly or wholly of masonry, such as at Arundel, Clun and Monmouth in the thirteenth century, or New Carmarthen twice, in 1233 and on a different scale in 1415 (Figs 2.1, 2.3). At Chepstow (Gwent), a long wall was built in the late thirteenth century across the neck of the peninsula on which the town lay, to demarcate an area twice the size of contemporary Cardiff.

Gates of masonry were an essential part of defences, and a number survive (Fig. 2.11), though in most towns the circuit walls have been lost. In a further group of towns the gates were of masonry but the defences of earth and timber, giving both strength and prestige to the entry points into the town. This was the case, for instance, at Beverley (where a brick gate of 1409, the North Bar, survives), Cardiff (twelfth century, before the later stone walls), Coventry, Pontefract and Tewkesbury. At Banbury there were four gates, but no walls; Aberdeen and Glasgow also had gates across their streets, but no other defences.[34] These gates by themselves underline one of the main func-tions of town gates, to be a symbolic barrier and a collecting-point for tolls on merchandise entering the town.

Bond identifies three further types of urban defences which would make good research projects. The first are new medieval defences for towns which were subsequently deserted or destroyed; many are in Wales. The walled borough of Old Denbigh declined at the expense of its suburbs because it was virtually inaccessible; the division between the borough and the market out-side was mentioned in 1334. Towns at Dolforwyn (Powys) and Dryslwyn

(Carmarthen) were suppressed or destroyed by the English and Owen Glendower respectively; Glendower's forces also destroyed the town at Old Kidwelly (Dyfed), an important port with connections with Ireland, Gascony and Aquitaine.[35] A second small group of towns intended to erect defences, but they were probably never built or never completed, as at Holt (Clwyd), one of the largest Welsh boroughs in the early fourteenth century, or Woodstock (Oxon). This need not have been a result of lack of cash; at prosperous Salisbury, only two gates and very little of the defensive circuit were ever built. Thirdly, certain villages gained defences: were they unsuccessfully trying to be towns, or are we underestimating their medieval importance? Bond mentions in this context Bourne (Lincs), Pirton (Herts) and Pontesbury (Shrops).

Defences performed many primary and secondary functions besides defence of the town and exclusion of the outsider. Walling of towns along the south coast of England, or later on the east coast of Scotland, were part of a regional programme of defence against a neighbour (in the latter case, England). Gates were used as accommodation for civic officers, as chapels, lock-ups and meeting-rooms. Heads or quartered remains of condemned people who were well-known, and whose death had to be widely noted, were placed on poles above gates in London and the shire towns. The defensive system included fishponds at Stafford and York, and a lake at Edinburgh; at Hereford and Winchester water from the town ditch drove mills.

Defences (that is, the ditch, wall and bank behind) have several archaeological virtues. The ditches are often waterlogged, producing a different range of rubbish from that thrown in the waterfront zone along the town's river. The line of the defences often crosses earlier occupation, which is therefore sealed and preserved. Scrutiny and stone-by-stone recording (often by photogrammetry) of masonry gates and walls interlock with documentary evidence in identifying structures, techniques and extensions to the town.

Work in Canterbury provides an example.[36] Several excavations and observations of 1947–77 show that the medieval defences of Canterbury followed the line of their Roman predecessors, reusing three or more of the Roman gates. Twenty-four medieval towers, of at least two periods of construction, have been identified. An interesting sequence of archaeological deposits comes from an excavation of 1977 in Church Lane, on the defences by the North Gate. Most of the recorded periods of occupation are shown in one of the drawn sections (cross-sections through a number of deposits), which illustrates the pressure on space near major obstacles to expansion like a stone city wall (Fig. 2.12). This section was only of the wall and the layers behind it; any ditches in front had been removed by later activity.

Probably in the late third century, Roman occupation (layer 88) had been interrupted by the building of the first city wall (81, 82) and its bank or rampart (80, 77, 76, 75, 74). In the late Saxon or early Norman period an intramural street was laid along the back of the rampart, shown by the layers of pebbled street-metallings, resurfaced at least three times (66, 65, 62, 60; roadside gulley, 67). Five human burials were found in the small excavation; two of the graves can be seen in the section, with a general level of graveyard soil (54, 55, 53; later street, 52). These appear to form part of the graveyard of the church of St Mary-upon-Northgate which was built on top of the adjacent gate at this time; crenellations on the city wall, probably of early Norman

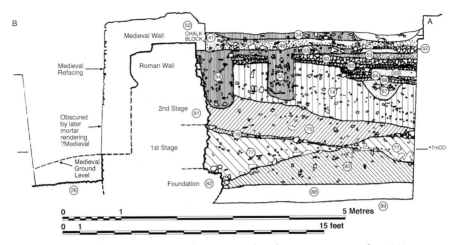

Figure 2.12 Canterbury: section of strata at Church Lane (Frere *et al.* 1982).

date, were embedded and fossilized in its north (exterior) side. The cemetery and streets were sealed by construction debris of the rebuilding of the city wall in the 1380s–90s (49); the original Roman wall was replaced with one in chalk with a knapped flint face (50). Medieval buildings immediately behind the wall also survive, in altered form, across the street.

Much archaeological work has taken place on medieval town defences in England and Wales, and a little in Scotland, but most of this work has been piecemeal and hurried, often ahead of bulldozing for ring roads and other modern necessities such as pedestrian subways. In avoiding historic centres which have clear amenity value, modern planners have destroyed large sections of medieval defences and the immediate suburbs. This may be inevitable, but it is certainly to be regretted. Towns were acquiring or refurbishing their walls late into the Middle Ages; the impetus rose from the insecurity of invasion or baronial warfare. But in the sixteenth and seventeenth centuries few defences were put to the test (except in the English Civil War), and town walls thereafter became an unwanted luxury. Churches have continued in use, and castles have proved difficult to eradicate; but defences were quickly overtaken by new pressures on space, and in Britain have largely disappeared. As a class of monument, they have become an endangered species.

The elucidation of the defences of medieval towns, the walls, ditches and gates (with or without adjacent walls) is one of the most significant contributions which archaeologists can make to the study of towns. Many towns laboured to complete their defences over a long period, and this is evident in the variety of forms of interval towers and other details, as at Hull, where the defensive circuit was rebuilt in brick over a seventy-year period. Documents are helpful, but rarely comprehensive. Many town extensions occurred in the eleventh to thirteenth centuries, when documents are scarce or non-existent. At this time especially towns attempted to define urban areas with walls or other physical boundaries, as a form of civic self-assertion, but also to have greater control over commercial transactions. A walled circuit, once completed, was a statement with regional or larger resonances: Norwich within its walls was the largest medieval city in area in England.[37]

Castles

A distinction should first be made between castle-boroughs, where an existing (often new) castle was the point of attraction for a new town, and truly 'urban castles', where castles were inserted into existing settlements.[38] In both cases there will be archaeological evidence for previous land-use; but in the second group, this will be already urban because part of the town was erased for the insertion of the castle.

The Norman kings and their subordinates built new castles which were physical statements of domination and at the same time powerful stimulants to urban growth. Besides offering security, any aristocratic residence would generate a market, and it is therefore not surprising that 80 per cent of all new towns in Wales and 75 per cent of new towns in England before 1150 grew up or were established next to a castle; the association of castle and burgh is even more marked in Scotland, where 31 of the 33 burghs founded by the king before 1286 were beside castles. There was a variety of factors influencing the siting of the castle and thereby the nascent town. At Ludgershall (Wilts), for instance, the twelfth-century castle seems to have adapted a prehistoric hill-fort, and the small town was laid out in stages below it; the castle environs included a designed landscape comprising two aristocratic parks for hunting. At Pleshey and Devizes, the design of the town in its defences suggests that both were founded at the same time; occasionally castles moved site, perhaps to encourage settlement in a better situation (as at Knighton (Powys) and Newport (Dyfed)). But in other cases the castle-borough failed, and several deserted sites in Wales and the adjacent border area show the form of these boroughs in their early stages. At Richard's Castle (Herefordshire), for instance, the large bailey of the castle contains a church, market place, and traces of burgage plots; the prominent defensive bank which surrounds the town was however not a primary feature, but added in the thirteenth century, perhaps when the settlement, like many others, was aspiring to be a town.[39]

A similar case is Saffron Walden (Essex), where the town has survived, but a period of building prompted by the lord of the castle failed to bring the hoped-for rewards.[40] In about 1144 the Mandevilles rebuilt the castle and enclosed a new town with two roughly concentric earthwork defences (Fig. 2.13). A market place and tenements were laid out within the outer circuit. In the early thirteenth century this nucleus was enlarged by the foundation of the new market place, within a grid of streets. But the enlarged town was never a success, and Walden remained a shrunken town, though quite large by Essex standards and certainly rich in the fifteenth and sixteenth centuries. In yet further examples, the economic future of the town lay away from the castle: at Salisbury and Thirsk protection was abandoned in the interest of better communications and economic prospects, and the town moved to a new site. Though castle-and-town foundations continued to be the norm in the frontier zone of Wales, England's relatively peaceful life after the civil war of 1136–54 meant that only kings founded new towns with the full defensive armoury of a castle.

In castle-boroughs the castle is usually on the edge of the town, often with its back to an adjacent river. Castles placed in existing towns were similarly on the edge of the settlement, often tied in to the Roman or Saxon defences (as at

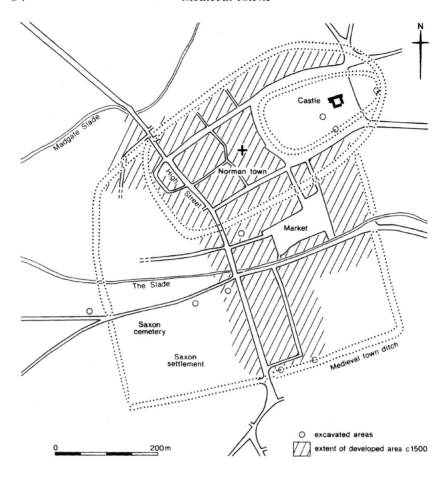

Madgate Slade

High Street

Castle

Norman town

Market

The Slade

Saxon
cemetery

Saxon
settlement

Medieval town ditch

N

○   excavated areas

⧄   extent of developed area c 1500

0   200 m

Figure 2.13   Saffron Walden, Essex: plan of the medieval town, with main excavations of the 1970s (Bassett 1982b). For amendments to the chronology after further excavations of 1984–7, Andrews and Mundy, in preparation.

Lincoln and London). At Stamford, the castle was placed outside the pre-Conquest borough, on a relatively high piece of ground next to the river and controlling the land routes which met at the place; here, between castle and town, the market place grew up. Elsewhere, the intrusion was more deliberate, involving the destruction of previous housing and streets, as in Exeter and Warwick. At Cambridge a church and a cemetery were swept aside. At Norwich almost a hundred houses made way for the castle, and here also two churches were demolished for the development of the cathedral. At Winchester, shortly after the Norman invasion, there was a wave of royal and institutional building which transformed much of the south part of the town: a castle, replacing fifty stone and timber houses; the extension of an existing Saxon royal palace, with consequences which can be seen in the street frontages today; and a new cathedral, one of the largest in Europe. Thus the construction of a castle should often be seen in a context of the appearance of

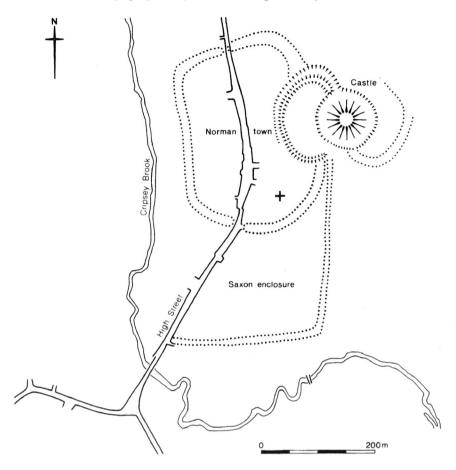

Figure 2.14 Chipping Ongar, Essex: suggested model of the imposition of the Norman castle and town on an existing Saxon settlement (Eddy and Petchey 1983).

a group of dominating, often monumental building complexes.[41]

Even clearer pictures of the process of imposition of the castle itself come from smaller places where later activity has not been great. Ongar (Essex), for instance, was an important centre, as a local moot (meeting-place) and market (Fig. 2.14); Ongar Great Park, west of the town, is the earliest recorded park in England, mentioned in 1015. What has been tentatively interpreted as a Saxon enclosure, later overlain by the castle, was sectioned in 1982.[42] A castle was imposed on this settlement, with the High Street running through its outer bailey, perhaps in the late eleventh or early twelfth century. At Pleshey (also Essex) the High Street also crosses the outer bailey of the castle, and a cross-route helps to form the market place in the bailey at Richard's Castle. There is, therefore, often a strong relationship between a major road, the castle bailey, and the subsequent capture of trade by the castle owner. In some towns, such as Launceston (Cornwall), the existing market was moved to be next to the new castle.

The insertion of a castle into a Saxon town, and its gradual assimilation into the urban topography, is also illustrated by work in and around the area of the castle at Oxford in 1965–73.[43] Here were two features of note: Saxon occupation including a timber cellar and pits pre-dating the Norman castle-mound built in 1071, and a catalogue of notable medieval finds, particularly of organic materials (i.e. shoes, clothing fragments and wooden objects), in the castle ditch. As early as the twelfth century, however, in a kind of urban reaction, properties along the street behind the barbican were already encroaching on the barbican ditch with their rubbish pits. It is as though the town is an organism, healing and gradually obscuring the scar of the new intrusion.

The castle often makes a major contribution to the topographical history of the place; it is a dominant feature in the landscape, and we can study its creation, rise and fall within the fortunes of the town at large. It is the residence of a local lord, and thus a centre of local business of all kinds and a place where luxuries would have been in comparative abundance. The castle may contain information about the town which is in as good or often better condition than elsewhere in the town, because the castle site has remained comparatively untouched and not affected by basements.[44]

Castles in towns were used for administrative purposes; usually as the sheriff's court and jail. When Lydford needed a court room and jail in the 1190s, the resulting building, which survives, was erected on a spur of an earlier ringwork, and became, at least in name, Lydford Castle.[45] Recent work suggests that the Norman Fleet Prison in London resembled a castle and was wholly surrounded by a moat formed by two channels of the Fleet river. Why there should be a royal prison on the west side of the City of London in the late eleventh century is not yet clear, but it matched the better-known Tower of London on the east side of the walled town. The establishment of the Fleet was perhaps part of the royal strategy to contain the city, England's largest town and a considerable if unruly asset.

With so many castle keeps having been cleared in pre-archaeological days, information on the residential aspects of castle history is now likelier to survive in the bailey or castle ditch, as at Pleshey.[46] Here excavations of 1959–63 in the bailey produced evidence of a twelfth-century rampart and defensive tower, overlain by two successive rectangular buildings, the second in stone and clearly the castle chapel, constructed around 1300. During the following decades, the chapel was embellished with painted window glass, a decorated tiled floor and architectural details in stone.

The disuse of the site in the post-medieval period has kept the archaeological strata in good condition, and it is clear that the chapel is only one of many buildings in the bailey; but it tells us much about the chronology and lifestyle of the noble household, in this case the de Bohuns, earls of Hereford and Essex, and later Thomas of Woodstock, seventh son of Edward III. The finds in and around the chapel included locally made floor tiles bearing several contemporary royal and noble coats-of-arms; correlation with those from two other prestigious sites indicates a working lifespan of 40–60 years for the tilery. The metal objects had a military flavour: spurs, knives and buckles. Significantly, perhaps, the original earthen defences do not seem to have been replaced; the place was a courtly residence, not a fortified stronghold. The pottery included imported wares from Spain and the Netherlands.

A castle was not only a noble residence, but probably much used for storing produce brought in from the countryside, and was therefore a centre of distribution, as suggested at Ghent.[47] The castle would have been the greatest employer in many towns. When a castle was destroyed for military or political reasons, the town would be affected. When royal interest and all the trappings of a royal palace moved away from Winchester in the thirteenth century, the town began a long period of decline.

In studying a medieval town, it is advisable to elucidate and then compare the building-dates of the castle and the town defences; were they constructed and repaired at the same time, or at different times, and does this reflect their relative signficance to the town? During the twelfth century some town defences and castle refurbishments went hand in hand, but from about 1300 many English urban castles declined as military structures, and towns' concern for safety concentrated on their own defences. In Scotland, on the other hand, towns did not in general gain substantial defences until the fifteenth century, and they continued to rely on castles for their defence.

Cathedrals, monasteries and parish churches as centres of social activity

The castle was only one type of large royal and religious building or complex of buildings which formed a nucleus of public life and traffic in the medieval town. The network of streets and lanes went through and around other complexes which by their size and often quality of construction formed dominant features in the topography of their neighbourhoods.

There may have been historic links between the castle in a town and a monastery close to it, also within the town: it has been noted that in 170 cases in England and Wales, mostly of the twelfth and thirteenth centuries, the castle and monastery were founded by the same person and were in close proximity, as at Abergavenny, Hastings, Pontefract, Thetford and Warwick, and a host of smaller places. But though these two centres of business and traffic may often have been in proximity, they vied for space and market custom inside the urban space. In some towns the meeting of main roads, and the market, was to be found at the gate of the monastery or cathedral church which has the role of epicentre of the place, elsewhere taken by a castle; and this would have an effect on the neighbourhood round the new centre. The Saxon town of Bury St Edmunds had been enlarged in response to the cult of St Edmund before the Conquest. Post-Conquest examples include Battle, Cirencester and Dunstable.[48] Reading lay at the junction of two important routes, connecting it with Oxford, London and Winchester. The founding of an abbey in 1125, with a market place developing at its gate, pulled the centre of gravity of the town eastwards. Its attraction to medieval pilgrims (including royal visitors) also ensured that St Laurence's church, next to the abbey, became wealthy. Any large church would attract traders to congregate near it, and market areas would form; in London, the goldsmiths established themselves at the west end of Cheapside, next to the cathedral precinct, during the thirteenth century. At Reims, the luxury trades in spices, gold and fine cloths were congregated near the cathedral; the oldest market lay right outside the west door of the church.

At Montpellier, many trades, including corn merchants, money-changers and fishmongers, had their stalls near the main church, and in time this led to the establishment here of the town hall.[49]

In similar but smaller ways, a parish church functioned as a public building or attracted public functions to itself. In England, new boroughs were often planted on the edges of existing parishes, and sometimes the church for the new place was dependent upon the mother-church; this often created difficulties (for example, the distance over which it was necessary to conduct funerals) and resentment. But where, as in the majority, there was a parish church or chapel, market life was also inextricably mixed with daily religious observance. Markets were held in or near churchyards, as at Llanelli or Haverfordwest; in many other places, churches lay in the middle of broad market streets.[50] When King's Lynn was extended northwards in the middle of the twelfth century, for instance, it acquired a second market place and a second church.

Towns also grew by the joining together of existing but separate neighbourhoods. When these localities joined to form a larger settlement, the churches stayed rooted in their ancient spots, communicating memories of the former arrangement of the place to the new generation. Sometimes whole parts of towns retained a preponderance of ancient churches, as at Reims. A church and its religious community or its prime purpose could also mould a whole neighbourhood or district. This is most evident in the cathedral quarters of towns, when they exist, but could be anywhere. Great churches on the edges of towns, such as the basilica of St Sernin at Toulouse, became rich and famous through being the goal of pilgrims; its fame had nothing to do with the town. The topographical impact of religious precincts and parish churches is considered further in Chapter 6.

Markets, water supply, secular public buildings and streets

The local ruler controlled the revenue of trade by encouraging a market within a town, often on only one site. In many cases there is documentary evidence for the 'establishment' of such a market, but this may only be the acknowledgement or attempt to control a process which had been going on for generations. Here archaeological work may explain why the market had come into being, long before a document mentions it. Many markets and fairs were set up in places already important, especially where people came together for legal or religious reasons; this is why some of the early markets appear to be badly sited with regard to road or river communications.[51]

A market emphasis would find archaeological expression in civic structures such as market buildings, toll-houses, the public weighing-beam, a town well or conduits, public quays and attention to city gates; but it is otherwise not easy to use archaeology to study markets. A characteristic of a market is an open space, used periodically, and therefore devoid of the features or deposits which might leave archaeological traces, except areas of gravel metalling; but this might have eloquent traces of the corralling of beasts. In Lund (Sweden), archaeologists have tried to demonstrate the location of trading areas by plotting the distribution of balance weights and scale pans, cloth seals and types of coinage. Over time, market stalls became permanent structures and buildings which in some cases survive today (as at Salisbury or St Albans). It was once thought that these buildings which encroached on a market space, and which are now represented by little adjacent streets in several towns, were private initiatives by tradespeople; but they are now demonstrated to be developments of the landlord.[52]

By the late thirteenth century covered specialized markets and civic warehouses for food, grain or cloth were to be found, mostly in principal towns; examples in the large cities of Bruges, London and Paris were considerable pieces of architecture.[53] Recent work has reconstructed the mid-fifteenth-century Leadenhall market in London from excavated and documentary evidence.[54] It also shows how the public functions of market and school were in this case intertwined. Leadenhall has been reconstructed from a fragment of wall surviving, to general surprise, within City office buildings of the nineteenth century; a series of truncated chalk foundations; and 177 loose moulded stones. These represented parts of arches, doors, two- and three-light windows and two spiral staircases. The complex comprised a large market space surrounded by arcades, with warehouses above; a chapel; and a grammar school, endowed by the rich mercer Simon Eyre (Fig. 2.15). The layout was established by comparison of the archaeological evidence for foundations with that from maps and plans; the reconstruction above ground (Fig. 2.16) by combination of the moulding details on the stones and engravings and sketches of the building before its demolition in stages in the eighteenth and nineteenth centuries.

There were few, if any, large open spaces for markets inside the City of London; the main streets were used instead. A similar arrangement can be found at Lincoln, where a single street formed the town's main market. This started at the Stonebow, a ceremonial gate opening onto the river Witham to the south, and finished at the gate into the Bail, the bailey of Lincoln Castle, which lay to the north. Looking back down the hill, one saw first the fish market, also known as the High Market, then the Poultry, and then the corn market. The skin market was off the main road in Hungate and the Drapery or cloth market was in a road parallel with the Strait. The lower part of the main street was occupied by the butchers in the late Middle Ages, and a further market was on Ermine Street in the suburb of Newport, around a market cross. At harvest time this was the appointed place to hire reapers and servants. Many of the Lincoln markets had originally been held in churchyards adjoining the streets, into which they were officially moved in 1223. Streets also turned into markets when large fairs came to towns: at Hull, a horse fair took place in the Ropery, the cattle fair in Mytongate, and the sheep fair in Salthouse Lane.[55]

As markets grew, so they specialized. First, it was possible to split the market so that different kinds of produce would be on sale on specific days: livestock, fish and so on. This is not likely to be recognized in the archaeological record. A second development was regional, in that some medieval towns specialized in a commodity which became a regional speciality. The third type of specialization was inside the settlement. Those selling certain produce would congregate in certain areas of the market: this may be the origin of street names such as Milk Street and Bread Street in London. These

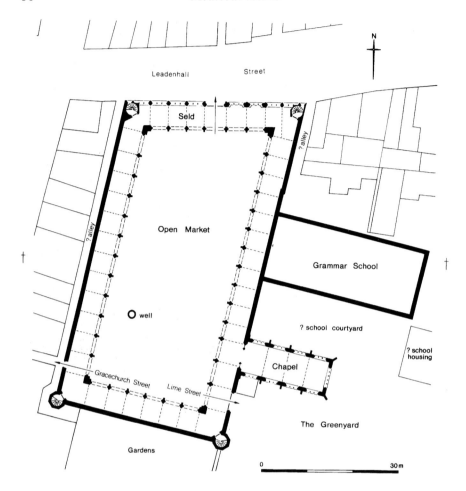

Figure 2.15 Leadenhall, City of London: plan of the market of 1440, which included a chapel and a school. This had open arcades on all four sides of its large courtyard, reminiscent of bastide towns but also perhaps of Les Halles in Paris (Samuel 1989).

may not reflect the activity of the streets themselves as much as that of the sections of the main market of Cheapside where the streets branched off. In the fifteenth century the market at Newmarket (Suffolk) was divided between butchers, drapers, ropers, mercers, tanners, ironmongers, cheesemongers and cordwainers (though this was exceptional for such a small town). Such a division of space might be perceptible in excavations of market areas. Fourth, in the larger centres, there were more than one market for each commodity; in London there were four principal grain markets by 1300, and in Paris by the fifteenth century, five or six principal butchery markets. As a town developed, markets would also change site: at St Andrews the market cross was moved in the 1190s from near the cathedral to its present position on Market Street.[56] The topic of markets and the related zoning of trades is considered in more detail in Chapter 5.

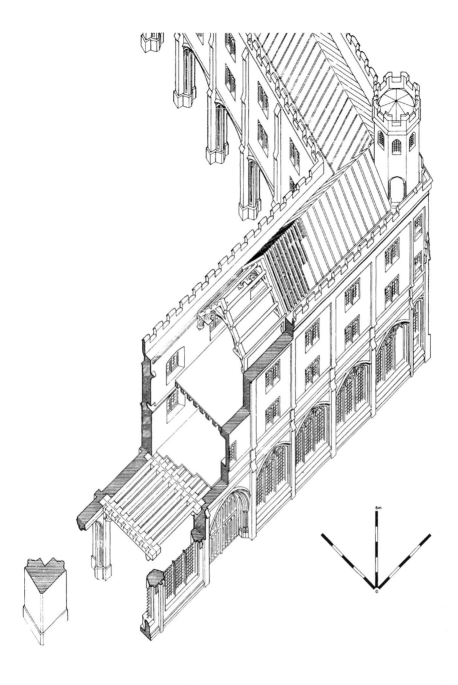

Figure 2.16 Leadenhall, City of London: axonometric drawing of north range (Samuel 1989). Above the market were two floors of storage space, initially at least for grain. This building was a proud civic statement, but it also had battlements, however symbolic, and watch-towers on the corners.

The lord took the tolls from markets; but what were people paying the tolls on? Current opinion favours the idea that the proliferation of markets in the twelfth and especially in the thirteenth centuries was for the disposal of rural surplus; and although the buoyant economy of the time prompted demand for manufactured goods and services by the local population, there was little stimulus for industry in the small towns.[57] Besides the new boroughs, villages also had their markets, and in some counties such as Leicestershire and Nottinghamshire there were more markets in villages than in towns. There were also many communities on the borderline between villages and towns, so the distinction cannot be forced. Some markets reflect specialized influences: the spread of markets along the Essex coast indicates a rapid growth of coastal trade in thirteenth-century Essex, though in time a good roadside location was better than a coastal one.[58] Only in larger market centres could money be spent on luxuries such as wine, spices, armour and quality textiles. These centres were provincial capitals, big fairs and ports.

Besides providing a market place, sometimes with covered stalls, the town or its lord was concerned to supply clean water, essential both for consumption and for industries such as textile production; running water drove corn- or fulling-mills (the latter are known in several European countries by or shortly after 1000). Major European towns organized a public water supply during the thirteenth century, often following the lead set by religious houses such as the friaries. London's first civic water supply of 1237 has been described as the first documented provision of fresh water in pipes in a medieval European city, to be followed by Breslau in 1272, Lübeck in 1294, Nuremberg in 1331 and Brunswick in 1334; but several other large cities and towns had piped water before London, such as Bristol by the early thirteenth century, so this list is incomplete. Nor was a piped supply the only solution: at Gdańsk, Antwerp and many other places, canals were built to bring water into the town for drinking as well as for industrial uses. At Salisbury, as already noted, water channels were a feature of the town plan in the 1220s, and they can still be seen in the back streets of Winchester. Some important towns relied on everybody having access to a well; York did not have a piped supply of water until the seventeenth century.[59]

The siting, appearance and efficacy of wells, fountains and washing-places (both for domestic laundry and industrial purposes, e.g. in the cloth industry) were of significance in the town's inner life.[60] The market place often contained a water supply, though not as often in English towns as in those on the Continent. At Coventry and no doubt elsewhere, the conduits were locked at night, along with the town gates; this would discourage people from walking the streets. A great number of public wells have disappeared, but formerly they provided points of public congregation at street corners or in public spaces. Here the presence of people, coming for water, may have influenced the volume of traffic into nearby shops and therefore affected their value as properties. One would suppose that a special correlation might be demonstrated between better buildings and the location of public wells and conduits. Similarly certain industries which constantly required water, such as brewing or dyeing, often congregated around access-points to water, and this sometimes caused friction with domestic consumers. Yet other wells were sited within churchyards or outside one end of a church, and they can be seen in later times in engravings, as parish pumps. There is no obvious reason why public wells should be next to churches; it may be partly because the church functioned as a local centre of life and therefore provided necessaries both for the spirit and the body.

During the early part of the twelfth century, in larger towns such as Exeter, London and York, there is mention of a guildhall. Townsmen pushed for and enjoyed some autonomy from the local lord through establishing a group called a guild, or later a guild merchant, which often became a precursor of a town council. Similar moves are documented in Scottish towns, where the guildhall is called a tollbooth. A town was where justice was to be had, and the building which embodied that principle could assume a civic style. Some guildhalls in small towns were adaptations of houses; others, like Thaxted in Essex, had a market space below and a civic chamber above (Fig. 2.17). In the fifteenth century, some major towns in eastern England rebuilt their guildhalls in stone, as at London (which had had one in stone since at least about 1270), Norwich and Lynn (Fig. 2.18). That at London was embellished with statues of civic virtues, a form of self-assertion by the city fathers which is matched by similar statuary on town halls in major continental towns (though there the statues tended to be of princes and kings, to draw attention to their official and dynastic attachment to the place). In larger towns of Europe generally, there was a development from the fourteenth century for the town hall to be separated from the market, and for a public space next to it to function for civic occasions and processions; this separating of functions might be looked for in smaller towns. But in general the archaeology of guildhalls is not developed.[61]

The public life of the medieval community revolved around its central institutions, and these may have been given special prominence, grandeur or increased accessibility to enhance their appearance and function. A parallel here can be made with Islamic cities, where public architecture (chiefly the congregational mosque, the central public bath and the central market place) were foci of great artistic and constructive energy. The major institutional buildings or areas may be located near each other for practical and other purposes; the streets to them from the main city gates may be of a wider, more stately character.[62] Apart from those new towns noted above, which being late arrivals were always small, there was little effort in the larger and long-lived centres of medieval Britain to widen streets or create formal squares. It was different in France and Italy. A concern with the careful ordering of public space in medieval towns extended from market buildings to squares and even street widths, especially in French and Italian towns. The central square (*la place publique*) was in many ways the symbolic centre of town life: here was the market hall, the public well, and sometimes a belfry which regularized and therefore helped organize the working day. It is therefore no surprise that the square is also the setting for modern civic monuments such as war memorials. The streets of the bastides were usually carefully graded as to their widths: at Monpazier, the longitudinal streets, which connected the central square to the gates, are 8m wide, the transverse streets 6m wide, and the connecting alleys about 2m wide.

Civic projects and civic regulation on both the use of amenities and building standards increased together in the second half of the thirteenth century,

Figure 2.17 The fifteenth-century Guildhall at Thaxted, Essex. This picture, taken in 1981, shows how even today medieval public buildings are used to celebrate royal occasions.

especially in Italian towns. At Perugia in 1275–6, the commune embarked on a truly ambitious urban renewal programme: over the next decades it constructed an aqueduct and fountain providing a public water supply, a new cathedral, and improved the access to the town by road. But access to these amenities had to be controlled, so regulations were widened and increased in number. At Bologna in 1288, the water brought into the city was restricted in its availability. Channels in the streets could not be flooded between May and September except with official consent, and from September to May householders could only take water from the channel to clean their alleys two days a month, and that at night-time, not in the day.[63]

An archaeology of civic management of the urban environment might study how far local regulations concerning orderly streets, or fire-proof materials, or the disposal of rubbish were observed in practice. There may have been some

Figure 2.18　The Holy Trinity Guildhall, King's Lynn, Norfolk. This stands in the Saturday Market, the ancient economic centre of the town next to St Margaret's church. This hall replaced one nearby in the years after 1421. The ground floor is a stone undercroft (the previous guildhall had been destroyed by fire); it was used to store wine and millstones, and later became the town jail. It was originally entered through the central openings which were later changed into windows. Above the building was of brick, with this fine chequerwork façade to the market. It was once adorned with statues. The civic porch was added in 1624 (Parker 1971).

form of what is now called development control in ninth-century Canterbury, where a Saxon bye-law required a space of at least two feet (0.6m) between each house. Comprehensive building regulations were common throughout European towns by 1300, and in some centres date from before 1250. At Dijon in the 1240s, the mayor had to look out for the alignment of buildings on the street; the perambulation of royal judges through the London streets, which contains early references to jetties (the overhanging storey) which were to be moved back or rebuilt, survives from 1246. Here, fire-break party walls and roofs of durable materials had been demanded in regulations of about 1200. There has not been much archaeological study of streets in medieval towns, perhaps because they mostly lie under their modern counterparts and access is difficult. Work in Winchester suggests that street surfaces were made of flints, and that in wet weather 'most streets and lanes must have been at least ankle-deep in refuse'.[64]

Suburbs

The previous sections have dealt with topographical elements conceived and created by the town or major institutions within it as statements of their presence or intentions: defences, major nuclei and the streets which articulated that organized space. There are two further boundaries to the settlement which reflected growth as experienced in the lives of ordinary people, and which spread around the institutional constraints: suburbs and the waterfront.

Growth or decline in the suburbs may be a reflection of the town's fortunes, and of its position in the hierarchy of neighbouring towns.[65] The form of suburbs was usually dictated by existing approach roads and by the location of markets immediately outside the town gates, as illustrated most vividly by the space called St Giles outside the north gate of Oxford. Nearby is Broad Street, another market which was able to expand over the outer edge of the city ditch. This also happened in Stamford and Worcester.

During the eleventh and twelfth centuries many of the older towns such as Canterbury, Winchester and York expanded their suburbs to reach their largest extent for several centuries. Prominent churches or bridges would be rebuilt as signs of prosperity. Suburban expansion can be identified by areas of town called Newland, as at Banbury and Gloucester. After 1300, few if any towns expanded further, and many contracted in size. By the time of the earliest maps around 1600, great parts of their suburbs had reverted to fields.

Dangerous or obnoxious trades were often banned to the extramural areas. Blacksmiths, potters, tanners and fullers were found here, either banned because of their smoke or noise, or taking advantage of the relatively open space (the bell-founders and tilers could dig for the special types of earth they required, the clothworkers stretched their cloths on frames called tenters).[66] When the hospitals and friaries came, they often limited rather than encouraged further growth.

Most suburbs were relatively poor, but some early developments were conspicuously wealthy, for instance in the western suburb of Winchester (where in the thirteenth century smaller properties were being amalgamated into larger units, as shown by substantial boundary ditches) or outside the north gate at Gloucester. The guildhall of St Mary at Lincoln survives as a reminder of the social independence of the men in the suburb of Wigford; this settlement, a long street south of the Roman town, had started developing in the ninth century, and in the medieval period was virtually a town in itself, with three stone gates of its own and twelve churches.[67] At Beverley, the canal of 1115–30 was instrumental in developing a new suburb, Beckside, with its own market on a quay, a church, and a range of industries taking advantage of the location: boat-building, rope- and sail-making, and the making of pottery, bricks and roof tiles. In a few cases the town centre moved to what had previously been a suburb: at Hereford and Northampton, for instance, the extramural market became the commercial centre of the town, as already mentioned in the case of Kidwelly, and the later expansion of Leicester was around the East Gate. In some towns the market lay by the castle, but later moved to the periphery of the built-up area when links with the countryside grew stronger.

One type of building often found on the periphery of towns or in the surrounding villages was the mill, which has been mentioned several times already; Domesday Book (1086) records over five and a half thousand mills in England. In a small place, townspeople were required to use the lord's mill and oven; in Winchester, a larger town, there were at least nine mills by 1200 – five on or outside the walls, but four inside the city, near the cathedral. Most of the early examples would be watermills, but windmills are known in other European countries from the early thirteenth century, and were common in southern England by 1300. Though most mills of both types were used for the grinding of corn, some were also used for the fulling of cloth, a practice which spread from Normandy in the twelfth century. A spread of mechanical fulling after about 1350 has been related to a decline in grain milling: the stagnant grain mills were taken over and productivity increased.[68] Here is an item on the agenda for medieval urban archaeologists, since excavations of mills near or in towns have not occurred in any number.

Suburbs have several archaeological merits: their boundaries, being the boundaries of the whole settlement, indicate the general prosperity or decline of the town; and suburbs often offer clean-slate sites, where the occupation will be easier to understand because it is on virgin soil. This occupation is often of an industrial character. Main suburban streets, with their narrow properties, look like main streets inside the town, but they lie in a rural setting and are usually without defences. This concentration of housing identifies the major axis routes to the town, and if the date of this settlement can be established by archaeological and other means, the date of development of that route (a trading route out to the hinterland in a particular direction) can be explored.[69] Equally important are the areas formerly on the edge of the urban settlement, but later incorporated inside defences; they can show when and how human occupation spread. This is illustrated by the excavation at Alms Lane, Norwich, which is treated in detail in Chapter 3. In the tenth century the site lay north of and outside the Saxon town, and until about 1275 was used as a refuse dump for the crafts, as shown by the artefacts. Wetland plants and bones of frogs and toads indicate the environment. From the late thirteenth century, as shown by archaeological and documentary evidence, the site was owned and used by workers in leather, skinning, bone-working, and especially iron-working. About 1375, however, the land was levelled and became the site of housing expanding from the city, and suburban or peripheral industries were pushed out.

Parallels between British and continental towns are immediate and instructive. Work in Marseilles, for instance, has elucidated the creation and purpose of medieval suburbs, founded at the end of the twelfth century and abandoned in the middle of the fourteenth. This expansion corresponds to a period of economic growth and importance of the city as a staging post for the Crusades. Excavations have revealed an industrial quarter of the thirteenth century entirely dedicated to pottery production. Around 1350 this area was erased, like other suburbs, to be replaced by new defences against external menaces.[70]

The waterfront

Besides spreading out along approach roads, the town often spread in a rather different manner into the adjacent river or sea. A waterfront zone often developed as a narrow strip of reclaimed land along the river bank or shore, modifying it to suit the needs both of landing and exporting of goods, and in time for housing, warehouses and other buildings; even churches. Thus many towns actually increased their area – in the City of London, perhaps by as much as 15 per cent – over the medieval period by pushing out into the water.

Waterfront archaeology has been one of the most significant developments of the last three decades within European urban archaeology. In this chapter we deal with the overall topographical significance of the reclamation process; the other main products of excavations on waterfront sites are the vast array of dated artefacts in the rubbish used to fill in behind the revetments (see Chapter 4) and the revetment structures themselves. Here three points concerning overall topographical development in the waterfront area can be made: (i) the chronology of reclaiming the land tells us about significant centres of human activity within the town; (ii) there was a range of motives for the reclamation, and (iii) waterfront sites furnish evidence for changes in river and sea levels. The most intensive study of waterfront reclamation has taken place in London, as a result of the complete change in land-use of the present waterfront within the City over the last thirty years, and the main results from this continuing campaign of excavations can be used as a model to compare with results in other places.

All the present land south of Thames Street, which runs for a mile from the Tower of London in the east to Blackfriars in the west, is a reclamation zone; it began in the Roman period and came to an end largely in the fifteenth century, though pieces of reclamation have been added up to 1962. The third-century Roman quays extended along much of the city's shoreline, but were in decay and eroded by the rising river throughout much of the Saxon period. The creation of new land south of Thames Street probably radiated out from three centres: the two Saxon landing-points for merchandise at Etheredshythe (later Queenhithe), first documented in 899, and Billingsgate, recorded *c.* 1000; and the pre-Conquest foreign settlement at Dowgate, later the Steelyard (Fig. 2.19). By the twelfth century churches were established south of Thames Street at Dowgate (All Hallows the Great and the Less), the bridge (St Magnus) and at Botolph Wharf, just above Billingsgate and perhaps originally part of the landing area (St Botolph). These remained the only churches south of the street, indicating that by the time of the formation of parishes in the twelfth century these points represented substantial areas of reclamation, occupation and activity. Thus we can suggest that a combination of public landing area + church + early reclamation = important place in the network of communications and business within the town. Again a church is centre stage,

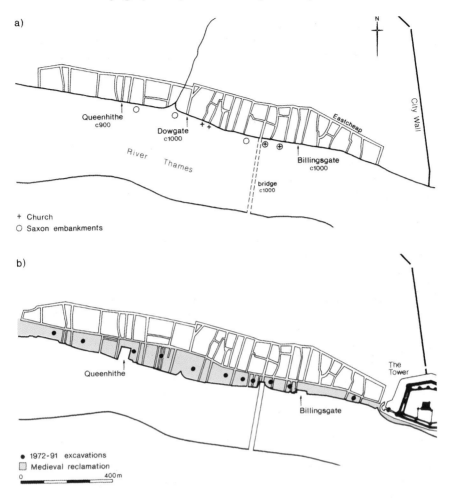

Figure 2.19 London: main Saxon reclamation points and churches on the waterfront, and the area of medieval reclamation which followed. This zone has been the subject of many excavations in 1972–91, the main ones of which are shown. The indentations of Billingsgate and Queenhithe mark public landing-places for goods and persons; the private properties had pushed out further on either side of them by 1400.

and it is difficult to be sure which came first: church or place of landing and its associated market. Though the stimulating effect of international trade in developing towns from the tenth century is currently downplayed, it might be suggested that trade of some kind, perhaps predominantly local or regional, helped to develop medieval street patterns by the waterside, and even that in some towns like London and Lübeck, this widening development only later reached the central parts of the town. Such reclaimed areas, though usually without churches, have been excavated at British ports such as King's Lynn, Newcastle, Norwich and Hull, and in many continental ports. In an extreme case, such as at Ribe (Denmark), the harbour was moved, and the town rebuilt

Figure 2.20 The Great Crane at Gdańsk (Danzig), Poland. This has been rebuilt after damage in World War II, but is on its fifteenth-century site. It was used for raising masts of large sea-going vessels. A fourteenth-century example, also restored, stands in Lüneburg. Medieval cranes of various designs are known from graphic representations such as panoramas of towns. Riverside walks are now a feature of many historic ports; they preserve the medieval units of reclamation beneath.

itself around the new centre of business.[71] In many ports buildings and quaysides survive, no longer used for industrial purposes, but now part of the historic heritage (Fig. 2.20).

It is also clear that reclamation proceeded at different rates at different times during the medieval period, and there must have been a range of motives behind different pieces of reclamation. In London, the greatest distances between successive revetments is in the period 1100–1350; thereafter, though revetments decayed quickly and were often replaced, it was on the same alignments or only a few feet further, and thus the rate of reclamation was now more gradual. In addition, river walls in stone, found from the twelfth century at larger ports such as Dublin[72] and London, became more common in the latter from about 1300; not requiring constant repair, these walls tended to put an end to the reclamation process itself.

The process of reclamation has been studied over a large area at the Trig Lane site, now beneath the new City of London Boys' School and south of an urban motorway, the construction of which in the early 1970s sealed waterfront deposits of the twelfth and early thirteenth centuries at the heads of properties stretching south of the medieval Thames Street.[73] South of the new road, the area excavated in 1974–6 revealed revetments and river walls dating between the end of the thirteenth and the middle of the fifteenth centuries on several properties (Figs 2.21–2). When dated by a combination of stratigraphy, dendrochronology and coins, the site demonstrated how individual private properties extended riverwards at different times, using differing forms of construction for the sometimes elaborate timber structures which held back the new man-made land. Finally, a stone wall formed a unified frontage in the mid fifteenth century, when documentary evidence confirms that the Armourers' Company had bought up the properties to form a desirable single riverside investment. The archaeological sequence goes back 200 years before the acquisition of the land by the Company, and in large measure explains their choice.

Certain merits of waterfront structures, such as what they have told us about medieval carpentry and the inclusion in them of many fragments of boats, are discussed in their proper place in other chapters. The rich survival of archaeological strata and especially finds in a waterfront zone gives the area a general importance for greater understanding of a town's history in a number of significant ways. First, the wealth of finds, especially of organic materials such as wood, leather and bone, is often accurately dated by a combination of dendrochronology and coins. The finds often include trade waste (unfinished products) or industrial scrap. The waterfront revetments constitute dated groups of medieval finds representative of life in the wider city, since backfilling the revetments acted as private and civic rubbish-tips. Second, in many ports, the strip of land along the river has often been raised several times against the rising river, and this action buried many medieval buildings whose fairly complete plans may be recovered by excavation. In certain towns such as London and Hull, the buildings and the finds in and around them may be further illuminated by documentary study of their owners and occupiers, including people of different social standing and of different trades. Third, overall, it is reasonable to suggest that the rate of reclamation in cubic metres is indicative of activity and growth in the city at large; so that as our information increases from a programme of excavations, we may be able to relate the volume of reclamation (measured by archaeological contexts) with periods of growth in the city itself. It is for instance noteworthy that the greatest period of reclamation in many port towns was during the twelfth and thirteenth centuries, when they were comparatively well off and growing. These general correlations show how the waterfront zone is an index or comprehensive sample of the archaeology of the whole medieval city.[74]

Figure 2.21 London: Trig Lane, showing the excavations of 1974–6, looking north-west (Museum of London Archaeology Service). The reclamation progressed from top right to bottom left, and each stage was filled in with large dumps of earth containing trade and domestic waste. These dumps are dated by the dendrochronology of the timbers in each revetment.

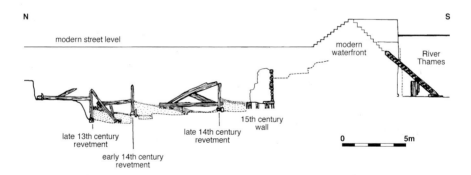

Figure 2.22 London: Trig Lane, simplified section showing the stages of reclamation from the late thirteenth to the fifteenth century (Milne and Milne 1982). This section, which also shows the relationship of the medieval revetments to the present River Thames, is of the east side of the excavation, which is beneath the photographer's position in Figure 2.21.

Analysing the main topographical components of a town

The best way to get an idea of a town's main topographical elements is to walk across it. The tourist can walk around medieval Paris, though here some imagination is required; but there are a cathedral and parts of two royal palaces, several sections of defences of two medieval periods, at least fifteen smaller churches and parts of three monasteries, and several houses or undercrofts of medieval date; there are two modern 'archaeological crypts' where medieval foundations and walls are displayed.[75] London has a similar selection of medieval remains *in situ*, though fewer because of the Great Fire of 1666. The centre of Rome, by contrast, comprises a large archaeological site with people living in it, but the medieval buildings and features are not highlighted for tourists.[76]

Even when much has survived, such as in Britain at Canterbury (Fig. 2.23), an impression can be gained through an energetic day's exploration. Besides the cathedral and its associated buildings, in a precinct which occupied a large part of the town, there is about half the Roman and medieval city wall and its towers remaining, with Henry Yevele's west gate of the 1380s; within the walls, the eleventh-century royal castle keep, the twelfth-century Eastbridge Hospital, several parish churches, and buildings which were once part of two friaries, as well as many medieval and Tudor secular buildings. Beyond the walls is St Augustine's Abbey, its precinct larger than that of the cathedral, with remains of several periods from the sixth to the sixteenth century,[77] and elsewhere fragments of extramural hospitals. Now tourism is important for the town's economy, and its exceptional historical monuments are displayed and cared for.

A contrast to Canterbury is provided by Norwich. Here is the best case from Britain of archaeologists, in conjunction with historians, elucidating the early development of the town. A programme of excavations and research over the last thirty years has developed hypotheses, tested them, rejected some and developed others, so that now the late Saxon and Norman town is in clear focus (Figs 2.24 an 2.25). Norwich developed from the tenth century as a collection of middle Saxon hamlets, and in the eleventh century was centred on Conesford, and undefended town south of the river Wensum; suburbs then developed, and the Normans arrived and transformed the place. They created a ceremonial secular and religious centre of power, and started Norwich's role as an international trading centre. Norwich is a fine example of how archaeology can put together the stages of growth and place in context the main topographical elements, both known (such as the cathedral and castle) and only surmised (such as tenth-century urban defences).[78]

Conclusion

Archaeological work in Britain, especially since the 1970s, has greatly extended knowledge, previously based on documents, of the siting, phases and layout of many medieval towns. In each town, one of the main objects of study should be the outline of each new topographical element; and then what happened to it. From this we may be able to both deduce the intention behind

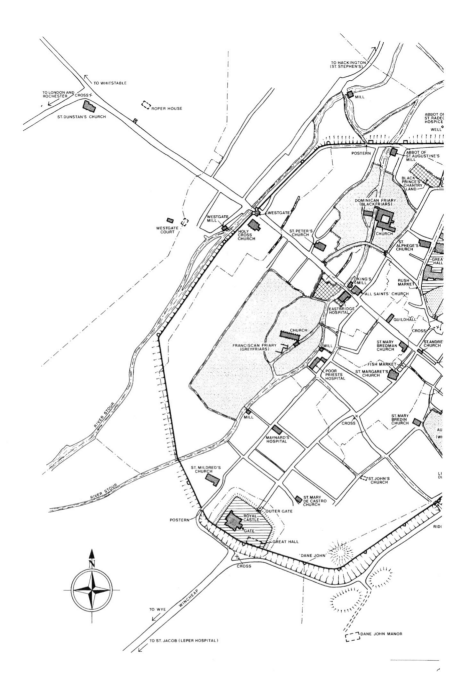

Figure 2.23 Map of Canterbury about 1500 (Canterbury Archaeological Trust). Here the medieval fabric has survived particularly well: the cathedral, St Augustine's Abbey, the Eastbridge Hospital, the defences and the castle are prominent sites; some parish churches and fragments of secular buildings can also be seen today.

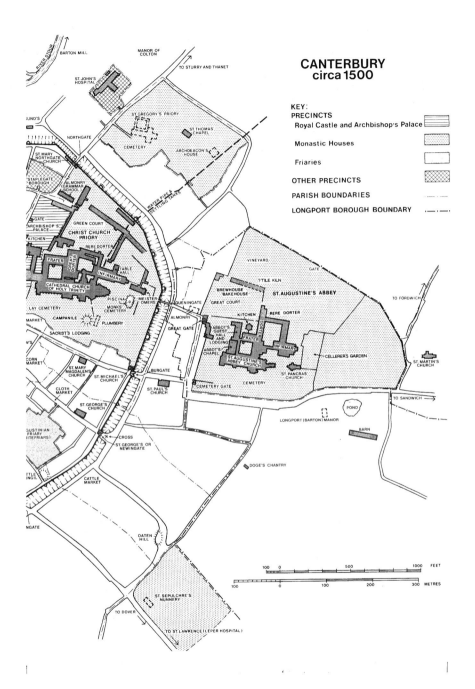

CANTERBURY
circa 1500

KEY:
PRECINCTS
Royal Castle and Archbishop's Palace
Monastic Houses
Friaries
OTHER PRECINCTS
PARISH BOUNDARIES
LONGPORT BOROUGH BOUNDARY

BARTON MILL
RIVER STOUR
MANOR OF COLTON
TO STURRY AND THANET
ST. JOHN'S HOSPITAL
GUND'S
ST. GREGORY'S PRIORY
ST. THOMAS CHAPEL
NORTHGATE
CEMETERY
ARCHDEACON'S HOUSE
ST. MARY NORTHGATE CHURCH
STAPLEGATE BOROUGH
ALMONRY (GRAMMAR) SCHOOL
WATER PIPE & SETTLING TANKS
GATE
ARCHBISHOP'S PALACE
GREEN COURT
VINEYARD
GATE
KITCHEN
CHRIST CHURCH PRIORY
RERE DORTER
TABLE HALL
FRATER
CHAPTER HOUSE
DORTER
INFIRMARY
LITTLE KILN
CATHEDRAL CHURCH OF HOLY TRINITY
PISCINA
MEISTER OMERS
QUENINGATE
BREWHOUSE BAKEHOUSE
GREAT COURT
ST. AUGUSTINE'S ABBEY
RERE DORTER
TO FORDWICH
LAY CEMETERY
MONKS CEMETERY
KITCHEN
ALMONRY
CAMPANILE
PLUMBERY
GREAT GATE
SACRIST'S LODGING
ABBOT'S GUEST HALL AND LODGING
FRATER
DORTER
CELLERER'S GARDEN
CORN MARKET
ST. MARY MAGDALEN'S CHURCH
ST. MICHAEL'S CHURCH
ABBOT'S CHAPEL
ST. AUGUSTINE'S ABBEY CHURCH
INFIRMARY
ST. MARTIN'S CHURCH
CLOTH MARKET
BURGATE
ST. PAUL'S CHURCH
ST. PANCRAS CHURCH
CEMETERY
CEMETERY GATE
TO SANDWICH
ST. GEORGE'S CHURCH
AUGUSTINIAN FRIARY (WHITEFRIARS)
CROSS
ST. GEORGE'S OR NEWINGATE
POND
LONGPORT (BARTON) MANOR
BARN
TTLE UNGIL
CATTLE MARKET
DOGE'S CHANTRY
NGATE
OATEN HILL
ST. SEPULCHRE'S NUNNERY
TO DOVER
TO ST. LAWRENCE (LEPER HOSPITAL)

100   0   500   1000   FEET
100   0   100   200   300   METRES

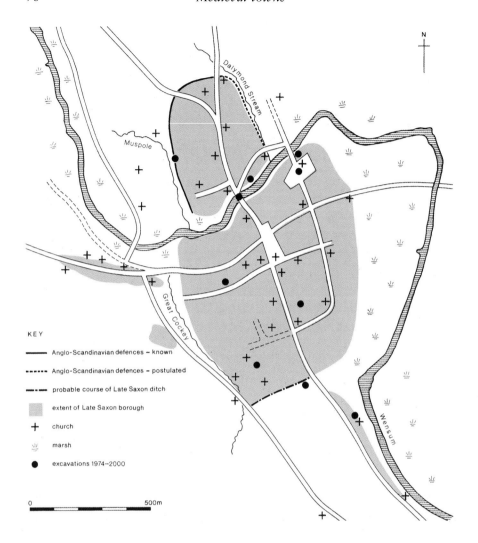

Figure 2.24 Map of Saxon Norwich; after Ayers 1994b, with further information supplied by Brian Ayers.

its formation and judge how successful it was. Some of the boundaries to the urban settlement, such as gates and defences, were meant to delimit, and had a constraining influence; other boundaries, such as the extent of surburban growth or expansion of the town into the adjacent river as reclamation, were a result of forces pushing against the previous constraints and flowing round them. The length of sequences of archaeological strata in towns permits and encourages this topographical study; it is seldom available for smaller settlements.

How can topographical elements be identified by archaeological means? Some elements have distinctive characters, such as castles, churches and

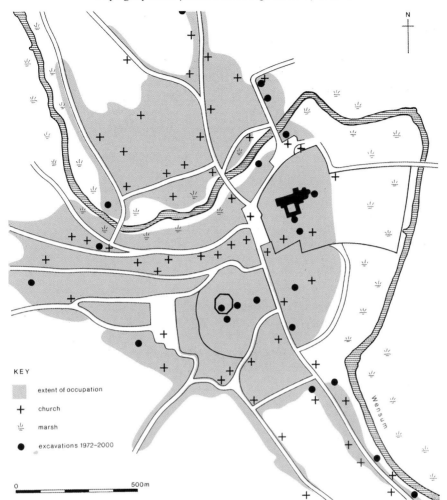

KEY

- extent of occupation
- + church
- marsh
- excavations 1972–2000

0   500 m

Figure 2.25 Map of Norman Norwich; after Ayers 1994b, with further information supplied by Brian Ayers.

markets. Others, such as the suburbs and waterfront, are perceptible zones where occupation derived from the need for access to roads or rivers, and where the pattern of properties and buildings is often relatively crisp and clear because in either case they were being laid out afresh. A third kind of spatial element can be identified by breaks in the grid of streets, or grids of different proportions in different parts of the town. This is particularly important when studying the successive expansions and areas of growth of the town.

From a knowledge of the development of the town and of its parts over time, we can hope to move further. Every new topographical element prompted a change in emphasis within the town, and we can therefore ponder the ways in which geographical shifts might reveal organizational shifts in the society which comprised the town itself. This is one of several themes to be explored in the following chapters on housing, crafts and industries, commerce, and churches and other religious institutions. Second, we should study the relative importance in medieval townspeople's lives of the commercial, religious and political buildings. It seems likely that the commercial were far inferior to the religious and political structures in grandeur, symbolism and meaning. Many, if not most, social values and actions are reflected in material forms; the town is a book to be read.

But for urban archaeologists there is another duty which has become apparent especially in recent years. We have to contribute to the debate about the future, in our own century and time, of the historic fabric of medieval towns.[79] Such a conservation argument is not restricted to medieval remains or to towns, but the main topographical elements which form the structure of the town are prime candidates for protection. The main parts of the town outlined in this chapter are of significance to the present town, its inhabitants and all who use the place for working, living or visiting. How the town looks or seems today is a product of its past, and it is the archaeologist's job to clarify the ways in which previous initiatives in the town's history by its residents or an imposed authority have contributed to the present townscape. Understanding will lead to appreciation.

3 Houses, properties and streets

The questions

To understand how the main kinds of secular buildings such as houses, shops and inns functioned in the medieval town, several questions can be posed. We would like to know the framework of streets and property boundaries which constrained the spread of buildings and governed their disposition and size; what the earliest buildings of stone and timber looked like; and, over time, whether they formed a range of types or preferred arrangements on the plot. Although the main discussion will be of domestic accommodation, we can briefly examine other types of building which shared domestic characteristics, and which were adapted from houses: taverns and inns for example. The appearance of these buildings can be illustrated by evidence of their construction technique, materials, decoration and internal or external fittings. And finally, we can ask what contribution archaeological study can make to an understanding of three kinds of environment in the medieval town: the built environment (its bulk, shapes, construction), the social environment (how rooms were used; how economic and social factors resulted in differences in the evidence), and the perceived environment (how medieval townspeople regarded their homes, notions of privacy, and mental arrangement of spaces around them). Space is a form of material culture, and therefore patterns in the use of space, or differences in attitudes to space, may be significant.

The number of excavations of medieval house-sites which have now been published, in either final or interim form, allow us to compare the quality of information between a large city such as the City of London and smaller towns. In London, continual and intense digging into the ground at all periods means that apart from along the waterfront, archaeological evidence of structures from which plots might be reconstructed is scattered and sparse; it is largely confined to the distribution of deep foundations such as sunken timber cellars, the foundations of stone buildings and the lower parts of cesspits and wells. In smaller towns, by contrast, the strata often survive in longer sequences, but not necessarily in more volume. Secondly, in towns away from the present industrial or commercial centres, standing buildings of the period are available for examination. A third source is reconstruction from documentary evidence; for direct comparison this depends on density of information over a long period, and sufficient information of the right type (e.g. measured dimensions) which occur rarely and fortuitously from the twelfth and thirteenth centuries. This evidence tends to occur in the larger towns and cities.

In this chapter we consider the house as a domestic unit, but also what activities besides domestic ones went on in it. Two main functions, to provide settings for domestic and trade activities, often overlapped in medieval buildings.

Formation of properties and early buildings

A first matter to explore is the manner in which properties and buildings formed among streets once the latter had been laid out, whether in the eleventh, thirteenth or fifteenth centuries; how prominent buildings formed first encroachments and then points of permanence in the development of streets; and, thirdly, whether distinctive buildings might congregate in particular areas of towns.

Several of the arguments in this chapter are illustrated by three excavated sites around Cheapside in London: one in Milk Street on the north side, and two sites in Bow Lane to the south, at Watling Court and Well Court. From the mid eleventh century, pit alignments at Milk Street, at right angles to the street, seem to indicate property boundaries; the pits left an undug strip between their lines, perhaps indicating a property boundary (Fig. 3.1). The formation of properties can be seen in more subtle ways through the disposition of rubbish pits, and in particular, cesspits (i.e. latrines). At Watling Court, properties were undoubtedly physically separate entities from as early as the late ninth or tenth centuries, on the evidence of (i) pits spaced at regular intervals which presumably lay behind surface-laid buildings fronting onto the streets (and which, in the city centre, have otherwise been destroyed by modern basements), and (ii) the use of many of these pits as cesspits; here we presume that in general spatially separated cesspits (i.e. one every five metres or so) indicate separate properties.[1]

In *c*.1050 Bow Lane can be visualized as a street of timber buildings, without cellars but otherwise of unknown character, with occasionally a substantial range behind and at right angles, of which the timber-lined cellar survives to be recorded (Fig. 3.2). This would imply a certain density of occupation and a similarity of construction between properties. It would also imply the emergence of the right-angled medieval house plan by the mid eleventh century: a range parallel with the street, through which a gateway or passage led to a small yard or alley along the side of a major, usually sunken-cellared building set at right angles to the line of the street (as Building 3 at Watling Court). A similar degree of rectilinearity and organization of properties, including gradually finer definition of access to the internal spaces, is found at this period in Northampton, Lincoln and Durham. At Northampton, the St Peter's Street site demonstrated a reorganization of street and buildings into a rectilinear arrangement, replacing the former loose configuration, in the late eleventh century; at Flaxengate, Lincoln, this period saw a denser level of occupation and the appearance of an L-shaped range of buildings bordering the street and running back from it. At Durham the late eleventh century saw the establishment of fences towards the rear of late Saxon properties, presumably parcelling out a backland which was previously common and the site of large middens.[2] The division, perhaps by a town authority, of street frontages into narrow-ended properties and the consequent placing of principal dwellings at right angles to the street can be traced back to the tenth century at York and at Douai (France) or Ghent (Belgium); perhaps even further back, to the *wic* emporia of the seventh century. It is the most basic and clear evidence of an urban way of doing things, of the intention to have an organized and carefully ordered space which will function as a town.

Figure 3.1 Milk Street, City of London: rows of tenth-century and later pits indicate where a medieval property boundary may have lain, in the unpitted area of strata where the two photographic scales lie. The late Saxon and medieval street is at the top of the picture; in the section, a metre-thick deposit of the dark earth of the Saxon centuries (Museum of London Archaeology Service).

The grouping and positions of buildings also show how the plot was arranged, especially in relation to the street, and where the main building and therefore the social centre of the property lay. At Watling Court, a prominent stone building of the twelfth century (Building 6) coincided with the substantial timber-cellared building of the eleventh century (Building 3); a large building lay in the same place over a period of perhaps two centuries, and the destruction of the former was probably followed closely by the construction of the latter (Fig. 3.2). This indicates a continuity both of location of the main building within the property, and perhaps underlines that this corner property was substantial among its neighbours in both periods. Corner properties,

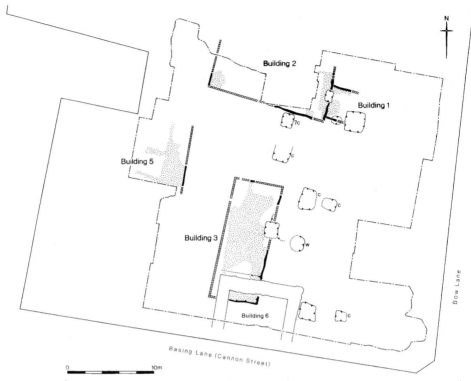

Figure 3.2 Watling Court, City of London: plan of the site in the eleventh century, with a twelfth-century stone building added. C = cesspit, W = well (Museum of London Archaeology Service).

whether built in stone or timber, were often grander structures, taking advantage of having two frontages. They thus formed local landmarks.

When working out the extent of medieval properties from excavated evidence, it is worth studying the position of the cesspit. The regularity of complaint by one London neighbour against another about leaking cesspits in the surviving rolls of Assize of Nuisance in the period 1301–1437 demonstrates that many cesspits were dug close to property boundaries. When a privy was used by more than one tenement, as is recorded in London from at least *c*.1160, the privy would presumably be sited on the tenement boundary. Stone-lined privies were generally located deep within the properties (i.e. towards the back); where relationships to recorded or vanished buildings could be suggested, the privies lay behind the buildings fronting onto the streets. In other medieval towns privies were similarly at the rear of buildings with gable to the street, either inside or immediately outside the building, as in thirteenth- or fourteenth-century Stamford or Southampton. Excavations at Worcester have found cesspits across small yards behind buildings on twelfth- to fourteenth-century tenements.[3] Surveys of London houses in 1607–12 show privies across small yards behind houses, in the same block as the separate kitchen, an arrangement which may date from at least the fourteenth century. Together, these configurations suggest that (i) stone privies of the thirteenth and fourteenth centuries were commonly towards the edges of properties, often deep within them; (ii) stone privies often replaced timber predecessors in the same locations (as is demonstrated on several London sites); (iii) timber-lined cesspits of tenth-century and later date are found near boundaries which are documented by 1300. It therefore seems likely that tenth-century pits can be used to infer boundaries in their own century.[4]

As towns developed, the shape and size of individual buildings contributed to the outline and definition of properties, particularly along street frontages. In some cases the frontage became indented or even slightly curved, taking account of encroachments or obstacles formed by prominent buildings. Some of these encroachments were buildings of stone, commonly with their gables against the street. The erection of a stone building by the street, often in the twelfth or thirteenth centuries (for example at Lincoln (Fig. 3.3), London, Winchester and Bury St Edmunds), would thereafter tend to anchor that part of the frontage for generations. Some stone buildings might be visible from the street, but placed back slightly within their surroundings of timber buildings; for instance, along the side of a plot and behind a street-range, as at Brook Street, Winchester. Documentary work on Canterbury houses has shown that they often occupied properties which, although not large, were nevertheless commodious. One house (Burgate) is first mentioned *c.* 1180 and several others *c.* 1200 or in the early thirteenth century. Properties were all shapes and sizes, though generally rectangular; for example, 52 × 90ft, 70 × 70ft, 60 × 106ft, 65 × 80ft and 42 × 74ft. One house occupied an entire plot 40ft square and another house had a frontage apparently of 60ft to a major street, forming the front end of a property 153ft long.[5]

Where timber cellars of the tenth and eleventh centuries have been found, they were entered from courtyards, and generally away from the street. The stone building with gable to the street must be seen as the successor to the cellared timber building of the eleventh century, with the innovation that the ground floor of the stone structure now communicated directly with the street. But this cannot have been the only pattern; timber buildings without cellars are found along streets, and often at right angles to them, from the tenth century. Many stone (and on the Continent, brick) buildings against the street must have destroyed their timber predecessors. Occasionally, the lower parts of the timber buildings were reused, and thus show that thirteenth-century stone houses were of the same plan as the previous in timber, as at Nijmegen (Holland).[6]

A wider question concerns the overall distribution of early medieval stone buildings in medieval towns. In cathedral towns, one concentration will be around the cathedral, where the higher office-holders (the bishop, dean and canons) had quality residences; these have been studied in some English towns, for instance Lincoln and Salisbury. In many cities in France, the organization of the area around the cathedral or other large collegiate church began in Carolingian times in the ninth century, and the number of medieval stone houses of the canons and officials of the chapter (the organizing body) had a considerable effect on the topography of the town around the church; this can be seen or traced today in a number of places, such as Aix-en-Provence, Angers, Autun, Limoges, Lyons, Metz, Toulouse and Tours.[7]

The other concentrations of twelfth-century stone houses indicate the central commercial area (or areas, in a large place like London) of the town, such

Figure 3.3 Lincoln: reconstruction of stone houses on the Flaxengate site in the fourteenth century (S. R. Jones and Lincoln Archaeological Trust). These stone houses overlay earlier timber buildings and presumably indicate an upgrading of the properties. These lay in the lower town, away from the cathedral close and its high proportion of stone buildings.

as the busiest areas of the waterfront. In Colchester the known fragments of early medieval stone buildings are found within two blocks of the High Street. In Canterbury, the 27 known stone houses are almost all to be found in the centre of the town (i.e. the High Street and streets north and south of it. Fragments of at least three 'Norman', probably twelfth-century, stone houses have been recorded in Bristol; one still partly stands to first-floor level. Some stone houses are associated with Jews in towns up to their expulsion in 1290, but this is probably not a useful way of looking at buildings. It is more important to register that Jews settled close to the principal commercial areas of the towns where they dwelt, as shown at London, Norwich, Winchester and York.[8] In Norwich the excavation of a notable late twelfth-century stone building on the waterfront at St Martin at Palace Plain, probably related to the adjacent cathedral, has occasioned a survey of early secular stone buildings in that city. Only two are physically extant, but records principally of the fourteenth century speak of at least sixteen probable examples. Twelfth-century Norwich was a port with continental connections; and an apparent concentration of stone structures on King Street, bordering the Wensum on the southern approach to the town, is notable and invites comparison both with London (New Fresh Wharf) and stone houses on the expanding waterfront in King's Lynn.[9] The St Martin at Palace Plain house in Norwich, which is now preserved under the County Court, has been reconstructed as possibly of three storeys, or two over a basement; if so it is probably the first three-storey Norman stone house below the level of a castle to be recorded in Britain. But it may not have seemed unusual among European towns: in Rouen a twelfth-century example has been recorded which had three floors above a basement, the ground floor rising through the equivalent of two floors so it would have looked higher still.[10]

Stone houses of the twelfth and thirteenth centuries are found in many continental towns; usually only one or two in each place, but sometimes far more. Over a hundred stone buildings of the thirteenth century have been recorded in Zürich. In Ghent, 115 medieval houses have been recorded, many of them largely of stone. Alternatively, and probably more widely, buildings were a mixture of stone, brick and timber elements. Stone towers were added in back courts to timber buildings which fronted streets from the late eleventh century at Zürich, Basle, Lübeck and Riga (Latvia). Stone cellars were dug in the thirteenth century towards the back of the house, beneath timber ground-level structures, in Minden (Germany) and Riga. Many timber-framed medieval houses in German towns have stone basements.[11]

In many European towns, a vaulted undercroft of stone or brick may be the only part of a more extensive and prestigious medieval house to survive into the age of recording, whether by engraving, excavation or through the happy chance of survival (there are some even in London and Paris). Many of these vaults were used for the storage of wine, and mapping the occurrences of the undercrofts in the medieval streets will provide information on the distribution of wine as a luxury import. In Paris, for instance, the cellars of the wine merchants were numerous in the streets around the main landing place on the Seine, la Grève.

While stone houses were no doubt symbols of wealth and the residences of substantial citizens, their survival in some towns should not obscure the need to study the development of timber buildings, which were originally the majority in north-west European towns. From about 1300, standing buildings begin to show us what street frontages in medieval towns looked like, but we await a body of evidence to work with for earlier centuries. In French towns very few houses with timber-framed storeys dating to before 1400 have survived, so that the spectacular stone houses of Cluny or of brick at Cahors (Fig. 3.4) today give only a partial impression of the total medieval townscape.[12] Archaeological work can make a significant contribution by two kinds of study: highlighting the contribution of those sites with extensive survival of evidence for timber houses, such as for instance Waterford (Ireland), where the remains of at least 118 houses, mainly of timber, have been excavated; and study of timber parts of buildings reused in waterside constructions, preserved by the waterlogged conditions adjacent to streams and

Figure 3.4 House at rue de la Daurade, Cahors (France). The top floor on the right is a later addition. The town has several thirteenth-century houses in brick, comprising shops below and a hall or tower above like this. Inside, traces of wall paintings have been recorded. In comparison to similar buildings in north European towns, the function and arrangement of the parts are the same; the style is nearly the same; only the material is locally derived. This restored building continues to function in the town; its ground floor is a restaurant.

rivers, whether still apparent or with their courses now buried underground.[13] These studies of both kinds are relevant to the whole medieval period, but are especially important for providing the history of buildings between the eleventh and thirteenth centuries, before the date of earliest survival of fragmentary standing buildings in towns.

Types of houses

By 1300, archaeological evidence is growing for a range of house-forms and arrangements of buildings on the plot. As with the other topics covered in this book, we only have space to present a British (and largely English) typology, and to suggest parallels at points with houses in other European countries.

Any typology of medieval urban house-plans must build on the work of

W. A. Pantin, who based his analysis on 40 medieval houses from 17 English towns.[14] He was concerned with the hall as the central feature of the tenement and the problems of adaptation on restricted urban sites, and he therefore deliberately omitted both the smallest houses, in which development was only vertical, and the largest ('such as Arundel House in the Strand, or the Bishop's Palace or the Old Deanery at Salisbury') where space allowed full introduction of the 'rural' manor-house plan. The archaeological typology must now be wider, dealing with these extremities of the continuum, and Pantin's types fit within the middle range. We must also attempt to see if houses were different in Scotland and Wales, and abroad.

Some of the larger houses in major towns such as London, York and Edinburgh were town houses of a distant lord, whether lay or religious. There were two purposes for such a house: the provision of accommodation for those engaged in the everyday affairs of the house or the see, such as the selling of produce or the buying of goods, especially luxuries; and as the residence of the institution's head when in town. These urban depots of religious institutions from out of the town, whether based in another town or in the countryside, are found in many of the larger centres. One such is York, where a hospice of Nostell Priory with fourteenth- and fifteenth-century buildings has been restored (it is now called Barley Hall and plays a part in the presentation of the past to modern audiences). Another is Edinburgh, where the sites of fifteenth-century ecclesiastical town houses produced an unusual amount of imported German pottery; many of the forms, particularly drinking mugs and jugs, were not available in local pottery wares. In addition to houses which were at least in part a town-house for the monastery, there were many properties in towns which belonged to monastic houses and were of major importance in their economies by being rented out: in Scotland, for instance, by 1296, about 24 religious houses had property in about forty towns. Fifteen Scottish monasteries held property in Berwick, on the Tweed and on the border between Scotland and England. But presumably these 'ordinary' properties would not be different from their neighbours archaeologically.[15]

Coming to London, for many religious and secular lords, also meant attendance on the king at Westminster, though the function of providing an urban base in the largest city had a longer history. By the end of the medieval period nearly two hundred 'Inns' of this kind can be identified in London or its immediate environs; their heyday was the thirteenth and fourteenth centuries, and they must have been a potent mechanism for distributing luxuries from the capital to the countryside and to lesser towns. In the 1350s for instance Elizabeth de Burgh, Lady of Clare (Suffolk) had a London house actually in the convent of the Minoresses outside Aldgate, to be used when she stayed (and entertained) in town. Accounts from the 1330s until her death in 1360 show that basic foodstuffs came from local tradesmen and her estates around Clare, but London provided parchment, Spanish iron, fish of many kinds (especially salmon, sturgeon and lampreys), wine, spices, cloth and furs. She also bought wine at Colchester or Lynn, and when at her house in Usk, from Bristol. An example of the accounts of a monastic house is that of successive cellarers of Battle Abbey (Sussex), responsible for providing their brethren with food and drink, who have left accounts for the period 1275 to 1513. Dairy products came from the abbey farms, and meat from the local market; wine came through Winchelsea, but spices and delicacies from London, where the abbey had a large house on the south bank of the Thames in Southwark.[16]

The town house of a lord, whether religious or secular, is a common feature of many continental towns, both large and small. In France, prelates were attracted to Paris after its establishment as a capital by Philippe Auguste in 1190. Bishops' residences in towns were often of imposing dimensions, and clear statements of wealth, power and prestige.[17] In north Italian towns, where clan warfare was rife, the noble compounds often included a high tower; these were demolished by town authorities to curb the nobles, for instance in Florence or Rome (which had several hundred), but remain in other towns such as San Gimignano, Siena, Lucca or Bologna.

In the vast majority of cases where their plans can be ascertained, the houses of religious and noble leaders in north European towns were of courtyard plan (Fig. 3.5: Type 4). The hall of the property lay normally at the rear of a yard, though occasionally to the side on restricted sites, with a range of buildings (often separately let) fronting the street. Leaders of the merchant community in major towns, such as those who dealt in wine or some other aspect of royal service, also aspired to the style of house with a courtyard and an open hall of lofty proportions. Pantin saw the type as one species of 'parallel' house, in which the hall lay parallel to the street, and described fourteenth- to sixteenth-century examples from Exeter, King's Lynn, London, Norwich and Oxford.

A town with a good number of surviving medieval buildings, such as Salisbury or York, or a corpus of house-plans such as those of properties in London in 1607–12 provided by the surveyor Ralph Treswell, demonstrates a variety of forms of medium-sized and smaller houses. Two main types may be proposed (Fig. 3.5: Types 3 and 2).[18] In this typology, for the moment, we are concerned with buildings on restricted sites towards the middle of towns; in peripheral or suburban areas, where plot width allowed the house to stand side-on to the street, further designs were possible.

The Type 3 house (filling a whole property, and of three to six rooms in ground-floor plan) did not have a true courtyard with a formal gate to the street, though it might have a yard with buildings along one side, or an alley running the length of a long, narrow property. The latter arrangement is illustrated most clearly by properties on waterfront sites, such as in King's Lynn or south of Thames Street in London. Many had an alley down one side, and in consequence buildings were usually arranged down the side of the plot behind the street-range which commonly comprised shops, sometimes let separately. Along, usually at the side of, most waterfront properties ran the access alley from the street to the river and the main water supply. This originated for the most part as a private thoroughfare, in some cases becoming public through time and custom.

Smaller, and more uniform in its characteristics, was a house with two rooms on three or more floors (Type 2). This type is known from documentary and archaeological evidence in London from the early fourteenth century; in several cases such houses form a strip, two rooms deep, fronting but separate from a larger property behind. Examples have been excavated on the New Fresh Wharf site, and houses of this type at Abchurch Lane in London, used as the examples in Figs 3.5 and 5.4, may have been those built on the site shortly

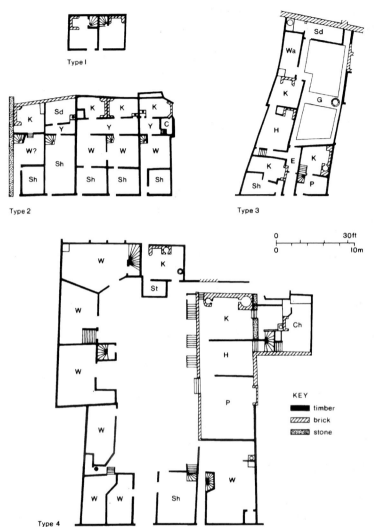

Figure 3.5 Types 1–4 of house plans from the London surveys of Ralph Treswell in 1607–14 (Schofield 1987; 1995). These plans from surveys, slightly later than our period, are used because nothing like them has yet been produced from archaeological work. The proposal behind their use is that the layout of buildings and rooms within them shown here is largely medieval. The majority of walls (shown in black) were timber-framed; brick is shown by diagonal hatching.

Key to room and space functions

B	Buttery	P	Parlour
C	Cellar	Sd	Shed
Ch	Chamber	Sh	Shop
Co	Coalhouse	St	Study
E	Entry	W	Warehouse
G	Garden	Wa	Wash-house (for scouring yarn)
H	Hall	Wh	Waterhouse
K	Kitchen	Y	Yard

before 1390. In Type 2 houses the ground floor was a shop and warehouse, sometimes with the two rooms thrown together to form one, or a tavern. Because the ground floor was given over wholly to trade, the hall lay usually on the first floor at the front, overlooking the street. In the late fourteenth-century examples at Abchurch Lane, the kitchen was a separate building across a small yard; but elsewhere in the capital the kitchen was often placed above ground in the main building, as structures occupied every inch of the small plots. Pantin traced the Type 2 form in the post-medieval period in Oxford and it is also found in other towns such as Exeter, Norwich and York from around 1500.[19]

The houses of the medieval poor have largely been destroyed without trace in almost every town. These humble dwellings did not survive into the era of engraving, and as they commonly lay along street-frontages, archaeological excavation has not uncovered them because of later street-widening and the digging of cellars, especially in the nineteenth century. Sometimes the existence of buildings, probably forming continuous façades and one room deep, are inferred from the absence of rubbish pits near the line of the street, as has already been noted; such spaces are found near major streets in eleventh-century London.[20] One-room timber-framed houses of thirteenth- or early fourteenth-century date have been excavated at Lower Brook Street, Winchester, and more substantial examples in stone of the fifteenth century at St Peter's Street, Northampton (though it is probably an error to say they were poor).[21] Others are examined in the case study of Alms Lane, Norwich, below.

In back streets of larger towns, and even along major streets of smaller towns, houses could also stand with their long sides or eaves to the street. Examples are provided by the Norwich and Northampton sites, and sometimes there is a mixture of buildings with their gables or sides to the street, as at Flaxengate, Lincoln (Fig. 3.3). Sometimes a throwing together of two properties, after an acquisition, would result in the building of a street front-age which was in effect two properties wide and which would be roofed parallel to the street. Never assume that the outlines of properties seen in towns today, or on nineteenth-century maps, were the original medieval outlines. The golden rule for the archaeologist is: check it on the ground.

A distinctive form of house, called the Wealden by modern students, is found in several towns. The first-floor chambers are jettied at one or both ends of the central, open hall, to give the hall itself a recessed appearance. Nine form a rent of Battle Abbey, *c.*1468; other examples are at Coventry and Canterbury. One at 49–51 Goodramgate, York, is a hall range at right-angles behind a street frontage. The form dates from the late fourteenth century to perhaps the 1530s; and may be an urban form exported to the countryside, where it is found sporadically over much of south-east England. The identification of at least 28 examples at Coventry has led to the suggestion that they may be a characteristic form of building especially in new areas of housing during the first half of the fifteenth century.[22] As the distinctive architectural features are at first-floor and roof level, this form is impossible to predict from archaeological remains in the ground.

It is important not to assume that a street was full of rich buildings, or poor ones, just from the excavation of single house sites or the survival of single buildings. The usual picture was that rich and not so rich mingled on the same street. In Scotland, about two hundred examples of small domestic buildings of the twelfth and thirteenth centuries have been excavated, a quarter of which come from one site on the High Street in Perth. Most of these were single-storey, of one room or rectangular with internal divisions, their walls of wattle. But they also included three examples of larger aisled halls, running down the plot; and one stone house of the thirteenth century, set back from the street.[23] Such is the general picture in many towns when archaeological investigation of an area is large enough: the few stone structures which survive today were originally surrounded by timber buildings themselves ranging from grandiose to ordinary.

Other types of building with domestic characteristics

There were other types of secular building which often looked like houses, and usually grew out of them. In medieval towns, there were three main types of victualling house: in ascending order of size and status, the alehouse, the tavern and the inn, though the distinctions were often blurred. As a rough analogy, in a sample of Canterbury drinking-houses of 1560–1640, alehouses had a mean number of 4.8 principal rooms, taverns 10.0, and inns 14.0.[24]

The brewing industry developed during the fourteenth century and prominent London brewers could maintain one of the earliest recorded company halls, bequeathed to them in 1408. The introduction of hops for the brewing of beer, from at least 1420 in London, made it necessary to incorporate storage areas into brewhouses, since, unlike ale, beer made with hops could be stored and transported. Brewhouses of the fifteenth century were evidently sometimes large establishments: in 1463 the Saracen's Head in Aldersgate, London, included a well-furnished brewhouse, a hall with two glazed windows, two privies and three refurbished stables. The largest examples contained horse-mills, to grind the malt; but otherwise brewhouses were evidently similar to dyehouses in the character of their installations, since there are cases of dyers and brewers using the same lead troughs and vats. In the next section of this chapter will be a discussion of a small tenement which may have functioned at least partly as a brewhouse at Alms Lane, Norwich.

Taverns were drinking houses where wine was drunk. Taverns are known in undercrofts by the early fourteenth century in London and Oxford. Some undercrofts were evidently built to be drinking-places from the start. The Peter and Paul tavern in Paternoster Row, London, rebuilt in 1342, comprised an undercroft provided with fireplaces and therefore presumably for drinking, and drinking rooms or partitioned areas on both ground and first floors.[25] During the fifteenth century the main drinking areas seem to have spread to the ground floor of buildings, and then the cellar was abandoned; the Cheapside area in London was thick with taverns which must have had a frequent trade in company meetings and feasts, possibly in special chambers. On the other hand, smaller late medieval taverns, with their drinking rooms at ground-floor level, often resembled private houses and modifications from one function to the other were probably minimal.

Inns were naturally extensive establishments, and provided accommodation of some comfort. By 1345 a guest could obtain a single room, at least in

London; in 1380 the custom of the realm, it was noted, was that the keeper of a hostelry was responsible for the goods left by the guest, who should also receive a key to a single room. Inns were to be found in numbers immediately outside gates, where custom concentrated and where long properties could incorporate stable yards; or near other major entry points to a city, such as from the Thames into London at St Paul's Wharf, where in 1390 a nearby inn could offer a suite of rooms comprising hall, chamber, buttery and kitchen. Archaeological work on inns has often been based on surveys of standing structures, such as at Canterbury, Newark and Oxford.[26] The work on the New Inn in Cornmarket, Oxford, its surviving frontage of 1386 now known as Zacharias's, has prompted the observation that inns seem to become more numerous after about 1350. Given the equally large number of travelling persons, for instance on pilgrimages, where did they stay in the twelfth and thirteenth centuries? In London there were many 'hostels', their rooms taken over by royal command when the court came to Westminster. But there is no information about their form. The origins and predecessors of the fourteenth-century inn remain obscure.

Another peculiarly urban development was the Row. From shortly after 1300, the word is used in London and other towns to describe blocks of shops or houses-cum-shops which must have had some kind of unified architectural character. A surviving example is Lady Row, Goodramgate, York, built in 1314: two storeys high, jettied on the first floor, and with simple living accommodation above a ground-floor shop. Three London contracts of 1369–73 indicate the nature of unitary blocks of shops in the later fourteenth century; these also appear to have contained living accommodation in the form of halls or solars.[27] Such blocks or rows were often built by institutions such as religious houses, both those in the town and outside in the countryside, seeking an income from rented premises in the towns (this was the probable reason for the Row in Goodramgate, the developer in this case being the church behind). These blocks contained both domestic and trade rooms.

Excavated sites: Norwich, Hull and Hartlepool

The typology of urban houses outlined so far, and the variations of form found in inns and shops, is based on a combination of standing buildings, which tend to be the superior sort of construction (they must have been, to survive to the present day) and post-medieval plan evidence. How much is this typology corroborated by medieval archaeological sites? The following examples are taken from three towns in eastern England where survival of medieval houses and their yards was extensive.

In Norwich, a site at the junction of Alms Lane and St George's Street, north of the river Wensum, was excavated in 1976.[28] Until the mid thirteenth century the area was waste ground on the margin of the settlement, used for rubbish dumping and quarry pits. In the first of three periods considered here (Period 4, c.1275–1400), a building interpreted as a brewery was established on the Alms Lane frontage, with the rest of the site occupied by an iron-working complex (Fig. 3.6). On the Alms Lane frontage, a clay floor lay around a large hearth (Building A1); ground into the floor was ash and large quantities of germinated,

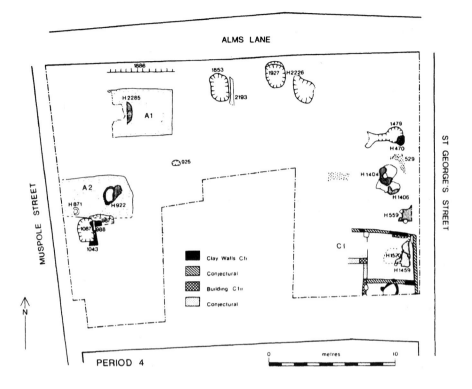

Figure 3.6   Alms Lane, Norwich: Period 4 plan (Atkin 1985).

burnt barley. South of this lay another building (A2) with a similar hearth (H922); a later small smelting furnace (H871) and deposits of slag indicate that ironworking was going on here. Slightly later, on pottery evidence, Building C1 was built at right-angles to St George's Street to the east. It comprised two rooms, was possibly tiled, and had two possible smithing hearths in it. A third room was added in a period of rebuilding. Towards the end of this period Buildings A1, A2 and C1 were allowed to become derelict, and a malting oven (1479) and hearths and furnaces (H1404, H470) were constructed to the north.

The industrial, as opposed to residential, character of the structures is mirrored in the pottery from this period: there was a higher proportion of local unglazed bowls in comparison to cooking-pots. Though much of the pottery was local, there were already (around 1300) imports from Holland and Langerwehe on the Rhine. Smallfinds included blacksmiths' tools (including some from later demolition layers, but thought to originate in this period), and a block of sandstone, unique to the site, which may have been used for sharpening them.

In Period 5 (*c.*1400–50), the site was divided into three tenements, with clay-walled houses on each property (Fig. 3.7); these divisions may have been inherited from the earlier periods. The occupation was now in part domestic, though strata still contained much iron-working waste and coal probably from

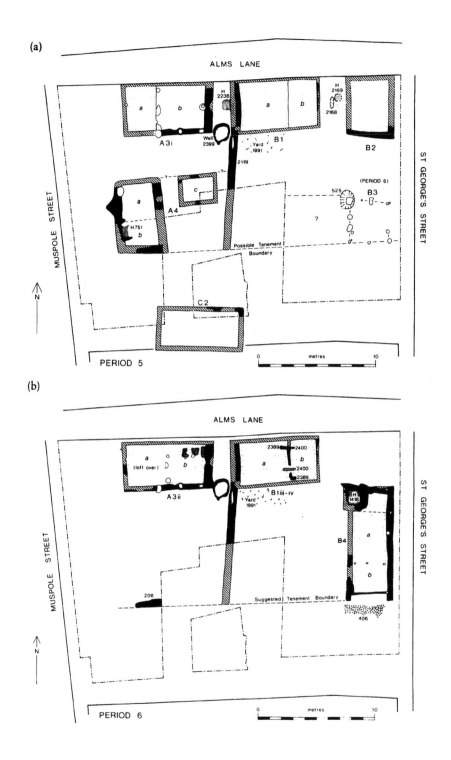

Figure 3.7 Alms Lane, Norwich: (a) Period 5 plan; (b) Period 6 plan (Atkin 1985).

smithing activities. On property B to the east lay two buildings, B1 and B2. As its strata contained Langerwehe stoneware from Germany, B2 was probably constructed later than the buildings on property A (the imported pottery is conventionally dated nearer the middle of the century in Norwich). On property C, to the south, small traces of a further building (C2) were also recorded. Here were also several fragments of a pottery vessel which may have been part of distilling apparatus. Buildings B1 and B2 produced implements used in domestic crafts, such as a bone spindle-whorl, and dress ornaments.

In Period 6 (*c.*1450–1500), houses extended along St George's Street, and there is the first evidence of buildings with upper storeys, by adaptation of the existing structures (Fig. 3.7(b)). This sign of increase in status is underlined by better contemporary pottery. The appearance of Raeren stoneware in this period dates the period to the end of the fifteenth century; other imports were Dutch redwares. The standard of house fittings, personal implements and jewellery (nail-cleaner, strap-end and pin from a brooch) was higher now than previously. For this site documentary evidence is available but limited from about 1290, and makes no useful contribution to the interpretation of the structures.

The second example is from Hull. As part of a campaign of investigations in the 1970s, two sites in the south-east part of the Old Town were excavated, in High Street and Blackfriargate; we are concerned with that in Blackfriargate, a site now beneath an orbital road. The excavation lay within a single medieval property on the north side of the street which led from the medieval market place and butchery (Marketgate, Queen Street) on the west to the High Street in the east and, as a continuation of the street, Rottenherring Staith on the river Hull.[29]

Six periods of activity (called phases by the excavators) account for the years between about 1250 and the end of the fifteenth century. Phase 1 (mid thirteenth century, after 1250) consisted of flood strata and a gully. Phase 2 (late thirteenth/early fourteenth century) comprised a three-bay building along the street, its bays shown by padstones which would have supported the main structural timbers, and a number of pits within the property, though their investigation was terminated by the flooding of the present river Hull during the excavation. This was probably the property of a Simon Wytelard in 1293. In Phase 3 (first quarter of the fourteenth century) the buildings were rebuilt, furnished with hearths and extended, and more pits were dug behind the buildings.

Phase 4 (second quarter of the fourteenth century, before 1352) saw a major rebuilding after about two generations (Figs 3.8–3.9). The buildings based on padstones were replaced by new ones with sills of brick, which had been used elsewhere in the city wall and the church of Hull since before 1300, and timber frames. They formed a central bay and an entrance parallel to the street with two wings at right angles, filling the street frontage of the property. The eastern wing comprised a hall with central hearth, and the western wing included what was probably a kitchen or outhouse, provided with a succession of ovens.

By this phase the tenement boundaries had been fixed, partly by stone walls; they survived to the twentieth century. This fixing reflects the increasing stability of life within Hull as an urban place. The excavators argue that highly

Figure 3.8 Blackfriargate, Hull: the Wytelard property in the early fourteenth century (Phase 4) looking south (the extended wing on the right is an addition of Phase 5 in the mid to late fourteenth century) (Armstrong and Ayers 1987). Plans of the site are given in the next two figures, but the photograph must be read as looking from the top of each plan.

skilled brick building was taking place on many sites in Hull during the first half of the fourteenth century; models may have been taken from continental northern Europe. Far from being a second-class substitute for stone, brick in England was used positively and for prestige.

The buildings of Phase 4 were probably owned by a Robert de Swanland in 1347; he divided and sold the property in 1352. This division was also shown in the archaeological record as Phase 5 (mid/late fourteenth century, after about 1350), when the large building of Phase 4 was subdivided to make two smaller dwellings (Fig. 3.10). This changed the former gateway or entrance and a room next to it, interpreted as a shop, into small rooms with identical central hearths of brick. The division of 1352 is also very useful for pottery dating studies in Hull, as it provides a fixed point or *terminus ante quem* for the styles and vessels found in the Phase 4 layers: local and North Yorkshire wares, and imports from Saintonge, the Low Countries and Spain. In Phase 5 further imports appear, including Siegburg and Langerwehe wares from the Rhineland. In Phase 6 (fifteenth century) the building to the west was repaired and possibly incorporated small-scale industrial facilities, but that to the east was dismantled.

In this case the writers of the excavation and finds report do not bring out the significance of the many objects in stone, fired clay, glass, iron, copper, lead, wood, leather and textiles from the site described and from a nearby site published with it. The reader must work from individual finds in catalogues to contexts on the site. It would have been useful to know if the excavators thought, for instance, whether the few fragments of medieval window-glass

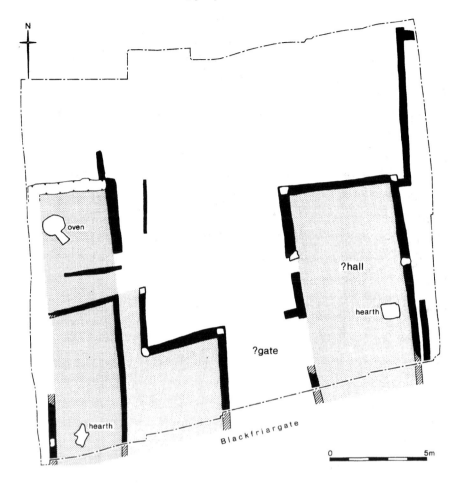

Figure 3.9 Blackfriargate, Hull: Phase 4 plan of the Wytelard property, early four-teenth century (Armstrong and Ayers 1987).

from the site might indicate glazed windows for the houses there. A small number of decorated floor tiles were found in layers of the Phase 3, Phase 4 and Phase 6 buildings, and probably came from use in them. The tiles were of types made in Nottingham, but the occurrence of two fragments of tile kiln waste on the Wytelard property, one in a layer behind the Phase 3 buildings, corroborates documentary evidence that East Midlands tilers were working in Hull in the fourteenth century.

To travel further north for the third example: at Hartlepool, excavations at Church Close in 1984–5 found Anglo-Saxon monastic occupation immediately north of St Hilda's parish church, and after a distinct break in occupation marked by deposition and cultivation of a sandy soil, a number of properties were laid out in two periods: the first possibly part of the initial founding of the medieval town in the late eleventh and early twelfth century, and the second in the mid to late thirteenth century.[30]

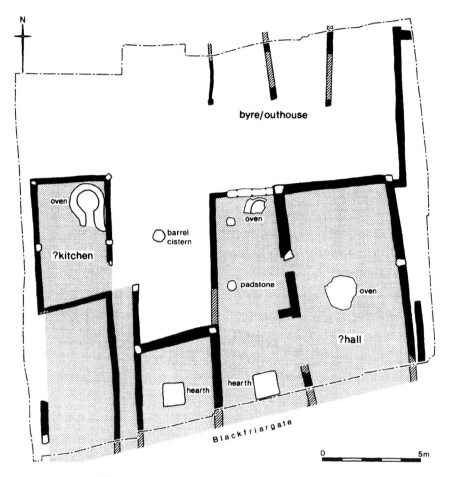

Figure 3.10 Blackfriargate, Hull: Phase 5 plan of the Wytelard property, mid to late fourteenth century (Armstrong and Ayers 1987). The new buildings presumably indicate a greater density of occupation along this part of the street. For reconstructions of these buildings, see Figure 3.15 below.

　　The earlier phase comprised two properties with buildings of slot- and post-hole construction, said here to be another rural tradition which went well with signs of cultivation in their backyards. During the twelfth century and up to about 1250, these buildings were extended and the yards became enclosed, dug with pits and hearths; urban lifestyle was taking over. By the end of this period some of the buildings were on sills of stone. In the second period (Fig. 3.11), three long stone buildings (II, IV and V) were erected on the northern property, their individual rooms reached by two alleys and with a common yard at the back. From the absence of tile on the site, they must have had thatched roofs. A similar building (III) was constructed on the southern property, much less of which lay in the area of excavation. This building preceded the others, and may have served the church to the south.

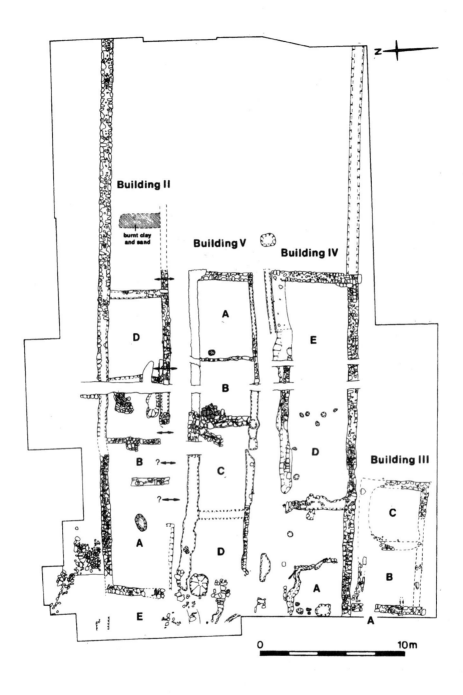

Figure 3.11 Church Close, Hartlepool: plan of properties in the late thirteenth century (Daniels 1990). The letters were assigned to rooms during the course of the excavation, and do not have any chronological significance.

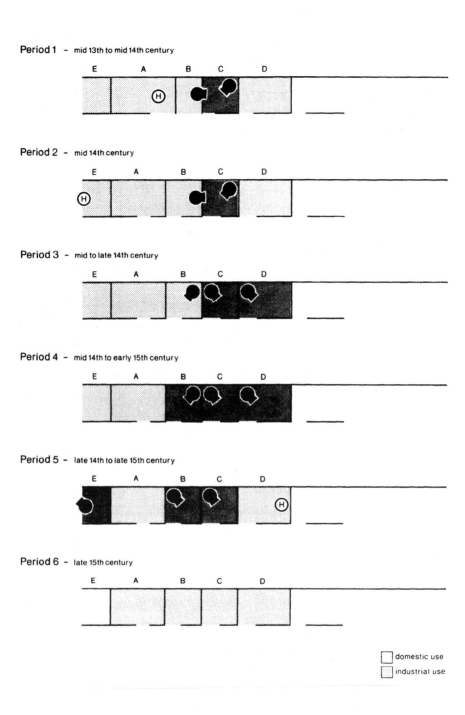

Figure 3.12 Church Close, Hartlepool: diagram of tenement use of Building II (the name given to a range of buildings on a property), from the mid-thirteenth to the late fifteenth century (Daniels 1990). The industrial use is suggested by the character of the ovens.

Building II, from its stouter construction, may have been of two floors, with the others only having one ground floor. A number of sill and jamb stones from it suggest it had freestone door- and window-frames, though the windows were in the main not glazed. From the suggested sitings of doors (Fig. 3.12), it seems that Building II also had an alley to itself, whereas the other two buildings shared an alley. Building III on the southern property had been demolished in the mid to late fourteenth century. The buildings on the northern property shared a history of adaptations, in the form of room expansions and contractions, the insertion or removal of hearths, and movement of partitions and doorways until the late fifteenth century, when they were demolished and ploughsoil once more covered the site.

On this site the excavator has attempted to analyse the function of the various rooms in the three parts of the northern property, which on structural grounds we can call individual tenements (Buildings II, IV and V). Their front rooms (not completely excavated because of proximity to the modern pavement, as is usual in urban excavations) had drains which ran into the medieval street; presumably they were shops (i.e. workshops). Building II had a larger number of domestic items than the other buildings in its component strata. The remains suggest that the house comprised a shop (room E), a hall with central hearth (A), a service room (B) and kitchen (C). Though Building II was thus domestic in function, several of the quickly changing phases of its use included ovens which may have had industrial purposes, and many stone containers were found in and around the building; these are shown diagrammatically in Fig. 3.12. They appear to have been at first domestic in scale, for baking already processed food (the only seeds found around the ovens were of heather, used as fuel) and possibly processing fish; quantities of herring and whiting bones were recovered. When, however, ovens were built first in room D and then in room E, it is possible that food preparation had reached commercial proportions. Buildings IV and V had a similar mix of domestic and industrial features, but they were more on the industrial side: in the mid to late fourteenth century the yard behind IV was the site of a lime kiln, a rare feature in Hartlepool where none of the domestic buildings so far known had mortared walls. Much more domestic refuse probably lay in the rear parts of the medieval properties, but these strata had to be removed by machine in order to examine the Saxon levels beneath.

These three examples of excavated sites show that there was great variety in the forms of medieval secular buildings, in the way they were laid out on plots, and especially in the ways they changed shape and position over quite short periods. When stone buildings were erected, the changes might thereafter be slower, but they still occurred. Thus there is a danger in seeking an over-rigorous typology of house-plans, and it is better to explore the range of shapes and sizes while keeping in mind the broad categories outlined above as Types 1–4 (which are solely derived from the Treswell London plans, a snapshot of building use in the early seventeenth century), or those described by Pantin (which were based on surviving buildings surveyed in the twentieth century, always altered several times since the medieval period).

Changing use of properties over time: Worcester

Archaeological work in towns, being founded in the sequence of usually many strata, documents changes in land-use over long periods; and these changes can have a variety of reasons. When several properties have been excavated, analysis of the finds provides some clues to differences. This has already been demonstrated in the three cases so far, but here is a fourth which has been taken further: excavation at Sidbury, a street in Worcester. Here medieval properties, particularly away from street frontages, were relatively undisturbed because they had not been subjected to the need for basements or large buildings.[31] The post-Roman use of the site began in the tenth century, when it is assumed that timber-framed buildings were erected at right-angles to Sidbury, the street which led to the cathedral. Three narrow properties or tenements (labelled A–C) are indicated (Fig. 3.13). From structural (bowl furnace, outdoor hearth, kiln), artefactual evidence and the few available documents, it is suggested that by the twelfth century there was a boneworker carrying out his trade on the central tenement B; bronzeworkers were active on all three properties in the fourteenth and fifteenth centuries. In 1976 Tenement A still had the first floor of its timber-framed front building, of around 1300, to be recorded. The diagram in Fig. 3.13 shows how these conclusions, largely based on archaeological excavation, enable us to see the three properties being subjected to pressures which changed their character as a group, first from residential accommodation to bone-working, and then to bronze-working. It would be illuminating to know if this reflected the history or needs of the nearby cathedral and its large community.

The third part of this chapter looks ahead to the ways in which archaeological study of secular buildings in medieval towns can be developed. Three important topics can be summed up in the questions: (1) what can be deduced about the physical nature of the built environment in towns, from the materials and other factors influencing construction of secular buildings? (2) what parts of houses were influenced by factors such as the needs of trade or the wish to make a statement about one's position in urban society? and (3) can archaeological investigation in the medieval town throw light on more personal matters, such as the developing wish for privacy, or the way in which the house might be more subtly divided between public and private areas, or even male and female domains?

Built environment, construction methods

The nature and quality of the built environment was influenced largely by three factors: the variety of building materials, the technological sophistication of construction methods, and urban building regulations.[32]

Houses in medieval towns were built out of four basic materials: timber, stone, brick and earth. The range of materials available had a profound influence on the types of building possible, on decoration and on life-span. Exploitation of timber is discussed further in Chapters 4 and 7; the sources and species of wood were largely local, even in London, though by the four-

Period		Tenement C	Tenement B	Tenement A
X4.2	1600	BRONZESMITH	BRONZESMITH	BRONZESMITH
		stone mould for	outdoor hearth	(bell-maker)
	1475	bronze casting		kiln for moulds
		many bronze		
		objects		
X4.1	1475	BRONZESMITH	BRONZESMITH	?
		bronze lumps	bowl furnace	
	1400	bone off-cuts	bronze objects	
	14thC	Site frontage levelled and lowered; City wall built at rear		
X3.3	1330	BONE/BRONZE-	?	BONE/BRONZE-
		WORKER	bone off-cuts	WORKER
	1300	timber-framed house		timber-framed house
		crucible		well, pebble yard
		antler off-cuts		bronze lumps
	c. 1300	Site frontage levelled and lowered		
X3.2	1300	Residential	BONE-WORKER	Residential
	1250	? timber-framed	clay tile and	pebble yard
		house	window glass	
	*c.*1250	Site frontage levelled and lowered		
X3.1	1250	Residential	BONE-WORKER	Residential
		? timber-framed	bone, horn and	? timber-framed
	1100	house	antler off-cuts	house
X2	100	Residential	Residential	Residential
		? timber-framed	large oak timbers	post-holes, daub
	*c.*900	house (shown by	cesspit	
		space)		

Figure 3.13 Sidbury, Worcester: archaeological summary and interpretation of three medieval properties excavated in 1976 (Carver 1980).

teenth century Baltic timber was also used in towns. The stones used in medieval buildings in towns were from the immediate region when available, but for prestigious buildings such as churches and hospitals, building stone and stone roofing flags or slates were brought long distances. Former Roman towns had a great stock of Roman building material within their walls, which was dug out and reused especially up to the end of the thirteenth century and occasionally later. Houses largely of stone were always the prerogative of the rich, and seem to have been a feature of the thirteenth and fourteenth centuries, as shown by the number of arched foundations of stone found on archaeological sites; thereafter however houses of stone are rare, except in towns near good quarries such as Burford in the Cotswolds. Brick was locally produced in parts of eastern England during the thirteenth century, but was in general use only from the early fifteenth century.

The structural character of foundations of domestic buildings from the eleventh to the fourteenth centuries in London has recently been examined in detail, in the light of excavations both in the area around the northern end of London Bridge and around Cheapside. Twenty-eight early medieval timber buildings have been grouped into three main types: (i) earthfast; (ii) ground-level; and (iii) foundation-bed (pad-stones, rubble platforms or mortar-capped rubble- or gravel-filled trenches).[33] The stone buildings introduced from the twelfth century were sometimes greater in area than the largest timber cellars which preceded them, and in every case much heavier. New foundation techniques were employed: the use of piles and, from perhaps the mid thirteenth century, arches in stone. Three different types of foundations were developed, and the period of use or fashion of each can increasingly be specified by the dating of archaeological examples: (i) chalk and gravel foundations without mortar, sometimes with piles (in use before the eleventh century, to some time in the thirteenth century) (Fig. 3.14); (ii) arched and mortared foundations (from the mid thirteenth century, rare by the sixteenth century); and (iii) mortared foundations without arches (from the twelfth century onwards). Thus a type-series of foundation styles is being developed, covering the tenth to sixteenth centuries. In towns generally, the changing character of foundations and basic methods of building walls can be seen as progress to better standards, or at least to more economical use of materials by making them last longer (Fig. 3.15).[34]

Timbers, whether from standing buildings or from waterlogged deposits on archaeological sites, can often be dated by dendrochronology, the most significant advance in dating since radiocarbon dating; indeed, it is more precise, and of more use in the medieval period. Timbers with at least fifty annual rings are preferable, but this need not mean timbers with large cross-sections; some only 80 × 50mm in cross-section have contained more than fifty rings. The best timbers for tree-ring dating fall into two categories: those with the longest ring sequences which are used to construct a site master curve, and those with bark and sapwood, which are important in providing precise felling dates. Though the main species used in British medieval constructions, and the main focus of study, has been oak, scientists are extending their chronologies to include elm, fir and beech.[35]

Many standing medieval buildings in both towns and rural areas in Britain have had their parts dated by this means. Every year a list of new datings is published in the journal *Vernacular Architecture*. Dates have been provided for cathedrals (Angel Choir roof, Lincoln; Ely nave roof; Salisbury crossing vault), castles (Great Hall, Leicester Castle, arcade; Martin Tower, Tower of London), prominent civic buildings (Exeter Guildhall; the Governor's House, Newark, roof), inns (the New Inn, Oxford, jetties; the Cross Keys Inn, Leicester, roof), as well as rural buildings such as barns and farmhouses. The date range is throughout the medieval period, and the number of twelfth-century dates at least from the larger buildings is encouraging, since so much of the evidence for the early centuries of the period has disappeared above ground. We have already noted the increasing contribution of archaeology in the form of timbers reused in waterfront constructions; these often provide details of construction of buildings formerly standing on land. When a town has a good number of surviving medieval buildings, dendrochronology should be a major

Figure 3.14 An apparently simple foundation at Milk Street, City of London, has much to say about twelfth-century construction. Only the lowest part survived, most of it being removed by later activity. At the base were voids left by triangular piles; where wood remained at the points, it was beech. Above were two courses of stone: the harder Reigate stone, and above, chalk, interleaved with gravel. Since chalk breaks up in frost, medieval ground level must have been higher (Museum of London).

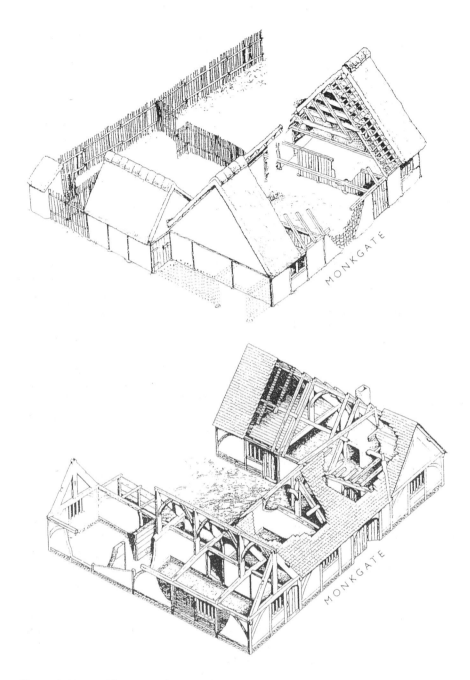

Figure 3.15 Buildings on the Wytelard property, Blackfriargate (formerly Monkgate), Hull, demonstrating changes in uses of materials. Single-storeyed buildings with walls based on padstones at intervals were set parallel to the street in the late thirteenth century. These were replaced within fifty years by a timber-framed house of 'interrupted sill' construction. The sill beams were carried on low brick walls; the roof, formerly thatched, was now covered with tiles (D. H. Evans and Humber Archaeology).

tool, as demonstrated at Chester: although the programme was limited, it provided independent evidence that several buildings in the Rows date from the second half of the thirteenth century or the first half of the fourteenth.[36] York has a good number of surviving timber buildings dated to the fifteenth century only on their general appearance; dating by dendrochronology might change this unsubstantiated perception and thus the history of the medieval town. In Scotland, samples were taken during urban excavations in the 1970s and 1980s, but not processed until recently for lack of a locally based laboratory. Now a start has been made, with analysis of tenth- to thirteenth-century timbers from excavations in Glasgow, Inverness, Aberdeen and Perth.[37] Towns in the southern German state of Baden-Württemberg and in Switzerland have produced eleven domestic buildings dating to before 1300, and another 52 from the period 1301–50. Study of medieval houses in Cluny included a programme of dendrodating which has produced sound dates for timbers in ten buildings in the town, ranging from 1322 to 1757.[38]

Many medieval buildings used bricks, usually for local infilling for timber panels to replace lath and loam, or for facilities such as chimneys and hearths. The scholarship concerning the early use of brick in Britain needs clarification. For large parts of the Lowland Zone in Britain there was a dearth of locally available sources of suitable building stone: this meant that any stone needed for building had to be imported, and consequently was quite expensive as a material. Brick had been used extensively from an early date in neighbouring parts of Europe which similarly lacked readily available building stone (e.g. the Low Countries and substantial parts of northern Germany); hence, it comes as little surprise that those parts of Eastern England which had the closest trading links with these continental areas, and which had similar access to suitable locally available clay supplies, were to develop their own brick and tile industries at a relatively early date.

Brick houses are found in towns in many parts of continental Europe, from the Baltic to Italy, from the thirteenth century. In the Netherlands and in Italy, there is development of typologies or chronologies of brick based on brick sizes.[39] Brick is a naturally more durable building material than timber, but is lighter and easier to shape than most building stone; hence it is cheaper than stone, but almost as long-lasting. It may therefore be suggested that, once in place, brick walls may have had an inhibiting effect upon change or innovation in the planning and evolution of a town. Certainly, in many continental towns in Northern Europe, the 'Hanseatic house' (or *Dielenhaus*), once established, has become a long-lived form – and is now an icon of cultural tourism in many of these towns, the principal manifestation of their long and proud histories.[40] In contrast, timber buildings had a more limited life-span, and because they tended to fall down or decay more quickly if badly maintained, towns which were dominated by timber buildings probably experienced more frequent flowering of new ideas in planning, construction or external decoration in their rebuilding.

The manufacture of clay roofing tiles had already begun in Eastern England by the middle years of the twelfth century (e.g. in East Yorkshire, Lincolnshire and East Anglia), and local brick manufacture was to start in the same areas within the next century. While limited production may have initially meant that the use of the new material was restricted to specific building projects, or even to limited use within a building (e.g. for brick hearths, or pad settings; or for door jambs and window surrounds within buildings made of other materials), by the early fifteenth century its use was far more widespread. In fifteenth-century Norwich brick was used both for the construction of complete brick undercrofts for timber-framed superstructures, and as a rubble core within the walling of many of the new parish churches, the exterior of which was faced with flint cobbles: even the spire of the cathedral (erected in about 1480) was largely built of brick, and then simply encased in stone facing – as also was one of the western towers of Canterbury Cathedral, at about the same time. Brick could also carry mouldings. By the mid fourteenth century, buildings in Hull were incorporating moulded brick jambs copying elaborate stone fillets (the Austin Friary at Hull, *c.*1340), and sophisticated arch construction that can be matched in contemporary structures in Lübeck and other Hanseatic towns; while by the early fifteenth century, there are surviving examples of ornately decorated niches, corniches, parapets and blind arcading (e.g. on the North Bar at Beverley, built 1409).

By the fifteenth century brick had spread more widely into other parts of the country, and it has been suggested that for the greater houses outside of the coastal zone brick building fell into distinct geographical areas that were centred on a rich regional patron and his circle.[41] It may be significant that the spread of brick buildings in London later in that century coincides with the adoption of brick in royal and episcopal palaces of which there were a great number in the area; similarly, in areas such as Lincolnshire the extensive use of brick in new prestige buildings, such as castles (e.g. Tattershall) and monastic buildings (such as the gatehouse at Thornton Abbey) helped to make the use of this material more fashionable. Houses totally of brick in towns were generally much later, for instance in the second half of the seventeenth century in Winchester.

Stone and brick also brought a measure of stability. Buildings constructed of such durable materials or having stone foundations beneath their timber frames survived to form relative points of permanence within the more rapidly changing surroundings formed by timber buildings. Thus the main buildings of some of the larger houses were a link with former topographic arrangements.

The built environment is also partly a product of building regulations in the town. From about 1200 in London the Assize of Building, a set of civic regulations, laid down requirements for party-walls and roofing materials (i.e. tile roofs), and made rules governing drains and disposal of sewage.[42] Thus we can study the effect of civic control on secular buildings, especially on wall construction (walls 3ft thick, as required by the regulation, are commonly found on City sites dating to after about 1200) and roof design. The civic regulations banned reeds, rushes, straw or stubble, and required roofs to be covered with tiles, shingles, plastered reeds or boards. In archaeological deposits, the standard rooftile or pegtile becomes common from the middle of the twelfth century, demonstrating that tiles were available and occasionally used fully fifty years before they were insisted upon in the written laws. Many other major cities had building regulations just as early, as noted in Chapter 2. Nuremberg had rules which ranged wider, covering consistency of style in façades (a feature normally associated with buildings of the eighteenth century), and specifying the allowed kinds of ornamentation and number of oriel windows.

The majority of secular constructions in British towns were of timber (as were some continental towns now known for their brick houses, such as Bruges); and certain developments in building construction in timber may be attributed to factors at work in the crowded town. The first developments are technological: around 1180 sawing was readopted, so that timbers were squared more accurately and therefore timber frames could be better built. Jettied buildings are mentioned in London in 1246, and these appear to be the earliest certain occurrences in the country; by 1300 jettied buildings were common in the streets of many English towns. Engravings show that jettied buildings were also formerly common in towns of the Upland Zone and in Scotland, but the passage of time has almost totally removed them. The exploitation of the roofspace, another need arising from density of living, is shown by the development of dormer windows in the early fifteenth century and of the side-purlin roof, presumably at the same time. The technology of the timber frame allowed easy expansion of building units to handle changes in circumstances, such as more functions within the domestic complex or more occupants. Overall, at least in English towns, the best use was made of town plots by increasing sophistication of carpentry rather than use of stone or brick, and archaeological study should reflect that importance. These refinements are found at broadly the same period in other European towns: jetties are recorded on buildings in the middle of the thirteenth century in Bergen and dendrodated to 1266/7 at Esslingen in southern Germany. In German and Swiss towns, timber cesspits were commonly being replaced by stone in the late thirteenth century, at the same time as in England.[43]

Thus, although there are regional differences in availability and use of materials, there seems to be a common timetable, in many European towns, in improvements to sanitation, quality of construction and innovation in form. Around 1180, as shown by archaeological work in many towns, stone buildings are occurring on street frontages and in properties behind. At the same time, waterfront revetments show that carpentry was improving, with a wider range of sophisticated joints which would allow buildings of several storeys to be built in timber. In this case, archaeology is showing that there was much building in stone, and technical innovation in construction in wood. This presumably means that people in towns were spending money on their houses, in a time of plenty, and developing their notions of suitable standards of accommodation. As we have seen, there is increasing evidence that the use of tiled roofs preceded their requirement by urban regulation. Perhaps therefore we are looking at the idea of progress in standards of urban buildings in too limited a way. It is not only a history of increased regulation from above for improvement, such as the documents imply; archaeological work shows that regulation codified and gave formal approval to what was already spreading practice.

Social environment: parts of houses and of properties

In some towns, standing medieval buildings survive from cellar to roof, and may be examined; but their interiors will have usually been changed, often drastically, over the centuries of their use, so that the intended functions of rooms in the medieval period is lost to us. Whole parts of the house have often been rebuilt, or chimneys, doors and stairs inserted or moved. Thus a standing building is often rather like a very ragged manuscript which is difficult to read. But archaeologists make the attempt in all European countries, with great success. For the eleventh and twelfth centuries, the standing evidence is largely that of stone buildings; but timber features are increasingly being dated to the middle and later parts of the thirteenth century, and it is only a matter of time before standing timber fragments of the twelfth century are identified in numbers in towns. Internal decorations such as thirteenth- and fourteenth-century wall paintings have been recorded in several towns.[44] In England, combined studies of inventories and standing buildings, predominantly in villages where more houses have survived, enable the picture after 1500 to be clearer, though both sources are not without problems.[45]

In many towns the medieval buildings have long disappeared, and the archaeological strata are all that are left. Occasionally, documentary evidence can reconstruct the buildings above archaeological remains; but not often. When they have survived, documents usually supply the name and trade of the owner (though not necessarily the occupier) of the property, some construction details (such as when a jetty overhangs a neighbour's property, resulting in litigation) and how properties were divided up between family members. Outside a few well-documented towns such as London, Winchester and Canterbury, the documentary evidence survives only from the thirteenth and especially fourteenth centuries; and archaeological work has repeatedly shown that the properties in question started forming up to three hundred years earlier. The following paragraphs consider what parts of medieval houses are usually seen by archaeologists, and what might be inferred about use of the rooms or spaces from artefacts and other evidence found within houses.

The position of the cellar or undercroft within the property seems often to reflect a need for easy access to the street; and here the expense laid out on vaulting (and presumably other kinds of colourful decoration) may have been intended to encourage business in or off the street. One type of undercroft, with its bays arranged in only a single row or aisle, lay along the street frontage, presumably beneath small shops, or occasionally down the side of a property with one end (and its entrance) by the street. This position with one end against the street had been established by some of the twelfth-century stone buildings. On prestigious properties a stone building in this position, on an undercroft of two aisles with columns down the middle (Gisors' Hall, London; Clifton House, Queen Street, King's Lynn; abroad at Lübeck and Arras) was presumably the hall or focus of the tenement. A third site was beneath the hall of the property, usually towards the rear of a wide tenement, but cellars in this position may have been vaulted far less often. The vaulted cellar was more usually tied to the street and as a result was often let separately from the buildings above and around it; a stone house in London had a cellar which was sublet before 1200, and at Chester streets of undercrofts or

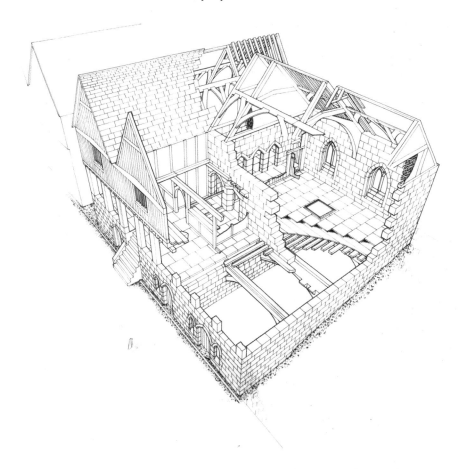

Figure 3.16 Cutaway drawing of the medieval house which largely remains within 38–42 Watergate Street, Chester (Graham Holme). This is the best example of at least three large houses in the Rows at Chester which had a hall behind and parallel to the street. At basement (street) level, three undercrofts run back from the street, two connected internally. At first-floor level, there were shops in front of the hall, which had a central hearth. This impressive building is probably of early fourteenth-century date (Brown 1999).

cellars, many of them probably separately let, formed the famous Rows during the late thirteenth and fourteenth centuries (Fig. 3.16).[46] In addition, less ornate cellars were entered from the land behind the street range; no doubt most towns had both kinds, like Waterford (Figs 3.17 and 3.19).

During the fifteenth century, perhaps as a result of the many economic troubles then being experienced by towns, undercrofts went out of use as places frequented by people coming in off the street. In Southampton, the thirteenth- and fourteenth-century undercrofts there combined the function of shop and warehouse, but undercrofts of the fifteenth century were for basement storage only; and their architecture reflected this change, as they became simpler, less embellished structures.[47] We do not know why undercrofts went

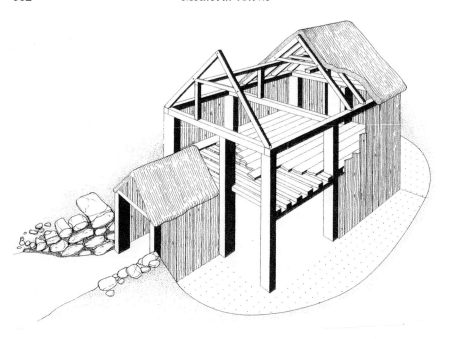

Figure 3.17 Isometric reconstruction of a late eleventh-century sunken building in Peter Street, Waterford, Ireland. The timber building had a cellar entered from the rear; and in this case probably also from the street, suggested top right. Such cellars in Irish towns may be Scandinavian, or may reflect an influx of English settlers (M. F. Hurley and O. M. B. Scully).

out of fashion as shops, and why the function was taken over by ground-floor shops. Perhaps there was less hoarding of goods in prestigious town-houses; and there is a notable concomitant development of the above-ground ware-house (especially for cloths) in larger centres in the fifteenth century. Cloths would suffer if stored in damp cellars, unlike the wine which needed cool temperatures. So perhaps the increased trade in draperies demanded, or at least influenced, a partial abandonment of the cellar and the increase in size of shops and warehouses at ground level.

Architectural historians of the post-medieval period sometimes assume that internal fittings of buildings are 'generally better indicators of changes in lifestyle and taste than are external features, since they were more readily adapted or added in response to variations in prosperity, social requirements or fashion'.[48] House fittings sometimes survive in and around excavated buildings; we can also attempt to deduce room or area functions from arte-facts. So far, however, study of furnishings, furniture and items such as heating and lighting equipment has really only got to the stage of cataloguing the artefacts. In reports from British archaeological sites there are few instances where room function can be deduced from or suggested by fittings or arte-factual evidence. This must stem from medieval houses, like their Roman predecessors, being composed of spaces which could be easily adapted for different purposes; in the ancient and medieval world there was a fluid mixture

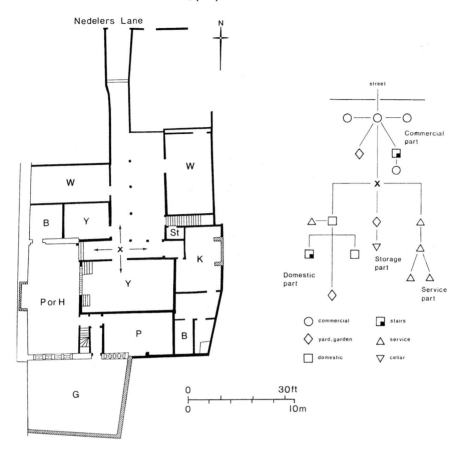

Figure 3.18 Left: plan of house in Needlers Lane (later Pancras Lane), London, in 1611 (Schofield 1995). Stone walls are shown by simple outlines. For the room and space functions, see key to Figure 3.5 p. 89. Right: access diagram showing the clear division into commercial, domestic, storage and service areas. The symbols are those used in a similar analysis of this property by Derek Keene.

of domestic and manufacturing functions within houses, but the processes rarely left structural traces. In addition, few rooms are excavated with their finds in their original places; even finds from dump layers which form floors are secondary, being broken and reused as building rubble and therefore of no use in reconstructing the function of the rooms themselves. Some suggestions have been made about room function from fittings such as hearths and ovens, as in the Norwich and Hartlepool cases already cited.

What factors may have influenced the use and form of rooms in urban houses? Some rooms, such as the shop, warehouse and especially the vaulted cellar or undercroft, changed their size, importance and perhaps function over time, presumably as a result of market forces which demanded different patterns of wholesale and retail trading. The chronology of the changing forms of these trade-related buildings can probably be seen as indicative of changing

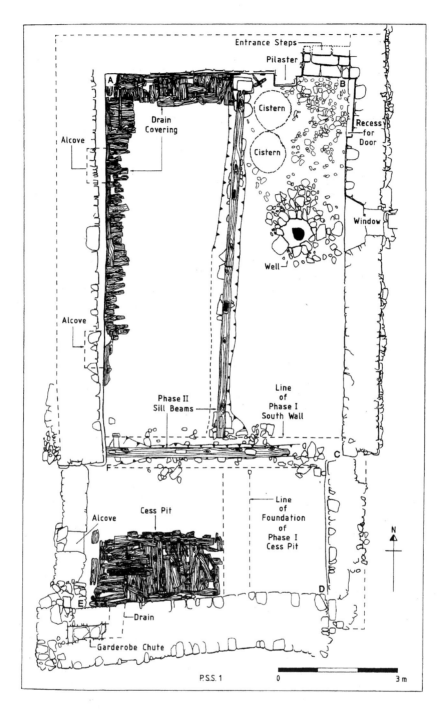

Figure 3.19 Stone undercroft of the thirteenth century on Peter Street, Waterford. This undercroft was entered from the street, and had windows; it also had cisterns and a well. The garderobe chute indicates that the house above had internal sanitary arrangements (M. F. Hurley and O. M. B. Scully).

emphases in the organization of both local and long-distance trade.[49] In small domestic units, the spaces allocated to domestic, trade and storage facilities would necessarily have overlapped. In the larger houses, these functions could be given separate spaces, which were separated by the access routes. This is most clearly demonstrated by the evidence of surveyed plans which survive from shortly after 1600.

A number of house-plans of early seventeenth-century London have survived in the work of the surveyor Ralph Treswell;[50] and given the conservatism of both building styles and the merchants who used them, even in the capital, it is probable that some of the arrangements perceptible in 1607–12 were in place before 1500 (Fig. 3.18). Here the ground-plan of a large house in the centre of the city, in Needlers (later Pancras) Lane, is analysed according to four general functions: commercial, domestic, storage and service rooms (kitchen and buttery). It divides neatly and significantly into these four zones or parts, with the commercial nearest the street, and a point (marked 'x' on Fig. 3.18) where the visitor decided which of the three other parts to enter. This house was carefully ordered in its spaces and in the matter of access between them; the only access between the four parts at ground level was via the central space (there may have been a communication route formed by upper chambers, since there were two staircases). Presumably this planning was deliberate.

This fine level of analysis seems at present a distant goal for archaeological study in towns, which starts with what is left in the ground, which is often the basement level. But careful excavation of sites rich in detail can begin to suggest the ways in which the lower parts of buildings, at least, performed a number of functions (Fig. 3.19).

Communication, perceptions and privacy; gender studies

Communication within properties was provided by courtyards, alleys and stairs. The origin of the internal court and the smaller alley, both of which could in time become public by custom, can be traced back to the early twelfth century and was no doubt older. In waterfront areas during the twelfth and thirteenth centuries, alleys grew in step with properties to articulate the space bordering the river (Fig. 3.20). When properties were subdivided, alleys which began at the former entrance to the tenement were formalized and extended to reach the new sub-units. In some tenements the alley went through to a second gate of the property, and thus became a common thoroughfare. This led to the building of separate dwellings on the backlands of properties, and the formation of satellite communities down the alleys. When they had their own well, there would be less need to go out into the street. Doors facing each other across a narrow alley or polygonal yard encouraged neighbourly conversation and mutual support. These informal communities are a feature of town life today where the old buildings and alleys survive, such as in parts of Lübeck.

Many of the smallest properties, however, had no adjacent private space, or very little, and were forced to grow upwards. This was especially true of the many houses which formed frontages to the street, with larger and separate houses behind. Stairs and staircases were developed to articulate this growth.

Figure 3.20   A river gate and stair at Skeldergate, York (York Archaeological Trust).

Can archaeological recording tell us about notions of privacy? The value of privacy in the home was developed by the thirteenth century in London; glass windows which were broken, and had therefore lost their opacity (for early glass was cloudy), were to be reglazed. In 1293 the Earl of Lincoln, having acquired the first residence of the Blackfriars in Holborn, granted a plot of ground next to his gate into Holborn on condition that the building to be erected contiguous to his own residence would have a wall 10ft high and with no window, arch or opening in it. From similar references for the fourteenth and fifteenth centuries, it is clear that the preservation of privacy was a concern, and it may have influenced the design of medieval houses, but comparatively few complete house-plans are so far known for the period up to 1600.

The final illustration is a second example from the Treswell series of London plans, a collection which provides a corpus of plans of whole blocks of property, in a snap-shot view of the townscape which is not paralleled so far by excavations in medieval London or elsewhere.[51] The whole block (Fig. 3.21), on both sides of Fleet Lane as it met the Fleet ditch on the west side of the city, was bequeathed to the Clothworkers' Company in 1538. Treswell names the contemporary function of many rooms and spaces such as hall, kitchen, buttery or garden, thus providing useful parallels for deductions about rooms or parts of standing buildings recorded on archaeological sites.

The large house is hidden from the street by a row of small dwellings. It is only reached down a narrow entry. Lady Wood's house (tenancy 1) then spreads out, and although rambling, is a series of carefully arranged spaces. If you trace with your finger the journey from the front gate at the street, through the yard, into the screens passage of the hall with its two doorways into the hall proper, you find two doors going out of the hall; the first, into a parlour which looks out over the garden, but has no door into it; the other, going via a yard and no doubt several locked doors, to the garden, which has only one entrance. The garden is the most private part of the house, up to eight doorways (and locks) from the street. Although there is now no way of knowing, it seems likely that the screen of small houses along Fleet Lane were not allowed to have windows in their backs, overlooking the garden of the large house.

Treswell normally supplies a written description, with measurements, of the upper chambers of each house. In this case, the text for the main house is missing; but there are many details about the smaller units and their tenants. So in this case we can see how poorer houses fitted in round the larger properties, at least around 1600. Blacksmith's Court, otherwise known as Flowerdeluse Alley, was tucked in between the great house and the Fleet Ditch; perhaps it had formerly been a back yard of the residence. In 1612 a narrow alley led to a small court around which were five houses, hard to disentangle. On the west side, towards the bottom of the plan, were a number of dwellings with only one room on each floor, stacked two rooms high with a garret above. Two houses were occupied by widows: numbers 12 and 15 on the plan. The former was only 12½ ft square; the stair in the corner led to another and separate bedsit on the floor above. These are the same sort of dimensions and areas which poor people had in nineteenth-century towns.

Can useful things be said about the medieval household? By this we simply mean the number of people in a house, how this varied between houses, and how the members of a household were composed (adults, children, servants, lodgers). A historian has recently concluded: 'we cannot be sure about how this most fundamental social institution was constituted. Most of the evidence is English, late and flawed.'[52] One example gives food for thought. A detailed

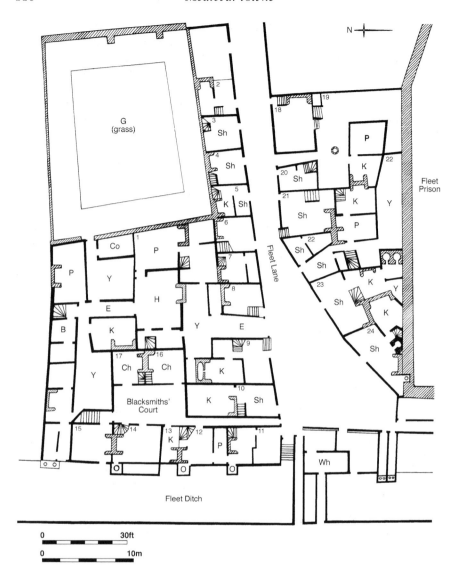

Figure 3.21 Fleet Lane, London, surveyed by Ralph Treswell in 1612. The 24 tenancies are numbered; Lady Wood is number 1. For key to room and space functions, see caption to Fig. 3.5.

documentary study of Coventry in the 1520s suggests that when households are graded by rent paid or by assessment of goods, they show that more expensive and presumably larger houses held families with more members, with more servants and with more children.[53] The surveys used also show that the number of people in a household differed according to the trade (and therefore generally the wealth) of the householder: the mean size of household was 7.4 persons for merchants, 4.2 persons for those in the metals trades, 3.2

for the building trades and 1.8 for households headed by women (usually widows). Such figures could be a starting-point for archaeological studies. We must be careful however not to project modern ideas of the family and family life into the past. With long working days, only a small proportion of a journeyman's day would be spent at home awake.[54] The household may have been of less social importance, particularly to men, than craft fellowship and relationships created and maintained at work. So far, archaeology has very little to say about these matters.

Material remains such as the building itself and any associated artefacts might display areas of the domestic unit which were used or occupied by one sex or the other. In this matter, so far, archaeological work and the related evidence of surveyed plans (which generally date to the late sixteenth century and after) are silent. Medieval women, at least in prosperous medieval London households, were often educated and given training in a trade; there were also independent women householders among all classes in many towns.[55] It may be that medieval and Tudor town-houses were not significantly ordered, explicitly or otherwise, into male and female areas. Further, to impose an idealistic dichotomy of 'male vs. female' on archaeological data may be over simple.[56] There may instead have been some household artefacts and spaces which were gender-fixed and others which were flexible, that is without gender connotations, in their use.

Conclusion

W. H. Auden once said that poets are people who hang around words; archaeologists are certainly people who hang around buildings. Research questions concerning the organization of domestic life take advantage of the considerable progress in recent years in the recording of medieval buildings by archaeologists, historians and students of vernacular architecture. But we still need to ask in the urban medieval context: what were the main sorts of houses? What building traditions were prevalent in the towns and in the countryside? What domestic activities are illustrated by the objects found? And can we reconstruct the standards of life of the mass of people who do not appear in documents?

As with all areas of archaeological endeavour, we should start with the topics about which we can be most confident: the size, shape and materials of buildings, their date (whether by artefacts or dendrochronology), and ideas about their function and status. From this archaeological work is providing the structural histories of properties, of street frontages, and of a range of house types and their component parts. By studying standing medieval buildings, often in the smaller towns, we can reconstruct the houses in three dimensions. By using documentary evidence when it is available, we can place an excavated property or a portion of a street in its urban setting. And by pulling all this information together, we can make a contribution to the study of factors in the arrangement and development of buildings which are not immediately evident in other sources, such as access patterns and division of the building into functional or even symbolic parts.

We are studying how social organization was reflected in buildings; and probably how buildings helped to order space and therefore society. Buildings influenced conduct and helped to impose rules; after a time, buildings created attitudes. Buildings do things to people.[57]

4 *Crafts and industries*

Introduction

This chapter examines one of the most characteristic elements of a medieval town, its wide range of crafts and industries. Those for which archaeological evidence is abundant include the working of stone (both ornamental and for mass walling), metals, pottery and tile, brick, glass, leather, textiles, antler and bone, and wood.[1] Indeed, the association of towns and industry is so clearly fixed in our minds that it is important to remember that many medieval industries were based in the countryside, taking advantage of the availability of fuel, raw materials, water power and lower land values. Medieval industries in general must have been labour-intensive, smelly, and, at a time when the bulk of urban housing was constructed of timber, a fire-risk. In this chapter and the next, the majority of archaeological examples are taken from work in London and Lincoln, the two places the authors know best, with brief allusions to other British towns such as Winchester.

A first question to ask therefore is why were artisans allowed to operate within or near a town rather than for instance in a forest,[2] where fuel, labour and water were at hand and there were fewer people to be offended or threatened by their activities? Among the possible reasons must be that towns, through the size of their resident population, were large consumers of goods. Furthermore, towns provided access to trade routes and merchants. However, there are cases where industries moved from town to country, and vice versa. Sometimes these moves appear to have been stimulated by technological considerations, such as the use of water power. The movement of the cloth-finishing industry out of towns, for example, is said to be the result of the invention of the fulling mill. In other cases movements may have been brought about through the land market. Rents in towns could be much higher than in the countryside (and indeed could vary dramatically from the main street frontages to the side streets and suburbs) and a shift in land prices could affect the location of an urban industry.

Trade routes and access to merchants would have been important not only in the marketing of finished goods but, for some crafts, for the purchase of raw materials. In addition, several medieval industries would have involved the investment of substantial capital and this too may have been more readily available in towns than elsewhere. The way in which artisans and their customers reacted to these conflicting forces provides one of the main interests in the archaeological study of industries, especially in those cases where the opposing pressures were evenly matched, so that a slight change in raw materials or technology might have a significant effect on the location and organization of an industry.

Before we can use archaeology to study crafts and industries, we need to define the terms of study more closely. Both the terms 'craft' and 'industry' imply the production of goods on a large scale, more than can be used within the household. Adopting the criterion of production for sale or exchange as a distinguishing feature introduces the first of many problems encountered in the use of archaeological evidence in the study of medieval crafts and industries. Whereas in the present day one might reasonably expect to be able to distinguish amateur from professional industry through the material evidence (for example by looking for a permanent workshop, looking at the scale of production, investment in equipment and so on) this may well be an inappropriate way of looking at much medieval industry, where we can expect there to have been less division between workplace and domestic accommodation, smaller-scale output and less investment in equipment than in the equivalent crafts today. Archaeologists therefore face two problems. First they have to demonstrate that a particular activity took place on or near a site, and second they have to argue for the scale of that activity.

To take one example, the bases of 'ovens' (hearths with evidence for a surrounding superstructure) are relatively common finds on medieval sites. These structures can vary in size, construction, the degree of burning to which they were subjected and their relationship with other contemporary features. Presumably the majority of these ovens were used for the domestic production of bread, pies and the like. Despite this, we know from documentary sources that professional bakers existed in towns and that their ovens were sometimes significant enough to warrant specific mention in property deeds. That significance might however be brought about by their size (in which case an archaeologist should have little difficulty in recognizing one) or their number (in which case only extensive excavation would prove the previous existence of professional bakers on the site). It may even be that commercial structures would have been constructed at waist height, so that all we find in the archaeological record is the base, without even any evidence that an oven was once present on that base. We should therefore be looking at excavated structures and their associated deposits with these questions in mind. Unfortunately there is little direct evidence in most of these archaeological finds for the original function of the oven. What is found within them is the last remnants of their fuel, not their products.

Though archaeological work has produced much evidence of manufacturing and places of manufacture, it has not often been brought together to develop the subject. For this reason the following survey is at a basic level, and comprises discussion of raw materials, fuel, manufacturing processes, workshops and industrial areas, the organization of urban industries, and finally technologies and styles of manufacture.

Raw materials

The raw materials of some industries were used in bulk and were therefore processed close to their source; an example would be the production of charcoal, which remained, until its demise in the early twentieth century, a woodland industry.[3] At the other extreme, some materials were unobtainable locally and had to be imported. Gold, silver, precious and some semi-precious stones (such as amber), ivory and furs were certainly within this category, but so were hard, fine-grained rocks suitable for hone-making. In between these extremes, the decision as to whether to place an industry closer to the source of raw materials or closer to the markets would have had to be faced. Major factors would have been land rents (which would have forced small-scale industries to the periphery of urban settlements, or out into the surrounding countryside), a water supply, the bulk of the raw material, the quantities which would be used and perhaps other factors such as the decrease in bulk involved in production and the quantity and nature of any waste. One might have thought that industries which produced nauseous smells (such as tanning) or hazardous smoke or flame would have been kept away from living quarters which, for much of the medieval period, were constructed of timber and were highly combustible. This seems, however, to have been only a minor concern to judge by where industries were actually located. There might also have been changes in attitudes over time: pottery and tile production was almost always a suburban or rural industry in thirteenth- to fifteenth-century England (for example, the tilehouse at Lincoln lay at the extreme southern end of the long Wigford suburb) and in France (as at Beauvais or Saintes), but high and late medieval pottery kilns occur in the centre of towns such as Bruges, and Siegburg (Germany) was quite literally built on pottery.[4] Do these differences have functional explanations, or should we be looking at cultural attitudes too?

A wide variety of raw materials were extracted from the ground, of which building stone was perhaps the most widely used.[5] Rural buildings were usually constructed using locally available materials,[6] but in a town the opportunities to find suitable building materials within the confines of a normal tenement were more limited. The use of stone in secular and religious buildings is discussed in Chapters 3 and 6. Stone quarries themselves are rarely located in towns, although many sites on the outskirts of the Bail in Lincoln have evidence for quarrying in the medieval period since that part of the city lies on an economically important bed of limestone which was used extensively in the town. Petrological studies of major medieval structures usually show that a hierarchy of stone types were used. Decorative details, window and door jambs were often produced in finer-textured stone than the ashlar wall faces, and these were often composed of different stone than that found in the rubble wall cores or foundations. Even so, all but a fraction of these stones would have had to be obtained elsewhere. Excavations in London showed that freshly mined flint and chalk rubble was being brought into the city, just for use in foundations. At Norwich and Beverley too chalk was quarried close to the town. At Norwich, as a result of the glacial overburden, chalk had to be extracted by mining rather than quarrying (skeletons of men who may have been miners are discussed in Chapter 7).[7] The lengths to which patrons were willing to go to obtain building stone are demonstrated by the cathedral at Ribe, in Jutland (Denmark), which was constructed almost entirely from volcanic tuff from the Rhine valley. Similarly, a survey of fonts and grave markers found at churches in towns around the Baltic Sea has shown that many were obtained from Gotland (Sweden). The fine freestone from Caen in Normandy was widely used in royal buildings and cathedrals in much of south-eastern England throughout the medieval period, but especially in the late eleventh to thirteenth centuries. These examples show that where suitable raw materials were not available locally it was quite possible to transport them over considerable distances, providing those places could be reached by water.

The most common evidence for the craft of masonry is the presence of layers of stone chippings, a by-product of the dressing of ashlar. These are most often found (or at least recognized) on the sites of major constructions such as castles and religious houses; at Baynard's Castle, London, a spread of chippings is interpreted as evidence for a commercial masons' yard next to the public wharf, where the stone would arrive for buildings of the royal wardrobe and probably for works at the cathedral, in the mid fourteenth century.[8] A further characteristic feature of urban excavations is the robber trench, often of considerable size, dug to extract as much stone as possible from previous foundations. The reuse of building materials could also follow on from the demolition of a building, and while there must have been a continuous trade in second-hand materials this would have produced more potential raw material at some times than others. Towns with Romano-British antecedents would have had access to large quantities of Roman building materials when first re-occupied in the late Saxon period. The amalgamation of some urban parishes in the fourteenth and fifteenth centuries and the subsequent decay and demolition of parish churches would again provide large quantities of reusable building materials, in this case not only ashlar and other stone but also floor tiles and window glass. This may explain the presence of decorated floor tiles in small quantities on secular sites of no apparent pretensions. Where timbers survive there is often extensive evidence for reuse, as has been demonstrated in the London waterfronts and elsewhere. Finally, the reuse of material from religious houses dissolved in the 1530s is starting to receive attention.[9] It is becoming clear that the presence of medieval moulded stone fragments on an urban site in a post-Dissolution context is no guarantee that a high-quality masonry structure ever existed on the site.

Stone was also used for smaller artefacts, either for use in the home or as personal ornament. Surprisingly, perhaps, there is evidence that in some cases the raw material was transported to a town to be worked, as shown in three examples from London. At St Alban's House, Wood Street, an assemblage of waste from the production of shale finger rings was found in a late eleventh- or early twelfth-century deposit.[10] Although the shale could not be reliably provenanced, the two potential sources were Kimmeridge in Dorset or Whitby in Yorkshire, each of which implies the transport of raw materials over a considerable distance. Both potential sources, however, were easily accessible via coastal shipping. Amber too must have been widely traded as raw material since debris from bead manufacture has been found in London (Fig. 4.1) while the potential sources are the east coast of England and, more likely, the Baltic, especially Danzig (Gdańsk). In this case, perhaps, the presence of the raw material might be a by-product of the much more substantial, and well-documented, trade in Baltic timber which both documentary sources and dendrochronology have demonstrated was used extensively in Eastern England in the late medieval period.[11] A third example consists of honestones, which had to be made from a hard yet fine-textured stone. From before the Norman conquest the major source of such rock, at least in northern and eastern England, was Norway. Schist from the Eidsborg region of southern Norway was exported in a semi-finished state, to judge by deposits of large quantities of waste flakes thrown into the backfill of the city ditch at Ludgate

Figure 4.1 Baynard's Castle, in London: pieces of uncut amber from a fourteenth-century waterfront deposit not far from Paternoster Row by St Paul's, where rosaries or paternosters, which used amber beads, were sold and perhaps made (Museum of London Archaeology Service).

in the late thirteenth century. How much of the trade in Norwegian schist in England was controlled by London artisans is unknown, nor is it yet possible to accurately chart the distribution of these hones, although they were clearly traded considerable distances inland.[12]

Stone mortars were used to grind herbs, spices, medicines and so on, and were an essential part of the medieval kitchen. They also had more specialized uses, for example for grinding bark for use in tanning or for preparing the raw materials used in glazing pottery. They are found sporadically in excavations but their rarity is probably due partly to the usefulness of a broken mortar as building stone or hard core. There is no archaeological evidence for the manufacture of these vessels and they were probably finished at the quarry site, or at least nearby, since there are typological differences which correlate with the petrological identity of the stone. For example, mortars of Purbeck marble with pierced handles are known from sites as far apart as Winchester in Hampshire and Ribe in Denmark.[13] The sources of these mortars are all quarries known for the production of high-quality ashlar and it is likely that the mortar makers exploited the same raw materials, skills and distribution routes as masons working at the same quarries.

Finally, mineral pigments were used in painting. Almost all would have had to be brought into the town, either from the surrounding countryside, as with ochres, or from farther afield, as with cinnabar (the crystalline form of mercuric sulphide), used as a high-status red pigment (as at the Austin Friary in Hull). Oyster-shell palettes containing a cinnabar-based pigment have been found in the City of London.[14] In general, too little is known about the extent and character of painted decorations in the majority of secular and religious medieval buildings, due to partial survival and the restoration over many generations of the grander examples; the archaeology of paint has yet to develop beyond occasional appearances in specialist reports.

A further common use of stone in towns was not for buildings or artefacts, but to make lime mortar. Medieval lime kilns have been excavated in towns, as at Bedford, and it may be possible to identify the source of limestone used if the lime had been incompletely heated.[15] The Bedford kiln was situated close to the castle, and it is likely that its primary function was in the production of mortar for construction works in that complex. Lime could also be used in the tanning process and another kiln from St John's Street, Bedford, was found just inside the defences of the southern half of the town. An ideal location for tanning would be on the outskirts of the settlement, with easy access to running water. Finally, lime was sometimes used to seal off noxious pit contents.

Metalworking and the making of metal objects were commonly carried out in towns but it is often difficult to establish the scale of the enterprise and the actual processes being carried out; though in appropriate ground conditions, many metal objects survive (Fig. 4.2).[16] The smelting of iron from its ore is likely to have been primarily a rural activity, governed by the location of the ore sources (although in north Norwich low-grade bog iron was roasted to extract the iron).[17] Smithing too produced large quantities of slag[18] and in towns with a substantial iron-working industry slag was common enough to be used as road metalling, as found at Gloucester, London and Worcester, or just widely dispersed as in Winchester. In among this smithing slag will be found 'hearth bottoms', formed where slag has pooled up during working, and tuyères, conical tubes of clay wrapped around the nozzle of the bellows in a forge to protect the nozzle from the heat. Copper alloys were produced from copper, zinc, lead and tin, each of which would most often have arrived in towns in the form of ingots, either of a single metal or already alloyed. Ingots of lead were found in a twelfth-century pit in London, perhaps destined for use in the manufacture of lead or pewter artefacts. More often, the raw materials of non-ferrous metalworking are represented by small offcuts from ingots, and moulds from the production of ingots. The latter are usually small and may alternatively represent a stage in the production of copper alloy artefacts on site, through remelting or beating. Chemical analysis of copper alloys shows that relative proportions of the major constituents were determined by the intended method of manufacture of the artefact so that items destined to be cast, beaten and drawn have differing compositions. Silver and gold were also worked in towns but here the raw materials have even less chance of entering the archaeological record than non-precious metals. Evidence for their use comes mainly from minute residues found within crucibles.

Glass-making was a rare urban industry in the medieval period and, indeed, a rare industry anywhere in the British Isles until the end of the medieval period.[19] Even simple decorated window panels could be imported from Flanders in the fourteenth and fifteenth centuries, despite their fragility. Here access by water to the coast was clearly an important factor, and it is possible

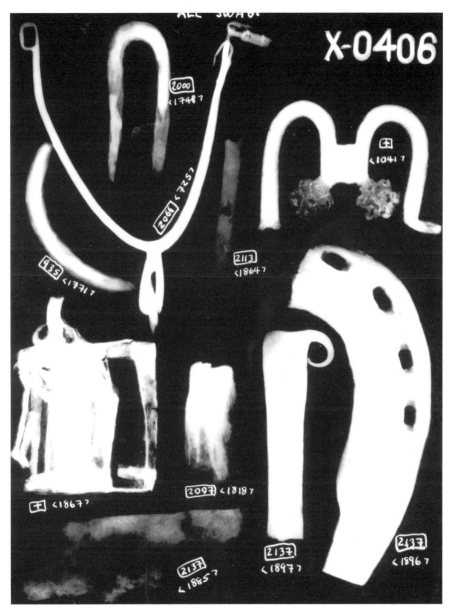

Figure 4.2 Metal objects from the waterfront excavations at Swan Lane, London, revealing their details on an X-ray photograph. Since most metal objects have corroded, the X-ray enables identification and careful conservation (Museum of London Archaeology Service).

that there was less danger of breakage transporting window glass from Antwerp or Bruges to London than there was in bringing glass from the Weald into the city. Nevertheless, there is both archaeological and documentary evidence to show that the craft was practised in the British Isles. Raw materials for glass manufacture include fragments of broken vessels or windows, known as cullet, small cubes or tesserae of coloured glass, quartz sand, a source of alkali (sodium or potassium) and finally colouring, or decolourizing, agents. Medieval technology in western Europe did not allow for the production of blue and red glass (coloured respectively by cobalt and reduced copper) which were therefore most often imported as small tesserae or cakes for remelting. Both documentary sources and analyses suggest that blue glass was produced by recycling Roman glass and, since the latter was made with sodium rather than potassium as a source of alkali, there is a difference in preservation. The blue glass often survives in much better condition.[20]

One source of alkali was from wood ash, used not only in glass production but, more importantly, in the manufacture of soap. Wood was also required in large quantities as fuel. Suitable supplies of quartz sand, which had to be relatively free of impurities, were also needed. All of these requirements led to the glass industry developing most often in wooded areas, often at some distance from towns, on or close to outcrops of white sandstone. Nevertheless, in the sixteenth century and later, urban glassworks became more common and with the replacement of stoneware bottles by glass vessels in the mid seventeenth century (and thus the creation of a mass market for the products) the industry was usually associated with towns. In this case the balance between production at source and production at the market was tipped by a change in the demand for glass and, perhaps, by changes in technology.

Clays were used in a variety of ways in medieval towns. Depending on the local building traditions they could be used for walling, in the form of daub, bricks or clay-lump, flooring (again either fired or not), building platforms and roofing (as fired tiles). Clay was used to line pits and other features to make them waterproof and clays were also, of course, the basis of the pottery industry as well as having a role in other industries in the form of crucibles and kiln structures.[21]

The majority of clays used in towns required no special properties and could be obtained either from clay pits on the edge of the settlement or even by quarrying within the town. All that was required was a clay in which the quantity of inclusions was not so great that the clay could not be moulded to shape or lose its cohesiveness. Petrological studies of burnt daub have consistently shown that this material could have been obtained locally, and within the town there would undoubtedly have been some trade and movement of clay.

By contrast, clay for use in pottery production was definitely imported to some towns. This can be demonstrated where the characteristics of the clay can be matched with a known geological outcrop or, more negatively, where a survey of local clay sources shows that none share the same characteristics. This importation was taking place as early as the late ninth century in Lincoln for the production of shell-tempered pottery. Similar clays were used at the nearby village of Potterhanworth by the fourteenth century and a survey of clays in and around Lincoln leads one to conclude that the clay was imported to the town, albeit probably only from a few kilometres away.[22] Clays with a low iron content which produced off-white vessels when fired could be found in association with the Coal Measures and appear to have been imported for use in urban pottery industries at a number of places, including Bristol and

Nottingham, in the later medieval period.[23] Longer-distance transport of raw clay can also be demonstrated in the Thames Valley. Surrey Whiteware pottery was manufactured from clay quarried from the Reading Beds, which occurs as a narrow outcrop around the rim of the Thames Basin, and yet in the thirteenth and fourteenth centuries kilns producing whiteware were operating in Kingston upon Thames and wasters from late fourteenth-century whiteware production have been found on the south bank of the Thames at Bankside opposite the City.[24] By the fifteenth century, however, both Kingston and Bankside had ceased production and the whiteware industry in the Farnham area, a rural industry which had existed earlier, expanded production to supply a large area of the lower Thames valley. Here, presumably, the competing forces which previously had favoured transport of raw clay to town-based potteries shifted in favour of rural production.

The raw materials used in brick and tile production can be studied using the same techniques as for pottery. The use of brick has a long ancestry in parts of northern Europe. At Ribe, for example, the use of brick began so suddenly in the middle of the twelfth century that its appearance in archaeological sequences can be used as a chronological marker.[25] Even the Danevirke, the boundary earthwork which marked the southern border of Denmark, was rebuilt (or refaced) in brick in the twelfth century. In the British Isles, brick and flat roof tiles were used from the middle of the twelfth century onwards, mainly in the south and east. This may be partly because along the west coast and the south-west peninsula slates could be used instead; the latter could be cleaved to form a much thinner (and therefore lighter) roof covering without the expense of digging, preparing and firing. An area occupied by the Beverley tile industry, at Grovehill, has been excavated and petrological analysis of the products has confirmed that they were made from local clay sources. For the same tilery, leases survive in the town's records which gave the tilers permission to quarry clay from the banks of the River Hill and Beverley Beck.[26] At Bristol, the same Coal Measure clay was used to make both ridge tiles and pottery, although the tile fabric is often much less well prepared. It seems that there, as was the norm, ridge tiles and roof finials were made by potters, using the same methods and raw materials, whereas when brick and flat roof tile manufacture started in the west of England in the sixteenth century new, more local, sources of clay were exploited.

Refractory clays, used to make vessels which could withstand heating in a furnace, have a more limited natural distribution. Several of the white-firing clays used for pottery, such as Stamford ware and Surrey Whiteware, were also suitable for use as crucibles and in these cases the crucibles, like ridge tiles, were produced by potters alongside other forms and sold to the metalworkers.

Many of the raw materials required by urban artisans would have been of organic origin. When organic production waste survives, however, it is often difficult to provenance, with the important exception of wood. Environmental archaeology shows that towns supported a wide flora, including trees and shrubs, but it is doubtful if any urban artisan could have existed using solely local material. Archaeological finds and documentary records show that structural timber was being imported from many sources. Such imports can be recognized archaeologically either by identification of the species, if that

Figure 4.3 Well-preserved oak timbers comprising a waterfront of *c.*1220 at Billingsgate, London. Waterfront structures provide much-needed evidence of the evolution of carpentry skills and of choice and use of timber. The boards used to form this reclamation unit wall were numbered, like parts of a medieval roof; the structure had been prefabricated in a yard on land (Museum of London).

species has a restricted distribution, or by dendrochronological analysis, which can show the likely source area of a timber (or more likely a group of timbers) by computing its similarity to tree-ring sequences of the same date from different regions. Using tree-ring analysis it has been possible to recognize the widespread use of Baltic timber for all manner of purposes, ranging from structural timbers to panels and coffins.[27] Wood was also required for house building and other structures (Fig. 4.3), furniture, vehicles,[28] machinery (such as looms) as well as for smaller, portable artefacts.

Most wood used, however, came from species which could have grown locally in the medieval period. Much work is being undertaken by specialists in ancient timber on the range of species used, whether or not there were preferences for particular species for particular purposes and the way in which the pattern of timber use changed through time. Tall, straight oaks grown in dense forest conditions, for example, seem to have become unobtainable in England even before the Norman Conquest. Documentary sources show that tree bark was used in tanning, and that the bark was harvested from living trees rather than felled timber. Once collected the bark was pulverized, that at Gallowgate in Aberdeen using a stone mortar.[29] Even where bark itself has not survived it might be possible to identify its presence in industrial quantities by characterizing the insect fauna which lived on it.[30]

Withies and reeds were required in large quantities in towns, for use in basketry and matting, as well as being used structurally, in thatch or as a backing for plaster. To date, archaeology has demonstrated (or confirmed) that basketry and matting were used but has not provided much information about the sources of raw material or location of production. Artefacts of these types were brought into town in a completed state, although obviously the raw materials were also being imported for use as walling and floor covering. The presence of large quantities of rush seeds in a soil sample taken from a pit in London was used to demonstrate that soiled flooring was thrown into this pit.[31]

Tanners required quantities of urine for the preparation and tanning of leather but the only archaeological evidence for its use is the presence of ceramic urinals, and jugs which appear to have been used as urinals. These vessels occur on domestic sites however and there is no evidence to show for what purpose, if any, the urine was being collected. Apart from this industrial use, for example, physicians used the colour and clarity of a patient's urine as an aid to diagnosis and the paper-thin forest glass urinals which they used to examine it are often found in late medieval urban cesspits. Dyers also used organic materials, such as woad, madder and other plants.[32] The plant remains themselves can be recognized if preserved through anaerobic conditions, in addition to which, the use of madder can be recognized by the characteristic staining it produced on the inside of vessels used as dye pots. These could be made of pottery. Theophilus, writing about 1122, recorded that madder was heated with lye (lime) in a 'raw pot' for staining ivory or antler.[33] Potsherds stained with madder are not uncommon finds in strata of the eleventh and twelfth centuries. Wooden vessels could also be used for dyeing, and fragments of timber vats and drains stained with dye have been found at Beverley. By the late medieval period there is documentary evidence for the large-scale processing and distribution of organic dyes (they are a common import recorded in port books) but the presence of pollen from such plants would be the only secure archaeological means of demonstrating that dyeplants were being grown within a town. Mosses, on the other hand, have very specific habitats and those used to stuff late medieval shoes from London have been identified as woodland species.[34] Given the abundant evidence for shoemaking and repairing in the Thames waterfront deposits it is more than likely that these mosses were being imported as raw materials.

The production of cloth from the fibres of the flax plant, linen, was a widespread and regionally important industry by the medieval period, for example in the north-east of England.[35] This is shown not only by documentary references to the industry but also by the presence of the element 'Lin-' in place names.[36] Flax seeds are a common component of botanical residues found in soil samples taken from urban deposits but, as with dyeplants, this is not necessarily to be taken as evidence that the flax plant was grown in towns as well as in the countryside. It could well have been imported in an unprocessed state to be retted (softened by soaking in water), leaving the required fibres. Several excavated structures have been postulated as being associated with flax retting (for example at St Aldate's, Oxford)[37] but positive archaeological evidence for the location of flax-production in towns, in contrast to that in the countryside, is rarer and consists of flax stems, seeds and capsule fragments, such as those of eleventh-century date which were excavated at Layerthorpe Bridge, York[38] or the similar finds from Eastgate, Beverley.

Animal products were another major source of raw materials for urban

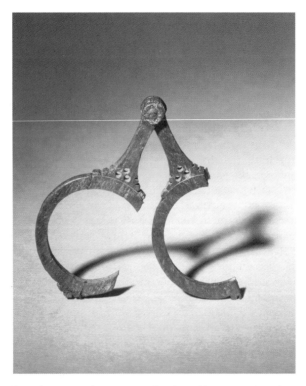

Figure 4.4 Fifteenth-century bone spectacles from Trig Lane, London; an important find in the history of optics. Bone was the medieval equivalent of modern plastics (Museum of London Archaeology Service).

artisans. Bone was used for the production of a variety of artefacts (for example a pair of spectacles found in a fifteenth-century dump at Trig Lane, London, Fig. 4.4; though they might have been imported) and waste materials, such as the sawn extremities of longbones or shoulder blades with holes left where circular blanks have been drilled from them, are easily distinguished from normal food debris. Some artefacts, such as pins made from pig meta-podials, use the whole bone, and therefore leave no manufacturing debris. It would probably never have been necessary to import bone as such to a town since the activities of butchers would generate more than enough raw material (antler, an exception, is discussed shortly). Hides for conversion to leather were sometimes traded although here too towns with a large population would have generated a large number of hides through butchery, leaving only the specialized hides required by white tawyers, for example, to be imported. The animal bone from tanneries can be used to indicate whether the hides were brought onto site with the feet and tails attached, since this leads to the over-representation of metapodials.[39]

Documentary records show that pelts were exported from Scandinavia and the Baltic for the manufacture of furs but the only evidence for this trade seems to be the occasional finding of bones from the extremities of fur-bearing animals which were left on the pelt after skinning, perhaps as a guarantee to the purchaser that the fur was indeed genuine.[40] A medieval pit excavated at Aylesbury, Buckinghamshire, contained the skeletons of domestic cats which had been skinned.[41] Silver fox foot bones were found in large quantities during the excavation of the Heumarkt in Cologne.[42] Beaver bones may also be evidence for a trade in furs and have been found at York.[43]

Antler, like fur, was also used in a number of industries.[44] In the eleventh and twelfth centuries it was used principally for the production of combs. Later medieval combs seem to have been made more commonly from wood while antler, although still used, declined in importance. Herds of deer were maintained for hunting in deer parks throughout the medieval period and if the base of the antler is found it can be seen whether it was shed by the animal and therefore collected seasonally or whether it was removed from the dead beast, as a by-product of the hunt. In either case it is clear that antlers are over-represented in urban archaeological deposits in comparison to deer bones and were therefore imported to towns as raw material for antler workers.

Cattle horn was used for several purposes, including the manufacture of combs, lanterns and windows. Horn itself rarely survives, except in anaerobic conditions, nor is it possible to determine the origin of the cattle or sheep from which it came. Deposits of horn cores, however, are a relatively common find, at least in early post-medieval urban excavations. The horn cores are all that survives from horn production, in which the horn and its bony core is boiled to make it possible to separate the horn, which is pliable when boiled. There has been some discussion about the significance of these deposits, in most of which the horn cores have been utilized to line pits but it seems clear that whatever their final function these horn cores were the by-product of horn working.[45] Since both horners and tanners used by-products of butchery in their crafts these two industries were often to be found in close proximity.

Wool formed the raw material for the weaving industry and because of its economic importance there is substantial documentary evidence for the organization of the cloth manufacturing process in the medieval period, at least from the thirteenth century onwards. The manufacture of cloth involved many discrete stages.[46] In between each of these stages there could be a change of artisan and location. First, the wool was shorn, collected from the farms where it was produced (often areas of limestone upland) and converted into yarn. The yarn was woven into cloth which was fulled and then dyed (if it had not been dyed before weaving) and finally made into clothing or furnishings. Each stage of this process was sufficiently distinct to give rise to its own occupational name: spinner, spinster, weaver, webster, fuller, tucker, tailor and the like. Similarly, it is possible to recognize archaeological type-fossils for almost every stage.

The collection and transportation of wool is perhaps the least archaeologically visible of these processes although a structure at Fountains Abbey has been identified as a storehouse on the basis of its heavily barred and shuttered windows.[47] In view of this building's later use in the fulling and finishing of cloth it is possible that wool was being stored in it in the twelfth century when it was first built. Excavations at the Abbot of Meaux's house in Blackfriargate, Hull, revealed a concentration of wooden bale pins, used to secure the wool bales.[48] The second stage, that of the production of yarn, is represented by carding combs and spindlewhorls. Yarn for worsteds was prepared from long-staple wool prepared using a wool comb. Such combs were used to align the fibres, thus producing a smooth yarn. Fragments of wool combs have been found on urban archaeological sites and the iron teeth from wool combs (also known as 'heckles' or 'hackles') are sometimes recognized among collections of iron nails.[49] Yarn for woollens, however, was prepared from shorter-stapled wool by being fluffed up so that all the fibres were randomly aligned. Initially this process was carried out using the prickly heads of teasels (also used later in the process to dress the finished cloth). By the fourteenth century, however, hand-cards were used instead. These were like large square brushes with a wooden base onto which were attached pieces of leather which had nails (later wire) inserted.[50] The combed or carded wool was then spun into yarn. Initially, this process was carried out using a distaff or spindle of wood. Medieval examples from England rarely survive, although there are a number known from Norway, but the bone, fired clay, lead or stone spindlewhorls used to give the spindle momentum are common finds. Most tend to be found in thirteenth-century and earlier contexts even though they were certainly used throughout the medieval period; a number of stoneware examples are known, produced at Raeren, near Aachen, in the late fifteenth and early sixteenth centuries, demonstrating that this hand spinning continued in use to the end of the medieval period. These late spindlewhorls are rare, however, and it is clear that by that date the spinning wheel had robbed us of information on the distribution of the process. From the thirteenth century onwards there is evidence from manuscript depictions for the existence of the spinning wheel but no archaeological evidence for the wheels themselves has been discovered, nor has any distinction between hand-spun and wheel-spun yarn been observed.

Until the tenth or eleventh century, the process of weaving using the warp-weighted loom involved the use of two characteristic artefact types which survive in some numbers; loom weights and 'pin-beaters'.[51] After that date, changes in technology meant that loom weights were not needed, although 'pin-beaters' are still found. These new looms were much more massive, involved a higher investment in manufacture and maintenance and sometimes required more than one person to work them. However, almost all parts of these looms were made of wood and therefore rarely survive in archaeological deposits. The clearest evidence for their use is likely to come from the fact that quite sizeable workshops were required to house the loom and that the former existence of such workshops might be recognizable from the ground plan of medieval tenements.

The next major stage in cloth manufacture was the finishing of the cloth. Evidence of surnames in medieval documents and street names such as *Walkergate* in Lincoln show the former existence of fullers, or 'walkers', who removed the grease and dirt from cloth by trampling it under foot in troughs with water, soap and fuller's earth. The mechanization of the fulling process, which had started by at least the late eleventh century, led to a movement of the industry out of the towns and to the fringes of upland districts, where adequate supplies of water to run the fulling mills could be found. The fulled cloth could then be dyed, if indeed the dye had not already been applied at the yarn stage as seems likely until the middle of the twelfth century, and the cloth could then be marketed.

Although most dyestuffs were of vegetable origin, one was obtained from an insect: the kermes shield louse, a native of the Mediterranean littoral, was used to produced a vivid scarlet colour for cloth. There is archaeological evidence for the use of this dye, and documentary evidence for its importation but, as yet, no evidence for the location of any workshops where it was used.[52]

Silk weaving was practised in at least one medieval city in the British Isles, London, and raw silk has been found on archaeological sites, albeit in small quantities.[53]

In general, where raw materials were of high value, and used in small quantities, they were imported to the towns where they were used. Where materials could be processed at the point of production or extraction, and especially where there would be a reduction in their bulk by doing so, this was done. However, within the medieval period there are a number of instances where an industry changed from being a rural industry to an urban one and vice versa. The most widely quoted example is that of fulling, where documentary sources have been interpreted as showing that the industry gravitated to rural areas with good possibilities of water power following the introduction of the fulling mill. However, if the technology of the fulling mill was already known on the Continent in the later eleventh century then this can only be a partial explanation. A more complex interpretation might have to involve a consideration of the social position of fullers in urban communities, the willingness of rural landowners to invest in fulling mills, the relative claims of other artisans to the power source, the contemporary economics involved in distributing the finished cloth and the changing demand for fulled cloth. In such cases, where archaeological and documentary evidence shows that the location of an industry was not governed by strict geographical determinants, there is a middle ground in which archaeologists and historians can work, elucidating the reasons why industries were located where they were and why they moved.

Fuel

Heat was a necessary element of many medieval industries. The way in which it was used, or at least the archaeological evidence for this use, is considered below. As with raw materials, the fuel would have had to be imported to the workshop, or the workshop located where the fuel was. Here too there were complex factors determining which option to take. In addition, there was the added problem of fire-risk and the nuisance caused by smoke and fumes. Analysis of ashes from industrial processes can identify the nature of the fuel. In the main, domestic fires utilized a range of fuels and probably consumed much wood and organic waste. Industrial processes may, however, have required the use of special fuel. Coal, for example, can have a high sulphur content which may affect its use in metalworking while documentary sources tell us that early post-medieval glassworks used pre-heated bundles of beech wood to fire their furnaces. Fragments of unburnt or charred coal or wood can be identified. In addition, the age and condition of the timber can be determined; in one case from Lincoln charred woodlice were found within the ash. It is probably not possible to distinguish charcoal ash from wood ash since they derived from the same source. Straw has been identified as the fuel used in some ovens (probably bread ovens) and the range of seeds found within another sample has led to the suggestion that spoiled animal fodder was used as the fuel.[54]

Peat was widely used as a fuel, to the extent that large areas of the Norfolk Broads consist of flooded medieval peat workings, and it should be possible, perhaps through identification of plant remains within the ash, to show that peat was the fuel used in a particular industry. If peat was stored before use it is possible that a distinctive seed assemblage or insect fauna might be found which could be used as an indicator. Such methods have demonstrated the use of peat at Hull and Beverley in the Humber basin whereas at Doncaster and Carlisle similar evidence may have come from imported turves.[55]

Analyses of ashes have also been carried out using X-ray diffraction to see if it is possible to use the range of minerals present in the ash as a means of determining the firing temperature. This work showed that the method was promising, although more primary research is needed to establish the accuracy of the method and to refine procedures for sampling and analysis.[56] Such a tool could be valuable in establishing the range of possible industries in which an excavated hearth might have been used and whether there is any correlation between the temperature achieved in the hearth and the type of fuel used.

Manufacturing processes

In some industries, a craftsman would carry out all the processes from preparation of the raw materials through to the sale of the finished goods, but in others varying degrees of specialization took place. Archaeology can sometimes reveal the range of processes involved in an industry and, by study of tools and waste products, which processes were carried out at which sites. Many industries used distinctive tools, although the humble knife could be used for numerous purposes; holes in medieval roof tiles and jug handles are of the same wedge-shaped cross-section and size as those of domestic knives. Where a specialized tool was used in an industry the archaeological discovery of that tool is potentially significant. Tools are, however, rare finds. Even today there is a market for second-hand tools and tools were often recorded as bequests in medieval wills. Two classic examples of the conservative nature of medieval artisans are to be found in the bell-making and tile-making industries. A set of moulds used to produce the lettering and decorative stops on inscriptions has been identified by the impressions left on surviving medieval bells. This set was first used in London in the fourteenth century, was passed from father to son in London and finally emerged in Exeter, where it was used some two hundred years later.[57] Studies of medieval floor tiles have shown that it is quite common to see cracks in the dies used to stamp the tiles, showing that the dies were used as long as possible, but in one case the tiler has gone to the trouble of adding extra wood to two sides of a set of dies so that they could be used on tiles of a larger size.[58] Naturally enough, therefore, many urban industrial sites produce no actual tools.

There are, however, a number of tools which have been broken or are small enough to be lost on the floor of a workshop. Leatherworking needles, for example, have a distinctive triangular cross-section which distinguishes them from those used on cloth and would be lost quite easily. They must also have broken often during use. Crucibles too were to some extent expendable. If a crucible was thought to be cracked it would be discarded, even while still complete, since if it broke during use the value of the lost metal would be much greater than the value of the crucible. The Museum of London houses a large collection of complete Stamford ware crucibles of varying sizes, all of which are unused and complete. They were found at Old Jewry, off Cheapside, and may well have been discarded because they were thought by the metalworker to be suspect. Industries requiring other pottery and glass vessels also produced relatively large quantities of waste. Vessels used in distilling and assaying, for example, sometimes occur with other, domestic, refuse but occasionally they are found in deposits of industrial waste. To date, however, such finds have mainly been from the sites of large establishments such as castles (as at Sandal, Yorkshire) or religious houses, where they may either have been used in alchemical experiments or in the production of medicines.[59]

Waste products are a common residue of urban industry. Metalworking in particular produced large quantities of waste whose study can be used to investigate the processes carried out. Slag is the most voluminous waste product, as noted above, but offcuts and spills of metal are also found. These can be used to distinguish metal casting from the working of sheet metal. Other industries which produced offcuts as a waste product were leatherworking and woodworking. The recyling of leather is revealed from the number of medieval shoes found with their uppers cut away for reuse. Since these are found alongside scraps and offcuts from fresh hides it is clear that shoemakers, at least, used a mixture of fresh and recycled materials. Studies of surviving medieval buildings also reveal evidence for the reuse of materials, in the form of beams with pegholes and mortises which could not have been functional in the beam's present position. Buried evidence for woodworking is less common, although probably originally accounted for a significant proportion of medieval urban archaeological deposits, as is indicated by excavations in Norway, where the climate has led to a greatly reduced speed of decay. There, wood chips form a significant element in most archaeological deposits and can even form the majority of the bulk of a deposit.[60] Where woodworking debris survives it can demonstrate the use of the pole lathe, which gave rise to characteristic waste products, such as the spinning-top shaped cores left over from the production of wooden bowls.

Unfinished artefacts are another rich source of information about urban industries. They can reveal details of manufacture removed from the finished product, such as casting seams, and can show the stages of production. Moulds too can reveal much detail of manufacturing processes. Stone moulds, made of fine-grained limestone or mudstone, were often reused. It is not uncommon to find several generations of moulds cut into a single block. Clay moulds, on the other hand, were less highly prized and in most cases were designed to be used once and had to be broken to extract the moulded object from them. Because of their size, bells and cast metal vessels gave rise to large quantities of mould fragments. Their study can reveal not only the type of object being cast (such as bell, cauldron, skillet, laver) but also, through organic chemical analysis, the nature of the wax used to make the initial model. Study of bell-mould fragments from Winchester has shown that horse dung was mixed with the clay to produce a porous, light mould.[61] Despite the undoubted value of industrial waste in the reconstruction of medieval urban industries, in many cases the only evidence for the industry comes from the finished products. Here, of course, one has to be wary of drawing the unwarranted conclusion that if an artefact was found in a particular town that was where it was made. Nevertheless, if artefacts of stone or fired clay can be shown by petrology or other characterization methods to be of local origin then their study can at least reveal the previous existence somewhere in the locality of workshops where they were produced and of the processes carried out there.

Archaeological analysis reveals much about manufacture of individual objects. A metallographic section through an iron edge tool, for example, can show the number of metal bars used in its manufacture, their composition, their hardness and any treatment that they may have received.[62] Sections through copper alloy artefacts can distinguish cast from beaten or drawn metal and, again, can reveal the existence of treatment such as annealing. Study of a pot can show whether or not the potter's wheel was used in its manufacture, and whether separate pieces of clay were used, and, if so, how they were assembled. Tools such as knives, roulettes (roller-stamps) and stamps of various kinds can all be identified from their impressions on the finished product.

Workshops and industrial areas

In many cases, the evidence for craft activity comes from typical domestic refuse deposits. Is this association a true indication of the way in which these industries were carried out, as yet another activity within the domestic household? Spindle whorls, for example, are common finds on urban sites and reflect the way in which the spinning of yarn was carried out as a domestic task by women, to the extent that being a spinster was synonymous with being an unmarried woman. In other cases, however, there must have been large-scale movement of the waste products (for example wasters from the rural kiln site at Danbury, near Chelmsford in Essex, have been found widely in the surrounding area, including the town of Chelmsford). It is therefore important to recognize the remains of workshops to establish beyond doubt that an industry was being carried out on a site, and to establish something of its scale and organization. In many cases, however, such evidence does not survive. By the late medieval period weaving, for example, was usually carried out in long upper chambers provided with good lighting in the form of numerous windows. These chambers can only be recognized if the buildings themselves survive. The groundplan of such a building may hint that it housed a weaver's workshop but the point may be incapable of proof.

Craft activity could take place within a domestic household, perhaps on the upper floor as noted above or within a shop on the ground floor. Equally, it might take place within an outhouse within a yard, or out of doors. The sort of evidence which will remain from this activity is likely to be difficult to interpret. Waste might be left where it fell, but the majority of structures will have been kept clean, tools will have been discarded along with domestic refuse, or taken away from the site altogether. The best hope of identifying a workshop or industrial area, therefore, is to excavate a large area, not a trench, so that the layout of a property can be seen. It may be that the position of hearths, pits, troughs, furnaces, drains, water sources and structures is more informative in combination than any one of these pieces of evidence might be if considered alone.[63]

If found in anaerobic conditions, timber yards might be recognized through a distinctive insect fauna or by offcuts, wood shavings or the iron axes, adzes, chisels and the like used in working the timber. Later medieval timber was often prepared using a large two-man saw. The tree trunk which was being sawn would have been positioned over a deep rectangular saw pit, in which would have stood one of the two men working the saw.

Rope-making similarly leaves little artefactual or waste evidence but may be identified from the distinctive shape of its workshops. Rope, made from bast derived from tree bark or from hemp fibre, was important in the shipping and fishing industries and consequently most medieval ports and riverine towns would have had at least one rope walk. The location of these rope walks is often shown on early maps or may survive as a place-name, as in the Ropewalk in Lincoln. In Scandinavian climates the whole operation had to be carried out indoors, so as to protect the hemp from damp. In most British towns, however, the rope walk itself was an open area, which needed to be about 6m wide and about 300 m long. From the early seventeenth century onwards the rope was spun using a large tread wheel and the finished rope was coated in tar which required a tarring shed to house large hearths over which copper cauldrons filled with molten tar sat. Naturally enough, these establishments were hazardous and were often located at the edge of settlements. In London, however, the Hanseatic League had a rope walk in the middle of the City, at the Steelyard.[64] Clothmakers also required large open spaces to stake out their cloths so that they could dry under tension. The cloths would have been tacked on frames using tenterhooks, a type of iron staple. These tenter yards are often recorded in placenames (as in Tentercroft Street, Lincoln) but at least one has been excavated, in Bristol. A distinctive find there consisted of copper alloy pins.

Urban salt production is known from excavations at Droitwich, in Worcestershire, and Nantwich in Cheshire.[65] Remains of twelfth- and thirteenth-century wich houses were excavated at the latter site and revealed clay- and timber-lined rectangular troughs within a wattle superstructure. This distinctive type of workshop may be expected throughout the extensive outcrop of rock salt in the northeast midlands, as indicated by the distribution of '-wich' and 'Salt-' placenames.

Bell casting required the digging of a large pit in which the mould for the new bell was made. This process is well described in medieval sources and from the discovery of bell pits. However, these pits are usually found on the sites of the churches or other structures where the bell was to be hung rather than at the bell-founder's workshop. Where such workshops have been recognized it is the vast quantities of bell mould and metal scrap which are the most obvious indicator, although given the reuse of bell mould, crucibles and slag as hardcore and metalling the simple presence of mould fragments is not itself sufficient evidence to prove the existence of a foundry site.

Other archaeologically visible industries include those which required the provision of heat, abnormally high quantities of water or other unusual conditions. Even here, it is clear that in many cases the archaeological evidence is capable of many interpretations and it is perhaps documentary evidence which is being used to determine which industry particular structures were associated with. Hearths are common finds on medieval urban excavations but most will have had a purely domestic function. Even the proliferation of hearths in a structure need not imply an industrial function. Excavations at Bartholomew Street, Newbury (Berkshire) revealed two rooms, tentatively identified as a hall and kitchen, where a large proportion of the floor space of the room had at one time or another been used as a hearth. Vat bases would have had a similar plan to bread ovens but instead of the circular area forming a dome it would have formed a cylindrical or slightly tapering chamber over which the copper cauldron or vat would have sat.[66] A group of such structures was found at Swan Lane, City of London, where they dated to the late twelfth century and are interpreted as having been used either for dyeing cloth or yarn (Figs 4.5–6); the vat bases themselves could be used in brewing, but in this case dyeing is suggested because of the survival of deposits of fuller's earth, used in the dyeing process. Clearly, a range of evidence is required before the function of such features can be positively identified from archaeological evidence alone.

Another major class of industrial feature found on medieval urban excavations is the pit or trough. There is no doubt that most holes in the ground ended up as convenient places to dump rubbish. However, they may well have had other functions first, of which the most obvious is the storage or disposal of liquids. Medieval tanners' workshops are known from Exeter and in the post-medieval period from both Gloucester and Exeter.[67] By this time tanners were using pits to contain slaked lime, which was used to remove the fat and hair from fresh hides. Further pits were needed to hold the hides while they were being tanned. However, unlike the lime pits these would not leave any obvious traces of their original function. One way to identify tanning pits is to look for groups of pits set within or just outside a structure, instead of at a distance from it, and where the pits were backfilled at the same time. This should be combined with the study of insect fauna and botanical remains which may produce an 'indicator group' for tanning.[68] Shallow rectangular troughs are often associated with metalworking and may have been used in annealing.

Dry material also required heating. Malt was produced by spreading out barley and leaving it until it started to germinate. Then the barley would have been gently heated to stop the germination process. By the early post-medieval period malting kilns were huge affairs, taking up the top storey of a building while a hearth occupied the lower level.[69] At some stage, perhaps in the post-medieval period rather than the medieval, the floors of these malt houses were formed of malting floor tiles, which have a series of conical holes pierced through them so as to allow the hot air to flow through the tile while retaining the sprouting grain. Malt was widely used in beer production and documentary records show that it was widely produced at a variety of levels: production in larger households for home consumption; production by

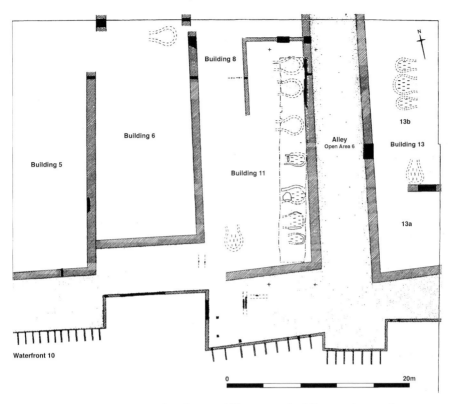

Figure 4.5 Swan Lane, London: late twelfth-century buildings and waterfront revetments. The first part of the excavation was a narrow trench in the basement of a functioning multi-storey car park, which found many hearths or vat bases (shown here inside Building 11); the wider watching brief found fragments of the surrounding buildings and revetments (Museum of London Archaeology Service).

brewers; and production for export. Charred grain ought to identify debris from malting but few deposits of germinated barley are known, and few in association with structures which might be malting ovens (see the discussion of the Alms Lane site, Norwich, in Chapter 3).

The location of pottery and tile kilns is normally revealed by the large quantities of waste found within and around them. Kilns with a wide range of sizes and shapes were used. The earliest post-Roman pottery kilns in England to date are those from Cox Lane, Ipswich, which are of eighth- or ninth-century date.[70] Later tenth- and eleventh-century pottery kilns were of similar size and are mainly found in towns such as Exeter, Leicester, Stamford, Thetford and Ipswich. Later in the eleventh century, however, pottery making began to shift from town to countryside although there were several major, urban potteries in the twelfth and thirteenth centuries, for example at Worcester and Doncaster. In many cases, however, the exact location of even major pottery industries is still unknown. This is the case with London-type ware which at its height was being traded widely across the North Sea and along the eastern seaboard of the British Isles. Some late medieval urban

Figure 4.6 Swan Lane, London: one of the vat bases, from the second half of the twelfth century. Such installations may have been for a number of industries, including dyeing and brewing (Museum of London Archaeology Service).

potteries are known, for example at St Mark's East in Lincoln,[71] but most pottery by then was produced in the countryside; often, as in the Surrey/Hampshire border industry, in marginal scrubland.[72] The St Mark's kiln is typical of the latest medieval kilns having a much larger cross-sectional area than earlier kilns and with multiple flues replacing the single or double flue/stoke hole.

Tile, by contrast, seems to have always been fired in rectangular kilns. These kilns had a raised floor, supported on arches, often themselves made of tile. Interestingly, in the middle Rhine it seems as though the location of pottery production is rather different than in England. From the late seventh to the late twelfth centuries pottery was produced in rural settlements on the west side of the Rhine (the Vorgebirge). In the thirteenth century these industries ceased and their markets were taken by urban potters based at Brühl, to the north of the Vorgebirge, and Siegburg, on the east side of the Rhine. Pottery then continued to be an urban industry, both at Siegburg and Cologne to the end of our period.

Blacksmiths' workshops must have been common in every town, and in many rural settlements too. A smithy has been found in excavations at Six Dials, in Saxon Southampton, situated at the junction of two streets and dating to the eighth or ninth century. A later example was excavated at Winchcombe (Gloucestershire).[73] The floor and surroundings of a rural smithy excavated at Burton Dassett in Warwickshire were extensively sampled to determine the distribution of hammer scale.[74] By this means the location of the forge itself was confirmed and details of the way in which the smithy operated could be recovered. Such methods are much more difficult to apply in urban situations, principally because it is less likely that the whole of the contemporary medieval surface would survive to be sampled. It is nevertheless quite possible to establish the location of a forge through the systematic sampling of surfaces of artefacts and deposits accumulated upon them. A study of X-radiographs taken of corroded metal objects at Flaxengate, Lincoln, several years after the excavation, demonstrated the presence of hammer scale and copper alloy metal droplets preserved in the corrosion products of metal artefacts discarded close to sites where metalworking was taking place.[75]

The organization of urban industries

Archaeological evidence provides details of the organization of urban crafts and industries. To return to the example of baking, the job could be undertaken at a domestic or professional level. If the remains of an oven are found how can we tell the status of its user? Only by observing a pattern: perhaps that ovens are not found on the majority of urban tenements or that there are a range of sizes in which the largest might be those of professional bakers and the smaller ones those of private individuals. Many other crafts may have been carried out on a casual, part-time basis, especially if the equipment and raw materials were inexpensive. Thus, the simplicity of lead-casting, or the re-melting of glass, should lead to caution in the interpretation of traces of these activities within an urban tenement. Furthermore, the quantities of slag produced by iron-smelting and the large volume of mould fragments resulting from the casting of bells, cauldrons and the like both make it difficult to be certain whether deposits containing these materials are the result of industrial activity on site or in extreme cases even in the same settlement. The carrying out on a site of many industries, on the other hand, can be completely invisible archaeologically. An example of this must be leather working. Waterlogged or otherwise anaerobic sites may produce abundant evidence for leather working, in the form of off-cuts, but with no other evidence for the craft. If those sites had not been anaerobic, in common with the deposits on most urban excavations in the British Isles, there would have been no indication of this activity at all.

Not only do some industries occur in towns and not in the surrounding countryside, but there may be distinct zones within towns; though this is by no means clear cut, and will vary from town to town. At Winchester, locational factors can be suggested in the grouping or concentrations of several manufacturing and food trades. Smiths naturally congregated near gates, but the only significant case of slag probably from a smithy comes from the courtyard of the bishop's palace. Work in other metals, and in bone, is indicated by archaeological finds but is not well described in documents. The three most identifiable groups on documentary grounds are workers in the preparation of cloth, the victuallers, and those in the leather industries. Clear-cut zoning of occupations was not, however, a feature of medieval Winchester, though the weavers tended to live and work near others in the cloth industry.[76] Documentary evidence also suggests that in fourteenth-century Ghent, many occupations tended to congregate in perceptible areas: carpenters, drapers, mercers, fishmongers, smiths, goldsmiths and leatherworkers. There were brewers and bakers throughout the city.[77]

The existence of manufacturing quarters (i.e. districts where artisans of several related crafts might have their workshops) in the twelfth century can be demonstrated in some places both by street names and also by the concentration of certain types of industrial waste, such as large brass-melting crucibles and bronze-casting mould fragments in certain areas of the City of London. In the eleventh century, streets off Cheapside, the main street of late Saxon and medieval London, were occupied by workers in metals and bone; nearby, the goldsmiths established their quarter, both on the main shopping street and near the cathedral, where from the thirteenth century there was an area of production of brasses and inlaid Purbeck slabs for tombs, which sent its products over much of England.[78] Thus the craftsmen who produced luxuries or household objects would tend to gather where patrons would be, or in the back streets behind markets.

Sometimes zoning within towns will be explicable in terms of the requirements of the industry. The fringes of a town will always be attractive to those industries which require large areas for storage or preparation, for example timber yards, tanneries and foundries. The borders of rivers were especially popular as industrial zones, as demonstrated in London and Norwich.[79] There may also be a symbiotic relationship between pairs of industries. Horners and tanners would have shared raw materials whereas the bark discarded by carpenters as waste could have been used by tanners as a raw material. Bladesmiths and scabbard-makers may similarly have found it convenient to work nearby. Collection of archaeological data on the range of industries represented on urban excavations ought to test and expand this short list as well as elucidate more of the detail of the inter-relationships of different crafts. Were different crafts thrown together by chance and mutual needs or did they seek each other out?

Just as some industries occurred together, so in others there were good reasons for keeping them apart. We have already mentioned the fire risk presented by many medieval industries and the nuisance caused by noxious smoke or fumes. Similarly, in some industries liquid waste was produced which would have polluted the water source for those down-river. Consideration of this problem seems to have led to zonation of industries along the river in Norwich around 1300.[80]

Technologies and styles of manufacture

Medieval industry was not efficient. First, there was an expensive wastage of resources. Fortunately for modern archaeologists, thousands of items of metal were discarded in towns with no thought of recycling or reuse, even though metals were often imported from far away in foreign countries. Second, some of the methods of manufacture seem labour-intensive to modern eyes. Several everyday dress accessories, for instance, were assembled from different elements, occasionally using different alloys, where there is no apparent decorative or functional advantage over using a single piece of metal. Punched decoration was occasionally added to cast fittings.[81] One obvious reason for this is that human labour, at least before the Black Death, was cheap with large numbers of people living in poverty.

At present there are some, though not many, significant technological advances or innovations known in the medieval period. In the pottery industry, which has been intensively studied, changes such as the use of lead glaze, the use of the wheel or of up-draught kilns were either introduced before the Norman Conquest or were adopted from other crafts.[82] A recent study of artefacts from the extensive excavations at Winchester suggests that there were a number of technological developments in some industries, but stagnation in others. The warp-weighted loom was displaced first by the vertical two-beam loom and then by the horizontal loom. Wire-drawing and the associated craft of pin-making emerged during the thirteenth century.[83] Candles with wicks of cotton replaced the open oil lamp with its flax wick; milling by the hand quern was replaced by machine milling, possibly following the introduction of the windmill in the late twelfth century. On the other hand, there was only limited change in the metal-working trades.[84]

When a large number of artefacts are recovered, developments of style and workmanship, and perhaps of craft control can be traced over long periods. This has been demonstrated in the City of London, for example with the study of scabbards (Fig. 4.7) and knives (Fig. 4.8). Study of nearly fifteen hundred medieval shoes from waterfront excavations in London has produced not only a summary of the main types in the period 1150–1450 (Fig. 4.9), but details of technical progress inside the manufacturing process (which in this case seems, from the abundance of shoemaking waste on many sites, to be local). In the twelfth century, rands (wedge-shaped strips of leather inserted between the upper and the sole) were introduced, perhaps to make the seams more waterproof. In the thirteenth century calfskin became the standard type of hide used in shoes, which were mass-produced in two pieces (the upper and the sole). Soles in two pieces themselves, particularly on the long late-fourteenth-century shoes called poulaines, would have made repair easier and could make better use of hides. In the middle of the fifteenth century the method of construction was changed, with the addition of heel stiffeners and an outer sole, in thicker leather, as a further component.[85]

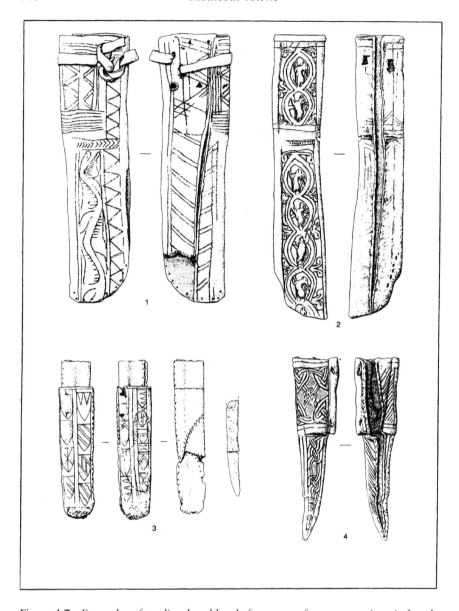

Figure 4.7 Examples of medieval scabbards from waterfront excavations in London. Some were made from a single piece of leather stitched together with flax thread. Thongs that survived were complex knots at the top (no. 1). The scabbards were decorated with engraving (no. 2), stamping, incising and embossing. Some have additional inner sheaths (no. 3) (Cowgill *et al.* 1987).

There is nothing yet to suggest strongly that these innovations occurred first in towns, though the sheer pressures of needs and availability of materials would make it seem likely.

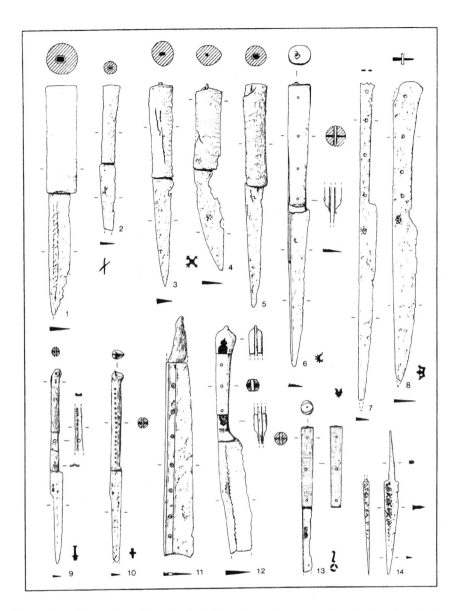

Figure 4.8 Examples of medieval knives from the excavations in London. Early twelfth-century knives represent the end of the Saxon tradition of wide blades with an angle at the back, sometimes decorated with pattern welding (no. 1). Late in the twelfth century these were replaced by more triangular blades embellished by a greater range of techniques, such as scrolls of silver wire (no. 14) or a single letter stamped into copper-alloy discs inserted along the blade (no. 11). In the fourteenth century there is an increased diversity of forms, coinciding with the introduction of the 'scale-tang' handles, in which two plates are riveted together on either side of the iron tang (no. 6). Previously, handles were simply fixed on a spike (no. 2). This new development allowed finer decoration. During the century also makers' marks became common (no. 8). Their use reflects an increase in the organization of the guilds which controlled the trade, but they cannot yet be identified with any London cutlers (Cowgill *et al.* 1987).

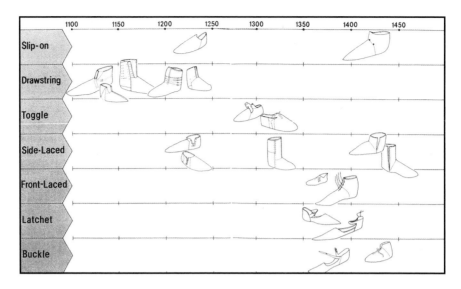

Figure 4.9   Summary of the main types of shoes, ankle-shoes and boots from London sites, largely the waterfront excavations of the 1970s and 1980s (Grew and de Neergaard 1988).

Archaeological and documentary evidence

From the thirteenth century onwards there are many kinds of documentary evidence about medieval crafts, especially (and largely) about crafts in towns; this large subject is not summarized here. But it seems profitable to compare archaeological and documentary evidence in an example from a British town.

In the thirteenth and early fourteenth century a major source of information about the distribution of urban industries comes from documentary sources, in the form of personal names.[86] Indeed, many occupations are recorded as personal names which have left no archaeological evidence whatsoever. Nevertheless, caution must be used. A 'plumer', for example, could be a dealer in 'plumes' or feathers but might instead be a plumber dealing in lead and its alloys.

A survey of published and some unpublished but transcribed documentary records, dating mainly from the twelfth to the fifteenth centuries, relating to the Lincoln suburb of Wigford, revealed very few direct references to industry, not surprising considering that the sources were almost entirely concerned with land transactions and therefore with property owners who might not necessarily be occupiers.[87] Occasionally the occupation of an owner, or the owner of a neighbouring property, might be recorded but in the main occupation has to be inferred from personal names, with all of the pitfalls that this type of evidence presents. Nevertheless, repeated occurrences of occupational personal names add up to a plausible pattern. Wigford, on the southern fringe of the city and with easy access to water, was the home to workers in the leather industry (23 per cent of the 110 industrial personal names), the wood

Figure 4.10 Medieval industries in the suburb of Wigford, Lincoln: the proportions of groups of trades, based on a sample of 128 references drawn from a range of documents (Vince 1993).

trades (10 per cent), fishermen (13 per cent) and the cloth trades (12 per cent) (Fig. 4.10).

The archaeological evidence, from about half a dozen excavations of moderate size carried out in Wigford over a period of fifteen years, is less able to stand statistical examination.[88] The leather trades are only obliquely represented in the archaeological record, through the related industry of horn working. This is to be expected since tanners, who were the most numerous representatives of this industry recorded in the documents, would have dug their tanning pits at the rear of properties whereas archaeological investigation has concentrated on street frontages. Horn working, however, is less noxious and the horners may well have operated in workshops incorporated into the frontage properties. Fishing is possibly represented by wicker enclosures erected on the river foreshore to confine fish. The cloth trades are again only tangentially represented, by sherds of pots which were probably used to dye yarn with madder.[89] These are almost all twelfth-century or earlier, after which date it seems that yarn was dyed in large metal vats, the evidence for which would consist of the ovens used to heat them. Professional baking, which accounted for 11 per cent of the documentary references, was probably not represented at all archaeologically; all the hearths and ovens excavated in Wigford are likely to have been for domestic use. The professional bakers of Wigford were concentrated in a small area to the north of the river Witham. The rough location of their ovens is known but most have probably been totally destroyed by the nineteenth-century and later construction of deep cellars for department stores and banks since that area became the commercial core of the modern city.

Evidence for non-ferrous metalworking was present in some quantity on at least one excavation but is hardly represented in the documentary sources for Wigford at all. The only possible reference to metalworking is the family name of 'Marshall' (which originally meant 'smith'). Pottery and tile production is represented by only three documentary references while the archaeological evidence for this industry is extensive, consisting of a pottery kiln and tile kiln from one site and pottery waste on several others. Neither the archaeological nor the documentary sources for Wigford have been exhausted and it is possible that further work on both will show a wider measure of agreement.

Archaeological evidence, when interpreted cautiously, can both provide useful confirmation of the range of crafts and industries being practised in a town and extend our knowledge beyond the documentary sources. In addition, it can produce a body of data on the raw materials used, the range of processes being carried out, the tools and workshops and, perhaps, the organization of the craft which is more detailed and with a greater chronological depth than that likely to be available in written sources. It is in particular clearer from archaeology than from documents that the mid to late twelfth century was a period of change in the organization of several industries, including making pots and tiles, dyeing, and non-ferrous metalworking.

Conclusion

In this chapter the archaeological evidence for medieval urban crafts has been examined. This evidence has been looked at sceptically since it seems to us that there is a temptation to latch on to certain interpretations and to make many assumptions which the evidence alone would not uphold. This is not to say that urban archaeology cannot answer questions about medieval urban industries, or that it can only be used as an adjunct to documentary research. Rather, we would argue for a critical approach to the evidence and for the more extensive and problem-orientated use of scientific analyses, especially in anaerobic conditions.

A major difference between medieval rural industries and those in towns derives from the increased pressure for space in the urban environment. There was a more rapid change of land use in the town and more effort was taken to dispose of waste. There was also more opportunity to use waste products for other purposes. Medieval slag heaps may survive within the Weald or the sites of medieval forests (some now below arable) while their urban equivalents have long since been flattened and their contents dispersed or reworked.

In addition to this methodological problem we have also emphasized the geographical determinism which can lead to trite statements about medieval industries. The decision to locate an industry at the market rather than at the source of the raw materials seems to have been geographically determined in a minority of cases. In the majority we see the medieval artisan balancing a number of economic, and no doubt also social, forces.

5 *Trade and commerce*

There has always been a strong connection between towns and trade. Towns required provision of food, fuel and clothing, and of the raw materials for the non-agricultural enterprises in which townsfolk were engaged. Traders required nodes at which goods could be passed on to the next stage of their journey from producer to consumer. The fortunes of a town often depended on the success of its merchant class in encouraging and exploiting local production and selling this produce, either as raw materials or manufactured goods, to others. The extent of trade in a town could vary from the exchange of rural produce within a small district to the export and import of goods throughout western Europe, if not beyond. Since a large group of documentary records has survived from the thirteenth century dealing with import and export taxation, or with local trade disputes, the historical evidence for commerce at the local and national level is strong, though it tends to be about the larger places. From a large body of work, historians have constructed several competing models of economic development in the medieval period. With the advent of computers, they are able to study very large datasets with ease, and are now tackling regional questions.[1]

With trade, we are forced to consider the town in a wider area, and not as the only centre of things at all. At the start of our period, towns were a relatively recent introduction, or reintroduction, into many parts of northern and western Europe. Goods were produced for local consumption or exchange with neighbours and trade was carried out to a great extent without the use of towns. It is likely that the institutions developed during this pre-urban period did not disappear immediately towns were founded in a region and that non-urban trade continued alongside that in towns for much of the medieval period.

Archaeology can be used to study trade and commerce through the characterization of artefacts and the analysis of their distributions; through study of the infrastructure required to facilitate trade and commerce, such as specific structures erected for the use of traders; and through the provision and regulation of coinage. There were few crafts or industries which depended entirely on towns for their existence and many which were carried out both in urban and rural locations; with trade, however, we come closer to the core of a town's economic and social existence.

Much has been written about the importance of trade to towns, especially in their formative years in the seventh to eleventh centuries.[2] A major function of towns was to facilitate the redistribution of goods both within a region and between regions. It is also clear that users of towns could be discriminating when they had choices. The aristocracy, for example, could bypass local towns and markets and purchase goods directly from the ports, thus ensuring that in an economy where problems of distribution meant that there was always a surplus of customers to goods (a seller's market in modern parlance), they could ensure that they obtained the goods they wanted. The almoners of religious houses and the bailiffs of rural manors ignored the closest towns in favour of regional centres. Clearly, therefore, not all towns offered the same range of goods and services. Further, some rural settlements were towns in all but legal status, to judge by the range of occupations in evidence. A challenge for archaeology is to produce a critical apparatus which will allow us to compare the trading contacts between one town and another, to say something about the frequency or intensity of those contacts, to distinguish local, regional, national and international exchange networks, and to use that data to address the question of the link between trade and the fortunes of towns.

This chapter is divided into two parts. The first examines the evidence for urban hierarchies and city-based regions and the interaction of towns and their markets (although this is such a huge topic that it is only briefly mentioned here); then the mechanics of trade, such as the provision and maintenance of currency, market places themselves, shops, the means used to transport and distribute goods, and the archaeological traces of the merchants who orga-nized and controlled the whole process and the communities in which they lived. The second part considers some case studies in more detail: the use of pottery as an indicator of long-distance trade, the supply of pottery to and from urban markets and finally how the archaeological and documentary sources compare for an English port, Hull. As in Chapter 4, the examples are almost all from Britain, because what is required is careful thought about the meaning of local evidence before we make wider connections.

The urban field

A useful concept for the comparison of commercial functions of towns is that of the *urban field*. This is a modern-day geographical concept which describes the interaction between a town and its hinterland. An urban field, like a magnetic field, can be thought of as a force whose intensity declines with distance. In the medieval period, such a field had a social dimension as well as a geographic one. The size and shape of medieval urban fields can be suggested from archaeological data such as the sources of goods found in a town or the presence and amount of goods in settlements in that town's hinterland which were probably obtained in the central town.

One example of an urban field is provided by toponyms, where during the thirteenth and first half of the fourteenth century in England people were often given surnames which referred to places, presumably their places of origin, such as 'of York' or 'of Bristol'. Such 'bynames' are generally taken to denote the places from which people or their immediate ancestors came, for people up to about 1350. These names were used to study the origin of the inhabitants of Stratford-upon-Avon.[3] Stratford derived most of its immigrants from nearby villages and increasingly fewer immigrants came from more far-flung places. A similar study of medieval Winchester suggests that the majority of immigrants came from villages within a twenty-five-mile radius.[4] In the East Midlands a study has been made of the toponyms found in selected towns in the Lay Subsidy Roll for 1327–8, as part of a wider study of Lincoln and its region.[5] This broadly demonstrated that for most rural settlements there was little immigration; but that all towns had a proportion of household heads with toponyms. Nottinghamshire, for example, had 23 towns in the study. Of these, 21 had between 6 and 14 toponyms, Newark on Trent had 31 and Nottingham itself 68. In the smaller towns the toponyms indicated that most immigrants came from within 15 km of the town. For Newark, they came from up to 80 km and for Nottingham from up to 115 km. There was little evidence that the smaller centres had discrete urban fields; immigrants were travelling past several other similar-sized towns before reaching the town of their choice. Immigration was not constrained by county boundaries and only marginally by relief (Nottinghamshire is bounded by the Hatfield Chase on the north, the Trent Valley on the east and the Pennines on the south-west). Only absolute distance seems to have had any impact on immigration to these smaller centres. For Newark and Nottingham, however, immigrants not only came from further afield but there was some evidence for two components: a central zone of similar size to those of the smaller centres and an extensive outer zone, although the urban field of Newark was entirely within that of Nottingham (Fig. 5.1). Finally, the urban field of Lincoln covered not only the whole of Lincolnshire but also Nottinghamshire. In terms of immigration, therefore, the fourteenth-century towns of the East Midlands seem to show two components: a region in the order of 25–30 km around the town (although slightly greater for Lincoln) and a zone of varying size which was largest for Lincoln (135 km) and increasingly smaller for Nottingham and Newark. This wider zone was absent from the smaller towns. One interpretation of these patterns is that the central zone represents immigration by those using the town and its markets for selling their rural produce and purchasing both manufactured goods and types of rural produce not available locally, whereas the larger zones represent immigration by members of the merchant class, who had bigger plans.

Throughout north-west Europe we can see evidence for such hierarchies of towns based on their trading activity. At the apex of these hierarchies were regional centres involved in long-distance trade by sea and over land and with the redistribution of goods to other ports and inland towns. Such towns include Lübeck, London, Paris and Bruges, as well as lesser places such as York and Lincoln. Many of these places were located on navigable rivers, often at or just above the tidal head. Initially, this location gave these river towns an advantage in that traders could easily bring goods right into the heart of a territory, but with the increasing size of sea-going vessels and their deeper draughts, outports grew at the expense of their inland partners (for example Hull at the expense of York and Boston at the expense of Lincoln). Similarly, some ports could not develop deepwater harbours and went into decline. This seems to have been the fate of Ribe, on the west Jutland coast; and perhaps also Schleswig on the east coast, whose predecessor, Hedeby/Haithabu, was a much more important trading centre. None of these superseded towns was abandoned, and indeed there is abundant evidence for prosperity in the later Middle Ages at all of them, but the contribution of overland trade to their wealth evidently declined.

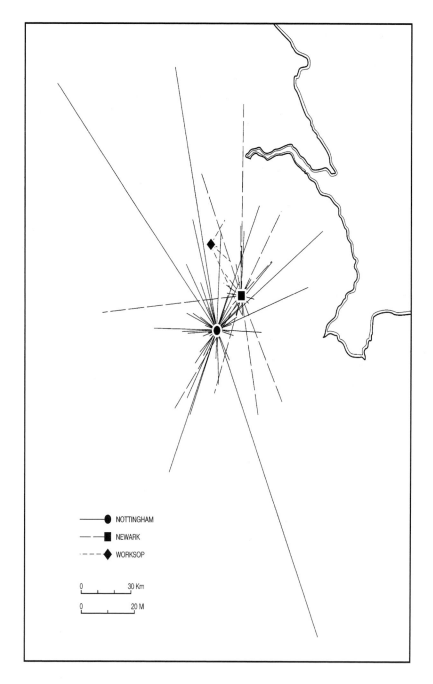

Figure 5.1 Urban fields of Worksop (a small town), Newark and Nottingham in 1327–8; each line represents one or more people from known villages and towns as suggested by their surnames ('toponyms') (from work by P. Bischoff).

Traders and trading communities

A definition of a trader can be wide, signifying anyone who earned a living by the exchange of goods or services, or can be more restrictive. Documentary sources make it clear that there was much blurring of roles, and yet there was a wide difference between, say, Aaron the Rich, the medieval Jewish merchant and financier from Lincoln, and the general run of tinkers and hawkers who are rarely recorded by name but whose activities are reflected in the distribution of mundane, mass-produced goods (such as pottery or copper alloy dress-fittings) often over large distances.

Identifying merchant communities as discrete entities in medieval towns is extremely difficult using archaeological evidence. The houses of native rich merchants were largely indistinguishable from those of nobles or prominent churchmen, and they did not usually congregate together, but lay dispersed through the town behind façades of smaller buildings (Chapter 3). The existence of foreign communities in a medieval town is sometimes suggested by documentary sources, place names (especially names of streets) and church dedications. These quarters could occur through the natural tendency of immigrant or ethnic groups to stick together, especially, as with the Jews, when they were under constant threat of persecution; sometimes, as in London, legislation was passed restricting the areas where foreigners could live. In yet further instances it was the occupation or economic interests of the immigrants which drew them together: Flemish weavers, for example, lived in a suburb on the south-east side of Beverley, and in the fifteenth century Southwark, across London Bridge from the City of London, was home to a Dutch community, attempting to evade the rules and regulations of the craft guilds in the city itself. They brought a range of new and useful crafts, including large-scale brewing with hops.

Merchants in foreign lands might stand out because of their material culture. Within the British Isles, this would include English merchants in Irish or Welsh towns, where the English culture was part of an almost colonial mindset. In Wales and Ireland, use of pottery is seen as an Anglo-Norman trait and is thought to be more common on the sites of the planted English towns, castles and monasteries than on contemporary native settlements. Use of coins was also perhaps a specifically Anglo-Norman practice in Wales in the thirteenth century.[6] Cooking vessels may be particularly sensitive indicators of cultural differences since, even if the same ingredients were used by native and immigrant groups, differences in preparation may be reflected in the type of vessels found.

A possible example of archaeological evidence for a foreign enclave may have been excavated at Dowgate in London, a site known from the twelfth century as the location of the Steelyard, the headquarters of the Hanse in England.[7] The deposit consisted of a large quantity of pottery, much of which was Rhenish stoneware jugs and beakers and blue-grey ware cooking pots and ladles. These types are relatively common in London excavations but only as a small proportion of the pottery found. Here at Dowgate they accounted for most of the assemblage. When first found, the assemblage was thought to have been evidence for cargo, broken in transport and discarded during the unloading of a ship. However, a detailed study of this assemblage showed that

a high proportion of the vessels bore signs of use; the ladles were sooted from use over a fire while the frilled bases of beakers and pitchers of Pingsdorf ware showed signs of chipping where they had been used at table.[8] Here perhaps we have the tableware of the German merchants, who (at least in later decades) lived a withdrawn life, guarding their morals and trading secrets behind a high wall which enclosed living quarters, a dye house, wine cellar, and gardens.

Relatively high quantities of imported pottery are also found in some thirteenth- and fourteenth-century pits and cellars in Southampton, and in one case the identity of the owner is known. Without this documentary evidence one might have postulated that the owner was French. However, unlike the case of the Dowgate pottery the forms and presumed functions of the Southampton pottery were no different from those of locally made wares although the pottery was of better quality. High-quality imports could enhance the status of their owner whether he or she was English or foreign. In sum, therefore, we can identify broad trends, such as the foreign culture of the thirteenth- and fourteenth-century burgesses of Wales and Ireland, but would find it difficult to identify the presence of small numbers of foreigners within English towns through archaeological means alone.

Coins, tokens and jettons

Goods could be exchanged and transported over large distances without the aid of an exchange medium but there is no doubt that the existence of such a medium would have made it much easier for trade to flourish. Stray coin finds earlier than the late twelfth century are rare or absent in large parts of the western and northern fringes of Europe. Even in those areas where the habit of coin use stretched back for centuries there are fluctuations in stray coin finds which suggest that there were times when coins were not used in all transactions.

Monetary exchange depends on the authority of the issuer of the coins but coins themselves were made of precious metal: at the beginning of our period mostly silver but towards its end including higher-value gold coins. Thus, silver coins could circulate outside the area in which they were minted, providing that the traders could be certain of their silver content. This could vary for several reasons: the silver content could be deliberately reduced, debasing the coinage; coins could be faked, consisting of a lead-alloy core with a thin coating of silver, or they could be clipped, removing minute amounts of silver from the edges of the coin. Fragments of silver or gold could be used as an exchange medium and in the western and northern fringes hoards of 'hacksilver', composed of broken fragments of jewellery or plate and small ingots of metal, have been found. Silver and gold, therefore, were being used as an international exchange medium which, providing that no new sources of metal were discovered, could provide a common, agreed standard.

Two other things were required to make this system work, a means of gauging the silver or gold content of a lump of metal (whether minted into a coin or not) and weights. A simple method of testing the purity of gold was to use a touchstone. It consists of a small smooth pendant of dark, fine-grained metamorphic rock with streaks of metal running across it. Analysis of these streaks shows that they were gold of differing purity. The touchstone was used by making a streak of the item to be tested on another stone and comparing that streak's colour with those on the touchstone. Weights would have been required when dealing with hacksilver or coin as well as for measuring the weight of traded goods. Most traders would have used a small, hand-held balance of similar character to those known from the tenth and eleventh centuries in which the two arms of the balance are of identical length.[9] The weights themselves would have been constructed out of metal and to judge by written sources there would have been both international and local standards used, depending on what was being weighed.

The production and regulation of coinage was a right that was sought after and protected in the medieval period. To be able to accept a coin by its face value, rather than having to test its actual metal content, would have made transactions smoother and quicker. Coins also provided a medium for propaganda, for example in the depiction of the ruler by whose authority the coins were issued. Almost from the reintroduction of coinage to north-west Europe in the sixth century, coins were often marked with a mint mark, following the custom of the Roman Empire. Such marks did not become the norm in England until the reform of Edgar in 973 but by the start of our period they were standard, together with the name of the moneyer. Where these mints can be identified they appear to have been in towns and the mint output seems to be proportionate to the size of the town, enforcing the view that the primary purpose for producing coinage was for trade (rather than taxation or the payment of alms, or of government officials, all of which also took place). Nevertheless, many English mints are known solely from coins struck during the period when English kings were paying Danegeld to Viking armies and by the late eleventh century the number of active mints was much lower than in the preceding century.

The function of the mint was to take bullion and coins which were not legal tender, to produce official coins and to produce a profit or farm for the mint authority. An English moneyer could only use official iron dies which were obtained from London and by ensuring a regular issue of new dies the king could keep control of the moneyers and ensure a regular income, since every new issue would involve the withdrawal of the previous issue, with a consequent profit for the king and the moneyer. This Old English system survived until the Anarchy of the second quarter of the twelfth century, after which Henry II introduced a new coinage. This involved reminting, during which period about thirty mints were employed, spread throughout the country. By the end of this coinage in 1180, less than half of these mints were active. They were distributed across the country, with approximately one mint in each region. This demonstrates that the provision of mints under Henry was decided nationally although even then the requirements of trade may have led to the provision of five active mints in East Anglia: Bury St Edmunds, Colchester, Ipswich, Norwich and Thetford.

Most mints were located in county towns, in which there was a Norman castle; but the location of minting within a town is not often certain. At Winchester, documentary sources suggest that moneyers operated in the High Street, at one end of the street market, and in Lincoln the city's moneyers certainly held land fronting onto the High Street. Despite this, a die used in the

Figure 5.2   Two pennies, a half penny (one side folded over) and a quarter-penny or farthing, from the excavation at Billingsgate, London, 1982 (Museum of London Archaeology Service).

Lincoln mint in the reign of Aethelred II was found on a site at Flaxengate, some way from the High Street.

At various times and places, attempts have been made to control the use of foreign coins. If the coins had a higher precious metal content than local issues then they tended to be driven out of circulation through hoarding and selective melting down whereas if they were of baser metal then they would probably not have been accepted. This left a number of currencies where the fineness and weight standards were sufficiently similar for coins to pass outside their legal limits. Many foreign pieces are found at port sites and the interpretation of these finds is slightly more complicated. A foreigner or traveller returning home from a foreign trip would probably not discard coins which were legal tender, even if they could not be used. Most coins at this time had a high silver content which gave them intrinsic value. There may well have been an unofficial acceptance of certain foreign coins within ports and this may account for their concentration there rather than in the inland hinterlands. Finds from medieval Southampton, for example, include an eleventh-century hoard of French deniers as well as single finds of other twelfth-, thirteenth- and early fourteenth-century French coins. Coins from Germany, Ireland, Scotland and Portugal as well as French pieces were present in waterfront revetment dumps from London, forming a small but significant proportion of the coins recovered.[10]

For much of the medieval period a single denomination formed the vast majority of coins in circulation in England, the silver penny. Halfpennies and farthings were rarely issued but were frequently produced by shearing pennies into halves and quarters (Fig. 5.2). The London waterfront excavations produced a high number of cut pieces, apparently much higher than in contemporary hoards, and these suggest that coinage was used in London, and probably elsewhere, for small transactions as well as large.

From the time of Edward I's 'sterling' coinage (1279 onwards), halfpennies and farthings were issued and are found on excavations. In addition, a larger denomination coin, the groat (worth four pence) was issued. Gold coins were issued in the reign of Edward III (the florin, or double-leopard, the half-florin

Figure 5.3 Late thirteenth-century tokens from Swan Lane, 1981; they were probably used as fractions of pence, prior to the issue of official halfpence and farthings (Museum of London Archaeology Service).

or leopard, the quarter-florin or helm). These were worth 6 shillings, 2 shillings and 1 shilling respectively. These were replaced by a system based on nobles (6s 8d, i.e. one third of a pound). Such pieces rarely occur as archaeological finds.

Tokens and jettons made of non-precious metals (tin, lead alloy and copper alloys) were also used in trading. The use of tokens as unofficial currency is suggested by the character of their designs, many of which have simple symbols on one or both faces. These symbols are taken by analogy with seventeenth-century trade tokens to represent the alehouse where they could be redeemed (Fig. 5.3). The study of tokens, which began in the nineteenth century, has revived in recent years following an exponential increase in the number of finds, both from controlled excavations and from the metal detection of spoil from waterfront sites in several large ports, notably London and Dublin. The concentration of finds of tokens at large international ports may or may not be significant. No such pieces were recovered from Colin Platt's excavations in the thriving medieval port of Southampton but excavations at Montgomery Castle on the Welsh border did produce a couple of pieces.[11] Here too much more information is needed about the type of sites where these pieces were used and about their relative frequencies before one can determine the way in which they were used; the presence of tokens on a castle site might suggest that they were used in gaming or gambling rather than for exchange.

The function of jettons is, by contrast, well understood. These copper alloy counters were used with the reckoning board (also called a counter) as a means of accounting. Each jetton placed in a particular column on the board represented a corresponding sum of money, and additions and subtractions could easily be followed even by the illiterate.

Production of these jettons seems to have been limited to a small number of centres. The earliest pieces found in the British Isles can be dated to the early fourteenth century since they were sometimes struck with the same dies used to make official silver coins. There is no indication, however, that jettons were ever intended to be used for exchange. Some, indeed, had a hole punched through the centre to make it quite clear that they were not coins. Later in the fourteenth century supply in England was supplemented and later probably surpassed by supply from France and the Low Countries. There the influence of official coinage on designs can be seen. In the late fifteenth century German manufacturers took over the supply and by the middle of the sixteenth century the market seems to have been dominated by makers in Nuremberg.

Jettons are widely distributed on medieval sites, both rural and urban. Although they would have been used in sets, they seem to occur in small numbers as a part of general refuse deposits; there are no known instances where a complete set was discarded or lost. One would postulate that the use of the reckoning board would be limited to the middle and upper classes since the majority of the population had no need for accounting. But although they are common on castles and monastic sites, there is no overwhelming concentration of jettons on middle- or high-status settlements nor on particularly wealthy or commercial tenements in towns. Again, it is probably only the collection of quantified data from a variety of types of site which will enable patterns to be seen.

Archaeological work, therefore, can elucidate the stages by which medieval Europe adopted coinage for all kinds of transactions in the Middle Ages, as a market economy took over from one based on subsistence. This is largely because money circulated in towns, and was lost in towns more than in other forms of settlement. The greatest number of coins from medieval London come from the silts around public landing places on the river.

Markets, fairs and trading buildings; craft halls and shops

Although the legal and, to a great extent, the archaeological evidence for trade is closely correlated with towns, it is clear that trade was not limited to towns. Among the earliest sites for international trade would have been beach markets. Sites which might have been such markets have been identified at a number of places. Most appear to have been much earlier in date than our period but by looking at the archaeological evidence they leave we can identify similar but later structures. A number of coastal and riverside sites in England, for instance, have produced concentrations of Anglo-Saxon coins. Most predate nearby towns and are likely to have been superseded by them but others appear to have coin lists continuing into the later eleventh century or later. These sites are being studied mainly by numismatists using finds recovered by metal detectors.[12]

The equivalent sites inland were fairs. The right to hold such fairs was granted by the king but many would have been held by customary right and therefore did not require royal assent, unless to change the location or date. Typically, they lasted two or three days and were held once a year, often on a saint's feast day, and were probably a mixture of religious, social and commercial activity. More than one fair could be held in a place per year but this is at best only a crude indication of the importance of that place as a trading centre since even large regional centres might have just two fairs per year while small places such as Marten, on the Trent in Lincolnshire, had three. In Lincolnshire there appear to have been three preferred durations for a fair. The most common was three days (almost half of 166 recorded durations) followed by eight days (13 per cent) and then between 15 and 17 days (5 per cent). This latter group consists of small riverine and coastal ports: Burton Stather, Crowland, Gainsborough, Grimsby, Spalding, Torksey and Wainfleet.[13] Their fairs were held between late May/early June (3 examples) and December. The sites of fairs often lie on the outskirts of the town on land in the town's fields or common but sometimes they were held in market places, as seems to have been the case with the Newport Fair in Lincoln which was held on Newport Green, a long cigar-shaped market place on the north side of the settlement. In Scotland the fairs were largely confined to the towns, which took care to have any competing ones suppressed;[14] clearly fairs were a great asset to towns, when they could look to their national and international connections.

An important element of any market would have been the maintenance of weights and measures. From the middle of the thirteenth century onwards we have evidence in England for royal attempts to standardize weights and measures.[15] The need for this seems in part to have come from the increased interaction between the various parts of the kingdom and the complications and confusions brought about by the use of different standards in those regions. The holder of a market had the responsibility for maintaining weights and measures and one tangible result of this was the public weighing-beam, or steelyard.[16] This was a balance with asymmetrical arms which would have been suspended from a superstructure rather than held in the hand like the much smaller equal-armed balances mentioned earlier. That balances did not need to have equal arms was known in the Roman period but apparently forgotten until the mid thirteenth century. From that time onwards steelyards were in use over much of England. A large number of weights from these beams also survive. They were constructed of latten with a lead core and usually bear heraldic devices. The majority of these bear the arms of Richard, Earl of Cornwall and Poitou, or his son Edmund. Others are known with the arms of Eleanor of Castile or the arms of England. The strong connection with Richard, Earl of Cornwall, is thought to be either related to his monopoly on the farm of the coinage, established in 1244, or his role in gaining a charter for the Hanse in London, in 1260. Subsequently, the 'official' steelyard weights of the late thirteenth century were supplemented or replaced by copies. Chemical analysis of these copies shows that they were made of a different metal, a leaded bronze, and were probably made in several centres. In 1350 the use of the steelyard was forbidden, providing an end date for these weights.[17]

Merchandise was also taxed, often at the point of entry to the town such as a gate or a public wharf. A series of pre-Conquest and early Norman lead objects struck with coin dies previously identified as 'trial pieces' used by moneyers to test their dies may be related to the collection of customs dues.[18] They date between the ninth and the mid twelfth centuries and are usually coin-sized flans stamped on both sides with official coin dies. They are highly unlikely to be forgeries, or trial pieces (in some instances the lead piece is demonstrably later than a silver coin struck with the same dies) and they are most likely to be tax receipts, issued to traders who had paid duty on goods. This interpretation is supported by two finds of lead tokens from the banks of the Seine in Paris which were marked *aquite sui* (I am quit [of tax]) and *lesco liberes* (pay the tax).[19] The findspots of the English pieces supports the idea that they were issued as proof of having paid tax and would have been given up to another official when the goods entered a market for sale and then returned to the moneyer who struck the piece for melting down (and to prevent reuse). Of 58 pieces known in 1991, 39 were found in the locality of the mint which struck them, the remainder being of uncertain mints. The only definite exceptions were a piece from Winchester, stamped with dies from an East Anglian mint, and a one from Coppergate in York stamped with dies from Chester. These finds probably represent goods landed at Chester and an East Anglian port, such as Ipswich, and carried overland to the place where they were to be sold. In the later twelfth century a new system, involving the issuing of sealed parchment cockets, *visi compoti*, replaced these lead receipts.

When the goods arrived, they had to be stored and then sold. Facilities for storage such as cellars, some with vaulting, have been described in Chapter 3; the appearance and development of ground-level buildings expressly for storage of merchandise, which we call warehouses, in the fifteenth century at larger ports merit more study. Permanent buildings for the primary purpose of retail trade (i.e. shops) are likely to have been common in the larger towns by the twelfth century.[20] Such structures are rarely mentioned in the type of documentary records available, and until this time timber was almost universally used as the main building material, so it is doubtful if the origin of the medieval shop can be proved to predate this period; although when evidence is found for craft activity on properties fronting the streets of a town, there is a strong likelihood that the goods manufactured on that site were also being sold from it. If so, then there were probably shops in tenth-century Gloucester and Lincoln.

Shops in the modern sense would have been a common feature of the larger towns from the beginning of the medieval period onwards and by the end of the period would have been found in small towns. They could be found in twelfth-century stone buildings; parts of some still survive in Canterbury, where they function as parts of modern boutiques.[21] The Norman House at the junction of Steep Hill and Christ's Hospital Terrace in Lincoln, immediately outside the South Bail gate, is a building in which shops were an integral and original part of the design. It was originally occupied and probably built by one of Lincoln's Jewish community, Moseus of York, from architectural evidence in the third quarter of the twelfth century. It contains an undercroft, a row of shops on the ground floor and a first-floor hall; originally it was part of a larger complex of buildings. The shops had no original access to the rest of the complex and must therefore have been designed to be let out to shopkeepers. The house is known through thirteenth-century and later documents as the urban seat of a succession of minor country gentry.[22] By the thirteenth century, shops would have lined the main streets and many side lanes in the majority of European towns.

We should, however, be wary about the term 'shop' (*schopa*, a term used from at least 1080); it also meant workshop throughout the medieval period, since many artisans made and sold their wares in the same place. When a London document of 1422 refers to 'my lane with 20 shops in it', that is not an early shopping mall, but an industrial alley. So what are the archaeological characteristics of a retail shop? If a room fronts onto a main street, has no evidence for access to other rooms behind the frontage and has no evidence for a hearth used for cooking it is likely to have been a shop. Variants to this general scheme exist; it was also possible for a shopkeeper to rent a storeroom or workshop on the street frontage where there was a connecting door, the lock of which was only usable from the owner's side. Furthermore, the sale of cooked foods would have required the existence of hearths and ovens within the shop. In towns where medieval buildings survive, traces of fittings and partitions which indicate shops are often recorded, sometimes during refurbishment to meet the shopping needs of the present century.[23] Documentary and plan evidence tells of a variety of shop forms by the opening of the seventeenth century (Fig. 5.4); many were simply the front room of a domestic building, that is the living-place of the shopkeeper. But the archaeological evidence for medieval shops has not been brought together, so that overall we know more about shops in Roman towns in Britain than we do about their medieval successors.

General market buildings have been briefly touched on in Chapter 2; London and the larger continental cities had specially built market buildings, for butchers or fishmongers, from the late thirteenth century. Further indications of mercantile traffic are specialized buildings associated with a specific trade or group of trades. These are of at least two kinds. The first were halls or building complexes which acted as wholesale markets, like later exchanges, predominantly for cloth; these were in several medieval towns such as Norwich, where the surviving fifteenth-century Dragon Hall in King Street dates from 1436. It stands next to the River Wensum and has an arcade facing the river, for ease of transport (Fig. 5.5).

The other kind which can be briefly noted is the craft hall, sometimes called a guildhall, which was a central place for one specific profession, whether in manufacturing or trade. There were more than fifty in the City of London, where they are known as livery company halls (such as those of the Merchant Taylors (the only one with substantial medieval fabric surviving), Mercers, Drapers and Brewers). Outside London such individual craft halls are rare, and the prominent tradesmen might meet in one hall that served the whole town. The crafts attempted to uphold monopolies, administered their apprentices, had feasts and later accumulated estates for charitable purposes; they also ran almshouses for their retired members or their widows. The archaeology of the craft hall or the London livery company is not yet developed, though one approach has pointed to the possibility of using the surviving medieval buildings as subtle indicators, through their structure, arrangement of spaces and decoration, of contemporary attitudes to fellowship and charity.[24]

Surviving accounts show that the transport of goods in the medieval period could involve several stages and that each would add to the cost of the goods to the consumer. For local transport within a town porters might carry goods

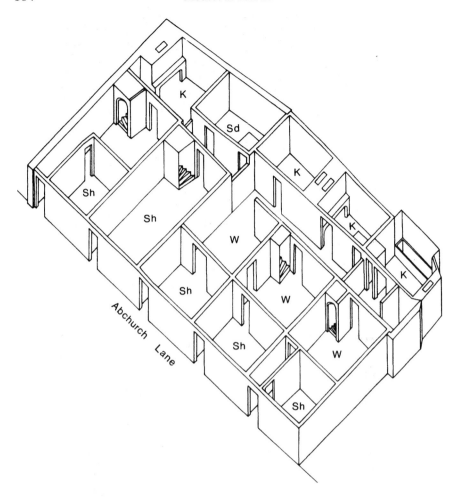

Figure 5.4 A variety of forms of shop around 1600, in Abchurch Lane, London; from the Treswell surveys (Schofield 1987). This block may have originally been built about 1390, but the partitions and even doorways may have been moved in the intervening period. Key: K, Kitchen; Sd, Shed; Sh, Shop; W, Warehouse (the terms used in 1600).

on their backs whereas for longer overland transport a carter might be employed. The fourteenth-century version of the *Lay of Havelock the Dane* shows that porters would wait at the High Bridge in the centre of Lincoln to be hired. Goods might also have to be transferred from large sea-going craft to smaller ones suitable for rivers and canals. The distances over which goods were carried overland were probably limited as much by the costs of man-handling goods at each of these stages as by the difficulties of land transport. Generally, as one might expect, large, bulky goods (such as stone or tile) travelled shorter distances overland than did small items.

Figure 5.5 Interior of the Dragon Hall, King Street, Norwich, built 1436 (Norfolk Archaeological Unit). This was almost certainly built by a rich cloth merchant, Robert Toppes. On the first floor was this enormous hall, with an office at one end; survey and excavation have shown that behind it a lane led to the river. Special facilities for trading and storage like this are one of the best archaeological traces of the beginnings of capitalism, and are found in large medieval towns.

Long-distance trade as demonstrated by pottery

Pottery is theoretically an ideal medium for studying long-distance trade. Sherds of pottery vessels are ubiquitous on medieval excavations; and pots, once broken, were usually not repaired or recycled but discarded. It is possible to distinguish many types of pottery through their form and decoration; by the use of scientific analysis to distinguish imports from local copies made in a foreign style. The geological source of the clay used in apparently featureless body sherds can often be identified using thin-section analysis where the fabric is coarse and contains rock and mineral fragments in its temper, or by using chemical analysis for the finer, untempered wares.

Much work on the identification of medieval long-distance trade involving pottery has taken place in the British Isles, and similar work is now appearing for other parts of western Europe and Scandinavia.[25] There is a major difference between sites with direct access to the sea and those inland as regards the range of imported pottery. The obvious reason for this is that pottery was relatively light, but bulky and fragile, and clearly did not have great monetary value. Consequently, it could find its way onboard ship; usually, to judge by port book records, as a part of mixed cargoes rather than the main item of trade, and would then be sold and used at the markets where the ships landed but not usually redistributed far inland. This dramatic decline in the access of the medieval population to imported pottery has been demonstrated in a recent study of the hinterland of Southampton. On sites within the port of Southampton itself imported pottery was used in large quantities, mainly for display (such as vessels for serving wine) but also for utilitarian purposes (such as cooking or storage) and is found on sites of all kinds. A few miles inland, at Winchester (14 miles), imported pottery is relatively scarce and appears most often on sites of high status. By the time one reaches the small market town of Newbury (41 miles), through which the main medieval road to Oxford and the Midlands passed, imported pottery is almost completely absent.[26]

The absence of imported pottery is therefore no guide to the overland trade of imported goods and the presence of imported pottery on inland sites is as likely to be a reflection of the purchasing power of the owners as it is to reflect the ease with which these vessels could be obtained. At coastal and riverine ports it is, by contrast, an extremely useful guide to trade. At Lincoln a survey of the medieval pottery from over two decades of excavation has shown a sudden decline in the frequency of imported pottery in the mid thirteenth century. To a certain extent this might be related to a decline in prosperity brought about by the collapse of the local cloth industry, but late thirteenth- and early fourteenth-century Lincoln was still a large and prosperous town. The main reason for the decline in the frequency of pottery imports seems to be that following the growth of Hull and Boston, foreign ships unloaded goods at those places, to be transported inland on smaller river craft. Excavations at both Hull and Boston have demonstrated that imported pottery was in common use at both ports.

The sources of pottery imports found at ports in the British Isles and around the North Sea are varied, and show some changes over time. In the late eleventh and twelfth centuries the main sources were the middle Rhine, the Meuse valley and the Seine valley. Rhenish imports consisted of a range of high-fired, unglazed vessels often decorated with red paint. The vessels included beakers, pitchers and storage jars all probably connected with wine drinking. The Meuse and Seine valley wares were lead-glazed jugs, also used for serving wine. In the second half of the thirteenth century, however, pottery from south-west France started to appear, joined towards the end of the thirteenth century by the distinctive Saintonge polychrome jugs (Fig. 5.6). Such vessels have been found on port sites as far north as Trondheim in Norway and as far west as Cork in Ireland. They were probably exported from

Figure 5.6 Saintonge polychrome jugs from London. These distinctive jugs were produced in the Saintonge region of south-west France in the late thirteenth and fourteenth centuries. Their distribution in the British Isles, especially in ports, is closely related with evidence of the Gascon wine trade (Museum of London Archaeology Service).

ports such as Bordeaux and La Rochelle alongside Gascon wine and salt. These Saintonge wares effectively superseded Rouen products on sites in the British Isles and Norway but Seine valley products, late Rouen ware, occur at sites in Jutland and the Baltic Sea littoral. Taken on its own, this pottery evidence indicates two trade routes: one running north-south along the Norwegian coast, then following the east coast of Scotland southwards to England and the other hugging the western European coastline and past the Ore Sund into the Baltic Sea. Documentary sources, however, reveal a much more complex set of relationships. For example, merchants from Ribe seem to have sailed across the North Sea to ports on the east coast of England, such as Great Yarmouth, then sailed south, crossing the channel to French ports and finally sailing back to Denmark, via the Low Countries. Pottery seems to have formed part of their cargo only on the last leg of a triangular trade. By the late fifteenth century there is documentary evidence for the importation of stoneware mugs, made at Raeren near Aachen. An initial interpretation of the pottery distribution would be that these vessels were being imported at numerous ports on the south and east coasts of England and from there were being traded inland. The documentary sources, however, indicate a London monopoly with re-export from London inland and around the coast. This Raeren stoneware is the earliest ware found in the British Isles to be marketed nationally.

A similar but slightly different pattern is found in the distribution of Spanish lustrewares from Andalucia, Malaga and Valencia. These vessels were decorated with lustre, a thin metal paint suspended in the surface of a tin-opacified lead glaze. The techniques for producing these vessels were not known in north-west Europe and in any case required considerable skill and investment. Such pots, therefore, were highly prized and it is no surprise to find fifteenth-century examples decorated with the coats of arms of the European aristocracy. The lustreware finds come from a small number of places with the majority coming from sites in London, followed by places such as Southampton, Bristol, Perth, Exeter and Boston, all of which were important ports. However, the list also includes Leicester and Coventry and rural aristocratic sites, such as Weoley Castle in Warwickshire. With valuable products like Spanish lustrewares we might have difficulty in deciding whether the presence of a pot was due to the ease of access to the coast or to the wealth of its owner, and the main reason for this uncertainty is that much of this pottery probably belonged to the merchant elite in these later medieval towns. This appears to be confirmed by the fact that the earlier ware is more common at Southampton than at any other site other than London, whereas the later ware is most common at London, Bristol, Coventry and Leicester, all towns which flourished in the post-Black Death period.[27]

In summary, the long-distance transportation of pottery was affected by a number of factors which hinder its use in reconstructing trade routes and practices. Where documentary sources survive they make it clear that actual trading practices were more complex than we might guess from looking at the surviving archaeological evidence. Nevertheless, this evidence survives in places where documents do not, and over much of north-west Europe.

The town's supply of local pottery

In comparison with the imported pottery there has been much less interest taken in the supply of pottery to a town from local sources; but in many ways the study of local supply can be just as informative. First there is the question of the introduction of pottery itself. In large parts of north-western Europe and Scandinavia in the eleventh century, pottery was not used. Within the British Isles, these aceramic areas were in the 'Celtic west': much of Ireland, Wales,

Scotland and probably substantial parts of northern England. Pottery was introduced to these areas along with towns and castles as an aspect of Anglo-Norman colonization. The earliest medieval pottery used in towns such as Exeter, Chepstow or Hereford was obtained from sources some distance further east.[28] This suggests that for several generations, in the case of Hereford to the end of the twelfth century, these towns lacked the integration into the local rural economy which was the norm further east. It is quite likely that pottery use itself was mainly an urban characteristic, reflecting the cultural differences of the town's inhabitants. This is a very difficult thesis to test, since pot scatters found during field-walking are our best means for discovering rural settlement sites. It seems likely that in other parts of north-western Europe where towns were being introduced during this period they were also foci for cultural change, of which increased pottery use may be one indicator.

In contrast, analysis of the standard black, handmade cooking pot of the type used throughout much of southern England in the eleventh and twelfth centuries shows that most were made in the countryside, probably as a seasonal activity by peasant farmers.[29] Many small towns relied on a single production area, but London in the eleventh century was supplied by a ring of these small production centres, circling the city on both sides of the Thames. The failure of many of these early centres to grow tells us something about the organization of their craft and the trading of their products, which was probably carried out seasonally by the potters themselves.

In the second half of the twelfth century some of these centres grew bigger, presumably involving more people within the settlement and perhaps involving the emergence of specialist traders. Whereas eleventh- and twelfth-century coarseware potters were trading their wares over distances of twenty miles or less in any direction, their successors might be trading their wares over thirty miles or more. This inevitably led to a reduction in the number of pottery centres. A good example of such a centre is that in the Malvern Chase, in the Severn Valley, since the products were tempered with a coarse gravel containing igneous rock from the Malvern Hills.[30] This distinctive temper allows the pots to be positively identified. Malvern Chase pots occur at Shrewsbury, Worcester, Tewkesbury, Gloucester and other towns on the Severn, and were traded overland to Hereford in one direction, and through the forest of Arden and the Cotswold hills in the other.

By the late medieval period a number of areas specialized in pottery production. The Malvern Chase was one such area and the Surrey/Hampshire border, supplying London, another.[31] The distribution of such wares shows that they were being carted overland over distances of thirty to forty miles. Greater distances were occasionally covered but by and large forty miles seems to have been a limit which was presumably related to the cost of overland transport in relation to the sort of price which a pot might command at market.

Alongside this relatively restricted trade in utilitarian pottery was a trade in glazed finewares such as jugs. In the eleventh and twelfth centuries these were rare, made at few centres and traded over long distances. In the second half of the twelfth century, however, the demand for glazed jugs grew considerably, and the following century saw the production of elaborately decorated and glazed vessels, such as London-type ware.[32] These were traded widely, with overlapping distributions, and it is quite clear that specialist traders, as opposed to the potters themselves, must have been involved in their marketing.

Study of local pottery marketing can reveal the use made of river transport, the existence of local and long-distance overland routeways and how such uses changed with time. As with imported pottery transported by ship, we have to remember that locally made pottery was not an expensive item and that if there is archaeological evidence for trade in pottery it is probable that other goods, now not visible to us, were being carried over much longer distances.

A port and its trade: Kingston-upon-Hull

We turn now to evidence of trade in a single place, the port of Kingston-upon-Hull. Founded in the late thirteenth century at the mouth of the Humber estuary, Hull rapidly rose to become the second most important port on the east coast of England after London. It is a typical example of a number of later medieval ports in England which rose to prominence, or were actually founded, during the high Middle Ages at the mouths of navigable rivers. Ships had been able to sail up the Humber and its tributaries reaching York, Bawtry, Gainsborough, Torksey and even Nottingham but the increased draft of sea-going ships favoured deepwater harbours. In addition, rivers were becoming more difficult to navigate as a result of bridges and weirs.

Nevertheless, even in the fourteenth century it was possible to travel by boat along the inland waterways from Torksey, on the Trent, to York.[33] It seems that where bulky goods had to be transported then rivers were used whereas if speed was important then roads were better. We might therefore expect this principle to be reflected in the source of artefacts found in Hull. The town's foreign trade is well documented through the port books in which customs duties were recorded.

The town is better known than most through its archaeology.[34] Not only do the archaeological levels survive, they have also been excavated on numerous occasions and the finds have been studied and published. Here, then, is an opportunity to compare what archaeology and documentary sources can tell us of the commerce and trade of an important medieval port.

The town was built on low-lying ground, some of which at least was reclaimed mudflats. This gave rise to near ideal circumstances for archaeology. First, the high water table led to excellent organic preservation. Second, there was a tendency to build up the ground level to protect buildings from possible flooding. This gave rise to large areas of stratigraphy consisting of layer upon layer of refuse, thrown down at regular intervals. Third, there was much less reworking of these deposits through pit digging or cellaring than would be found on a site with a lower water table.

The pottery from Hull excavations includes a variety of imports. French wares are mainly from the south-west of France but vessels from the Seine valley and from Normandy also occur. From the fourteenth century onwards Rhenish and Meuse valley stonewares are found and Low Countries wares of various sorts are common; the latter include plain red earthenwares, decorated red earthenwares and plain unglazed greywares. Finally, Iberian wares, such as Merida-type ware from southern Portugal and lustrewares from Malaga

Figure 5.7 Large casks of Baltic oak on the waterfront at Blaydes Staithe, Hull, of about 1490; perhaps for storing live fish (D. H. Evans and Humberside Archaeological Unit).

and Manises, have been found. The striking feature of this imported pottery is its high frequency, often forming between a quarter and a third of the pottery found in a deposit. Within these imports, south-western French Saintonge wares are by far the most numerous, outnumbering Low Countries and Rhenish wares by some considerable margin. The remaining pottery is from sources within the Humber basin, such as Beverley, Holme upon Spalding and West Cowick, or traded downriver to Hull, such as North Yorkshire white-ware from the Hambleton Hills or Rawmarsh, or evidence for coastal trade both north (Scarborough) and south (Toynton) of the Humber. In some cases it is not possible to identify the route along which pottery travelled to Hull, as in the case of Potterhanworth ware, which could have been carried overland from the Lincoln area to the Humber, down the Trent or via Boston.

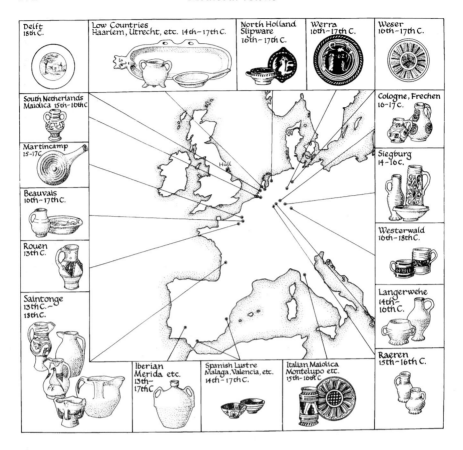

Figure 5.8   A traditional view of Hull's import trade between 1200 and 1700, compiled *c.*1980. Because it is based on pottery alone, it gives a misleading and partial view (compare Fig. 5.9). Major trading areas such as Scandinavia, the Baltic and Scotland are not represented because the trade was in perishable goods (D. H. Evans and Humberside Archaeological Unit).

Other traded objects whose source can be determined are hones (mostly from the Eidsborg district, in southern Norway), floor tiles (including examples made in Nottingham), lead alloy pilgrim badges (from Pontefract), and timber (where wood of Baltic origin can be recognized through its dendrochronological signature). Large casks of Baltic oak, dating to about 1490, from a site at Blaydes Staithe appear to be custom built for holding live fish (Fig. 5.7); some trades required special installations or distinctive buildings.

From the archaeological evidence Hull was a centre for the importation, mainly, of Gascon and Rhenish goods, with some evidence for coastal trade within the British Isles, and for inland connections with the vale of York, south Yorkshire and the Trent valley. But the archaeological picture only deals with a tiny fraction of the trade. A study of the Hull customs accounts suggests that 99 per cent of the port's exports and perhaps as much as 95 per cent of its imports would have been in goods which either leave no archaeological trace

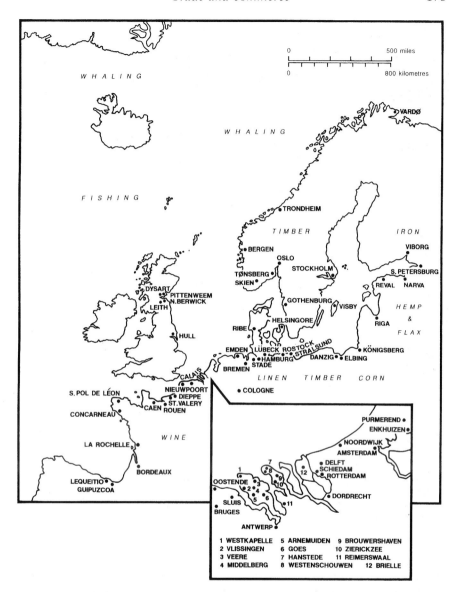

Figure 5.9 Hull's trade 1200–1700 when the main centres providing Hull with perishable commodities, known from documentary sources, are added (D. H. Evans and Humberside Archaeological Unit).

or which cannot at present be provenanced. Further, in this case the limited or incomplete nature of the archaeological evidence is plainly shown, when a picture of Hull's import trade between 1200 and 1700 is first presented purely on pottery evidence (Fig. 5.8) and then based on the inclusion of the main centres with which Hull traded, as mentioned in accounts, and especially taking note of perishable commodities (Fig. 5.9).[35] This is not to demean or diminish the archaeological evidence, which is comparatively profuse, but to argue that it must be placed in context if the broader picture is to be attempted, as it must.

Conclusion

From the market places around which many new towns of the Middle Ages were built, to the houses of their prominent citizens grown wealthy on trade, commerce was the driving force which brought those towns into existence and ensured their survival. The archaeological contribution starts with the study of merchant communities, both native and foreign, in towns; with coins, jettons and tokens; weights and measures; and with buildings or parts of buildings given over wholly or partially to trade. Yet there are many aspects of the process which are difficult to study using archaeological sources. From our case study at Hull we can see that archaeology reveals only a fraction of the trade passing through the port, both because the goods being traded were ephemeral and because many never stayed in the town but were in transit, being transhipped or transferred to carts for inland distribution. Pottery may be the best archaeological indicator of trade at present, but archaeologists throughout Europe are still a long way from confidently interpreting the mass of pottery from non-local sources in a town as reliable indicators of trade.[36] Archaeology can supply information on what was traded, where the goods came from, and to a lesser extent who was trading; this was no longer the exclusive province of documentary historians. But there are problems about forming conclusions about local, regional and international trade from the mass of information now available across Europe. The archaeological argument has still largely to be constructed.[37]

So what is the way forward? First, even in the best-documented parts of our period there are large aspects of trading which were not covered by documents. There was, for example, no reason to make official records of coastal, riverine or overland traffic since no duty had to be paid on goods transported from one part of a kingdom to another, only on foreign trade. Second, if we can understand the biases in our archaeological sources in circumstances where they can be compared with documentary evidence, then we stand a better chance of being able to understand the evidence we find for commerce and trade in times and places which were never documented or where such documentation does not survive. Third, the archaeological evidence spans towns and their hinterlands, kingdoms, literate and pre-literate societies, and covers the entire medieval period. We can place the documents, detailed though they sometimes are, in a wider and richer context. This is what archaeologists dealing with medieval towns all over northern Europe are now doing.

6 Religion in towns: churches, religious houses and cemeteries

The social order of the medieval town was pervaded by a set of religious beliefs which was given its official form in the thirteenth century, and which infused the language, ritual and even fabric of urban life until much of it was swept away at the Reformation. Thus the manifestations of religious belief in towns in our period are of great interest. Churches are not only buildings for a specific function – worship – but they may have acted as mirrors to the communities they served, and because of comparatively little disturbance over the centuries in comparison to secular sites (apart from the cataclysm of the Reformation) we may still be able to see those reflected images. By studying churches, cemeteries and religious artefacts such as pilgrim badges, we can begin to understand some aspects of what medieval people in towns believed.

Archaeological assessment and recording of churches

A *church* can be either a parish church for a town or village, or the building specially used for worship within a wider complex of buildings occupied by a community of people dedicated to a religious life (monks, nuns or friars). Larger churches in towns might have communities of priests attached; cathedrals, the seats of bishops, would normally have several other buildings with set functions adjacent to the church or nearby. The archaeological assessment of the church itself as a building can pick out features which are found in many or all of these types.

Is it possible to recognize a church on purely archaeological grounds? The answer is usually yes, for the church as a building or as a complex of stratigraphic units (layers, walls, floors) has a distinctive character (Fig. 6.1). Both inside and immediately outside the church will be human burials; and, by comparison with sites of secular buildings, the smallfinds will include large numbers of floor-tiles, fragments of decorated window glass and moulded stones (Fig. 6.2).

Churches are usually extremely long-lived sites. Of 24 English urban parish churches excavated in recent years, only three or four might date in origin from after 1100. Further, the earth within a church is a particularly rich and complex archaeological site, the layers inside it (apart from burials) are often crisper than those outside the building due to lack of animal action or leaching. Four categories of archaeological evidence can be identified: the structural development of the building; the evidence of construction methods (scaffolding, mortar-mixing areas, bell-founding pits); floors, furnishings and

Figure 6.1 The excavation of a typical small town church: St Peter, Waterford, Ire-land. After possible traces of a wooden church, and burials, the first stone church erected in the early twelfth century went through fourteen phases of alteration which lasted to the nineteenth century. This view, looking west, shows the apsidal extension of the chancel some time also in the twelfth century; the first stone chancel is seen behind, and the first nave is beyond that. To the sides and in the foreground are later foundations of aisles and a further eastward extension of the thirteenth century. The rectangular stone feature is the base of an altar, at the east end of the square chancel. Two stone-lined graves can be seen within the area of the apse, but stratigraphically they preceded it and must have been dug immediately east of the square chancel. In this cemetery stone-lined graves were common throughout, suggesting such burials were a local custom rather than special (M. F. Hurley; from Hurley *et al.* 1997).

fittings; and burials.[1] From this we can reconstruct the growth of the church in its various stages and their reasons, the relationship of archaeological strata to medieval liturgy (i.e. practices of worship), the interaction of church and society as demonstrated by patronage of embellishments such as stained glass and monumental brasses, and the care taken over burials (and thus the beliefs and intentions surrounding them). Human skeletons as illustrative of health and disease among medieval town-dwellers are considered in Chapter 7.

   Two particular features of churches as archaeological sites are that, on the one hand, the excavations often take place within the building itself (Fig. 6.3); and, sometimes as a consequence, the excavated fragments are displayed in

Figure 6.2 St Nicholas Shambles, London: late medieval walls (or in this case, a post-Reformation wall when the church had been demolished) often contain moulded stones from phases of the parish church.

special underground chambers thereafter (usually in the larger churches such as cathedrals). There are examples in most European countries (e.g. Lund (Sweden), Cologne Cathedral (Germany); one at Grenoble (France) figures in Chapter 8), though not so many in Britain (the remains of several periods below York Minster are noteworthy). There is an effort to present the fragments of several previous periods of the history of the building. Such a permanent display means that the church will form an important part of the town's presentation of its past to the resident and visitor.

The growth of a church and its various uses

The archaeology of the church, and especially the parish church, in Britain is a creation of the last thirty years. In the early 1970s, writes Richard Morris, 'the origins of Britain's parish churches were virtually prehistoric. Like ridge and furrow, no-one quite knew when they came into existence ... '.[2] Now, as this chapter will show, much is known and understood about the origins, development and meaning of parish churches.

Figure 6.3 Excavations in progress in the cathedral at Geneva (Switzerland). The remains have since been covered and made into an archaeological crypt, open since 1986. The intention from the start to preserve the most didactic or spectacular remains has consequences for the collection of information about all the periods on the site (Service cantonal d'archéologie, Geneva).

A distinction must first be made, in terms of numbers, between pre-medieval towns and towns founded in the medieval period. By 1200, towns both of Roman origin (such as Gloucester, Exeter, Winchester or York (Fig. 6.4)) and of Saxon origin (such as Ipswich, Norwich or Thetford) possessed many parish churches. In 1300, for instance, a person walking the one and a quarter miles from one side of the City of London to the other would pass the doors of 16

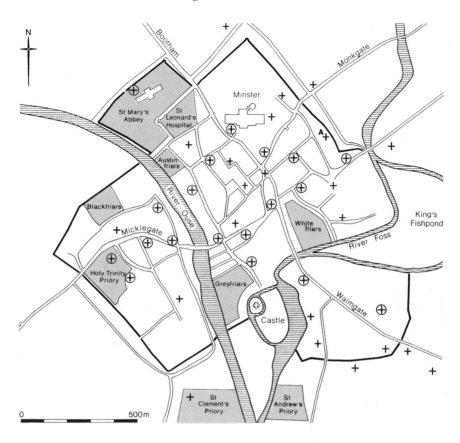

Figure 6.4 Map of medieval York, showing all the parish churches and religious houses (after York Archaeological Trust). The circled crosses indicate parish churches which survive today. A = site of St Helen-on-the-Walls.

churches (out of a total of over a hundred (Fig. 6.5)); there were even greater concentrations, by square mile, at Lincoln (32 churches by 1100), Norwich (57 by 1200) and Winchester (57 by 1300).[3] The high number of churches reflects a great period of church building by secular patrons in these towns during the tenth and especially eleventh centuries. By 1300, and especially after 1400, the number of churches was in fact declining slowly, particularly in smaller towns. In addition, towns founded after about 1100 normally had only one church; so that more than 50 per cent of the English places which were urban at the time of the Norman conquest contained more than one church, but only 4 per cent of the boroughs founded in the following two centuries.

In Wales, also, older foundations had more churches, though on a smaller scale. Chepstow had three churches besides the priory, Haverfordwest had three, and Cardiff had two churches and a chapel at the entrance to the castle. Several pre-existing Celtic or early Anglo-Norman churches were instrumental

Figure 6.5 Part of the riverside area of the City of London, just above the bridge, around 1550. Many parish churches are shown, but precisely because of their number it is difficult to identify most of them from these sightlines. In the foreground on the waterfront is Fishmongers' Hall, a notable piece of secular architecture taking advantage of its riverside site, like the Guildhall in York (Ashmolean Museum, Oxford).

in determining the sites of Welsh towns and English boroughs. Scottish burghs tended to have only one church.[4]

We can therefore make an easy but crude distinction between older towns like London or Winchester, where there were many usually small parish churches, and newer towns, particularly those which flowered in the late Middle Ages, which have one large and fine church (Fig. 6.6). There were also towns such as Hedon (East Riding, Yorks), Stamford and Reading which lie somewhere in between.

Let us take an example, St Mark's, Lincoln.[5] Excavations of 1975–7 after demolition uncovered what remained of the parish church of St Mark's, on the west side of Lincoln High Street, about 450m south of the walled city in the suburb of Wigford, which has already been mentioned in Chapter 4 (Fig. 6.7). The church and its graveyard were probably established between the late ninth and the eleventh centuries, with the mid tenth century being the preferred date; a small rectangular timber building south of the later medieval church is probably the original church.

In the mid eleventh century a new church of stone was built next to the timber church. It had two spaces or cells, the nave about twice the area of the chancel (Period II). It reused masonry from local Roman buildings in its fabric. The chancel was floored with flagstones, and the nave with beaten earth. Two north–south sub-rectangular robbing-pits inside the chancel may be indicators of successive positions of masonry altars; they were not dated, but the excavator suggests that they show a migration of the altar from the chancel arch (where it met the nave) to the east end of the building, as is known in other churches and which seems to have been a product of the elaboration of the communion service during the twelfth century.

The church was probably burnt in a city-wide fire of 1122. A western tower

Figure 6.6 The town church at Lavenham, Suffolk. What do these churches prove?

on massive foundations (Period II) was added shortly afterwards, presumably so that heavy bells could be hung and used. It is also possible that the tower was used as a baptistery, but evidence (in the form of a font or a special drain for the holy water) did not survive. Two generations later the ground plan was expanded by the rebuilding of the church with a new north aisle and an enlarged chancel (Period III). St Mark's demonstrates how phases of construction can be inferred even when direct evidence such as foundations has been lost: reused in the foundation of the north aisle were moulded stones from a mid-twelfth-century door, which joined with others found somewhere round the church in 1871. They probably came from the Period II north door of the church. Other blocks reused as rubble may have been from the chancel arch. The door mouldings are similar to others on the doors of Lincoln Cathedral of the 1150s or 1160s; it can be proposed that the style of the cathedral masons was diffusing among the smaller parish churches.

The need for a larger church could have stemmed from requirements for more space for processions, burial spaces for prominent parishioners, or the profusion of subsidiary altars. Traces of foundations or robbing-trenches suggested that an altar stood at the east end of the north aisle, and that a rood screen divided the new nave and chancel, another common thirteenth-century development.

After this substantial rebuilding, the church stayed much the same in form for the rest of the medieval period. This is typical of the Lincoln churches, whereas those in York and Norwich underwent thorough rebuilds in the fourteenth and fifteenth centuries. St Mark's did acquire a chapel, extending the north aisle, which was used as a mausoleum by a leading family of the parish in the early fifteenth century. A mortuary chapel sited on either the

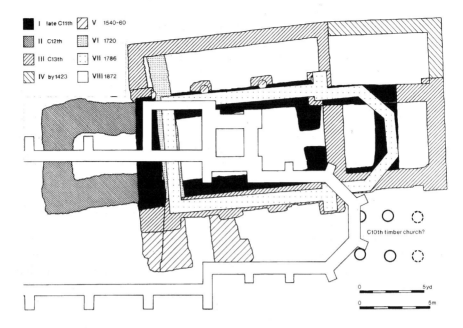

Figure 6.7 Development plans of St Mark's, Lincoln (after Gilmour and Stocker 1986).

north or south side of the chancel is another well-known phenomenon in medieval urban parish churches throughout the country (examples from London are cited below). In the 1550s or 1560s a two-storeyed porch was added on the south side, built largely of reused graveyard monuments and architectural fragments probably from other sites, a vivid reminder of the destruction of many religious sites at the Reformation. Careful excavation and analysis of the results have therefore produced much about the growth and liturgy in a small suburban church, and a little about its use by prominent persons in the community.

In smaller towns and villages such a piecemeal history of building would be typical because of the sporadic availability of funds. The town with several, or many, churches provides further scope for ascertaining broad trends in church-building which would otherwise have to be sought over a wide region. Did the churches develop individually, or was there simultaneity in architectural development over the town – did all churches get towers, or aisles, or lengthened chancels at roughly the same time? In larger towns such as London and York, the fully developed church with three aisles was common by the end of the fourteenth century, though in York in particular this was overtaken by further rebuildings in the next century; in Norwich, however, three-aisled churches appear to be rare before 1450. This would fit with a generally held view that Norwich's period of spectacular growth was in the late Middle Ages.[6]

A first set of factors at work in designing and ordering the building was institutional. Traditionally there was a division of responsibility for rebuilding and upkeep of the parish churches, the division marked by the chancel arch. The choir to the east was the responsibility of the rector (the lord or institution which had the right of appointing the priest) and the nave to the west that of the parish. This is one reason why in surviving churches the chancel arch is often the oldest part of the fabric; it formed a boundary between responsibilities. At St Bride Fleet Street in London, the excavated church maintained its chancel arch in the same position through several rebuildings from the tenth or eleventh century until destruction in the Great Fire of 1666.[7] At St Mark's Lincoln the chancel was paved but the nave was of beaten earth. Archaeology has not yet made much of this; the division of responsibility seems to have been practised more in some parts of the country than others.

Some patterns of use within the church were the work of parishioners. The fourteenth and fifteenth centuries saw the widespread establishment of chantry chapels, in which a prominent sponsor endowed the church to provide for a priest to say daily masses for himself and his family. Such chantries could take the form of a simple altar against a pillar, or the sharing of a chapel, or in exceptional cases screens of wood and even stone demarcated an area within the body of the church. Very exceptionally, the chapel was built at the sponsor's cost as an appendage of the church.

In the 658 wills surviving on the London Husting Rolls from the earliest example in 1259 to 1300, 59 perpetual chantries are recorded as being founded in parish churches. From 1300 to 1402, in the same series of wills, an average of 28 permanent chantries were founded every ten years. Though it is rarely stated that the testator had improved the church, either in its architecture or by donating fittings or ornaments, it does seem likely that the period of the greatest number of chantry foundations, the fourteenth century, should also be the most likely period of architectural embellishment on that account. A similar development has been suggested for Florence, where the desire for private chapels was the major catalyst that brought about a boom in church construction after the mid fourteenth century.[8]

While it may be commonplace for chapels to have been erected towards the east end of the parish church, some London churches show that the chancel area may have been embellished with chapels added to the north and south before the body of the nave was given aisles, to produce a winged effect in plan, probably during the fourteenth century. In two cases they were on special undercrofts with external entrances. This seems to be a feature of large towns; here there were people with enough money to build their own personal part of the church, naturally around the holy epicentre, the main altar.[9]

Town churches were also patronized by the crafts. The earliest dates at which this tended to happen in towns need further research, and depend at the moment on the survival of documentary evidence. At least ten medieval guilds are recorded in Stamford, for instance, and they were associated with seven of the parish churches. Most have left no physical record of their uses, but a prominent donor provided most of the expense for the surviving fourteenth-century north chapel of St Mary's church, which was probably used by the Corpus Christi guild. In the early sixteenth century Holy Trinity, Coventry, housed not only the archdeacon's court but also nine chapels, three associated with trade groups: mercers, tanners and butchers (Fig. 6.8). Chapels attached to several London parish churches, though they may have originally been

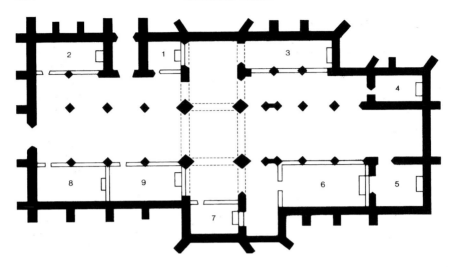

Figure 6.8 Plan of Holy Trinity Church, Coventry, with its nine chapels: 1, St Thomas Chapel; 2, Dyers' Chapel (?); 3, Mercers' Chapel; 4, Lady Chapel; 5, Trinity Chapel; 6, Butchers' Chapel; 7, Corpus Christi Chapel; 8, Jesus Chapel; 9, Tanners' Chapel. The screens are conjectural (Cook 1947).

sponsored by rich individuals, were taken over by the donor's guild and used to maintain and express a link with a parish church; sometimes guild equipment such as a chest for valuables or banners for pageants would be stored there.[10]

The origins of the urban parish, and the growth of parish churches, are equally important archaeological themes on the Continent. In the eighth and ninth centuries, in larger centres such as Mainz (Germany), nobles required their dependants to attend their own churches; generally, the parish was a creation of the twelfth and early thirteenth centuries as in England. It was also, as everywhere, used as a unit of civil administration, especially for local and national taxation. Comparison between the archaeologies of medieval town churches in Britain and those on the Continent might usefully concern relative sizes, to examine an impression that English towns at least had individually more churches per acre and that the churches were therefore generally smaller. Hamburg had only four parishes, Cologne had 12, Toledo 28, and Verona 52; but London had over a hundred churches. This meant that a church in Toledo had on average about 1,800 parishioners, and a London church about 450.[11] British and continental churches should be compared not only for their size, but for clear similarities: their uses by craft groups, use as the places where civic standards of measurement were officially carved on walls and pillars, and uses by prominent townspeople (both men and women) for personal statements in their burial monuments.

Fittings, patronage and architecture: church interiors

The interior of a parish church contained fixtures such as the rood, font, pulpit and pews; glazing and images (either paintings or statues); floor tiles and monuments. Popular devotion and ritual practices inside the church are virtually invisible in written sources before the thirteenth century, and evidence of the religion of the parishioners, rich or poor, has to come from archaeology.[12]

Up to the twelfth century, in England, it was usual only for priests to be buried inside parish churches; noble and civic dignitaries were being buried in monastic churches from the later part of the century. By the middle of the thirteenth century effigies of knights are known in parish churches, and monumental brasses survive from the 1270s; latten images let into stone are recorded from 1208. Alabaster seems to have come into use during the second quarter of the fourteenth century, and its frequency increased in the decades after 1350; it was carved into small reliefs, sometimes grouped in wooden frames to form reredoses or retables, and effigies.

From the late thirteenth century brasses, or simpler brass crosses, could be ordered by all richer persons including prominent tradesmen; the workshops also produced monuments or monumental decorations in Purbeck marble.[13] The main production centre was London, with clients in southern England and East Anglia, capitalizing on the growing population and an increasing preference for burial in the church. After about 1400 there was another fashion for prominent tombs within the aisled church, around the east end. To some extent this overtook the practice of building whole new chapels.

Just as trading groups demonstrated their faith and social cohesion by sponsoring windows (as can still be seen especially in York churches) or repainting roof timbers of churches, so prominent individuals made private chapels into family mausolea, and in so doing sometimes brought about the rebuilding of parts of the church to accommodate their tombs. During the fourteenth century a rich merchant could commission effigies of himself and his wife in alabaster, to lie on an eye-catching tomb as big as a table. In some cases the tomb is next to an altar or its piscina, and the two items are clearly meant to be thought of and used religiously together. At the same time the prominent tomb was a social statement, a reminder to the living of the local connections of the people who were dead but still present in effigy.

Among the most numerous artefacts available to the archaeologist from churches are moulded stones; the individual carved blocks forming arches, doorways, tombs and pillars. Certain types of moulding can be dated to within twenty years, for example window tracery; studies forming data banks of mouldings, for instance at Warwick University, have correlated dated examples. The position of the moulded stones in their strata can be significant, since the degree of articulation of stones forming a window or doorway helps interpretation of the demolition layers. When stones have been preserved in the soil, perhaps after destruction of the building or monument of which they formed part, they often retain their original paint. Evidence for tooling on the stones is of limited value, since tools were long-lived and conservative in design; one or two tooling textures are roughly datable, for example the diagonal striations of the twelfth century. Regional groupings of mouldings are beginning to be noticed, and some geographical concentration of distinctive styles, such as the 'Yorkshire School' of twelfth-century parish churches. In this case a common repertory of carvings showing literary themes (Labours of the Months and symbols of the zodiac) is shared by a number of churches which were in the hands of members of York minster chapter, the archbishop of York, or else were possessions of prominent religious houses.[14]

Moulded stones tell us about vanished buildings, and sometimes about buildings in other parts of the town. At York, excavations of 1973–80 on the site of the Vicars Choral of the cathedral, at Bedern (see Fig. 1.3), produced over four hundred fragments, the great majority brought to the site as rubble and reused in walls. A large subset of this material came from masonry originally cut in the 1160s or 1170s for the new choir and western towers of York Minster, a seminal building in English architectural history and one of the first buildings in the Gothic style in northern England; but lost because these features had been destroyed by later rebuildings at the Minster.[15]

The interiors of churches, especially the larger ones for which we have both physical remains and documentary records, tell much of the changing requirements in liturgy or the conduct of religious services, though changes in architectural style in churches cannot always be attached to changes in liturgy.[16] In larger churches with communities of canons or monks, the twelfth century saw the expansion and elaboration in architecture of the choir. From the late twelfth century, two developments were even more widespread: the need to provide more altars for the growing multiplication of daily masses and of the cult of the Virgin resulted in the focus of liturgy spreading out of the chancel area into transepts and chapels. Further, in the majority of the largest churches (such as at St Albans or Chester), after Canterbury Cathedral began the trend in the 1180s, relics became important generators of income from pilgrims, and a shrine would be inserted or added in a sacred area behind the high altar.

The altars formed stopping-places in elaborate processions which wound in and out of the church. In the thirteenth century, Salisbury Cathedral had seventeen altars; apart from two parochial altars in the nave, the others were in chapels along the eastern arms of the transepts (three on each side), in the extra choir transepts, and around the high altar. These processional ways might be detectable in archaeological excavation, but church floors are usually honeycombed with later graves and vaults, so the evidence does not survive.[17] It is however important to appreciate that a large church was not a monolithic, unchanging structure, but served as a framework of meanings through which people, often in hundreds or sometimes thousands, constantly flowed; and much of the structure and decoration was geared to that movement. At Salisbury and other cathedrals, an elaborate west front incorporated a gallery where the choir sang on major occasions such as Palm Sunday; such fronts, brightly painted and with statues of saints sometimes with welcoming gestures, encouraged the townspeople to enter the church, which stood for the heavenly city.[18] Within, the church was a living pattern-book of architecture and artistic patronage; though much of its finery was removed at the Reformation, excavation both inside and outside churches finds glass, painted plaster and pieces of tombs. One hardy and colourful item is often recovered by the archaeologist: parts of tiled floors. On rural monasteries, large areas of such floors are either still *in situ* at guardianship sites, or are found in excavation; in urban churches, tiles have been much moved about through constant grave digging and re-arrangement of the floor. Patches of tiles, reset, can be found in many rural parish churches and a few urban ones. Tiles were made at a few centres, and evidently widely marketed, or at least sought out by religious houses over wide geographical areas: the types found at two Chester houses, the Benedictine nunnery and the Dominican friary, are found in other houses over a wide geographical area, from Dublin to Derbyshire.[19]

Burials; cemeteries

Much can also be learnt about both the surrounding topography and about the management of the individual church and its land from study of the cemetery which nearly always accompanies the parish church (though in some towns, such as Exeter and Winchester, the reservation of burial rights by a cathedral seems to have restricted the development of parish churches and their cemeteries). Here we are concerned with the rituals of burial, monuments and organization of the cemetery. Many graveyards have been excavated in recent years in Britain.[20]

In the eleventh and twelfth centuries, some burial practices apparently of the Saxon period lingered on in parish graveyards. The types of burial, and some apparent burial rites, can be illustrated by study of 234 articulated skeletons from the graveyard of St Nicholas Shambles, London,[21] with parallels from other excavated churchyards.

At St Nicholas, about half the burials were in the churchyard, and half within the confines of the church, though in the absence of horizontal strata it is possible that some of the internal burials were originally outside, to be covered by expansion of the church building. All burials avoided the first eleventh-century nave and chancel, confirming the prohibition known from documents against burial of laity inside churches until the twelfth century.

Most people were buried without a coffin, in an unadorned grave; in medieval times women were often buried in a shroud, for which the pin might survive near the bones, whereas men were sometimes buried in hairshirts woven from coarse two-ply yarn. Older men and especially older women might have stone pillows in the grave; often these stones lay to either side of the head perhaps as protection. Graves sometimes had simple trampled floors of chalk and mortar; slightly more prestigiously, dry-laid or mortared stone might line the grave in peremptory fashion.

There was evidence of two occasional burial rites. In three cases Roman tile was laid on the body, a practice noted at St Bride's in London and in Norwich in eleventh-century contexts. In four further cases a pebble had been placed in the mouth of a mature man and four comparatively elderly women (that is, over 38 years old; Fig. 6.9). Even in the middle of the capital city, folk rituals, it seems, were still prevalent.

We lack substantial archaeological work on a medieval urban parish cemetery which studies how the graves were laid out or grouped, or how paths went to and from the church. This is probably largely because urban cemeteries are greatly disturbed by constant grave-digging, up to the recent past in

Figure 6.9   St Nicholas Shambles, London: one of the cases of a burial with a pebble in the mouth (White 1988).

some cases (most medieval cemeteries were in use for eight hundred years or more). In urban cemeteries in the Roman period, which are less disturbed because they had a limited period of use, archaeologists can make suggestions about previous land-use before the cemetery, rows of graves, marking of graves and individual monuments, even clusters which might express group identity (family, patronage, trade affiliation); but we have still to attempt this for a medieval cemetery. Some first ideas about how cemeteries were laid out can come from excavation of sites where the graveyard was of short duration, such as those covered by establishment or expansion of castles, as at Trowbridge (Wilts) or Norwich Castle. At Trowbridge an eleventh-century stone church and 160 burials were sealed during the later twelfth century by expansion of a castle (Fig. 6.10). Several rows of burials west of the church could be discerned. At Norwich, an eleventh-century wooden church, rebuilt twice, was overlaid by similar expansion. Burials on its north side were only partly in rows, and by their positions suggest there was no north door. In this case, there was a grouping of child burials towards the east end of this north graveyard.[22]

We can outline some further questions or matters to be aware of. The pottery from parish church and cemetery sites is often of a peculiar character because it is largely brought in with soil or building material, rather than used on the site. The finds from graveyard soil may be significant, since cemeteries in medieval towns were used as playing fields, places of work or assembly, open-air courtrooms and as markets; several churchyards were arranged around a preaching-cross. Buildings in or encroaching upon the churchyard could include the rector's house, or a house for chaplains of the chantry endowed by a testator. Many churchyards had a well, sometimes built or

Figure 6.10   An eleventh-century graveyard under excavation at Trowbridge (Wilts) (Trust for Wessex Archaeology).

endowed by a worthy citizen. There seems to be a tradition both that parish churches were often built with larger, more public graveyards to the south, and that the north churchyard was assigned for burials of people who in some way were socially irregular or abormal (criminals, suicides, the unbaptized); these pieces of folklore or local custom should be tested archaeologically. Clearly there were many things going on in medieval churchyards which we only dimly understand.[23]

It is also possible to study burial location inside the church, though often the medieval graves will be badly disturbed (and many removed) by either digging up of bones to put in a charnel house, or later post-medieval burials (graves 6ft deep seem to have become standard in the seventeenth century, and urban churches commonly have many brick vaults, which begin in the early sixteenth century in Britain and two centuries earlier on the Continent). The practice of having a charnel house somewhere on the site, and not the excavated portion, will affect arguments from burial statistics arising out of excavated groups. Some remarks about internal burials will be made below, in the section on friaries, where the relatively undisturbed strata and the shorter timescale of use has made deductions easier.

Further questions about parish churches

In 1987, Morris suggested several objectives in the archaeological study of urban parish churches.[24] First, there must be complete excavations of selected churches and their precincts (to ensure that earlier churches are not 'hiding offstage'), and to recover sufficiently large groups of skeletons to make a worthwhile contribution to population studies. Second, the difficult question of dating simple plan-forms and masonry must be tackled, for instance by typologies of foundation-types and further studies of moulded stone designs; this also means more sites of short duration to isolate particular developments or snap-shot views of church development. Third, archaeologists should examine how churches had parts to play in urban environments: on walls and near gates (e.g. St John, Bristol, St Alphege in London, or St Mary Northgate, Canterbury), at the doors of greater churches, buried deep within housing (St Pancras, Winchester) and especially on streets. The parish church must be studied on the same three levels as a secular building: as a structure, to understand its variety of form; as internal space, to understand the functions that went on in it; and as a leading component of a neighbourhood street-scape, pulling people away from their other pursuits. Further questions and objectives were added in a survey of work in Britain of 1996.[25] Regionalism in churches has emerged as a significant and potentially fruitful area for future research; for instance, there are areas around towns which shared a spurt of church- or tower-building, as in the fifteenth century around Devizes (Wilts).[26]

Two questions concerning town churches may be mentioned in particular. In the older centres, the majority of parish churches began life as parts of private residences in the tenth or eleventh centuries. This often governed their sites, which would be set back from the main medieval thoroughfare. What was the process of allowing public access to and use of this private place? It is another case, in parallel with changes to secular houses, where we might study the changing balance of private and public access. Archaeological and architectural evidence, for instance, demonstrates that Winchester parish churches were being extended as early as the late eleventh century; but the population was declining or at least static, and parishes did not increase in area until much later. It therefore seems likely that the increase in size represents the change or extension from private chapel to a wider and more public parochial function.[27]

As far as English parish churches go, archaeologists and historians have not yet addressed Postan's remark that late medieval churches, often large and expensive, have nothing to do with the economy of the time, that is with what was happening in agriculture, industry or trade. In the thirteenth and early fourteenth centuries, many town churches were extended and embellished; they appear to have been an important recipient of the good fortunes then being enjoyed in towns. After the Black Death, expenditure on monastic and cathedral buildings fell sharply, and it seems that religious devotion turned from these large churches to the neighbourhood parish church. In these later centuries, it may be that embellishment of churches has more to do with an increase in piety than a general increase in wealth. Alternatively, pews, tombs and vaults can be seen as personal assertions of status by the richer families in the parish.

Pilgrimages and fraternities

There were other material manifestations of religious belief in the medieval period besides churches and their contents. Two which are susceptible to

Figure 6.11 Ampullae (holy water containers) of tin; souvenirs of a pilgrimage to Canterbury. Becket is shown at the end, his hand raised in blessing. From the Swan Lane site, City of London, thirteenth century (Museum of London).

archaeological investigation are the pilgrimage and buildings erected or used by groups of lay people for charitable and religious purposes.

The pilgrimage was both an act of faith (as it is today) and, by the fourteenth century, a social occasion that combined tourism and religion. Pilgrims bought souvenirs of the shrines they visited, either in the form of metal badges worn on the hat, or ampullae, small tin or pewter containers of holy water, which were worn on a string around the neck (Fig. 6.11). Many different types of souvenir have been found in Thames foreshore deposits, both medieval and modern, in the City of London. Those from recent excavations, for instance, at the Swan Lane and Billingsgate Lorry Park sites, included a number of badges from the shrine of Thomas Becket in Canterbury. Becket appeared on horseback (riding in triumph) or on ship (returning from exile), and in the fifteenth century pilgrims could buy miniature copies of the sword that killed him, complete with scabbard; there were other badges which were little models of the shrine and especially of the reliquary in the form of a bust of the saint (the original reliquary held a piece of his skull). Alternatively, the pilgrim could get an elaborate madonna and child associated with Our Lady Undercroft (Fig. 6.12). Although a large number of the badges found in London came from Canterbury, there were others which demonstrate both local and foreign religious journeys, for instance to the miracle-working image of the Virgin at the Whitefriars friary of Toulouse (Fig. 6.13) or over sixty other continental shrines. Nor are these interesting finds confined to London. Watercourses in Salisbury have produced an impressive array of pilgrim badges from at least 31 places in England, as far apart as Finchale and Canterbury, and at least 22

Figure 6.12   Madonna and Child found in the spoil from the Billingsgate site, London, 1983. This badge is associated with Our Lady Undercroft at Canterbury Cathedral. It is dated to the seond half of the fourteenth century from its context, and to 1360–70 from the style of the shoes of the king on the left. The architectural references are also of this time. This badge was carefully folded up many times before being thrown away, perhaps deliberately, into the river.

places on the Continent, from Vadstena in Sweden to Compostela in Spain.[28]

These badges are one of the best ways of understanding the beliefs of ordinary medieval people. Within a few years of Becket's murder in 1170, holy water containing drops of his blood was reputed to have brought people back from the dead. The ampullae were talismans which resolved all sorts of personal problems and fended off difficulties and dangers. The simple badges from a shrine which may be Our Lady of Willesden in north-west London (where there is still a holy well) show the Virgin standing on a crescent moon: whereas the moon is constantly changing, the Virgin is eternal. The glorious medieval shrines in pilgrimage churches have often disappeared without record, and the badges not only hint at their character, but in the case of Our

Figure 6.13 Thirteenth-century badge commemorating the miracle-working image of the Virgin belonging to the Whitefriars at Toulouse (France), from Swan Lane, London (Museum of London). Next to the Virgin, a kneeling figure is delivered of an evil spirit which emerges from her mouth, an allusion to a miracle which took place in 1265. Opposite, a cured cripple discards his crutches, and below, a friar kneels in prayer. The scraped background was to take paint, which has survived as a pinkish pigment. The Virgin and Child must be a resemblance of the real statue in the Carmelite friary of Toulouse, which originally came with the first friars as they moved from Mount Carmel in the Holy Land about 1238.

Lady of Walsingham, give crucial details not found in other sources about the construction of the shrine itself.

People banded together to go on pilgrimages; they also formed groups at home, called parish fraternities. Unlike the craft fraternities, these were solely charitable or religious in purpose and admitted women as well as men. Confusingly, they are also sometimes called guilds or gilds, and were so during the medieval period. The two-street town of Westminster, not a large place, had nine parish fraternities; the earliest known, in the thirteenth century, was responsible for ringing the bells in the abbey. Fraternities were generally associated with parish churches, though one Westminster group met in the hall of the archbishop of York, and several in York met in private houses or at the

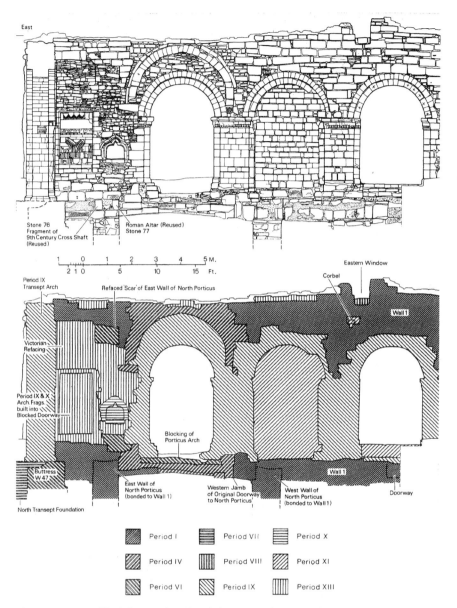

East

Stone 76
Fragment of
9th Century Cross Shaft
(Reused)

Roman Altar (Reused)
Stone 77

1 0   1   2   3   4   5 M.
  2 1 0   5   10   15   Ft.

Period IX
Transept Arch

Refaced 'Scar' of East Wall of North Porticus

Eastern Window

Corbel

Wall 1

Victorian
Refacing

Period IX & X
Arch Frags.
built into
Blocked Doorway

Blocking of
Porticus Arch

Wall 1

Buttress
W 47

East Wall of
North Porticus
(bonded to Wall 1)

Western Jamb
of Original Doorway
to North Porticus

West Wall of
North Porticus
(bonded to Wall 1)

Doorway

North Transept Foundation

Period I	Period VII	Period X
Period IV	Period VIII	Period XI
Period VI	Period IX	Period XIII

Figure 6.14 Half of the north side of the nave of St Oswald's priory church, Gloucester. Above is the elevation, below is an interpretation by period (Richard Bryant). This piece of wall includes work of eight periods from about 900 to 1866. Note how the Period I walls of the Saxon church (c.900) are both at the bottom and top of the drawing. At this time there was a transept or porticus coming out from the wall towards the viewer. In the early eleventh century (Period IV) the arch into the porticus was rebuilt into the arch seen in the ruin (the large one in the eastern bay); in the early twelfth century (Period VI) the porticus was demolished, along with a matching southern one seen in excavation, but little of this phase survived because the arch was to be re-opened later. In the early or mid-twelfth century (Period VII) new building works were largely elsewhere on the site (notably a new transept on the east). In the

Austin Friars. In Westminster, York and elsewhere such groups ran small hospitals and almshouses, and for Westminster it has been suggested that their vigorous social work made the parish church as central a feature of social life as the town hall. Some of the more well-heeled religious fraternities rebuilt or erected buildings for themselves, and in this they are difficult to disentangle from craft fraternities, since they shared a similar agenda; there is some merit in studying them together.[29]

Religious houses and cathedrals

Just as the number of parish churches in a town is one barometer of urban intensity (at least up to 1200), so the number of religious houses (including hospitals) may indicate regional centres, not all of them large towns today. In Britain at the Norman Conquest, urban religious institutions, often dominating their respective towns, were either Benedictine monasteries (Canterbury, Chichester) or secular colleges (Beverley, Ripon). Foundations continued, so that the largest number of urban religious houses in towns, by 1300, were Benedictine. From the early twelfth century houses of the Augustinian canons, and other minor orders of canons, spread through all kinds of town. They undertook pastoral work and the care of souls, and therefore took responsibility for the sick and insane, and provided for the aged and lepers. Leading churchmen may have actively promoted the establishment of the Augustinians in their dioceses during the twelfth century as a means of wresting the control of parish churches from their predominantly lay owners, at a time when the parish structure we know today was not developed. Thus the Augustinians are interesting as having functions within the secular town outside their precinct walls.[30]

Some towns which are small today must have been formerly of greater significance, as measured by the number of their religious houses. A list of

period 1150–75 (Period IX) a Romanesque arcade was inserted along the wall (the outer wall of the new north aisle was already in place, near the viewer). Evidently this was constructed without taking down the tenth-century wall entirely. In the thirteenth and fourteenth centuries (Period IX) two new bays were added at the west end of the church, off to the right (only half the elevation is reproduced here). A thirteenth-century piscina (recess for placing and washing the holy vessels) can be seen fitted into the wall near the east end, but this would have been too low for use when compared with the thirteenth-century floor levels, so its insertion must be later, possibly even Victorian. The last two periods are post-Dissolution: in 1540–1656 (Period XI) the second arch was blocked as the north aisle became the only usable part of the church: the nave was demolished. There appears to have been a doorway at the east end, later blocked with medieval material. The precise end-date for this period is given by documentary evidence: the church was largely demolished in 1653–6. In its ruin period of 1656–1866 (Period XII), there were various consolidations. Thus a long and complicated history has been deduced from the wall itself or its immediate surroundings.

This piece of arcade wall was intended, in 1967, to become a feature in the middle of a new traffic island. This plan was later shelved, and the ruin is now a Scheduled Ancient Monument, with the outlines of related excavated buildings laid out on the ground nearby (Heighway and Bryant 1997).

towns in Scotland which had two or three friaries and several hospitals each, for instance, identifies the political, ecclesiastical and academic centres: not only Edinburgh, Aberdeen, St Andrews and Berwick, but now smaller places such as Dumfries (seven institutions), Elgin and Haddington (six each). A study of the relationship between religious houses and Yorkshire towns suggests that foundations of hospitals and friaries are the better index of urbanization, rather than monasteries as a whole; the former show the vigour and extent of twelfth-century towns, the latter reflect fortunes and intentions in the thirteenth century.[31]

Some more important Saxon churches, often called minsters, survived to be major churches in towns, with dependent churches bound together in a ritual cycle of festivals and processions. In some small towns, the minster site transformed into a town between the ninth and thirteenth centuries. Both in parish churches and in what remains of some older urban monasteries, Saxon work can still be seen mixed with the work of later periods. Only careful stone-by-stone recording will elucidate the many phases, as demonstrated at St Oswald's priory, Gloucester, where recording of a large standing fragment and excavation next to it in 1975–83 have unravelled a complex history from the ninth or tenth century to the present (Fig. 6.14).

But in towns chosen by the Normans to be cathedrals, the story is different. There is today no certain pre-Conquest Saxon work to be seen above ground in any English cathedral; the Normans erased it everywhere, as a statement of religious and therefore secular authority.[32] Some cathedrals were replanned in such a way that their previous relationship to the inherited Saxon street-plan was destroyed. This is the case, for instance, at Wells, where the west front of the Saxon cathedral (now beneath the cloister) looked directly onto the market place, but the present church and main buildings of the late twelfth to early thirteenth centuries are aligned more strictly west–east by twelve degrees. Other cathedrals expanded over adjacent streets, especially in the late eleventh and twelfth centuries.

Large religious houses within towns often had a delicate relationship with their townspeople. In medieval Canterbury, for instance, many of the inhabitants made their living out of the monks, either as servants, or as suppliers of luxuries, food and building skills or labour. At the same time, riots and pitched battles between town and monks also occurred; in Canterbury in 1188, a difference of opinion between monks and the archbishop resulted in a year-long siege of Christ Church monastery. Thus religious institutions were commonly surrounded by high walls. In the late thirteenth century, as major towns put effort into their defences, so the major churches within towns fortified their precincts in stone: Norwich in 1276, York, Lincoln and St Paul's in London in 1285, and Canterbury in 1309. In the first half of the fourteenth century, these precincts were embellished or emphasized by prominent gates with a new architecture of octagonal turrets (the earliest probably that at St Augustine's abbey, Canterbury, in 1308). Elsewhere the precinct did without walls, at as Beverley, where the cluster of prebendal houses near the Minster had at least two symbolic gates on its approach roads. And the influence of the church sometimes stretched further into the urban topography: some lanes near great churches may originally have been laid out as processional ways, as suggested for Winchester.[33]

The present cathedrals, in Britain and abroad, are nearly all in origin religious communities within towns, some going back to the sixth and seventh centuries. As they are now living and used churches, the building works of maintenance and occasional development produce much of archaeological interest: not only the history of the building from excavation beneath its floors, but important examples of high-class standards of construction and decoration from floor to roof, as well as some of the best-quality information on the uses of different stones, sometimes from quarries far away.[34] Within the close, the cathedral or monastic complex comprised many buildings, and their variety of detail will not be pursued here. There are many archaeological guide books which take the interested reader round monasteries, pointing out the function and appearance of the various buildings.[35] A technical distinction can be made between urban monastic cathedrals where all the associated domestic buildings of a resident community were necessary, such as Durham, Chester or Worcester, and 'secular' cathedrals, where the canons (the equivalent of the monks) were not resident and buildings such as cloisters or dormitories were more formal than necessary, such as Wells, Salisbury or St Paul's. But the two types are best studied together: the cloister at Salisbury was one of the largest in Europe, surpassing that of many monasteries.

In France, comparatively little evidence of the buildings around medieval cathedrals has survived, and here archaeological work has made great progress; similarity with large churches in other countries, including Britain, is evident. The cloister appears in the ninth century, and as in England, during the Middle Ages it was taken up by cathedrals, to dignify their existence and to become the site of prestigious burials, both religious and especially for lay patrons. The precinct was often completely walled, sometimes with towers (Viviers), or walled on three sides with a river forming the fourth (Lyons, Vienne). At other places, however, the close was more supple or permeable, without its own fortifications, such as at Chartres, Laôn or Paris. Within the close, some buildings were specially situated because of their prime function: the house of the provost or dean controlled the access to the cloister (as at Westminster Abbey), and the refectory was placed so that it could be used for administering alms or food handouts to the urban poor and pilgrims.[36]

An area of current British interest concerns what happened in the outer courtyards of monastic houses and friaries, in that these would be the spaces where the house conducted the majority of its business with the outside world. A second yard or zone would have represented the storage and provisioning area of the monastery, where the food and other produce of the estates would be stored and processed. Urban precincts often included stables, brewhouses and accommodation for lay people. In the small town of Waltham Abbey (Essex), excavation reminds us how many buildings must have crammed into the spaces between the stone structures we now see in cathedral closes. Excavations of 1970–2 near the church, in an outer monastic close called Veresmead and in the Grange Yard, uncovered twelve medieval and two post-medieval buildings. In the outer close stood a two-bay timber-framed aisled hall and a store; nearby stood two successive dove-cotes, and beyond a large fish-farm of ponds. In the Grange Yard were a twelve-bay aisled timber-framed barn near a dock, a hay barn, a brick building with stalls and a solar end, three successive farm entrance lodges and a forge.[37]

Figure 6.15   Holy Trinity Priory, Aldgate, London: a newly discovered chapel in 1985 from the west, on the site of the lift shaft of the future building (Museum of London). It survived 3.5 m high partly because after 1532 it became a cellar at the end of a garden, and then lay partly beneath a Victorian cobbled courtyard. It was a surprise find, and lay on the site of a future corporate headquarters building.

In the majority of cases, apart from some of the present cathedrals, monastic buildings have been destroyed and the originally large complexes lie under several streets, so that one end of the priory church, underground, might be in one street and the other end in another. Many fragments of monastery buildings still hide behind stuccoed or brick façades in the town. Other fragments are revealed within buildings or under courtyards when development of secular properties takes place, and then their preservation is an issue. Unlike the majority of Roman, Saxon and medieval buildings which were constructed of light or perishable materials, these stone fragments seem to argue for their own continued survival (Figs 6.15 and 6.16). One solution, moving the ruin, is not new. Attractive fragments from cathedral or monastic churches have been moved across towns (though in pieces, not intact) since the eighteenth century: St Thomas's Porch was removed from Salisbury Cathedral by the architect James Wyatt in 1791 and rebuilt in the grounds of St Edmund's College; what was probably the chancel arch of the Benedictine nunnery at Chester has moved twice. Conservation thinking now argues that if research is carried out before a development takes place, such movements should not be necessary and should if possible be avoided.[38]

Figure 6.16   The chapel is raised on a concrete raft and moved across the building site during construction works by developers Speyhawk. Though greeted as a bold solution at the time, this is now cited as a case where prior research might have helped bring about a better solution. It is clearly not ideal for masonry (or any historic structure) to be moved. In this case, however, the chapel was only discovered encased in brickwork during the excavation which followed the granting of planning permission. It is now in a basement room nearby, available for study (Museum of London Archaeology Service).

Friaries

The urban order *par excellence*, and therefore in themselves an evidence of urban vigour, were the friars, especially the Dominicans (Blackfriars) and Franciscans (Greyfriars). The placing of their houses shows where they expected greatest spiritual (and financial) custom; besides the obvious larger towns, both orders had sites in medium-rank places such as Beverley, Berwick, Lincoln, Norwich, Northampton, Oxford and Bristol. The Dominicans were also active in the far north, in Edinburgh, Perth and Aberdeen. The formation of the Franciscan and Dominican orders in the early thirteenth century has been called the most distinctively and uniquely urban contribution made by the church in the long history of Christianity.[39]

Because of the almost total destruction of their written records, we know little of the social setting of the British friaries. Only 10 per cent of the sites of English friaries can now be identified by fragments above the ground, and very few are as extensive as a typical monastic ruin kept in guardianship. Friaries are especially noteworthy for two reasons: the information they may provide about previous land-use beneath their precincts, and the nature of the buildings of a peculiarly urban religious order (Fig. 6.17).

Figure 6.17 Work in Canterbury in 2000 revealed much of the Austin Friars (also known in Canterbury as the Whitefriars); the project continues to 2004. This view shows the north side of the church, looking east. Medieval foundations are overlaid by modern ones. The square structure by the human figure may be a later addition in the corner between the north aisle of the nave (foreground) and the reduced width of the chancel (the north wall of which is under the further part of the modern building) (Canterbury Archaeological Trust).

The normal (but by no means universal) extramural siting of friaries, when there must have been plenty of cheap land within the comparative security of the town defences, is demonstrated by the Welsh towns which were additionally in a troubled frontier zone. At Cardiff, the Blackfriars and Greyfriars both lay outside the town, but near the castle (Fig. 2.1, the sites marked F); in other Welsh towns friaries lay at the water's edge (Haverfordwest), across rivers (Brecon), at the limits of settlement or off suburban roads (Carmarthen, Denbigh, Newport (Gwent)); that at Rhuddlan, in existence adjacent to the Norman defences by the 1260s, was left in the countryside when Edward I had the new borough laid out on the far side of the castle in 1281–92 (Fig. 2.3).

The fact that friaries often settled on marshy land (which may have been used as a rubbish-tip by the adjacent town) should produce archaeological dividends, for in these waterlogged conditions the survival of organic materials, as well as seeds, insects and parasites, should be high. In the case of the Austin Friars at Leicester (to be examined below), an ecological history of the site before, during and after the occupation by the friars can be sketched out.

Some friaries, however, were occasionally also sited within towns, and near market places: at Maldon, or Lichfield (Fig. 6.18), for instance. The great church of the Greyfriars in London was also next to the Shambles or meat market in the middle of Newgate Street, in Hull the Austin Friars had their church next to the market place, and in Canterbury the Austin Friars had a gate into the nearby High Street; here, as at Chester and York, all three friaries were within the walls (Figs. 2.23; 6.4). In several French towns it has been noted that friaries first settled outside the walls, but then moved inside later; perhaps their particularly urban mission was calling them closer to the markets and places of public resort. Indeed, Pope Clement IV eventually had to issue a papal bull in 1268 commanding that there should be a distance of about 500m between the mendicant convents in any town.[40] Change of site by friaries should therefore be looked out for in British towns; unlike the other orders, the friars needed the market place to perform their spiritual functions.

The friars were determined to preach to the largest audiences possible, and this directed their choice of locality for their church (a populated town) and the development of their church architecture. Sometimes the cloistral plan would be arranged so that the church, the principal focus of the complex for townspeople, was near the principal approach road; the cloister and other friary buildings would be placed on the other, private side. At Chester work of 1976–83 has elucidated for the first time the layout of the Franciscan and Dominican friaries, which lay on the west side of town up against the city wall. This meant that the public buildings, normally at the west end of the complexes, were not on the town side. The Dominicans solved this by constructing a walled alley from the town, on the east, which went past the more private areas and buildings of the friary and along the side of the church to the public spaces at its west end.[41]

Usually, by the fifteenth century, the church was a large aisled nave without appendages such as private chapels or large transepts. This style, in which the church is a vast rectangular hall, may have started with the London Greyfriars in 1306; it resembles not only the large friaries in towns like Florence, but their contemporaries, the loggias and meeting places for merchants in Italy and Spain. The friary church was divided into two unequal parts by a solid screen

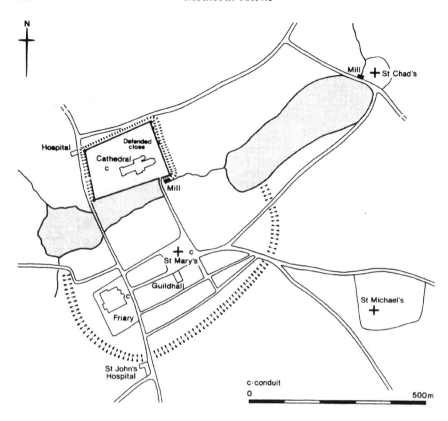

Figure 6.18 Lichfield at the end of the Middle Ages, showing the sites of both the cathedral in its defended precinct and the friary, near the market place and next to the town conduit (Gould 1976).

or pulpitum; the choir was kept within the bays east of this screen, to allow the maximum space for movement around the church. Between the choir and nave, supported by two parallel walls or arches which crossed the church, was usually a steeple or belfry containing one large bell. The architectural emphasis of these walls and the adjacent pulpitum formed a natural break in the building for through-traffic and, later, partial demolition after the Dissolution. When some great friary churches were allowed to survive as parish churches, it was only by cutting them in half along this line and reusing one half, usually the eastern with its greater religious resonances and meaning.

The domestic buildings of friaries also had their own character. Often the cloister was moved slightly away from the body of the church, so that a lane or alley ran between. The position and size of the cloister is much more a commentary on the success of the friars in obtaining land to build on than upon any planning instructions they were working to. The walks of the cloister were often built over with rooms above: not only the dormitory and special rooms such as a library, but also sometimes the refectory. Archaeological excavation, concerned often with foundations and below-ground evidence, may not detect these first-floor functions and is likely to be most fruitful when investigating the drains and trying to identify the kitchen. We should also keep an eye out for the industries or crafts which the friars may have practised to keep themselves; and several friaries built wharves into their adjacent rivers.

Friaries in many towns have been examined in recent decades: the following is a brief survey of some of the results. In 1974 excavations on the site of a brewery on the outskirts of medieval Guildford uncovered the cloister and ranges on its north and east sides, the choir and most of the nave of the church on the south side, and part of the churchyard to the south of the church of the Dominican friary.[42] With the exception of a chantry chapel and an extension to the chancel, all these buildings were laid out in a single operation. The nave had a single additional aisle from the beginning, but apparently never needed to expand further (as was the case in some other friaries, e.g. at Beverley). The area beneath the choir stalls produced a large number of bronze objects: jettons, pins, strap ends, book studs and lace tags. The excavators suggested that these were the debris of bored friars, fiddling with anything to hand and often losing it.

Further information from friaries concerns the pattern of burials within them. At Guildford, only the nave of the church and the cemetery to the south were investigated. The 28 burials in the nave included wooden coffins, and one case of a lead coffin with the body of a young woman. Outside in the cemetery, coffins were less frequent. The few skeletons found in the cloister walks were male and almost certainly friars. In the graveyard south of the church a boundary wall may have divided a main cemetery of the friars, to the east, from lay burials (which included women). Female burials were also found in the nave, where burials were generally of richer patrons. Here, however, areas kept clear of burials included the altar and the area around the probable site of the pulpit. At the Dominican friary in Chester, excavation found that there was clear zoning in the single north aisle: towards the west end, burials intercut each other and were more numerous; towards the east end, there was careful planning, fewer graves, and possibly a greater use of memorial stones. Of the twelve burials at the east end, the sex of six could be certainly suggested; and only one of these was female. Burials at the Dominican friary at Oxford seem to have divided into friars in the cloister walks, lay people (probably dignitaries, or at least rich tradespeople) in church, and a main cemetery north of the church. Several children were buried at the west end of the chapter house. At the Franciscan friary at Hartlepool, more people were buried in the church than outside to the north, and there was more evidence of coffins inside the church than outside, a probable distinction of status.[43]

The development of a friary site over time is the main point of interest at Leicester. The site of the Austin Friars, immediately outside the west gate of the town (Fig. 6.19), was well-preserved due to its being a garden in the eighteenth century and the site of a railway station in the nineteenth. The friary also lay on an island in the river Soar, which ensured the exceptional survival of material which illustrates the lifestyles and some aspects of the economy of the friars.[44]

The excavation site lay to the north of the friary church, and ten phases of activity charted the development through time and expansion across the site of its associated religious buildings (Fig. 6.20). Pottery wasters suggest that the

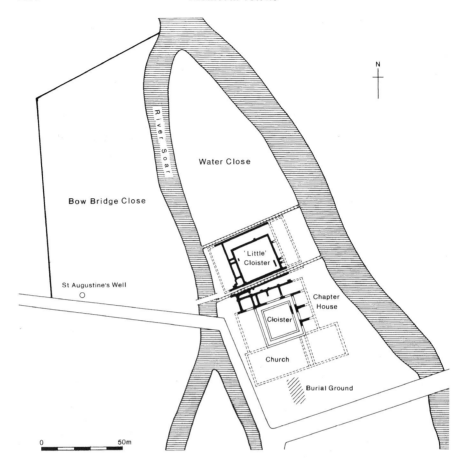

Figure 6.19 Overall plan of the Austin Friars, Leicester, on its island in the River Soar (Mellor and Pearce 1981).

pre-friary land use may have included kilns. The friars arrived in phase 2 (1254 on documentary grounds), dug a drainage ditch to limit the site and put up two buildings, one of timber. They made and repaired shoes; refuse in the ditch included wooden table vessels and fragments of clothing. A high number of cereal pests in samples from the ditch sediment suggests grain stores nearby, and household pests appeared for the first time.

Finds and environmental material from the site contribute to a detailed impression of life in the friary. Much of the building materials had been removed, but in the destruction levels were many pieces of painted window glass; the buildings were roofed in clay tiles and local Swithland stone slates, the ridges adorned with ornamented pottery crests. Floor tiles were laid in the south cloister alley, shown by loose fragments and tile impressions left in the mortar. Three sources were identified by X-ray fluorescence of the clay: from Nottingham, north-east Warwickshire and Northampton. The friars' meat diet was mainly cattle, sheep, pig, chicken, goose and duck; the pigs may have

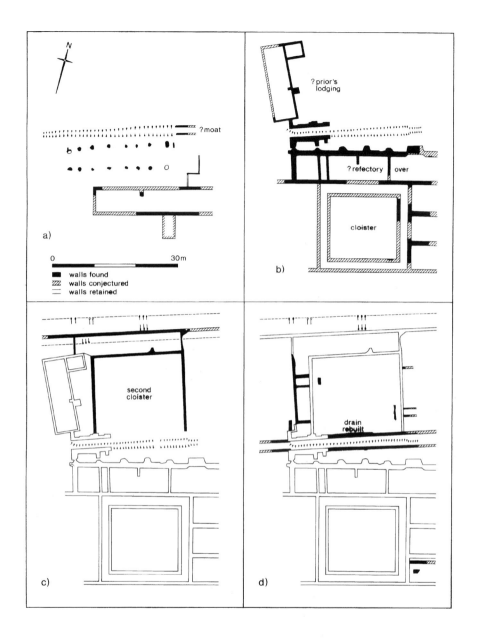

Figure 6.20 Successive period plans of excavated buildings north of the church at the Austin Friars, Leicester (Mellor and Pearce 1981): (a) phase 2 (late thirteenth century, after 1254), (b) phase 3 (early fourteenth century), (c) phases 4 and 5 (middle and later fourteenth century), (d) phases 6, 7 and 8 (fifteenth century). The first friary phase (2) includes a timber building. This is overtaken by a proper cloister in phase 3, with buildings of two floors indicated by buttresses; a period of expansion continued into phase 4, which was probably abruptly halted by the Black Death. By the end of phase 5 around 1400, however, this part of the friary had reached its grandest extent, with rich tile pavements comprising heraldic designs (of local families where identifiable). In 1372 the friars were hosts to a general chapter of their order.

been slaughtered on the site, as bones from most parts of the animal's body were recovered. Fallow deer were similarly introduced in one piece; they were the only wild species showing butchery marks. Eleven species of fish were eaten, of which nine were marine; they may have come in salted form. The insect assemblages reflected building on the site (wood-boring beetles), nearby grazing animals (dung beetles) and, after a flood sediment of the early sixteenth century in the drain, a complete absence of food pests. At its dissolution in 1538, the friary had only four inmates.

Friaries, as the particularly urban form of religious community in Britain, have much to contribute not only about an important facet of medieval religious life but also about many aspects of life in towns. Even when outside the walls, and especially when within, friaries were placed near major thoroughfares, and therefore routes of transportation may be glimpsed through their situations; like market buildings and gates, they may indicate the major axes of the town. Second, since friaries, unlike monastic orders, did not rely on a system of providing food from rural manors and granges in the possession of the house, but had to get their food where and when they could from the town itself, so friaries must have shared the town's sources of food supply; this has been demonstrated by analysis of animal bones from the Dominican priory or friary at Beverley.[45] Thus excavated evidence of diet will have an urban character, and the comparatively well-isolated assemblages possible on friary sites may stand as reference material for the usually more jumbled evidence on house sites in the town.

Hospitals

Besides its friaries, any reasonably vigorous town could expect to maintain three or four hospitals. Since the main enthusiasm for hospital foundation dates from the early twelfth century, study of the position of hospitals in the town can give clues as to the extent of built-up areas and lines of defences; though some hospitals were sited within towns, most were on the edges, and some, such as leper hospitals, were deliberately placed at some distance from the town. The majority of hospitals looked like the monastic infirmaries from which they were derived, with a wide, undivided hall; but some leper hospitals may have given their inmates individual cells in a single range, and by the fifteenth century the courtyard plan is found in hospitals as it was then becoming usual in academic and secular colleges and almshouses.[46]

One example published in detail is St Mary Spital, an Augustinian priory and hospital founded in 1197 outside Bishopsgate to the north-east of the City of London (Fig. 6.21). The hospital was destroyed at the Reformation, and its extensive area covered by streets, but a number of excavations have revealed much of the hospital's plan and its development.[47] The recorded parts date largely from after 1235, when the hospital was refounded and the original church was presumably demolished. The main new building at first combined both church and hospital; the church had a choir but no nave, and a four-bay northern arm which served as the hospital. This may have continued to the south to give a T-shape to the building, as at St John's Hospital, Canterbury. Traces of a foundation probably for a rood screen (forming the entrance to the

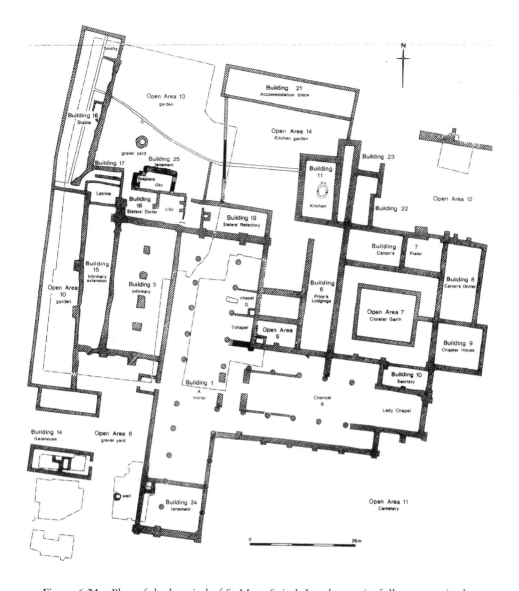

Figure 6.21 Plan of the hospital of St Mary Spital, London, at its fullest extent in the period 1400–1538 (Thomas *et al*. 1997). The walls in black are the only new features of this long period; virtually all the main buildings had been built some time before. Building 1 was the great T-shaped hospital building of 1235–80; Building 5 a new building of 1280–1320, built over one of the cemeteries. At this time also a courtyard of buildings forming the prior's house was added to the north-east (Buildings 6–9) and a sacristy added (Building 10). A gatehouse was built on Bishopsgate (Building 14). In a period of further expansion in 1320–50, Building 5 was extended (Building 15) and part of the street frontage developed (Building 16). In 1400–1538 smaller buildings were constructed on the margins, some as improved accommodation for the lay staff (Building 21). The hospital was surrendered in 1539, and by 1560 half the buildings had been demolished; the other half had become houses. This was the story of the Dissolution in every town: large imposing complexes vanished within a few years. The bigger the town, the more dramatic and unsettling it must have been.

choir) were found between two of the pillars. The floors of the church were of
mortar or clay, replaced many times during the lifetime of the building, and
there was no sign of floor tiles or their impressions (sometimes tile floors were
lifted in the medieval period, leaving impressions in their clay bedding layers).
An orderly cemetery was laid out between the church and Bishopsgate.

About 1280, however, a new infirmary block was built adjacent to the old
infirmary wing, over its cemetery. This new building was five bays long and
had an arcade down the middle; it was extended by half as much again to the
west in the 1320s. The old north wing probably reverted to being part of the
church, since burials were now made in it; a total of fifteen were recovered. To
the north lay stables and a drain; a latrine block and a long hall which may
have been a dormitory were added about 1350. North-east of the church lay
the thirteenth-century canons' cloister (i.e. not the lay sisters who functioned
as nurses) with further prestigious buildings on two sides, including the Prior's
Lodging, the canons' dorter, frater and chapter-house. The last two had fine
decorated tiled floors. In a garden west of the new infirmary, a sluice-pit
contained a large group of pottery and wooden vessels, shoes and seed evidence possibly of patients' food. The cemetery now lay to the south-east of the
infirmary, away from Bishopsgate; 102 skeletons were analysed. In this case
the study of human remains tells us more than the ailments or conditions of
individuals, or at least prompts further questions.

There were three groups of skeletons: the first, of 1235–80; the second, of
1280–1538; and a third small high-status group buried within the church of
the hospital, also of 1280–1538 (some fragments of tombs survived, and
names are known from documentary records). In the first group, a significant
portion were adolescents, evidence of the known specialism at this hospital
with orphans. There were also more men than women – why in a hospital?
One theory is that these were rootless migrants coming to London, but not
surviving long. The remains of skeletons buried in the church had the highest
level of dental disease, and were older; as one might expect from well-fed
prosperous citizens who wished for burial in chapels or near the altar in the
church. They also had the highest level of diffuse idiopathic skeletal hyper-
ostosis (DISH), a condition associated with a rich diet; about 20 per cent of the
skeletons, as opposed to a frequency of about 2–3 per cent in modern populations. This well-off group of persons had been less exposed to knocks and
skeletal traumas in their working lives than the other two groups who were
laid in the external cemeteries. Thus the study of human bones from St Mary
Spital is demonstrating how cemeteries in different parts of the complex show
differences which can be explained in terms of the groups of people who
patronized the hospital, both migrants (as it appears) and wealthy citizens.

Whereas the St Mary Spital project (which continues at the time of writing,
with study of several thousand more medieval skeletons) shows a hospital on
the edge of the capital, predictably extensive and architecturally important, a
contrasting collection of findings comes from the excavation of a small and
more typical hospital, St Bartholomew's in Bristol. Here a late twelfth-century
stone house was adapted as the main hospital building; a column from it
survives. Founded around 1232–4, St Bartholomew's was one of several
hospitals serving medieval Bristol; in 1445 it expanded to provide a home for
retired mariners. The gradual adaptation of the medieval buildings from the

twelfth to the nineteenth centuries was recorded in the masonry and below ground.[48] More archaeological studies of smaller hospitals are required; and they should be of the whole complex, as in this Bristol case, and not only part of a cemetery or whatever fragment of the hospital site became available for investigation. Because hospital studies (such as those of leper houses) rely for their effectiveness on study of human skeletons, it is important to excavate, if we can, more than a sample of the graveyard which is usually dictated by modern circumstances.

Behind their high walls, the grander religious houses were little towns in microcosm. Each house had a church usually larger than the local parish church, a centre for official administration with architecture designed for ceremony (the chapter house), and buildings for eating, sleeping, working and storage; many of them of stone, and with drains that worked. When civic leaders searched for models to improve the town, its standard of construction and perhaps the decoration and internal arrangement of its major buildings, they must have looked at the monasteries and friaries in their towns. Further, it is important to compare building styles, technologies and periods of construction between a town's religious houses and other forms of building which may have survived better, to avoid having a partial picture. The Rows of Chester are important testimony to the thirteenth-century prosperity of the town as part of the royal campaigns into Wales, but they were part of a building boom which included three now vanished friaries. It is one of archaeology's roles to restore this balance.

Conclusion

Whether it is a large church such as one in a monastery, or the smallest parish church, there is much for archaeology to bring to the study of medieval religion. Here the documents are comparatively weak; very few churches have an accurate or reasonably full history of their building works in the medieval period.

When we look at the specialized character and functions of the church building, whether a parish church or the centre of a religious community, four topics are noteworthy: how churches grew; how the building and its spaces helped to make the liturgy or services work; what the fittings and decoration tell us about patronage and the way people used churches as a form of expression for themselves and their families; and how churches reflected the resources, aspirations and failures of their locality. In these ways ceremony, ritual and forms of social organization fostered by the church expressed social structure and urban identity. When the Reformation swept much of this away, towns had to find a new symbolic vocabulary to represent themselves to the world, and to themselves.[49]

It is therefore important that once the outline of a church's development is known, its secular surroundings and any previous structures on the site should be analysed; and the same, on a larger scale, goes for the buildings comprising a monastery, friary or hospital. Documents are remarkably uninformative about the disposition of monastic buildings in the majority of cases, and excavation must usually provide the plan and its internal details. Only then

Figure 6.22 The Old Jewish Cemetery in Prague, established shortly after 1400. An interesting recording challenge for the archaeologist.

Figure 6.23 Façade of the Franciscan monastery of San Juan de los Reyes, Toledo (Spain), built after 1476. On it are displayed fetters and chains from Christian slaves recently released from the Muslims in Andalucia. Here religion and state propaganda are joined in a common interest at the shifting and uncertain border of the Christian world.

can we approach larger questions such as whether churches or monastic houses competed with other functions, or with each other, for space, custom or prestige in towns; or to what extent a monastery or a large parish church was the dominant factor in town life. And in the larger towns, it may be that we can learn about the spending power and taste of the wealthy burgesses as much from their patronage of religious art and architecture (especially their tombs) as from the design and decoration of their own homes. Burial in parish churches, hospitals, friaries and indeed all sorts of religious houses, whether inside or outside in a cemetery, was demonstrably ordered by the status of the deceased.

This chapter has not journeyed very far into continental Europe. We end with two illustrations to draw attention to research topics not touched upon. There were other religions besides Christianity in medieval Europe: notably Judaism in all European countries (Fig. 6.22) and Islam in a large part of Spain (Fig. 6.23).[50] These faiths are important for their influences on the mainstream Christian culture, through juxtaposition, antagonism and occasional acknowledgement. The border between Christian and Islamic ideas, expressed in architecture, artefacts and attitudes, helped to define Europe as a religious and therefore cultural and political entity.

7 *The environment of medieval towns*

...mental archaeology is a branch of the subject which includes specialists in flora, fauna, microbiology, dendrochronology and human bone studies.[1] The urban archaeologist has many questions of these specialists: the
appearance of the town site in its pre-urban phase (i.e. the pre-town landscape), the disruption to the environment caused by the initial settlement,
information on the town's phases of expansion which is provided by preserved
organic remains, the function and social status of parts of the town at various
periods, and specific aspects of use of individual buildings.[2] Here, besides
giving some answers to these questions, we review four topics: (1) the influence on medieval town life of physical factors (climatic regimes, air and water
pollution); (2) man's interaction with the environment (plants, insects, and
wild animals; woodland management, the effect of towns on their hinterlands); (3) biological factors affecting townspeople (dietary changes, infesta-
tions, viruses and disease); and (4) environmental consequences of social
practices within towns (overcrowding and other effects of urban living).

Physical factors

The high concentration of human activity and density of population in towns
have an effect on their climate and atmosphere.[3] The climate of the medieval
period in Britain can be reconstructed to some extent from documents (the
earliest weather diary describes the weather in Oxford in 1269–70), tree rings
and pollen assemblages. From this emerges a picture of general warming to
around 1000 and then cooling throughout the medieval and post-medieval
period. Around 1200, however, winters became noticeably milder than before.
During the thirteenth century there was a period of little rainfall, but the
fifteenth and sixteenth centuries were up to twice as wet, and there were
periods of extreme storminess at the end of each century. This increased
rainfall seems to have been one cause of a change in rural house construction,
from structures laid on the ground-surface to those surrounded by deep
external gullies under the eaves, drains on the inside of walls and construction
of some houses on platforms.[4] A discussion of the role of climate in English
medieval history concludes that long-term climatic changes had a limited
effect on the standards of living of the inhabitants of lowland England, though
settlements and arable land were given up in uplands due to increased rainfall
and the gradual drop in temperature.[5] The country lost thousands of acres of
land, but because of a drop in population, the land was no longer needed. In
contrast, short-term weather fluctuations had profound effects: poor harvests
meant widespread starvation, surges in grain prices and the danger of urban
unrest. The archaeological contribution to this debate is hesitant and self-

critical, as archaeologists are 'merely noting environmental and economic coincidences, and we need to develop our enquiry to see if they are related'.[6]

Further topics of interest are differences between town and countryside in temperature, wind velocity and visibility; and air and water pollution. We know that present-day conurbations such as Manhattan or the City of London generate their own micro-climate, largely because of the intense generation of heat (now central heating, but formerly thousands of fires and ovens). 'Heat islands' of this kind in late medieval Britain might have reached as much as 4°C above their surroundings. On the other hand, life in towns may have been less comfortable when it rained. Since stone and brick buildings and gravelled streets are more waterproof than rural landscapes, precipitation will run off quicker; and thus towns which had not developed wide storm drains would be flooded in storms. This flooding would contaminate drinking water, as we know from documentary references.

There are differences between town and countryside today in the ferocity of winds and visibility in the atmosphere; it is difficult to suggest how research on such differences might take us back into the pre-modern period. There are however some potential lines of enquiry concerning air pollution. Concern was expressed about the possible damage to health of coal smoke as soon as it became widely used in the thirteenth century. The smoke concentration over the City of London in the medieval period, for instance, must have been far higher than rural levels. During the post-medieval period of industrialization there was evident concern about the effect of fog and smoke in aggravating respiratory conditions, diminishing sunlight, damaging plants, buildings and clothing, but study of these factors has yet to be extended back into the medieval period. Worthwhile examinations might take place of corroded metal and stonework, and dust deposits, to give information on the nature of urban air pollution in the past.

A study of sediments on two sites at the junction of the Fleet River with the Thames, along the west side of the medieval City of London, has suggested correlations between events in the sedimentary record and pollution and climatic 'events' recorded in medieval documents.[7] Beneath 6m of man-made deposits, up to 4m of prehistoric and historic (pre-fifteenth century) sediments of the Fleet were sampled. From medieval sediments came many species of diatoms (microscopic unicellular algae), small molluscs, sponges, foraminifera and ostracods (a type of crustacean). The 140 species of aquatic organisms were a mixture of freshwater, brackish (salty) water and marine species. Two successive layers of sediment, both of fourteenth-century date, produced significantly different assemblages, suggesting something happened in between. The upper layer contained a higher proportion of a diatom associated with polluted water; at the same time molluscs, ostracods and mussels, which prefer clean water and were abundant in the lower stratum, suddenly disappeared from the upper. This evidence suggests increasing pollution of the Fleet, at the time when Edward III was repeatedly demanding that the mayor of London clean up the area. This study further claims that some of the brackish water microfossil organisms may have been deposited by tidal surges during periods of reduced freshwater flow, which are also mentioned in documents.

Molluscs can also indicate the ancient environment, particularly on virgin sites where the influence of settlement is still to be felt. At Oxford, the

Blackfriars covered the ground surface with a dump of clay, perhaps to raise their intended friary buildings above the adjacent river level. The thirteenth-century surface they buried contained aquatic molluscs, suggesting seasonally flooded grassland. Parallel exercises have studied the environmental impact of new towns in the Roman period, for instance the first-century development of Roman London.[8] There is therefore the potential within medieval urban archaeology, as with the archaeology of other urban periods, to study both the history of pollution and the effects of urban growth on the landscape by examination of diatoms, molluscs, plants and insects.

People and their environment: flora, insects and wild vertebrate fauna

Botanical evidence, assemblages of insects and of wild vertebrate fauna in towns (specifically small mammals like voles and mice) are grouped for consideration here because they reflect both the influence of the natural world on human habitats and alterations by people to their natural surroundings. Are such assemblages indications of natural habitats, or of human presence? The problem is, they could be either. Excavated plant remains (mostly seeds) or pollen may indicate what was growing nearby; or they may suggest cultivation or industrial uses. Similarly, insect assemblages may suggest natural happenings or the decomposition of human rubbish, sometimes of a particular character which indicates that the deposit is derived from trade or industrial waste. Bones of small rodents and other wild animals and birds may indicate, by their presence, the character of the immediate surroundings of the deposits.

The rich botanical results from waterlogged sites in Winchester and Southampton, for instance, have illustrated this fundamental problem.[9] These deposits preserve a wide range of seeds, but in many cases they could be from either human or natural sources, and could reflect long periods of residuality; where conditions are favourable, seeds can lie in the ground for hundreds of years without alteration. In addition, peculiar circumstances ensure the survival of certain restricted kinds of seeds: carbonized (burnt) material is often mainly cereals, chaff or associated weeds which have been exposed to fires, and mineralized material is also found in human faeces, reflecting those plants which have been eaten. Over five thousand samples from Winchester of the tenth to fifteenth centuries were examined, but the pessimistic conclusion was that detailed and reliable statistical analysis on pits of a particular century (i.e. to chart change) could not yet be undertaken. Current work in London suggests that there were no real changes in plant use during the medieval period, but emphatic differences between the medieval and the Roman periods. We have not yet said why this was so.

To make general statements, plants can be grouped by habitat or association, so that observed variations are between groups rather than individual species. Two groupings used by environmental archaeologists studying material from towns are presented here, from Reading and London (Fig. 7.1); in each case the preferred range of habitats of the plants is the basis of the grouping, but in the London case three categories deal with uses, and a further category is of cultivated plants. It is an open question, in our view, as to which classification is better.[10]

Reading		London	
A	arable	A	weeds of cultivated land
B	riverbanks	B	ruderals, weeds of waste places
C	cultivated land	C	plants of woodland and hedgerows
D	disturbed, wasteland	D	open environments, grassland
E	heath	E	plants of damp, wet conditions
G	grassland	F	edible plants
H	hedgerows	G	medicinal and poisonous plants
M	marsh	H	plants with commercial or industrial use
P	ponds, ditches (still water)	I	cultivated plants
R	rivers, streams (running water)		
S	scrub, woodland		
W	waysides		

Figure 7.1 Two classification systems for excavated plant remains, used in Reading and London (Wessex Archaeology and Museum of London).

The Reading classification is looked into below when we use excavations in that town as a detailed example of environmental analysis. Here we can see how the London classification works, with examples from the 1991 study of 106 samples from 60 tenth- to thirteenth-century features (pits, occupation layers, and hearths or ovens) on central sites.[11] Weeds of cultivated land are usually brought into towns with the cultivated plants with which they were grown. In this group of pits and other features, as in other towns, they included corncockle and fool's parsley. Plants of waste places and disturbed ground are probably the most numerous on urban sites, since they reproduce quickly: such species as goosefoot, nettle, thistle and dandelion. Plants of woods, scrub and hedgerows were not well represented in the London pits, except as edible fruit and nuts, which are better discussed as a separate group. Inedible plants in this category, such as stitchworts and chickweeds, may have been imported casually by animals or people. Grassland plants may also have been brought in accidentally. Some, such as sedges, were probably imported for flooring or thatching material, and seeds of the grass family (along with other species) may have been from hay. Plants of damp or marshy land included rushes and other plants growing on the banks of ditches or streams; they were also used for roofing or flooring. Edible wild plants included blackberry and raspberry. Edible woodland plants included wild strawberry, sloe and hazelnut; apples may have come from hedgerows or managed orchards, along with pears. Medicinal plants included opium poppy, which contains strong alkaloids, and henbane, which is a sedative; many other wild plants had some kind of medicinal property, if herbals and folklore are to be believed. Wild plants with other economic uses included elderberries which could be used in tanning; and weld, which produces a yellow dye but is also a common weed. At present, it seems that seeds of wild plants with uses in medicine, as food, and in industry rarely occur in large enough concentrations

Figure 7.2 Part of a large deposit of hop seeds excavated on the south bank of the Thames in Southwark. When seeds are found in large quantities, they may be for industrial uses, in this case brewing (Museum of London).

to justify interpretation as anything but weeds. Cultivated plants included carbonized peas, beans and cereals, together with cherries, fennel, grapes and figs. From the fifteenth century, hops were imported in great quantities for the brewing industry (Fig. 7.2).

The earliest appearance of new food plants or exotic fruits in documents can be compared with their earliest appearance in the archaeological record; this is one of the current approaches.[12] Imports from other countries in Europe are likely to have been a significant part of the diet and therefore of the archaeological debris. By the end of the medieval period, the level of imports in the larger centres was high. To take the most extreme case, import duties in 1480–1 in London were levied on ships coming from the Low Countries and Northern Spain, carrying almonds, aloes, aniseed, apples, barley, bay-tree (laurel) berries, cinnamon, cloves, dates, figs, flour, garlic, ginger, hemp, hops, mistletoe, mustard seed, nutmeg, nuts, oats, olives, onion seed, oranges, peas, pine-cone kernels, pomegranates, prunes, raisins, saffron, teazles, walnuts and wheat.[13] All these commodities would have spread through the capital to smaller towns; and to a lesser extent they were imported through many other ports. It is ultimately more important to know how people on an excavated site were using spices, cereals and fruit, rather than to know whether the produce was native or foreign. Generally, also, the range of seeds from archaeological sites is much smaller than that mentioned in documents.

Two main types of pollen spectra (graphs showing the variety of pollen in particular sample deposits) can be distinguished. The first is rich in pollen of grasses and Compositae (e.g. daisies, dandelions, marigolds), probably the result of natural transport and deposition. The second type is rich in pollen of cereals and sometimes of Ericales (heather, ling, heaths), and the deposits producing it are often well-fills or buried soils; thus it is probably a sign of human activity.

There are a number of caveats which have to be made. Some plants produce far more pollen than others, and clearly wind-pollinated plants such as dock, sorrel and nettle will produce higher amounts of far-travelling pollen when compared with insect-pollinated plants such as bedstraw or the herb avens. The pollen in any town deposit will be a mixture of 'regional pollen' from outside the town, a 'local pollen' component from features such as moats and ditches, and a third human component (Fig. 7.3).

Certain types of feature seem to have distinctive pollen spectra.[14] Ponds, wells and ditches have spectra with abundant evidence of grass and other plants which together derived from local sources. A second distinctive spectrum is characterized by a preponderance of cereal pollen, and one possibility is that this represents straw or chaff. This was the character of samples from a ditch at Bolebridge Street, Tamworth; a ditch at Nantwich; and a pond or dump in York. A third type has a large amount of Gramineae (grasses) pollen, together with signs that the pollen was dispersed by humans, and probably represents hay somewhere nearby (as from a sample from a barrel-latrine in Worcester). Fourthly, pollen of heather and ling is occasionally found in urban samples, and presumably reflects the introduction of cartloads of such plants for roofing or flooring, as also indicated by seed remains. Heather seeds inside pottery kilns at Kingston-upon-Thames (Surrey) must have been from fuel or kindling.[15]

As mentioned in Chapter 4, the plant product most used in the medieval town was, of course, wood; especially for buildings and constructions of all kinds, artefacts, and for firewood. By the thirteenth century, in England, woodlands were a managed resource.[16] Man expected to live off renewable resources, and woods were managed on this basis. Felling at set intervals and programmes of coppicing (an ancient practice, as demonstrated by archaeological research) ensured vigorous regrowth.

Oak was the most widespread timber used in buildings and other wooden constructions such as waterfront revetments; it was used for structural timbers, laths and boards. Oak for royal contracts, such as the roof of Westminster Hall, came from royal woods in Hampshire, Berkshire, Surrey and Hertfordshire; the leaders of the Church could also rely on royal or noble assistance for large structural timbers. Religious houses could use wood sent as part of the rents of their manors.

Elm was used for piles in waterfront structure, but was also supplied in the form of boards. It was used for doors and window shutters, privies, floors and for benches, dressers and shelving. Even in London, the sources of elm were local: the Bridge Account Rolls for the brief period 1381–97 mention eighteen specified places in Essex, Kent, Middlesex and Surrey as sources. Ash was used for handles of tools, furniture, the uprights in wattling and as planks in certain situations, especially pastry boards (the long table attached to the wall in many kitchens). Beech was used for laths, occasionally for shelving, and sometimes used for scaffolding or other forms of poles, as was alder (also used

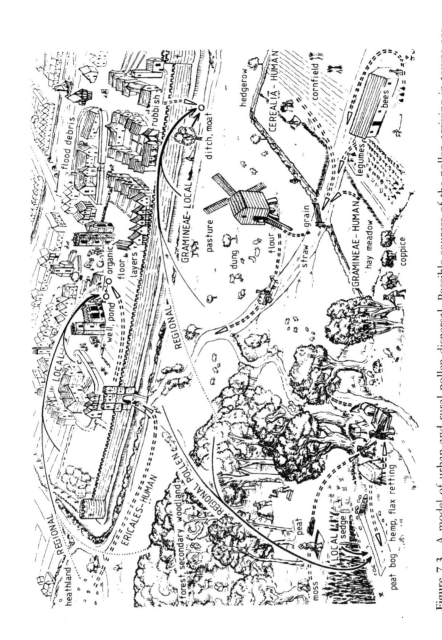

Figure 7.3   A model of urban and rural pollen dispersal. Possible sources of the pollen arriving in towns are shown by single lines; the pollen dispersal through human action, by double dashed lines (Greig 1982).

Figure 7.4 A twelfth-century rubbish pit lined with wicker, Milk Street, London (Museum of London).

widely for piles), fir and willow. Wicker (horizontal and vertical rods woven together) was used chiefly for fences, weirs and to line rubbish pits (Fig. 7.4).

Demand for timber from towns had a number of consequences. Firstly, areas around at least the major towns were denuded of a large part of their tree cover; as we have seen, most of the major species could be used either in construction or as fuel. This continuous and, in some towns, increasing need for timber led to the import of some species from mainland Europe, especially the Baltic, in the thirteenth century. Secondly, it is probably the case (though more work is needed on this to fill out the picture) that the possibility of finding larger trees for construction work became rarer as the period progressed, and therefore that the timbers provided for building work in towns gradually became smaller. This seems to be the case in London, where building contracts specify the sizes of many of the principal timbers. A range of documents suggest a general diminution in timber sizes between the middle of the fourteenth century and the latest, in 1602. This can also be seen in the archaeological record: because Baltic oak came from primary forest, it produced fast-growing tall straight trunks which were ideal for beams and boards.

Study of insects in the medieval period does not seem to have advanced as much as that for the Roman and Saxon or Viking periods.[17] In York, where much work has been undertaken, it is suggested that changes occur in typical beetle faunas through the medieval period; domestic species like furniture beetle, spider beetles and species which graze moulds becoming gradually more numerous than those found in rotting matter, and grain pests, common in the Roman period, appeared again in the late medieval centuries. Study of insect and small mammal assemblages is very site-specific, but can on occasion make suggestions as to the ebb and flow of the boundaries of settlement. The onset of urbanization on the west fringe of medieval Oxford, for instance, was revealed by insect assemblages. Samples from mid- to late-twelfth-century ditches at the Hamel contained insect faunas characteristic of damp grassland. Ditches and pits of the next two human generations contained urban faunas; the proportion of outdoor insect species fell. The insects had habitats such as rotten thatch, damp corners of buildings or decaying straw and animal remains. One pit contained many puparia of a bloodsucking sheep parasite, suggesting the washing of sheep or carding of wool on the site. It is also important to understand, however, that there are no special 'urban' species of insect, but rather insects which favour artificial (man-made) conditions in either town or countryside, and these can be classified by their preferences into indoor or outdoor species (Fig. 7.5).[18]

A detailed understanding of the appearance of some urban areas, especially open spaces, can be obtained by studying small mammals, such as mice, rats and voles. Principles developed from the study of animals on islands have been applied to medieval urban ecosystems, proposing that large gardens, church-yards and waste ground can be seen as 'habitat islands' or refuges for small mammals, separated by areas of dense human occupation without much greenery.[19] A greater range of species might be expected in open spaces near the edges of a town than in the centre, but this has still to be tested. Certainly analysis of a late-fifteenth-century well at Greyfriars, London, and fourteenth- to fifteenth-century pits in the collegiate grounds at Beverley (Lurk Lane), both peripheral sites in their towns, showed a variety of species: on both sites, rats, mice, fieldmice, field (short-tailed) voles, bank voles, pygmy shrews, water shrews and weasels; in addition, at London, yellow-necked mice and hedge-hogs, and at Beverley, moles. These habitat islands might therefore furnish much useful information on the history of small faunal species and their frequency in towns. But further, from their preferred microhabitats, we can reconstruct the immediate surroundings of the deposits in which their bones were found. Armitage and West suggested, from the range of small animals which had been trapped or had fallen into the disused well of the London Greyfriars, that the garden contained thick grass, scrub, water-filled ditches, possibly hedges and orchard; but all contributing to an impression of 'an overgrown and bankrupt garden'.[20]

It is currently thought that the more dramatic aspects of small animals, and in particular their role in the transmission of disease, would be difficult to recognize in archaeological bone assemblages.[21] House mice and rats form a significant pest of Roman settlements and are clearly transported by man. Although the black rat was introduced in the Roman period, extensive sieving at York of Anglian and later levels suggests that the species was not present again in this town until late in the Anglo-Scandinavian period; that is, it was re-introduced, perhaps reflecting trade with Europe or the Mediterranean. Since these small mammals are only hosts of the vector of many diseases, and their presence is esssential for some diseases such as the Black Death (in

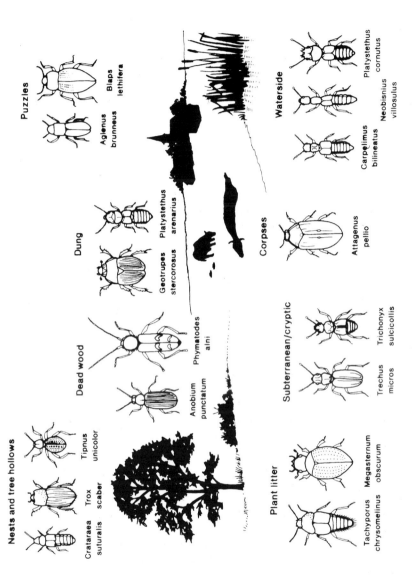

Figure 7.5 Some urban insects and their habitat preferences (after a drawing by Mike Hill in Hall and Kenward 1994).

epidemic proportions), their actual presence is not in itself an indicator of disease, although it may reflect hygiene levels and refuse disposal practices.

All kinds of site may produce evidence of seeds, use of timber, insects and small animals. But to advance, the discipline needs groups or assemblages which are tightly dated, low in residuality, exceptionally well preserved, large in sample size, and not too far removed from their original point of use or deposition (in other words, the 'more secondary' the deposits become, through being churned about or physically transported, the less reliable will be our conclusions).

Work in London and other medieval ports shows that waterfront sites often have all the required merits (though there has to be an assumption that the waterfront dumps were 'fresh' and therefore not removed too far from their primary state). Many deposits on each large site are dated accurately by dendrochronology of timber structures; if there are stone river walls, naturally, the tightness of dating is far less exact. Large samples from well-defined deposits should be bulk-sieved for bone, shell, pottery and other finds on a mesh of 2–4 mm; the resulting domestic animal and fish bone assemblages need to be sufficiently large for statistical comparisons. If several waterfront sites are excavated, we can document the chronology of introductions of imported foodstuffs as well as new types of pottery or other artefacts; though new species rarely appear in the archaeological record until some time after their first documented appearance, and it is more likely that the archaeological specimens are from the period when the species' use becomes more common. Further, both finds and environmental analysis in London have demonstrated that the dumps used to reclaim land reveal differences between sites which may reflect either nearby rubbish heaps from different social groups (royal households, poorer ones) or variations in local activities (including trade waste). The dumps may have incorporated rubbish from the tenement which was itself being extended, thus forming a reservoir of information to match the structural remains. Even better evidence comes when a building, often of timber, survives exceptionally well in the riverside deposits, and environmental analysis can make a contribution to the study of its function and appearance.

The excavation of a riverside area in Reading provides an example of a project where a range of techniques of environmental archaeology were used. This will illustrate both the merits and limitations of typical medieval material.[22] Reading grew around the River Kennet near its confluence with the Thames; its main centre was the Abbey, founded in 1121. The town developed in an area crossed by streams, which provided wharfage and water power, but also brought problems of flooding. Between 1979 and 1986 a number of excavations took place on the east side of the town, south of the abbey and on part of the abbey precinct along the waterfront. The excavations found timber and stone wharves along the Kennet and a stream called Holy Brook which functioned with the abbey mill, as well as buildings. The main site, Abbey Wharf, included waterfront reclamation of the kind already described in Chapter 2, in several phases from the early thirteenth century to the early nineteenth century.

Pollen samples were taken from a context of the late thirteenth century which was part of a reclamation dump; it may therefore have included some silt from the foreshore of the adjacent river, which would be earlier. There was a diverse range of pollen from trees, shrubs, aquatic and marsh plants, cereals and weeds. It is difficult to elucidate their possible sources. A large amount of cereal pollen perhaps derived from crop processing at the nearby abbey mill, and willows may have grown on the river bank.

The plant remains were far more informative. One hundred and forty-seven species were identified from the four excavations. They were classified as in Fig. 7.1 above. The flora of the river channels, the adjacent open areas and the grassland could be largely reconstructed. Hay meadows could be suggested from the presence of certain plants which favour such environments. More weeds associated with cereals were found in the period when the abbey flourished. 'More exotic' foods such as grapes, walnuts and figs, taken here to be high-status foods, were found in the abbey period. During this time the percentage of wasteground weeds dropped. Some seeds of hemp, flax and hops were found, but not enough to indicate that they were used on an industrial scale. A botanical view of the abbey and its gardens begins to emerge (Fig. 7.6).

On this group of sites the molluscs were also examined: oysters, mussels, whelks and cockles. These shellfish were consumed as food; the oysters were common from the early fourteenth century. The source of the oysters can be suggested from the prevalence of an infestation caused by a marine worm, *Polydora ciliata*, which is usually found on the east coast of England, from Suffolk to Kent. This was also the likely source of several whelks. Thus we can suggest that the monks of Reading had their shellfish brought in, perhaps by boat up the Thames and Kennet, from the coast.

Several wider conclusions arising out the environmental evidence were put forward in the Reading study. A period of increased deposition of silt in these non-tidal river channels partly corresponds with evidence for increased rainfall in England generally in the period 1150–1300. This would have necessitated the riverside revetments then constructed to control floods; one consequence of structures on an upstream site may have been to increase flooding immediately downstream. This reorganization of the abbey margin included mills and perhaps fish-ponds; this was a consequence of the need to control the floods as well as the developing structuring of the abbey facilities.

Beyond the boundaries of the town, natural or man-made, lay the countryside. One area of discussion between environmental archaeologists and economic historians should be that of the evidence from each quarter of the impact of a town on its hinterland, particularly on the conduct of agriculture. Archaeologists find seeds in towns and can study medieval farms; economic historians propose models for the growing and marketing of agricultural produce, particularly the staple foods of wheat, oats, rye and barley. Work on the grain supply of medieval London by historians, for instance, shows that an economic model suggested generally by J. T. von Thünen in the nineteenth century is broadly applicable to the supply of London around 1300. By studying the extent of London's grain provisioning zone and London's impact on the spatial pattern of grain production, the study was able to propose that the supply area normally extended to include market towns up to twenty miles away when only land transport was used, but up to sixty miles away when water transport could be used. Because grain production was influenced by

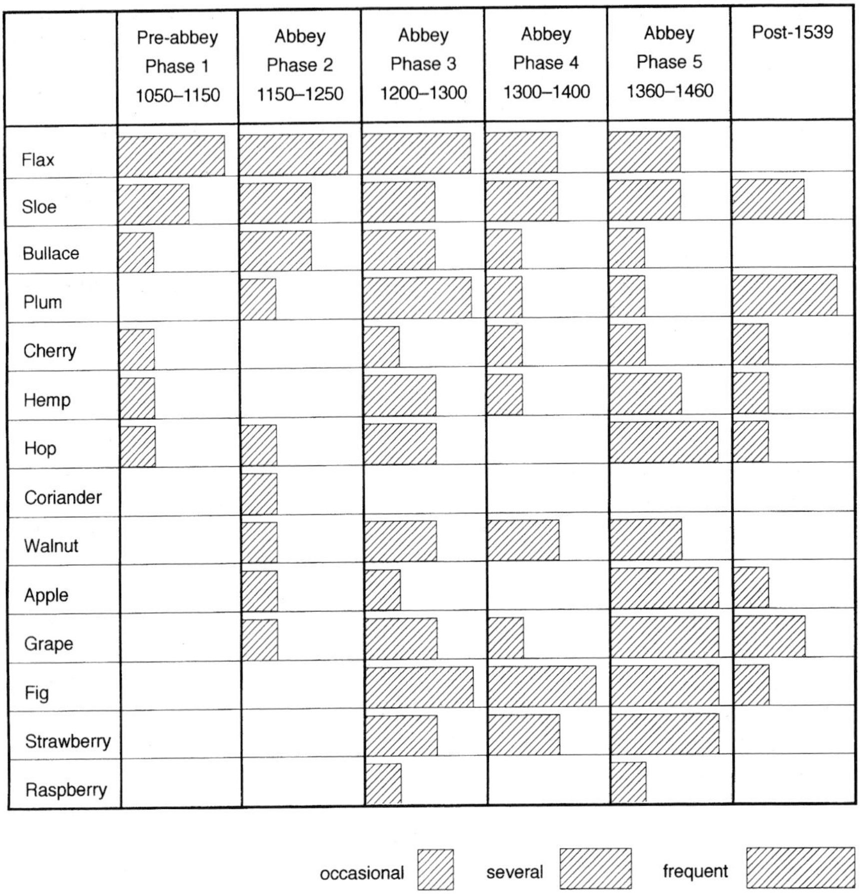

	Pre-abbey Phase 1 1050–1150	Abbey Phase 2 1150–1250	Abbey Phase 3 1200–1300	Abbey Phase 4 1300–1400	Abbey Phase 5 1360–1460	Post-1539
Flax	frequent	frequent	frequent	several	several	
Sloe	several	frequent	several	several	several	several
Bullace	occasional	several			occasional	
Plum		several	frequent	several		frequent
Cherry	occasional		occasional	several	several	several
Hemp	occasional		several	occasional	several	several
Hop	occasional	occasional			frequent	several
Coriander		several				
Walnut		several	frequent	several	frequent	
Apple		several	occasional		frequent	several
Grape		several	frequent	frequent	frequent	
Fig			frequent	frequent	frequent	several
Strawberry			several	several	frequent	
Raspberry			occasional		occasional	

occasional   several   frequent

Figure 7.6 Plants of 'economic use' from Reading waterfront sites (Carruthers 1997). The 'abbey period' is signified by an increase in species, mostly for food.

market demand, a series of concentric zones of land use, as proposed for an ideal town by von Thünen, could be seen, though the type of soil was also a factor. Oats, the cheapest of the grains, and much used for feeding horses, were grown near the capital. Rye, rye mixtures and barley were grown further out; and wheat-growing areas were even more distant.[23] If archaeological study could make a contribution to this, then it would be engaging in economic history, not just the elucidation of the medieval landscape.

Biological factors: diet

As the previous discussion has shown, the influences at work on the provision of foodstuffs in towns are several and intertwined. When towns are relatively small and depend for their food supplies on the adjacent land, the diet of townspeople and rural food-producers are very similar. Urbanization, however, moves towards abolishing the seasons, for town authorities try to store grain and other basic foodstuffs to offset seasonal variations in the availability of food. The meat diet of townspeople will perhaps be different from that of rural folk, since farmers will sell excess stock to town butchers, and the town itself may demand certain kinds of meat. Alternatively, the town may be fed with what the countryside around is producing for other purposes, as in the case of sheep reared predominantly for wool which are sold in town markets when they have outlived their usefulness.

Further, the increasing urban population puts a huge load on the surrounding countryside. Agriculture becomes more intense, since farmers can make money by supplying the towns, and rural estates thus begin to mirror prosperity in towns which they have helped to support. This section will deal with the provision of meat, which has to be transported, butchered and marketed. This part of the food industry has many by-products; urban manufacturing crafts use the waste from animal slaughter, especially tanners (who supplied the leather industry), horn- and bone-workers. We then append a few paragraphs on plants in the urban diet, but the text reflects the fact that more work has been done on animal bones and what they mean than on cereals, vegetables and fruit.

Discussion of bones must start with those of the main domesticated animals: cattle, sheep or goats (which are often discussed together, partly because of the difficulty of telling the bones apart), and pigs.[24] The first example shows how sites in a town demonstrate the exploitation of these species over time. At King's Lynn, ten thousand animal bones were identified; they represent however probably less than 0.025 per cent of the bone deposited in the town since the eleventh century. Here three periods covering the whole town were used: I, *c.*1050–1250; II, *c.*1250–1350; III, *c.*1350–1500.[25] The percentages of fragments of the three main domesticated species are shown in Fig. 7.7. By weight this indicates that beef was the main meat consumed; the number of bone fragments was similar in Period I, but a dressed carcase of beef probably gave 36 kg or more of beef or veal, as against 3kg for one of mutton or lamb.[26] The increasing availability of beef in King's Lynn over the medieval period is marked. This diet was varied with a wide selection of domestic and wild fowl and varieties of fish (of which more below).

A different pattern of meat consumption over time was found at Lurk Lane, Beverley, in a study of buildings forming part of the precinct of the medieval minster from the eleventh to the fifteenth centuries.[27] Cattle, sheep and pigs were the most common mammals; but when measured both by number of fragments and by minimum number of individuals (MNI) methods, the percentage of cow bones present fell during the twelfth and thirteenth centuries, to pick up again in the fourteenth. At the same time, the percentage of sheep bones rose, to fall back as the proportion of cattle rose again. Throughout, the proportion of pig bones stayed roughly the same.

The significance of the proportions of the three species was underlined by study of the age at death of the animals (i.e. when they were brought to market for butchery). Most of the cows were aged 3.5 years or older; they had presumably been used for milk production or, in the case of the old ones, as draught animals. Similarly, two-thirds of the sheep were aged three years or more, up to two years later than would be necessary to obtain the maximum

Medieval towns

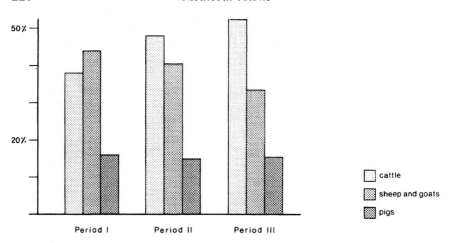

Figure 7.7 Main domestic species of meat-bearing animals from King's Lynn, by weight (Noddle 1977).

meat from the body. Pigs, on the other hand, were reared primarily for meat and were slaughtered as soon as a worthwhile body weight was attained.

Pigs were probably also raised in the backyards of the town, and were not subject to economic forces influencing the availability of cattle and sheep driven in from the countryside (i.e. their usefulness for other purposes). At Beverley, the relative increase in the sheep numbers in the twelfth and thirteenth centuries probably reflects the importance of the area for providing wool for the expanding textile industry. Similarly at Lincoln and York, although beef was also the main meat, the consumption of mutton increased at the expense of beef in the medieval period.[28] Since wool was an important export, it is seen to be a consequence that sheep became predominant in the urban diet – i.e. economic factors pertaining to an agricultural product, not a consequence of urban desires. In Oxford, near the Cotswolds, analysis from large samples on the St Ebbe's sites suggests that the townspeople ate meat from sheep which were surplus to requirements in a wool-producing area: that is, the young males and older females, which had presumably outlived their usefulness. Similarly most of the beef came from cows, not oxen, which probably had longer working lives as draught animals on the farms. In the fourteenth and fifteenth centuries there was an increased availability of veal, i.e. unwanted male calves, which has been noted in Exeter, Northampton and Oxford.[29]

Rabbit appears to have been introduced during the eleventh and twelfth centuries; it became a common food.[30] Wild mammals such as deer are occasionally to be found in early medieval deposits, but rarely in later towns. Study of wild species may provide information on the relationship between hunting practices and the town, domestication of wild species, and control of the landscape. At Lurk Lane, Beverley, for instance, hunting must have been responsible for a profusion of deer, hare, wild boar and wild birds: 28 species of birds were identified, three-quarters of which were edible (the others being scavengers), and half the species present came from wetland environments which surrounded the town.[31] In the age before refrigeration, meat from animals when killed did not travel far, so there was presumably a wider range of species on the table in small, rural towns.

Fish was an important element in the medieval diet, since the Church forbade eating of four-legged animals for up to three days each week and during Lent. Freshwater fish for institutions and households of status came from private fishponds; this seems to have given some species of fish a status which might seem unjustified on grounds of palatability. Towns on rivers could expect a variety of freshwater species in their diets: ten species were identified in a sieved deposit from Abingdon. But strata generally contain more evidence of marine species, even on inland sites. There was a flourishing inland trade in dried fish, and presumably these were predominantly marine; stockfish came in quantity from Iceland. Systematic sampling of many deposits on the Alms Lane site in Norwich in 1976 produced fish remains from 166 out of 244 samples. They were predominantly marine species, with almost two-thirds of the bones being of adult herring. There was also cod, whiting and flatfish; and of freshwater species, pike, roach, tench and perch; and eels which live in either habitat. The marine fish would be imported, and on this comparatively lower-class site, freshwater fish was comparatively scarce.[32] At ports and coastal towns, as one might expect, the variety of available fish was greater. At Great Yarmouth, where fishing was a staple industry, deposits of the eleventh and twelfth centuries produced nineteen species of mainly marine fish, incidentally proving the value of sieving; a previously excavated site at Baker's Lane in King's Lynn had produced eight marine species from normal retrieval (hand-picking of bones), and these tended to be the large specimens with heavy bones. The Yarmouth fish included species inhabiting both inshore and deep water, and those which live near the surface and in depths of over 100m. A variety of fishing techniques, with trawls, seine nets, and hooks (several of which were found on the excavation) is indicated.[33]

As with mammal bone, analysis should try to find out if there were spatial differences in the presence of fish bones, and whether fish consumption changed over time. Both these factors might have social as well as economic reasons. At Alms Lane there was little difference in consumption of fish between the tenements which were sampled. In Winchester, it is suggested that fish may have been an increasing part of the urban diet in the decades immediately before 1330, perhaps indicating a falling standard of living; when living standards rose after 1350, there were fewer fishmongers resident in the town.[34]

To revert to the major mammals, a problem is how to distinguish food debris from deposits left by butchery or industrial processes concerned with animal products, for example tanning or horn-working (the latter briefly mentioned in Chapter 4). Serjeantson has suggested four criteria: the context is a residential building; the bones are exclusively or mainly of food animals; there is evidence of butchery; and the parts of the skeleton which have the most meat predominate. At Exeter, despite the variability in the groups, it seems likely that all parts of animal carcases were dumped on these domestic sites. This could be because either householders did their own butchery, or that they bought all parts of the carcase, even those without much meat, from the market. By contrast, in early medieval Southampton, the bones derived

from twelfth-century pits behind stone houses on the High Street were derived
from large joints or carcases, suggesting butchery on the site; but in the thirteenth century, as butchery became a specialized trade, with markets of its
own in the town, the size of the joints was reduced and the choice of meats on
this comparatively well-off site widened.[35] One feature of town life may be
smaller cuts of meat, which implies that people in towns were able to be more
discerning in their food habits.

A model of the exploitation of meat-bearing animals in Lincoln over the
period 850–1500 has been provided by O'Connor, using material from the
Flaxengate site.[36] He assumes that the studied bones came from both domestic
consumption and butchers' or slaughterhouse debris, and the relative absence
of luxury animals indicates that the site was of middling status. Hunting and
wildfowling were incidental providers of food; venison was rare. Fig. 7.8
shows how butchery practices for sheep changed in the mid eleventh century,
when also younger pigs appear noticeable in the diet; the rabbit makes an
appearance shortly before 1300.

When large numbers of animal bone fragments are studied, it is possible to
make suggestions both about the management of animals in the countryside,
and how they were kept in towns. The best archaeological evidence for the
management of sheep flocks in the countryside probably comes from urban
excavation. We have already noted that an increasing proportion of sheep
bones at Beverley may indicate an emphasis on sheep-farming in the area.
From a large sample such as the 28,000 bones now studied from medieval sites
in the St Ebbe's district of Oxford, Wilson has outlined the contribution of
animal bone studies to the study of the local economy and the organization of
the town. The high proportion of bones from cows rather than oxen suggests
that dairying husbandry supplied most of the cattle killed in Oxford, in turn
implying that arable farming was less prevalent in the area. The subsistence
economy of the town may have been geared to this farming style. The post-
medieval organization of butchery, in which cattle were brought long distances and fattened in meadows near the town, may have started in the
medieval period; along with breeding and husbandry improvements, this was
to result in larger animals (to identify evidence of improving the breed of
animals in the medieval and post-medieval periods would be a major step
forward in environmental archaeology). Within the town itself, pigs and calves
were slaughtered on the tenements; they may have been kept there. The
tenements would have had a superficial scatter of bone debris about them, but
most of the animal debris was safely buried in pits, and exposed bones would
be scavenged by dogs, rats, cats, foxes and birds. The investigation could not
demonstrate that fowl were reared on the site, since the bones could be from
birds bought in the market. The small size of the bones of domesticated animals during the medieval period points to poor feeding and housing conditions, especially meanness in provision of fodder.[37]

Further analyses can tell us about the way animal carcases were prepared
for the table, at least in major institutions such as religious houses. For
example, Levitan analysed bones from nine areas of St Katherine's Priory,
Exeter.[38] The study is also a warning, for each of the nine locations gave a
different view of the relative numbers of species over time; in other
words, small-scale excavation, say of one or two areas, would have given an

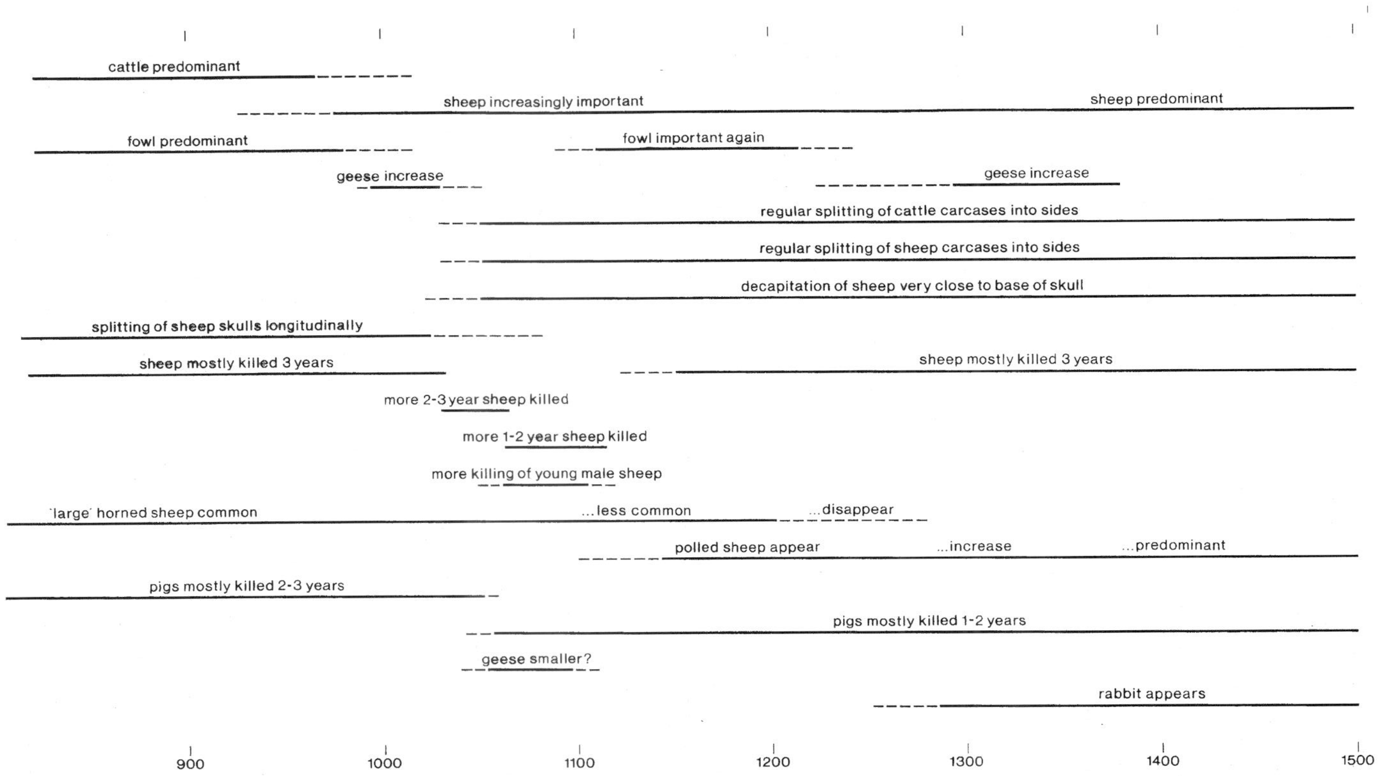

Figure 7.8 Chronology of some of the variables noted in animal bone assemblages, tenth to fifteenth centuries, at Lincoln (O'Connor 1982).

over-selective picture. The priory was apparently buying in carcases whole or halved, and much secondary butchery took place on site. The main results were that outside the kitchens, large bones were dumped as carcases were deboned and meals prepared. Smaller bones, which represent table waste, were found in deposits closer to the eating and living areas, and were perhaps disposed of in a more haphazard fashion. Monastic sites hold out the possibility of progress in this area because they are, to some extent, closed sites with limited functions (as opposed to the burgage plot, subject to many forces), but they generally seem to produce a small number of animal bones; perhaps the excavators are too keen on chasing walls.[39]

Can we detect differences in social standing between ordinary households from their diet? This question can be asked of studies of animal bones and of seeds. Sometimes, not surprisingly, there are no differences: a study of two adjacent properties in medieval Hull produced no clear differences and considerable similarity in the animal bones that were discarded. On the other hand, an instructive case comes from seventeenth- and eighteenth-century Amsterdam, where Ijzereef was able to suggest, from bones in cesspits, which households were Jewish and which not (5 per cent or more pig bones indicates a non-Jewish household), and although pottery and glass did not indicate much social differentiation, he proposed a range of rich to poor households based on 'rich' and 'poor' bone assemblages.[40] Rich meant the better cuts of beef, a high proportion of chicken, turkey and goose, freshwater fish and oysters; poor meant cattle skulls and metapodials, with bones often smashed open for the marrow, and fish skulls. If such distinctions could be found in British assemblages, and correlated with similar indices of social status in the artefacts (or possibly documentary records, if present), it would be a significant step forward. Differences in social status might also be indicated by differences in plant remains, for instance if there was a higher proportion or variety of imported plants or foodstuffs (grapes, figs; oranges probably from Spain or Portugal) on one property than on another.

The largest item in aristocratic budgets in the medieval period was food and drink. Further, modern anthropological studies show that socially defined custom is a major determinant of what we eat. In previous centuries, as today, food is a vehicle for social cohesion. It was and is used in rituals or on ceremonial occasions (the wedding feast, the wake); there have always been prestige foods which were only found at rich tables, such as venison, wild birds, and the rarer fish.[41] In medieval towns, the waste of food preparation and what was left on the table were regularly tipped into cesspits to join the human waste. A wide range of animal, bird and fish bones in such deposits might indicate a degree of wealth and feasting, as is suggested by documentary records such as accounts of foodstuffs for specific meals. The Carpenters' Company in London had feasts when the mayor was presented to the king at Westminster (November), on St Laurence's Day, and on a special Feast Day. Records of what was purchased for these meals each year survive for much of the period 1491–1521. The Feast Day meal in 1491, for instance, included a whole sheep, veal, beef, necks of mutton, two swans, 17 geese, 22 conies, seven dozen pigeons, nine pikes, as well as ingredients for sweet dishes. On other occasions variety was provided by lamb, kid, marrow-bones, and pork; other poultry and game included the occasional buck, chickens, peacocks, plovers, rabbits, sparrows and other small birds; and the fish included bloaters, bream, cod, crab, crayfish, dace, four kinds of eel, flounders, haddock, herring, lamprey, ling, minnows, mullet, oysters, roach, salmon, salt-fish, shrimps, smelt, sole, sturgeon and turbot.[42] This was not a royal or a noble household, but a prosperous guild in London; in general, there was a high proportion of animals and birds that had not previously served a useful purpose on the farm. One way forward may be to characterize such luxurious meal assemblages from documentary records and then look for similar groups in the archaeological record, starting with high-status sites.

The degree to which cereals, fruit and vegetables formed the diet of townspeople in the medieval period is by comparison far less well researched. There is a large amount of documentary material about baking and bread, marketing of garden produce and land given over to production of food both outside and inside town walls, such as orchards. Medieval cookbooks have recipes not only for all kinds of meat dishes, but soups and vegetarian meals and salads.

Cereals, which formed the staple of the medieval diet, are often found in the form of charred grains and chaff. Wheat was the preferred, and most widely used cereal in the lowland zones, followed by rye, barley and oats, as suggested in documentary sources.[43] The last two crops tended to be grown mainly for feeding livestock, although they were widely eaten in Ireland and Scotland, where the climate was less suitable for growing wheat. Peas, horse beans and lentils could be dried to provide alternative protein sources to meat throughout the year, and would have been particularly important to the poor, and members of religious houses. Remains of these have been found in a number of towns in England and Wales, but rarely survive except when charred, and so are very under-represented in the archaeological record. This problem is even more marked for leaf and root vegetables, which were widely grown in gardens and used extensively in soups and pottages, but were harvested before setting seed, and so usually leave no recognizable remains in archaeological deposits. Leek has been identified from epidermal material at several towns including York, and seeds and fruits from beet and brassicas (which include cabbage, kale and turnip) may also represent cultivated food plants.[44]

Evidence for wild and cultivated fruit in the diet is much more widespread, as their pips and stones are found, often in huge numbers, in the ubiquitous rubbish pits and latrines found in medieval towns. Remains of sloe, plum/bullace, cherry, apple, pear, blackberry, raspberry, wild strawberry and hazelnut are frequently recovered, while less common fruits and nuts include mulberry, walnut, gooseberry, peach and medlar. Grape and fig seeds are also found in large numbers, and while there is evidence for vineyards in this country, documents also testify to the importation of raisins and figs as dried fruit. Although an increasing variety of foodstuffs is recovered from later medieval deposits, archaeological records of exotic food plants often lag some time behind the first historical references to their cultivation or use in this country. This is probably because new introductions or imports would have been rare luxuries, used only by the rich, and the chances of recovering their remains from archaeological deposits is thus remote until consumption of these foods became more widespread.

One local but extremely useful area of plant studies is that of food plants which passed through the human body and ended up in cesspits (Fig. 7.9). The interpretation of some layers in these pits as human faeces is often supported by the occurence of human parasite ova (see below), though it is also clear that cesspits were used as general dustbins for the waste of food preparation in the kitchen (a topic of equal interest). The seeds from two medieval town cesspits are shown in Fig. 7.10. A third example is that of a cesspit attached to a fifteenth-century hall in the precinct of the minster at Beverley, on the Lurk Lane site: here much was deduced from samples from three layers.[45] The most abundant food residue was cereal bran, from wheat and/or rye, which had been ground into flour to make bread. Those who used the site also ate figs, strawberries, hazelnuts, apples, raspberries, sloes, the bullace (another member of the *Prunus* family), wild cherries and elderberries. Grape pips came from raisins, which we know were imported into Hull in the fourteenth century, though grapes were growing in monastic gardens. The food or drink was flavoured with fennel, coriander, poppy and possibly dill. All three contexts produced fragments of corncockle, a widespread weed in the medieval period; but not many, indicating the bread consumed was made from well-processed grain. Corncockle makes bread unpalatable and produces mild intoxication, and its ingestion has been associated with susceptibility to leprosy.

How good was the standard of living in medieval towns, as indicated by the provision of food and drink? Townspeople generally probably had a better diet than their neighbours in the countryside. If they had money, they could buy several kinds of bread, ale, wine, meat and fish. Fruit and vegetables came from town and suburban gardens. Over the period, there is some evidence that town-dwellers ate more meat (possibly cut into more ways), and less cereals or fish; after 1350, such a desire was part of the strengthened bargaining powers of the workers. In this later period, also, they apparently drank more alcohol; a general increase in production of barley for brewing had started before 1300, and this was now sustained by the reduced population, enjoying better standards of living. Similarly, there was probably an increase in the consumption of wood as fuel per head, as demonstrated by study of the provision of firewood to London.[46] Living standards, as far as they are measurable by environmental archaeology, were improving.

Biological characteristics of urban people; disease

Urbanization was perhaps the greatest social transition suffered by man since remotest antiquity, and some changes in man's health may well have followed from it. There might be alterations in nutrition, changes in the pattern and ferocity of diseases, differences in height, age at death, or changes due to the nature of urban living and work. This discussion follows the outline of Waldron.[47]

We are constrained to examination of the human skeleton for evidence, and only a proportion of conditions and diseases are manifest on human bones. Of vitamin deficiency diseases, only scurvy and rickets are detectable in skeletons. Scurvy (lack of vitamin C) is indicative of a restricted diet, and was epidemic in medieval Europe in winter months when fresh fruit and vegetables were

Figure 7.9 Thirteenth-century cesspit, Milk Street, London. Environmental analysis of the deposit in the pit (which can be seen below the vertical photographic scale) produced a great number of fruit seeds (Museum of London).

Milk Street, London,
1240–70

Fischmarkt, Constance,
Latrine VII, after 1301

barley	acorn	mustard (black and white)
black bindweed	almond	oats
black mustard	apple	parsley
black nightshade	barley	parsnip
blackberry	beans	pea
buttercup	black elderberry	peach
campion	blackberry	pear
cherry	bluebell(?)	pepper
chickweed	blueberry	plum
corncockle	camomile	pomegranate
dock	caraway	poppy
elder	carnation	purslane
fat hen	carrot	quince
fig	celery	rape
fool's parsley	chervil	raspberry
fumitory	columbine	red elderberry
hare's ear	coriander	rose hip
hazel	cress	rye
hedge-parsley	cucumber	sloe
knotgrass	dill	sour cherry
marsh marigold	dock	spelt (wheat)
mulberry	emmer	strawberry
oats	fennel	sweet cherry
oraches	fig	sweet chestnut
pale persicaria	flax	turnip
pear/apple	gooseberry	violet
plum	grape	walnut
raspberry	hazelnut	watercress
sedges	hemp	wheat
sloe	hop	
thistle	hyssop	
vine	juniper	
water pepper	lentil	
wheat	millet	
wild cabbage	mountain ash berry	
wild strawberry	mulberry	

Figure 7.10 Seeds found in two medieval cesspits, in London and Constance (Switzerland) (Davis 1991; Flüeler and Flüeler 1992).

unavailable. Rickets (lack of vitamin D) is a disease of children, enlarging epiphyses (the ends) of growing bones and causing bowing of the limbs; common among medieval skeletons, it was endemic in areas of low-incident sunlight, and perhaps therefore it might be more prevalent in crowded parts of towns. White suggests that there are no recorded archaeological examples in the early medieval period in England, indicating that people were sufficiently exposed to the high degree of sunshine then prevalent.[48]

Infectious diseases which might have been particularly rife in towns include leprosy, tuberculosis and syphilis. The first two were common in the medieval period, though it has also been suggested that the spread of pulmonary tuberculosis led to the decline of leprosy in the post-medieval period, since the tubercle bacillus seems to have given some immunity from the bacterium which causes leprosy. So far few sites in Britain have produced examples of leprous bones, though the disease was common enough for there to be about two hundred leper hospitals in thirteenth-century England. Five cases of tuberculosis and some possible cases of syphilis were noted at St Helen's in York.[49] A traditional belief that venereal syphilis was unknown in Europe until the return of Christopher Columbus from his transatlantic venture in 1493 has been the subject of increasing challenges. Isolated examples from medieval Kingston-upon-Hull and Rivenhall, Essex, have been supplemented by the multiple cases of treponemal disease noted during the excavations of 1997–2001 in the cemetery attached to the hospital of St Mary Bishopsgate (as described in Chapter 6), which will probably result in the confirmation that syphilis was not a disease imported from the New World.[50] The suggestion that tuberculosis and syphilis were particularly urban diseases (in that they spread more quickly in places with a higher density of people, especially those travelling to and fro) should also be tested. Differences in the prevalence of other types of infection between urban and rural sites have been observed: periostitis, a frequent response to trauma and infection of especially the lower limbs, was much more common in the urban site of St Helen-on-the-Walls than at Wharram Percy deserted medieval village (Yorks), where the corresponding prevalences were 22 per cent and only 9 per cent, respectively. Other diseases known to have been virulent in medieval Europe included amoebic dysentery and smallpox.[51]

Not enough is yet known about people's height in the medieval period to distinguish between rural and urban populations (Fig. 7.11), but it is notable that an observable decline in height among British youths in the nineteenth century could be related to industrialization and urbanization. We also do not have enough samples yet to form conclusions about differences in age at death; certainly people lived shorter lives in the past, but the only comparisons which can be made are between then and now, rather than between communities of the same historical period. More pessimism attends hope of distinguishing work-related conditions in the medieval period, since the actual occupations are never known; though in the case of an eleventh-century group recovered from beneath the levels of the bailey at Norwich Castle in 1979, widespread occurrence of deficiency in vitamin D (resulting in rickets) and a number of pathologies associated with lifting and labouring strains among the male skeletons suggested occupations where hard physical work was undertaken away from sunlight. This could cover many medieval trades, but in this case mining of chalk was suggested.[52] More success may be achieved by studies of post-medieval cemeteries, where documentary evidence, particularly name-plates on coffins and parish registers, may give details of occupations of the deceased. If they have problems with their bones, then comparisons could be made with similar pathological cases from medieval contexts.

Let us take an example. The cemetery of the small parish church of St Nicholas Shambles in London was excavated in 1975–7 and 234 articulated skeletons of eleventh- to twelfth-century date recovered.[53] A large proportion of adults could only be said to be 'over 17', and thus the finding that only 6.4

Site	Date	Heights		Sample size
		male	female	
Bidford-on-Avon	Saxon	5′7″ (171.4 cm)	5′1½″ (156.2 cm)	large
North Elmham, Norfolk	Saxon	5′7¾″ (172.1 cm)	5′2″ (157.2 cm)	20
Porchester Castle	Saxon	5′9¼″ (175.9 cm)	5′5″ (165.1 cm)	15
St Helen, York	10th–16th	5′6½″ (169.3 cm)	5′2″ (157.5 cm)	large
St Nicholas Shambles, London	11th–12th	5′8″ (172.8 cm)	5′2″ (157.5 cm)	94
Durham Cathedral	12th	5′7½″ (171.5 cm)	–	20
Pontefract Priory	12th–14th	5′7½″ (171.5 cm)	–	34
Wharram Percy, Yorks	medieval	5′6″ (168.0 cm)	–	large
Greyfriars, Chester	medieval	5′6½″ (168.8 cm)	5′3″ (161.0 cm)	20
Austin Friars, Leicester	medieval	5′10″ (177.8 cm)	5′2″ (157.5 cm)	13
Bordesley Abbey	medieval	5′8″ (172.8 cm)	–	19
Rothwell Charnel House, Northants	medieval	5′5″ (165.1 cm)	5′2″ (157.5 cm)	large
Dominican Priory, Chelmsford	medieval	5′7″ (170.2 cm)	5′1½″(156.2 cm)	25
Guildford Friary	medieval	5′8″ (175.0 cm)	5′3″ (160.0 cm)	56
St Mary's Priory, Thetford	12th–13th	5′9¾″ (177.2 cm)	–	5
South Acre, Norfolk	12th–14th	5′6″ (167.6 cm)	5′1½″(156.2 cm)	5
St Leonard's, Hythe, Kent	14th–15th	5′7″ (170.2 cm)	5′2″ (157.5 cm)	large

Figure 7.11 Mean stature heights for Anglo-Saxon and English medieval populations (White 1988), in feet and inches, and in centimetres.

per cent of the others reached 45 is probably unreliable (many in the broad 'over 17' group were probably over 45). Similarly few infants were found, a common feature of cemetery excavations where the small bones have probably been greatly disturbed. The skeletons of those identifiably under about 13 years old could not be assigned a sex (Fig. 7.12).

This group of town people was comparatively healthy, with few patholo-gical conditions evident on their bones. Only 12 per cent of the adult jaws were free from some kind of dental defect, mainly either a high degree of calculus deposit, indicating a lack of cleaning of the teeth, or caries (Fig. 7.13). On average people lost 7.6 per cent of their teeth during life. Nutritional disease was evident in 17 per cent of the skulls in a mild form of pitting of the

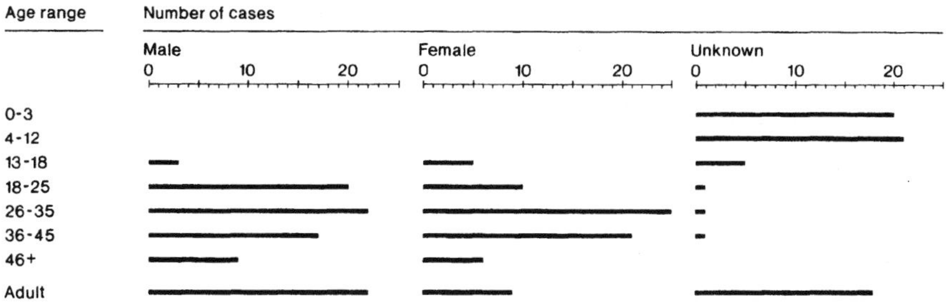

Age range	Number of cases		
	Male	Female	Unknown
	0 10 20	0 10 20	0 10 20
0-3			▬▬▬▬▬▬▬▬
4-12			▬▬▬▬▬▬▬▬
13-18	▬	▬	▬
18-25	▬▬▬▬▬▬	▬▬▬	▪
26-35	▬▬▬▬▬▬▬▬	▬▬▬▬▬▬▬	▪
36-45	▬▬▬▬▬▬	▬▬▬▬▬	▪
46+	▬▬▬	▬▬	
Adult	▬▬▬▬▬▬	▬▬▬	▬▬▬▬▬

Figure 7.12 Age at death and apparent mortality rate at St Nicholas Shambles cemetery, London (White 1988).

inside of the eye cavity called cribra orbitalia. Osteoarthritis, especially of the vertebrae, was found in many skeletons; at least 40 per cent of the adults were affected, men and women equally. Deformities of the toes might be a result of wearing tight shoes. Individual cases of note included a girl with a missing left leg who had survived to be a teenager and another, tall and probably overweight, who was left with a prominent limp probably through a congenital disorder of the hip joint called coxa vara (Fig. 7.14). One young woman died in childbirth (Fig. 7.15). A much larger group of 1041 skeletons has been published from the cemetery of St Helen-on-the-Walls, York, but the date range of this population stretches from the tenth to the sixteenth century, and conclusions can therefore only be of a general character.[54] The low expectation of life, with 27 per cent of the sample dying as children and only 9 per cent living beyond the age of sixty, confirms documentary evidence for high mortality rates all over medieval England. Unexpectedly, men seemed to outnumber women at all ages over 35, whereas in modern societies women usually have a higher expectation of life than men. It may be that females suffered poorer nourishment than males in medieval (and here, Tudor) towns, as well as the special hazards of child-bearing. In contrast, in the lay cemetery at the Gilbertine priory of St Andrew's, also in York, child mortality was high and half the men died before the age of thirty, whereas a good proportion of women lived on beyond the age of fifty.[55] More tightly dated groups of skeletons are required; and groups from different parts of the same town, to study local variations. This is beginning to be possible in the larger towns where much excavation has taken place, such as York and London.

Jews in England led an exclusively urban life until their expulsion under Edward I in 1290. Jewish cemeteries were generally established outside settlements and only one has been excavated, that at Jewbury, York.[56] The peak age at death was in the range 20 to 30 years for both sexes, but, as at St Andrew's and in stark contrast to the parish cemetery of St Helen-on-the-Walls in the same city, a significant proportion of women lived on into old age. The population revealed by archaeology were physically different to their neighbours in York with a generally distinctive skull shape and 'short' stature, especially for men (average 167.4 cm), perhaps the result of genetic differences or of religious isolation. The population suffered from infectious diseases including leprosy, tuberculosis and syphilis but also a high proportion of

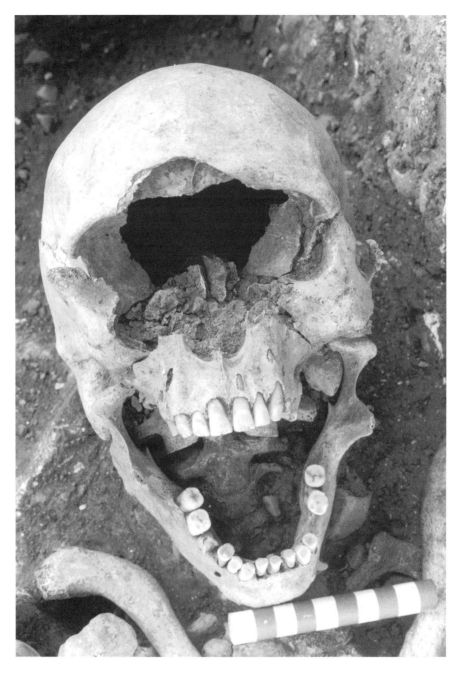

Figure 7.13 A good set of teeth on a skeleton from St Nicholas Shambles. A man aged 32–35, he had lost six teeth during life (White 1988).

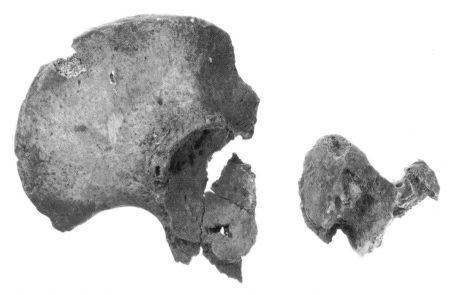

Figure 7.14 Detail of the congenital orthopaedic hip disorder *coxa vara* on a skeleton from St Nicholas Shambles. This woman lived to be 25–28, but her femur had been disposed to slipping in the joint through adolescence; this led to it growing distortedly, and some discomfort (White 1988).

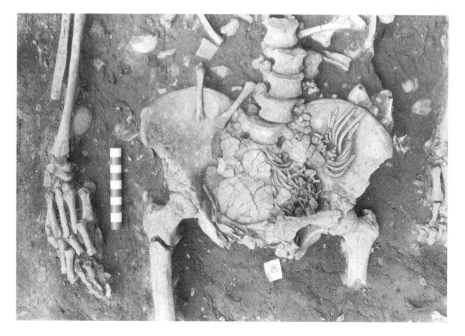

Figure 7.15 Detail of a young woman who died in childbirth, St Nicholas Shambles; the foetus was never born (Museum of London). The bones of small children are often dispersed by later digging in a cemetery, and thus their number is probably under-estimated.

sinusitis and a few cases of rickets, the latter two being far more characteristic of urban life during the industrial revolution.[57]

When archaeological survival is exceptional, a detailed medical and anthropological programme of research can produce far-reaching results. One such programme, for instance, is that being conducted on the human remains from two sites in Svendborg, Denmark, as part of a multi-disciplinary study of the medieval town.[58] About two hundred individuals were excavated. Child mortality was high; the average age at death was 33 for men and 28 for women, several of whom died in childbirth. The average height was 175 cm for men and 163 cm for women; at St Nicholas in London it was 173 cm and 157.5 cm (Fig. 7.11). The medieval Danes were also larger than nineteenth-century Danes; in 1850 when National Service was introduced, the average height of the first intake was 162 cm. Osteoarthritis was widespread, reflecting the hard physical labour and lack of labour-saving devices of the time. A notable feature of the Svendborg group is that 57 of the skeletons still had their brains, due to the anaerobic alkaline soil conditions. Scanning electron microscopy clearly shows the brain structures.

The level of hygiene on urban properties can be ascertained by study of human coprolites (faeces) and evidence of parasites such as tapeworms, which are found in both cesspits and floor layers. At High Street/Blackfriargate, Hull, for instance, samples from cesspits of thirteenth-and fourteenth-century date produced ova of intestinal parasites; floors produced parasite ova probably from rat and mice droppings. Human parasites included whipworm (*Trichuris* sp.) and maw-worm (*Ascaris* sp.), which have also been found in medieval faecal deposits in York and Beverley. Absence of the ova can also aid interpretation. At Beverley, for instance, a twelfth-century pit attached to an aisled hall in the minster precinct served as a dump for food waste, including fish bones and fruit stones; but the very low concentration of intestinal parasite ova ruled out the possibility that this was a cesspit – more likely the pit was dug simply for rubbish disposal, possibly during the demolition of the associated building.[59]

Towns were often ravaged by disease. The Black Death of 1348–9 cut the population of Britain by between 30 and 45 per cent.[60] It is estimated that in Europe, over a three or four year period, 25 to 50 million people died, a quarter to a third of the entire population. The plague was especially disastrous in certain towns, for instance Lübeck, where nine out of ten people perished. It may have been especially lethal because it struck at a population already weakened by chronic undernourishment after a generation of agrarian disasters and famine. Plagues occurred between 1328 and 1377, perhaps resulting in an overall fall in population of over 50 per cent; the population did not really resume an upward trend until about 1470. By the early fifteenth century, it seems that plague had become a particularly urban disease: by the 1420s the habit of fleeing to the country to avoid contagion was already well established. Between 1400 and 1485 only five plagues affected the whole country, whereas seven hit the capital. The Black Death has not been studied archaeologically, partly because it is difficult to identify a plague pit from skeletons alone; the plague did not affect the bones. A start is being made after excavation of what was certainly a special plague cemetery of 1349 at St Mary Graces, London.[61]

Were townspeople different genetically from those in rural areas? At any period, a proportion of town dwellers will be migrants from the countryside. Modern research suggests that migrants sometimes select themselves, in that they are taller. Whether it is a result of their genetic makeup or the urban environment, however, several modern studies around the world suggest that urban children grow up taller and heavier than rural children, and urban girls reach puberty earlier than rural girls; a feature observed in 1610 by a writer called Quarinonius. In one modern study, village children erupted their permanent teeth on average later than urban children. It seems probable that most if not all these differences are due to the economic differences between town and country dwellers, resulting in the better feeding of the well-off. Such differences might be apparent in medieval populations.[62]

Conclusion

This chapter has considered the ecology of the medieval town: the degree to which urban settlement affected its rural surroundings, the environment in towns, and the degree to which nature's products – the weather, animal and plant foodstuffs, and man's own biology – affected life in towns. It is evident that environmental archaeology has a great potential. From soil samples the archaeologist can extract a detailed description of how and under what conditions deposits formed. Pollen gives information on vegetation and land-use, diatoms on salinity and levels of water pollution, botanical remains on vegetation, diet, materials used in buildings, technology and fuel. Though useful, however, this is at present largely anecdotal evidence. Some broad changes can be seen, for instance in the consumption of varieties of meat, but we cannot yet say much about how, or whether, environmental factors actually contributed to change. It does appear to be the case that the environment of towns had an effect on people's state of health and perhaps exposed them to a wider range of conditions and possibly fatal diseases than living in the countryside.

Documentary evidence, for all its strengths, tends to give a short-term and very partial view of most matters now covered by environmental archaeology: long-term climatic and ecological change; human diet; the health of the population. Archaeology looks at matters such as the human diet from a long-term perspective. Environmental questions for the period which can be answered, at least partly, by archaeological study divide into three groups.

The first concerns processes involving human action. How polluted were the rivers near towns? What were the ecological consequences on the rural landscape of the increasing domination of farming by a town's needs? Similarly, what were the environmental impacts of industrial processes on local communities? Were these different in towns and in the countryside? The second concerns the feeding of medieval townspeople, and the effect of this need on the hinterland. What are the environmental indicators of increasing requirements on the countryside and agriculture? What were the consequences for the breeding of animals? Or for the management of wild fauna and fish? Third, some environmental variables had an effect on cultural systems. What was the extent of the arable area? What was the frequency of droughts? What was the pattern of flooding? All these would have had a profound effect on the conduct of agriculture in the region.

Because the study of the environmental archaeology of towns is still at a comparatively early stage, at least two other approaches could be taken. The environmental archaeology of a particular town might be arranged as a study in the progression from the rural (pre-urban) to the modern urban environment: colonization of the countryside, early food supply, commercialization of that food supply, development of secondary animal product industries. Within the town we would then pursue local variations in craft activities, development of craft control, and, in general, the late medieval migration to larger towns which produces density of urban population and its concomitant urban diseases.

There is secondly a potential within environmental archaeology to add a further dimension to the study of towns and their surrounding areas. Medieval urban archaeology uses concepts derived from economic history deduced from documents, and perhaps this should be resisted. The current emphasis on proportions of animal bones, meat weight, wheat varieties, and food storage and processing might be matched with studies into the natural history of the medieval farmyard and field or the ecological consequences of drainage or woodland clearance. What were the ecological effects on a village which was economically dominated by the self-interest of a nearby town? Instead of seeing the space around us, and around our archaeological sites, as a natural resource, emphasizing modes of production and systems of redistribution of wealth, we could see it as context for living and stress the finiteness of the resource.[63] This is a challenging new way of looking at the past. At all times we should explore the extent to which the bundle of variables studied as environmental archaeology will demonstrate that life in towns was different from that in the countryside.

8 *Unfinished business*

The discoveries and speculations surveyed in this book are the work of many archaeologists in medieval towns in Britain, especially in the last thirty years. Archaeologists have shown that towns can claim to be more representative of the nature of the society of which they formed part than any other type of site. In towns we are most likely to find archaeological evidence of both long-distance and local trade, of exploitation of natural resources, of specialization and of technological evidence in manufacturing, of social differentiation, of the means of political control, and of the religious aspirations of the population. This is our continuing agenda, and much remains to be done. We end with a series of suggestions for archaeologists to think about.

One critic of the first edition of this book said that it needed an intellectual framework and perhaps a small amount of appropriate theory. We do not claim to provide here an intellectual framework for the archaeological investigation of medieval towns. But we can describe why we have written the book, and how we think urban archaeology should be conducted; perhaps also what should happen next.

Every student and scholar is a prisoner of his or her own history, and so are we the authors. In the 1970s and 1980s, building on the achievements of the pioneers, archaeologists throughout Europe created the discipline of urban archaeology. In Britain, this was not done by the two institutions which had up until then directed archaeological endeavour, the universities on the one hand, or state archaeological services on the other hand. Rather, it was archaeologists attached to museums, or to planning authorities (the county council, or more rarely a town), or in new archaeological trusts, who worked out how to deal with urban development. They were also the largest employers of archaeologists, and one feature of the last three decades has been the resulting creation of archaeology as a full-time profession.[1] This book is a product and reflection of that exciting time; but now we must move on. The archaeological landscape of Britain, in terms of the attitudes, professionalism and procedures, some codified in law, is now completely different from that in 1970.

The work by many archaeologists reported here arose from a concern (occasionally an anger) about the needless destruction, often without adequate recording, of Britain's urban heritage, both medieval and early modern. This feeling was shared by architectural historians. Looking back in 1990, Mark Girouard felt acute pain: 'I went back to Chichester and found too many of the Georgian houses which had excited me as a child pickled and preserved as little more than a screen to hide the car-parks. I saw how ruthlessly two-thirds of the centre of Worcester, and most of the centre of Gloucester, had been mangled; walked from the station through the corpse of what had once been Chelmsford; discovered how Taunton had destroyed in a year or two the town centre so carefully and creatively formed in the eighteenth century ... and wept in the screaming desolation of Birmingham.' He went on to suggest that

Figure 8.1   Aerial view of the centre of York, showing the Minster and a high survival of medieval elements in the town: the defences, street patterns, churches and properties with buildings largely of recent centuries but on their medieval alignments. The archaeological strata (which includes these buildings) are often over 5m deep; in this case there is a Viking and Roman city beneath. In this medieval town, much of the evidence remains to be read (National Monuments Record).

'keeping and understanding the past makes for tolerance; it also makes for creativity, in devising ways of altering and adding to towns, for nothing comes out of a vacuum. It is hard to believe that those who made the running in English towns in the 1950s and 1960s would have done what they did if they had known more about them.'[2]

This study, which is a contribution to the spreading of that knowledge, has been primarily of what happened inside medieval towns; how the varied parts and the people who inhabited them interlocked together (Fig. 8.1). We have been able to make some progress in the areas of topography, secular buildings and religious buildings; but less progress in the study of crafts and industry, trade, and environmental archaeology. In these latter three areas, the archaeological agenda beyond the level of description has perhaps still to be formulated.

This book has not been about several other matters which might be thought relevant: how towns functioned in their regions (indeed, to what extent archaeology can define regions), hierarchies of towns, and of 'regional' or national differences between sets of towns. Sometimes we have alluded to these topics, but generally not. Somebody else can write that book.[3]

There has been little discussion of a slightly different question, the extent to which towns in general were different from their countrysides. Some historians have made this into a cause.[4] We agree that the town was perceived as different from the rural surroundings, both by its residents and by people in the countryside. Because there was division of labour in towns, there were more institutions to govern those different sectors, and therefore more bodies of knowledge which bred social differentiation, clashing interest groups and traditions. In medieval towns there were special buildings which were only present in towns, the original forms of hospitals, hotels, libraries, exchanges and banks, warehouses, government offices and shops; towns later spawned other specialized building forms such as railway stations and factories. The uniquely urban setting of many types of institutional and public buildings begins in the Middle Ages.[5] It might even be argued that towns drew on other towns as much as from their hinterlands. Perhaps this is going too far: some historians argue that there was no essential antagonism between town and country, nor did medieval towns radically transform the backward countryside either economically or socially.[6]

How should archaeologists study medieval towns? Here the two authors would make different or complementary points. Schofield says that in general, the archaeological investigation and study of medieval towns should go through four stages. These stages are (i) data gathering, (ii) the construction of chronologies and typologies, (iii) study of archaeological evidence of specific activities, and (iv) study of the archaeology of groups which functioned within towns, including their contacts with the region around the town and other towns. From description, we move to interpretation and explanation.[7] We then ask if towns across medieval Europe were sufficiently similar to be studied as a group, and if so, why that should be. Finally, we make some suggestions about the purpose of studying medieval urban archaeology, and how to present its results in a useful way to enhance conservation and to manage change in towns. The argument of this chapter, and ultimately of the whole book, is that recording leads to interpretation, which leads to policies about conservation of the historic environment (Fig. 8.2).

Vince says that there is another way of looking at towns. Archaeologists approach towns with a set of preconceptions as to what the place was like and how it operated. Once they start to excavate, or to study stray finds or try to establish the medieval topography through cartographic means, they start to test these ideas, consciously or subconsciously, against their data. Sometimes the data is entirely consistent, in which case no changes in the model take place, while at other times the new data causes a rethink. This is as true of medieval town plan studies as it is of pottery and smallfind typologies.

We do agree that archaeological work has two main objectives. These are to contribute to the study of past towns and their people; and to influence conservation of the remaining medieval monuments and strata in the present town. Understanding of the historic fabric of a town (including all those

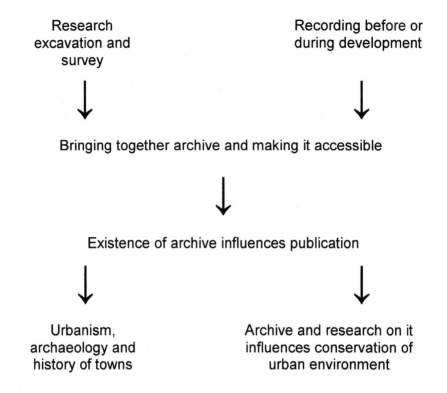

Figure 8.2   The progression from recording through the archive to publication, the study of towns and conservation policies.

activities which are now only traced by study of artefacts or ecofacts) leads to an appreciation of its value, which creates a desire for its protection.

Data gathering

If nothing or little is known about the archaeology of a town, then data must be gathered. This was the phase which many medieval (and pre-medieval) towns went through in the 1970s and 1980s as their centres were drastically altered. At this first stage, many would argue that there is really no appropriate archaeological strategy or question except Philip Barker's 'What is there?' Others would say, in contrast, that while it is important to produce consistent data over many investigations, it is also possible to apply research questions to the archaeology of a town, even where little is so far known. Archaeologists who work in towns reply that research questions are by their very nature selective and exclusive. An emphasis on the Roman period will inhibit data-gathering in the post-medieval period, as was traditional in British archaeology until the 1970s. By constantly unearthing the unexpected and yet significant, urban archaeology points out the blinkered perspective of over-rigid research designs. An alternative strategy is to let theory rise out of data;

and altering the question in a small but highly significant way to read, 'What is going on here?' This should not be to the exclusion of hypotheses to be tested, or questions posed from historical evidence or the growing weight of archaeological evidence itself. But we need to keep an open mind when we dig.

Excavation sites will continue to be dictated very largely by development pressures, and they will be all over the town. This should be used to provide a wide range of samples from different types of deposit – streets, backlands, churches, defences and waterfronts. The strategy must be to bring about, within the context of redevelopment, a comprehensive series of excavations sampling all the periods of the town in a wide variety of stratigraphic situations. We need to map the survival of deposits within towns, to chart the archaeological resource which is still available to be managed (either by preservation or by interrogation before destruction in building works). This resource will be greatest in certain parts of town, for instance along the waterfront, in churchyards and in zones not yet touched by comprehensive redevelopment. If we chronicle the earth-moving episodes in a town's history, as has been done for a handful of British towns (London, Stafford, Worcester, York), we not only have the menu of research possibilities (and an important tool in the necessary dialogue with urban planners), but the earth-moving operations themselves show us something about the town at those periods. The building of castle mounds or clearance of whole streets for public or religious complexes demonstrates power at work in the town; the expanding waterfront zone presumably reflects pressure on urban space, as a result of booming business, or rising population, or both.

At the same time as we gain a satellite view of the town's depositional history, we must use the close-up lens. The essence of town archaeology is the sequence of layers which form its stratification. From the sequence we can deduce change over time in building layout and design, in pottery and all other kinds of artefacts, and in the interaction of people with their natural environment. But layers in towns suffer from two kinds of interference. The first is the sheer weight of the actions of people over time, continually digging new holes and constructing new roads or buildings. In towns of the greatest age such as the ex-Roman centres, the medieval strata are often damaged, at least in part. Their buildings and yards, in any one period, are never complete. The second problem is residuality: an unknown proportion of the finds or inclusions (building material, bones, seeds or insect remains) within any stratum may have survived from a significantly earlier period and thus form a kind of misleading contamination. Bones, pottery and the hardier seeds or fruit-pips could be redeposited centuries after they were initially discarded. A 'background noise' is created, through which the true signals of each new period have to be heard.

To address both these problems, the archaeologist can use information from single-period sites, both individual building-types (an intact church or medieval house) and whole short-lived towns (i.e. a medieval town site which is now deserted) for comparison with the often more fragmentary remains excavated in the centres of living towns. The abandoned sites, often in the countryside, will in theory tell us what our fragmentary buildings looked like in their full plan.[8] But what these rural sites gain in extent of plan, they will lose in not having long histories and useful sequences of layers; and many short-lived sites were, almost by definition, failures. Often, therefore, dating frameworks will be from long-lived towns, whether pottery or artefact types, carpentry joints dated by dendrochronology, or moulded stones in buildings dated by documents. The key is the urban stratigraphy; hence the emphasis among urban archaeologists on the diagram of relationships between layers called the Harris matrix as the key to explanation and the starting point for interrogation of the archive, whether the site report or the multitude of finds.[9]

Nor is the background noise of residuality necessarily a bad thing; in long-lived towns we have to work with it. Significant information can be gained particularly about artefacts from study of layers later than the period in question. Recognized and tackled correctly, residuality need not be a problem. We must by preference distinguish the types of deposit which are low in residuality, and here again waterfront dumps, being composed of largely contemporary and often fresh rubbish, are apparently good candidates. It may be that waterfront dumps are better reservoirs of low-residuality than other secondary contexts such as pits on inland sites; the latter lay open for periods, whereas the process of dumping behind revetments was presumably quicker, being intended to function as reclaimed ground on which traffic and buildings could promote business. But there are reservations even about waterfront dumps as pockets of reliable information: there was widespread reuse of second-hand timber which makes reliance on dendrochronology hazardous, and uncertainty about where the rubbish came from.

At this first level of data recovery, there are some specific areas which require development. Two can be mentioned: how to deal with the sheer weight and variety of information from the larger (or even medium-sized) medieval towns, and how to deal with small towns, which may have even less archaeological survival than rural settlements.

Many of the large urban excavations of 1960–90 remain unpublished, largely for lack of resources. It is the same in all European countries, as far as one can see. What urban archaeologists must do is contribute to and maintain an archaeological archive for the town they work in, usually based on the local or regional museum. If the archaeological material was worth digging, it is worth storing for posterity. But it must be worked on, even after first publication of results. The availability of the archive, in some cases mountainous in extent, suggests that future publications may take a variety of forms. The increasing use of the Internet and internal computer systems means that we do not have to publish as we did when the finds were shipped off to a dead-end future in a store and in effect forgotten. The more that the archive is curated, made available and continuously questioned, the more previous archaeological work has meaning and the more academically effective will be future investigations. Spatial study of the great number of finds throughout an individual town is being helped by computers and their programs: the development of Geographic Information Systems (GIS), already used by many archaeologists in rural contexts, may be applicable in town situations. So far GIS applications in urban archaeology in Britain have developed as visual extensions of urban databases, i.e surveys of monuments; and in cemetery studies, since GIS permits extremely fast and efficient multi-variate analysis to test potential zoning of social groups in the cemetery (by gender, age, implied status through grave construction and the like).[10] It is also being used for the analysis of complex sequences on individual sites.

To emphasize the value of deep stratification of major centres is not to abandon the archaeology of small towns, which have their own considerations. Size, by itself, does not make a town (though some historians have thought so, and a few continue to do so). What differentiates a town from a village is a preponderance of activity concerned with manufacture, food processing and trade, both wholesale and retail. Borough status and other privileges, and the buildings to illustrate this local independence, will follow. The boundary between large or complex villages and small and simple towns is difficult to define, and may in any case have been fluid, as witnessed by the number of 'failed' market grants and borough charters held by what were clearly agricultural villages. Small towns are in some ways more difficult to study than larger towns; the stratigraphy in them is thin, and therefore extremely fragile and susceptible to damage from the lightest of foundations. Small town medieval society is less well understood, by documentary historians, than that of the manor and village.[11]

It has been argued that many of the archaeological models being developed by medieval archaeologists for larger urban centres are inappropriate when applied to small towns.[12] The conclusions of a survey of 64 medieval towns in Worcestershire, Herefordshire and Shropshire are instructive; one productive approach is to consider the towns in a region, however defined, as a group which form a landscape of connections and contrasting fortunes (Fig. 8.3). The authors of this survey argue that small towns have archaeological merits. In the Middle Ages, small towns had a narrower range of manufacturing crafts than large towns, and were more closely woven into the local farming economy. Some kinds of archaeological evidence might be better preserved in smaller towns: streets, backlands and religious buildings such as friaries, which survive on the fringes of towns where there has been no development. The processes of refuse disposal and intensity of land use characteristic of large towns are not found in their smaller counterparts, so stratigraphy is often much less, but it can also be comparatively less damaged by later intrusions.[13] Perhaps the authors of this book have been too influenced by their experiences in the larger, deeper towns; and we have to acknowledge that methodologies for the archaeological investigation and understanding of small towns have yet to be developed.

Construction of typologies and chronologies

Archaeologists in many medieval British towns have now reached a second stage. A body of data has been gathered, and questions are being put to it. These questions concern both topography ('How did the town develop into its present shape?') and artefacts ('What equipment did the people use? What did the insides of their houses look like?').

Archaeologists have always been at their most original and confident when studying street plans, building types and the distribution of debris. The debris will include evidence of manufacturing and trade, and the objects will represent a whole level of popular material culture which is representative of the life

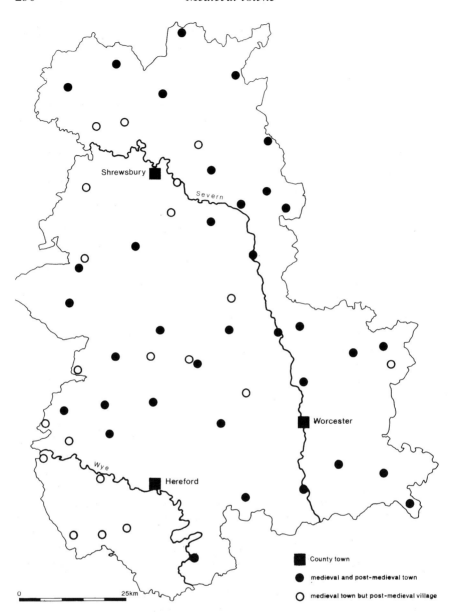

Figure 8.3 Medieval towns in Shropshire, Herefordshire and Worcestershire (Dalwood 2000). This shows the value of studying small towns in a region. Medieval towns which partly failed and which are now villages are predominantly in the west, but there is also a ring around Shrewsbury, a prosperous post-medieval town.

of the majority of people who do not appear in documents (and which have not figured in traditional museum collections). Spatial studies will be informed by dating of the layers which is provided by artefacts, coins and dendrochronology; and by careful use of the stratigraphic and dating evidence, typologies of individual forms of pottery or artefact – which type came first, and which later – can be constructed. These typologies, of which a pottery type-series is the most important for the town, can then be used to date artefacts in less well dated contexts, which are perforce the majority in both urban and rural excavations.

Some of these chronologies of individual artefact-types (including buildings) will be informed by dates in documentary records, and medieval towns have, to varying degrees, the additional benefit of more records per square mile than rural places, or than towns in previous centuries. The two sources are complementary. Archaeology gives more depth on individual sites, while documentary study is wider and can be more effective at the level of larger units such as street or town. Each group of investigators scrutinizes a different set of sources, and there is no overlap. Further, there is scope for much interesting comparison of results, even if (or perhaps, especially because) we do not yet know how the two sets of information will integrate in the short or long term.[14] It is also possible to produce social and cultural history without any archaeology at all.[15] The best archaeology uses documentary sources when they are available, and studies the interplay between them.

While remaining critical about the nature of the evidence from the ground or in standing structures, the archaeologist can produce an archaeological account of the stages in the life of a medieval town. The emphasis in this book on words like sequence and chronology shows the archaeological strength of urban deposits. Archaeological investigation excels in the recording of times of change and crisis. Strata and the activities they suggest, such as construction and demolition, above all indicate change, whether for good or ill. One building or waterfront or industrial process or circuit of defences is replacing another. Archaeological work in towns should therefore investigate evidence of change, and seek to suggest the reasons for change which have rarely been written down. Were these changes caused by social conflicts, or by new technologies, or by environmental factors such as a worsening climate and river silting? By concentrating on these crucial phases or turning-points in our urban history, archaeology will provide its own explanation of the past.

The medieval period in most of Britain, as we saw at the beginning of this book, falls into two parts: the rise of towns in 1100–1350, and crises and consolidations in 1350–1500 (or to some scholars, 1530). Of these two parts, the first is in some respects easier to study, as is its equivalent in the first two centuries of Roman occupation of Britain. Urban consumption, urban markets, new standards in housing, waves of religious orders are all clearly perceptible in the archaeological record. The economy was more commercialized, whether that is reckoned in terms of a simple increase in commercial activity, or an increase in commercial activity outstripping population growth.[16] The archaeology of medieval towns can be dealt with as a study of definable monuments and sites, since the larger topographical features were often clear and stark. There should be more work in Wales, Scotland and Ireland; many themes could be listed for treatment. But at least we roughly know what evidence survives, and how to record it. These clear objectives apart, however, each town will have its local archaeological puzzles and questions to address, and knowledge about the town does not necessarily grow incrementally through the centuries.[17]

The second part of the Middle Ages, from 1350 to about 1500, is by comparison poorly understood, in towns as in the countryside, and this is partly because we do not yet know effective ways to study it. In large and small centres, the strata of this later period are thin or non-existent (as at Lincoln or Godalming, Surrey); the waterfront zones are increasingly unhelpful, as stone walls take over from timber revetments and the dated groups of artefacts become far less frequent. In some cases, documentary evidence becomes the only medium of information for the site in this period (for instance, Fishergate in Norwich, or many sites in London).[18] In other places, such as Coventry, there is documentary evidence for decline, but the largest domestic site excavated so far suggests that building was taking place. The standard of living for manual workers such as artisans seems to have improved: more meat, more objects in metal and glass, probably better housing. In town and country, the recently increased availability of dendrochronological dates for standing buildings suggests that new construction and rebuilding continued after 1350.[19]

It seems the case that after the Black Death, because there were considerably fewer people in towns, several processes took place. Shops disappeared from central streets; some houses became larger, while the unwanted margins of settlement crumbled, decayed and were covered with their own version of dark earth, the deposit normally associated with the Saxon centuries. The amalgamation of properties into larger units can be seen in other European cities and towns. Within towns, we can expect that the poor and disadvantaged areas suffered disproportionately from the main urban plagues. From England to Italy, the Black Death was without doubt a proletarian epidemic; the rich escaped when they could, or lived in parts of town where the quality of life, and sanitation, gave them some protection. Thus the marginal areas will show more radical evidence of change to the archaeologist.

During the second half of the fifteenth century some towns recovered. They tended to be the larger centres (and above all, London), or those which could depend upon a rich hinterland for their industrial wealth. Others, like Coventry, Lincoln or Winchester, went into decline. Because there were fewer people around, there was less need for towns. But during the fifteenth century, and into the sixteenth, new centres of political, commercial and cultural influence and power attracted immigrants both rich and poor. After a period of stagnation and desolation, sixteenth-century towns looked for their future prosperity to a new network of connections, beyond Britain and Europe, to Asia and the New World. This had profound effects on towns in the Old World, at least on the western seaboard (Seville, Lisbon, La Rochelle, Plymouth and Bristol).

This study has had to have chronological limits, which were roughly 1100 and 1500. We have been unconcerned with these divisions, and have often gone before and after to either study origins or trends or to seek parallels. Much of the urban structure of medieval British towns (topographical, religious, cultural, social) has its origins in the ninth and tenth centuries; some of the medieval structure survived until the eighteenth and even nineteenth centuries.[20] The medieval period has a long tail, and often study of the transformations of the medieval town, such as at the Reformation, are a potent method of finding out what was going on in the earlier Middle Ages.

Figure 8.4 A thirteenth-century building reused in an eighteenth-century house, in Leadenhall Street, London; change the furniture, and this could be one of the surviving medieval undercrofts used by shops in Chester (engraving of 1825; Museum of London).

Certainly the period 1100–1700 in British towns is best studied as a single entity, as the playing out of a number of long themes. We should study how medieval buildings were adapted in the post-medieval period; some post-medieval sources, such as engravings, are the only sources for medieval buildings, whether churches, bridges or houses (e.g. Fig. 8.4). The medieval period in this longer sense ends with the Georgian city. Finally, some archaeological questions, particularly those concerned with environmental or climatic change, can only be answered by looking at one or more millennia.

Study of archaeological evidence of specific activities and groups

A town is a relatively dense and permanent concentration of residents engaged in a multiplicity of activities, most of which are non-agrarian; and any distinctive urban character emerges from this heterogeneous composition packed into a rather dense place. The archaeologist can study activities in towns, and the distinct groups which operated there.

A certain kind of study forms the bulk of archaeological reports today: excavations of the defences of town X, the cathedral at Y, the bridge of Z. Less common are studies of single facets of town life which bring together the evidence of several sites within the place. This is partly a consequence of a potentially over-rigorous division of archaeological reports, and of archaeological organizations, into site- and finds-specialists (a dichotomy encouraged by the development-led process of excavations, which requires a quick report on a single site to discharge a planning condition). There should now be a swing towards integration of structural and artefactual evidence, so that we can understand an activity – defence, or religious experience or making cloth – in its entirety. When the structures associated with an activity, the heavy plant, changed, did the mobile equipment also change? We do not seem to be asking such questions.

Between 1150 and 1340 an urban society is more evident in European towns. By this we mean a web or collection of groups which did not have their roots, power bases or fortunes in the countryside. It may have been there in the eleventh century, but so far there is little evidence. Many towns were autonomous or fought to be so, but these apparently united communities contained disparate groups and classes. Friction between these component groups often resulted in violence, as argued by some historians.[21] Other historians stress that although the allegiance and behaviour of town dwellers were usually determined by the sectional interests of their various groups, the town survived because there was an occasional 'realisation of a widely shared sense of civic community'.[22] Archaeology has an important role to play here in describing the extent and character of the material lifestyle of the various groups, and in investigating what an archaeology of the 'community' might mean. In this matter, there is a lot of talk, but few hard suggestions.

Some groups can be perceived relatively easily, such as the nobles who occupied distinctive and large town houses, or the churchmen and women in their walled-off convents. The ordinary people who made up the majority of citizens were dispersed and arranged through the town according to factors which are revealed by a combination of archaeological and documentary study. One model to follow, suggested by work in Winchester, is that change in local patterns of land use was rapid, but took place within a relatively static framework of streets and major standing buildings. Towns had large institutional complexes within them, but it can be argued that they had little more than a marginal effect on the actitivies of the citizens. Somehow the town absorbed these large complexes, and went on with its own life centred on the market place.[23]

Especially within larger towns, taxation records show that some areas were in general richer than others (Fig. 8.5). This may be because people in one zone were generally richer, or because the richer area had in it one or two very rich tax-payers; archaeological study of sites in both rich and poor areas may help clarify the fiscal data. But how can archaeology identify rich and poor sites, or rich and poor households? We have not yet worked out the criteria. Animal bones are one possible means, but we are not agreed on what was expensive or restricted and what was cheap. Ceramics were used in a wide variety of ways, and although the archaeologist can plot the sites of exceptional pottery such as imported items throughout the town, it is difficult to know what to make of it.[24] Assistance may be sought from study of the post-medieval period. In one large sample of English inventories of 1675–1725, richer houses had more clocks, china, pictures, books, knives and forks, looking glasses, table linen, earthenware dishes, saucepans and cooking pots than poor houses, in that order downwards.[25] What this shows is that normal archaeological finds,

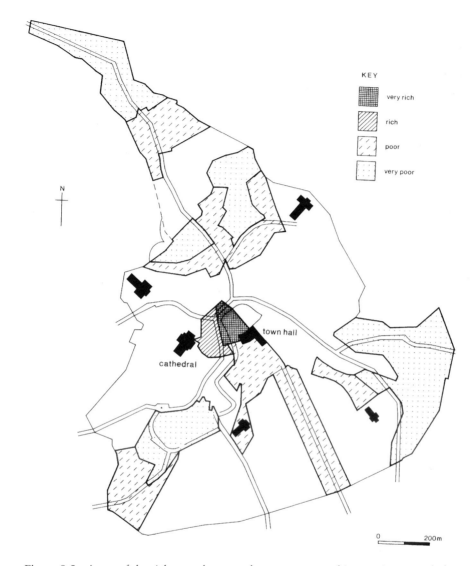

KEY

very rich

rich

poor

very poor

town hall

cathedral

0   200m

Figure 8.5   Areas of the richest and poorest houses as mapped in taxation records for 1318–20, Siena (Balestracci and Piccinni 1977). Such documentary records are valuable but blunt instruments, and should by enhanced by archaeological work on individual sites within these general areas.

especially pottery, were not particularly good indicators of wealth, and the archaeologist must look elsewhere to study this variable. There should be more studies of the 'bottom-up' view of the medieval town. Archaeology should not be solely a matter of fine workmanship and high-status sites. There is a need to investigate the mass market, where the majority of people operated, to establish the baseline of the archaeology of the ordinary. The poor formed an important and numerous part of the urban population, perhaps 25 per cent or more.[26]

Further, these dichotomies themselves may be of limited value; power is heterogeneous, that is, many people have power or authority of some kind (parents, schoolteachers, firemen, midwives). The idea of one group or class dominating another may be too simple; there may have been 'cultural hegemony', a prevailing consciousness or way of doing things which has been negotiated between groups and accepted by them.[27]

There may have been some activities or processes which were especially prevalent in towns, as opposed to the countryside. Three which may be mentioned as having unexplored archaeological dimensions are technology, literacy and consumerism.

A presently unanswered question concerns the role of towns in developing or promoting technological advancement. For some scholars, such as Sjoberg (1960), the main influence on the development of society from prehistoric to industrial times was technology. That is, distinctive types of social structures were associated with varying levels of technology, by which term Sjoberg meant sources of energy, tools and know-how. According to this argument, the shift from copper or bronze implements to those of iron opened the way for proliferations of cities throughout the Old World. With iron, better wheeled vehicles became a reality, shipping goods and food to markets in towns. Improved tools built better and more permanent houses, and money made an appearance.[28] But these ideas have not been applied to the medieval period with any force recently, and they should be reviewed by those knowledgeable in medieval technology, particularly as it might have been illustrated or clarified by archaeological work.

Literacy was the key to Islamic advancement, which was at least partly based on technological innovation and achievement. Islam was moreover primarily an urban civilization. Urban prosperity, local and international trade, literacy and a flourishing culture of science were all linked together; and further, the Islamic empire, which stretched from Delhi to Marrakesh, made Arabic a common language of scientists and allowed interchange of ideas in that language over an immense geographical area. Transferring this to our own area, it may be that constructing an archaeology of literacy would be profitable; and we will probably find that towns were, as some contemporaries thought, crucibles of literacy. This skill aided technological as well as other advances, the most important of which was religious questioning. The Reformation, all over Europe, was a literate movement which championed the written or printed word; it began and spread most fiercely in towns.

Third, can we talk of 'consumerism' in medieval towns? We take consumerism to mean a desire to possess articles for the sake of possession, a wish which goes beyond the dictates of fashion or enjoyment and involves virtually all sections of society rather than just the rich. This consumerism is said to be a feature of the eighteenth century in Europe and America: it is the age of Wedgwood. Conspicuous consumption, the term now used by medieval and post-medieval historians, was actually coined by the sociologist Thorstein Veblen to describe a force behind consumerism in upper-class people in late nineteenth-century America.[29] Some scholars have proposed that conspicuous consumption was a feature of Renaissance Florence, in the middle of the fifteenth century, and as such 'new in western history'.[30] It is always dangerous to claim that something is new.

What is the evidence like for Britain? In 1480, as shown by customs accounts, London was importing an enormous variety of miscellaneous household items and knick-knacks: thimbles, kettles, mirrors (some from Nuremberg), playing-cards, spectacles, candlesticks, brushes, laces, buckles, straw hats, imitation pearls, mistletoe beads, spoons, needles, sheep bells and ear-pickers. Though presumably most of these items were also made in England, somebody thought it worthwhile bringing them from Antwerp, Arnemunden and other Netherland ports. Much longer runs of such records survive for other towns such as Hull. But this cannot compare with the volume and variety of consumer goods in the eighteenth century. Perhaps consumerism in the Middle Ages applies only to a small number of facets of material life.[31] In a consumer culture, objects are thrown away more than before, so the waterfront reclamation deposits are useful again – they are a material catalogue of what was thrown away by townspeople, and it is evident that they threw a lot away in the twelfth to fourteenth centuries, when towns were growing in their commercialization and urban life seemed good.

The idea of Europe

Are medieval towns all over Europe sufficiently similar to be studied together, or are there significant regional differences? It seems to be an assumption of historians and archaeologists that the European town was broadly similar from Waterford in Ireland to Novgorod in Russia. The rise of Europe as a centre of civilization in the medieval period, and afterwards in the Renaissance, is the theme of many studies, for instance by the influential French historian Fernand Braudel.[32]

Braudel said a number of interesting things about towns. He was writing principally about the period 1400 to 1800, and the relation between 'civilization', that is towns, and the emergence of capitalism. In his famous phrases, 'towns are like electric transformers. They increase tension, accelerate the rhythm of exchange and constantly recharge human life'.[33] He firmly believed all western European towns shared common characteristics; Islamic towns (at least all the big ones) shared peculiarly Islamic characteristics. Further, following Lewis Mumford, 'capitalism and towns were basically the same thing in the West'. Whatever meaning one attaches to the term capitalism, it can be traced to thirteenth- and fourteenth-century cities like Florence and Venice. Here people said 'always reinvest your profits' and even 'time is money', a phrase associated with Benjamin Franklin in the eighteenth century. Large cities contributed to a first European world-economy, 'an economically autonomous section of the planet able to provide for most of its own needs, a section to which its internal links and exchanges give a certain organic unity'; and the centres of this world-economy in the Middle Ages were the large number of towns in the Low Countries, among them Bruges; the trading routes of the Hanse merchants, especially through the Baltic; and Italian cities, especially Venice and Genoa. 'The birth of Europe, that monstrous shaper of world history, took place not in 1400 ... but at least two hundred years earlier.'[34]

We suggest that the archaeological version of this European story can now be told. As our introduction in Chapter 1 implied, we have concentrated in this book on a zone around the northern boundary of the former Roman empire. The study has suggested that towns developed in similar ways in this zone, from Ireland to Romania (though we have not been able to say much about towns in the eastern half); and from Scandinavia to the Alps. During the medieval period, there was a great cultural and economic coherence about this zone. By the twelfth century, for the first time since the Roman period, all western Europe, outside the Iberian peninsula, was Christian (and there would be expansion with religious motives into north-eastern Europe in the following two centuries). Romanesque architecture is found throughout; specialists argue for local variants, but they are always basing these assertions on the grandest buildings. Simple churches were the same throughout northern Europe. As we have seen, towns in different parts of Europe developed improved standards of construction and urban hygiene at roughly the same time. Many artefacts and bulk materials circulated throughout the zone, a process lubricated by 'international' trading corporations such as the Hanse. A British site report which studies simple artefacts in reasonable depth, such as one of the sites we have been using at Eastgate, Beverley, finds useful parallels in other towns throughout Britain, on rural sites, and often abroad (Fig. 8.6). At this level of material culture, all Europe shared the same kinds of objects at work and in the home.

This European cultural zone was bordered by others which defined it; in particular, the world of Islam to the south, which occupied much of Spain until 1492, and at an earlier period had occupied Sicily. There was a chain of great cities from one end of the Islamic world to the other: from Cordoba, Seville and Granada in the west, through Fez, Marrakesh, Cairo (with a population of half a million in 1300, more than any European city) to Damascus, Aleppo and Baghdad in the east.[35] In many ways the Islamic city resembled the European: there were markets, walls and gates, craft streets, religious buildings, and sponsored fountains. Perhaps there are no real archaeological differences at all, at least in the public aspects of town life. Within the household, it was perhaps different, but archaeologists can handle that.[36]

There are therefore many similarities between the archaeologies of medieval towns across and within Europe. We study the same processes, attitudes and often the same artefacts. Our computers should increasingly speak to each other, as should archaeologists themselves.

The future: managing change

Many towns across Europe have a substantial surviving element of their medieval architecture (Fig. 8.7); this forms both a commercial asset for tourism and a source of pride and identity for the townspeople. In an even larger number of towns, there are occasional medieval buildings or constructions (houses, bits of defences, bridges) still *in situ* but divorced from their original settings, odd reminders of the past in the modern townscape.

As far as buildings above ground are concerned, there is a healthy and fairly widespread concern now to preserve and enhance standing medieval buildings

Object(s)	Parallels
bone and antler pins	York, Northampton
bone comb	Birka, Ribe, Wolin (Poland), Shetland, York
bone objects used in textile production	York, Lincoln, Waltham Abbey, Birka
bone writing instruments	Whitby, York, Oxford, Boston, Hull, Northampton, Guildford
bridle bit cheek piece	York, Thetford
buckles and strap ends	Writtle (Essex), London, Hull
carding combs	Northampton
copper alloy brooches	Castle Acre (Norfolk)
glass vessels	London, Hull
horseshoes	London
jet brooch	Lincoln, York
knife	Lincoln, Southampton
mirror-case	Perth, London
pewter brooch	York, London
pewter ring	Worcester, London
pins	London
shoes	Durham, York, Dublin, London, Århus, Novgorod, Lincoln, Oslo, Amsterdam
spearhead	Lund
spoon	Bergen, Oslo, London, Carlisle, Netherlands
stone cresset lamp	Southampton, Bergen, Oslo
stone hones	Lund
textiles	Newcastle, London

Figure 8.6 Parallels cited in a report on objects found on the site at 33–35 Eastgate, Beverley, excavated in 1983–6 (Evans and Tomlinson 1992).

in towns (Fig. 8.8). Conservation of historic centres of towns is government and European policy. But it does not take sufficient account of the archaeological dimension, and the fault may lie with archaeologists for not constructing their argument and sufficiently entering the discussion.

In 1975 the Council of Europe declared that the structure of historic centres is conducive to a harmonious social balance and that by offering the right conditions for the development of a range of activities our old towns can be helped to become a favourable environment for social integration. The concept of integration is central to further declarations, including the Malta Convention (1992), which took note of the fact that the growth in number and size of major urban development projects made it necessary to find ways of protecting the heritage through 'integrated conservation methods': this means rehabilitation in old centres as a factor of social cohesion and economic

Figure 8.7 Rue aux Herbes, Chartres. How should we protect our medieval town centres? Why are we protecting them?

development. Generally protection of the heritage involves respect for the historic context in terms of volume, scale, form, materials and quality of design; protection of views, vistas and settings, and street layouts; safeguarding of areas of archaeological importance, open spaces and historic parks.[37]

How is this done? Architects and planners prefer to make a living city rather than a museum town. First, restore meaning to the town and a sense of pride to its inhabitants through restoring historic monuments; then the needs of tourism become secondary. Making tourism the first priority is dangerous, since tourist industries can dominate the range of functions in town centres, and have a negative impact.[38] Next, historic centres are meaningful only if inhabited; free-market forces must be kept in check to prevent cities and

Figure 8.8 Medieval stone buildings on a modern street, Rothenburg ob der Tauber (Germany); no intrusive modern signs or large new buildings; tasteful conservation to make the old buildings work in the present town. It is important that reused ancient buildings do not become a tawdry tourist trap and drive the residents away; the old buildings should function as they used to, as shops for the locality and as houses, with only a few given to selling souvenirs.

neighbourhoods from losing their identities, and old city centres must function to improve the conditions for inhabitants. Some of the built heritage conservators go as far as to declare 'our heritage has not been built for the purposes of admiration, it was built to be used'.[39]

This increased drive for protection of the built environment in medieval and other old towns is admirable, but the archaeological component is rarely included.[40] The archaeologist can sign up to the list of duties of the building conservator, that is to (1) contribute to a policy framework for integrating conservation objectives within the aims of sustainable development; (2) minimize the depletion of non-renewable heritage assets; and (3) define the capacity by which the historic centre can permit change.[41] In general, urban archaeologists all over Europe do the first two, but the third may be something new and a challenge.

We must now construct a language which gets from 'this must be conserved' to 'these are the ways in which archaeological investigation can inform the future management of historic areas, or even new developments, within the town' (Fig. 8.9). We must use the results of the work of the last thirty or forty years to develop guidelines on how to enhance the town itself and make it more attractive, otherwise present forces leading to depopulation of old town centres will prevail.

Figure 8.9 Excavation in Walmgate, York, of foundations of medieval buildings; across the street, rather stranded in the modern townscape, is a standing medieval building (York Archaeological Trust). Archaeologists must develop the arguments so their work influences the conservation of what remains above ground, and helps to fit modern buildings in with the old.

Figure 8.10 Winchester Cathedral: the outline of the seventh- and eighth-century cathedral, excavated by Martin Biddle in the 1960s, marked on the ground next to its medieval successor (John Crook).

The present or future townscape should not strain to look medieval. There was much about the medieval town which should not be imitated; standards of hygiene and construction are now completely different, and it is important not to be sentimental about historic towns. Parts of medieval towns probably had over twice as many households per hectare as modern planning policies allow. The guiding principles must be that new developments must not affect the grain of the place, but fit new buildings within the town's existing frame. At

Figure 8.11 Long-term excavations since 1978 within the redundant church of Saint-Laurent in Grenoble have addressed the question of whether any one period of a building's long history should take precedence in display over another. The archaeologist's proposal here, according to a philosophy that is widely shared, is that intelligible remains of all periods should be conserved and displayed; if that makes understanding of the sequence difficult for the ordinary visitor or citizen, then archaeology is difficult (F. Pattou, Musée Archéologique, Église Saint-Laurent, Grenoble).

the same time the form of the town must respond to the rapid changes all towns are now undergoing, a result of the combined and sometimes competing forces of depopulation, changing work structure, immigration and consequent hardening of local, often ethnic neighbourhoods.[42] Archaeologists study all these factors at work in the past, and could make useful contributions to future improvement or good design.

Figure 8.12 Recording strata in front of the twelfth-century (though restored) keep of Norwich Castle, before a public lift is inserted into the mound to make the interior of the castle more accessible (Norfolk Archaeological Unit).

There are already some ways in which archaeological work is contributing to the present townscape. One is to draw attention to or supply the forms of past buildings, to be etched in the ground (Fig. 8.10). This is a widespread technique, for usually monumental buildings or complexes such as cathedrals and monastic buildings, gateways and defensive walls. Another is to conserve part of a medieval building outdoors; again usually part of a large complex, or successive complexes, such as at the east end of the cathedral at Lyons, excavated in the 1970s. A third possibility is to make an archaeological crypt, as outside Notre-Dame in Paris or inside or near cathedrals, such as Antwerp, Barcelona, Geneva (Fig. 6.3) or York. Here the remains can be seen underground in their original positions, though in some cases there is little relationship with the above-ground surroundings. A fourth method is to use the present building itself, often a church, as a shell for a display of its long history using the remains excavated within, as at Saint-Laurent, Grenoble (Fig. 8.11). And in many places an internal fragment of a medieval building is displayed *in situ* in a corner or beneath a glass floor; or a modern building has a medieval cellar. All these are legitimate ways of giving the ancient fabric a voice in the present townscape. In most European towns, when medieval features are revealed during reconstruction of an old building, they are preserved in the future building if possible and often displayed. This is not only generally required by local and national policies concerning the built environment, but enhances the property in its new role.

New development can enhance the historic environment in a modern way if it is seen to understand its urban context. Archaeologists can provide this understanding, and during the action of helping to manage the urban asset of monuments and strata can promote the archaeological contribution to the history of medieval towns (Fig. 8.12). What we have not done yet, and must now do, is to move from description to explanation of medieval towns in Britain and in their European setting. This is not only because we wish to understand them, but also because most of us live in them.

Notes

1 Introduction

1. For historical studies in English of towns on a European-wide scale, see Nicholas 1997a, 1997b; Friedrichs 1995; Hohenberg and Lees 1985. Some surveys in other languages are noted in Appendix 1.
2. Bruce-Mitford 1956, xxiii; Grimes 1968. For Norwich, Jope 1952.
3. For Hull in the 1960s and 1970s, summary in Evans 1993, 1–4; Southampton: Platt and Coleman Smith 1975; Stamford: Mahany *et al.* 1982; Winchester: Biddle 1967; 1974; Beaumont James 1997; Worcester: Barker 1968–9.
4. Heighway 1972.
5. Jones 1984 chronicles the main developments in rescue archaeology in Britain in the 1970s. The work and influence of the Norwich Survey, which ran under Alan Carter's direction from 1971 to 1978, is described in Carter 1978 and Atkin 1993, and in Atkin and Evans 2002.
6. Simpson 1972. For reviews of how Scottish urban archaeology developed since then, Hall 1999; a historian's view, Ewan 1990, 15–39; for a review of work in Aberdeen to 1987, Evans *et al.* 1987.
7. Biddle and Hudson with Heighway 1973.
8. Some of the county and individual town archaeological surveys of the 1970s are noted here. Berkshire: Astill 1978. Dorset: Penn 1980. Essex: Eddy and Petchey 1983. Oxfordshire: K. Rodwell 1975. Somerset: Aston and Leech 1977. Surrey: O'Connell 1977. Sussex: Aldsworth and Freke 1976. Towns: Boston: Harden 1978. Gloucester: Heighway 1974. Lichfield: Gould 1976. London: Biddle *et al.* 1973. Newcastle: Harbottle and Clack 1976. There is also a detailed bibliography for rescue archaeology in the 1970s in Jones 1984, 159–62.
9. Aston and Leech 1977, Leach 1984. The quotes are from Aston and Leech, pp. 136–9.
10. Schofield and Palliser with Harding 1981. This comparatively rare text can now be found on the CBA website. It contains many local references and speculations about their towns by a large number of archaeologists, at an exciting time.
11. Addyman 1992; Harris 1979.
12. Flüeler and Flüeler 1992, 19 (Stuttgart); Bräuning 1999, 107; Jurion-de Waha 1999. For Europe-wide archaeological reviews, Barley 1977; Gläser 1997a; Council of Europe (ed. Leech) 1999; and see Appendix 1. A sympathetic historian's view of the archaeological contribution of 1950–1992 to the study of European history is Verhulst 1994.
13. Bradley 1984; Barry 1987, 2; for the archaeology of medieval Dublin, see now Duffy 2000; Cleary *et al.* 1997 (Cork); Hurley 1997 (Waterford).
14. Fehring 1985; 1990; for building recording, see especially a volume of papers called *Hausbau in Lübeck*, Jahrbuch für Hausforschung 35, Sobernheim 1986.
15. Sarfatij and Melli 1999; Sarfatij 1990a; 1990b.
16. For early reporting of the work at Bergen, Herteig 1975; for Amsterdam, Baart 1977; Baart 1997 contains a full bibliography of work up to 1995.
17. Paner 1997 on Gdańsk; Pärn and Tamm 1999 on Estonia.
18. Oexle 1999; on Novgorod, Brisbane 1992, Brisbane and Gaimster 2001.
19. M. Gautier writing about Bordeaux in Tours 1982, 372.

20. Council of Europe (ed. Leech), 1999.
21. The archaeology of the Crusades is not dealt with here. For a detailed survey, Pringle 2000; for historical summaries, Riley-Smith 1987, Maalouf 1984, Prawer 1972.
22. This phrase 'preservation by record', invented in the 1970s and already out of date by 1990, has unfortunately been taken to mean the same as 'a pig-headed wish to record as objectively as possible as an end in itself' by a number of writers on archaeological method, both concerning strata in the ground and building recording. These critics confuse objectivity with consistency. The archaeological units in Britain which developed recording systems in the 1970s and 1980s never said their systems were objective, but they did strive to be consistent.
23. Oxley 1999. Compare this approach with that of the previous twenty years and its results, for instance in Hall 1996 and 1997.
24. Hall 1999, looking back at the previous 25 years.
25. For archaeological methodology which has arisen largely out of the urban experience in Britain, see for example Roskams 2001 (excavation methodology) and Orton *et al.* 1993 (pottery studies); for recording manuals, Westman 1994 and as a continental example, Carandini 1991.
26. E.g. Corfield *et al.* [1999].
27. Eydmann 1999, 202.
28. Schiffer 1987.
29. For instance in the cases of London (Biddle *et al.* 1973), Worcester (Carver 1980), Novgorod (Dejevsky 1977; Brisbane 1992), Pavia (Italy; Hudson 1981) or Cesena (Italy; Gelichi *et al.* 1999).
30. Bureš *et al.* 1997.
31. Nydolf *et al.* 1992.
32. For the expansion of archaeological work into recording standing buildings in towns in Britain by rescue archaeologists, see Wood 1994 and now Pearson and Meeson 2001. Medieval buildings in towns had long been recorded by individuals and institutions created for the purpose, such as the three Royal Commissions on Historic Monuments (for England, Wales and Scotland); for Salisbury, RCHME 1980. Similar work on buildings has been undertaken by colleagues on the Continent, for instance papers in Carmiggelt *et al.* 1999. Further examples are given in Chapter 3.
33. Ebner 1991; for Cologne, Schütte 2000.
34. Pirenne 1925; for archaeological reaction to and modification of these views, Hodges 1982; Hodges and Whitehouse 1983; Hodges and Hobley 1988. Historian Adriaan Verhulst finally gives Pirenne's ideas 'a decent funeral' in Verhulst 1999; for a previous critique concentrating on the twelfth and thirteenth centuries, Hibbert 1978.
35. Barrow 2000.
36. Verhulst 1999, 42–3; Esquieu 1994. For Paris, Jehel and Racinet 1996, 24–5; Velay 1992, 88–9. The archaeology of the replacement of Roman buildings by a bishop's palace in the fourth to seventh centuries can be studied in the archaeological crypt at Barcelona, originating in excavations of 1931: Beltrán de Heredia Bercero 2001.
37. Verhulst 1999, 62–5; De Witte 1991.
38. Blair 2000, 248.
39. Hodges 1982; Hodges and Hobley 1988; Verhulst 1999, 24–43; Hill and Cowie 2001.
40. Ayers 1994a, 1994b; Hinton 2000; Demolon and Louis 1994.
41. Verhulst 1999.
42. Hinton 1990, 82–105.

43. Platt 1978, 1–29; Hinton 1990, 106–32.
44. Britnell 1996, 79–127; Astill 2000.
45. The small town of Wyke, which preceded Kingston-upon-Hull, is a striking example (Evans 1999).
46. Jehel and Racinet 1996, 195–6; Keene 1985a. For recent reviews of the large amount of historical and archaeological work on London, see Keene 2000a (the period to 1300); Barron 2000 (1300–1540); for a gazetteer of all sites excavated in the City in the period 1907 to 1991, Schofield with Maloney 1998.
47. Davies 1991; Soulsby 1983; Griffiths 2000.
48. Lynch *et al.* 1988; Stevenson 1988b; Dennison and Simpson 2000. For the annexation of Cumberland in 1136–8 by David I, and the links between urban development and a contemporary regional silver mining boom, Blanchard 1996.
49. Britnell 1994.
50. Keene 1985a; 1989.
51. Goldberg 1992.
52. For reviews of the archaeological evidence, Platt 1976a; 1978, 138–204; Hinton 1990, 191–213.
53. Hatcher 1996; Swanson 1999, 16–19. An example is Coventry: Phythian-Adams 1979, which argues for a general period of urban crisis around 1520, 'one of the major watersheds in the cultural, social and economic history of the nation' (p.4).
54. Soulsby 1983, 24–7; Griffiths 2000, 699–714.
55. Slater 2000 for summary of this debate and suggestions for new directions of enquiry.

2 Topographical factors in the growth of towns

1. For Scotland, Lynch *et al.* 1988; Ewan 1990; Dennison and Simpson 2000; Astill 2000, 44–5.
2. For continental Europe, Dickinson 1961; Barley 1977; Pardo 1982; Heers 1993; and see Appendix 1.
3. Keene 1985b, i, 42, n.5; Carver 1978.
4. For minor streams in Norwich, Ayers 1992; or Bruges, Verhaeghe 1994; Winchester, Keene 1985b, i, 166–7.
5. Butlin 1993, 115; Kowaleski 2000, 468.
6. Sarfatij 1997a.
7. Campbell *et al.* 1993, 60–3; Smith, *Wealth of Nations* (1777), ed. Skinner 1999, 122.
8. Kermode 2000, 446; Soulsby 1983; Keene 2000b, 548; Campbell 2000, 53–4. For the transport system in medieval England and Wales, Edwards and Hindle 1991; Miller and Hatcher 1995, 149–55.
9. Biddle and Keene 1976, 282–5. For a brief survey of mills in medieval England, Holt 1992.
10. Verhulst 1999, 108–9.
11. Slater 1987; Carus-Wilson 1965. For general study of the influence of bridges, Beresford 1988, 112–20. An archaeological and historical study of London Bridge, one of the largest in medieval Britain, is Watson *et al.* 2001.
12. Ayers 1994a, 1; Baker *et al.* 1979, 294.
13. Steane 1985, 109–15.
14. Eddy and Petchey 1983.
15. Hindle 1982; Steane 1985, 104–9. There seems to be no agreement among historians as to whether medieval roads in Europe were passable or bad.
16. Dyer 2000, 521–2; Nicholas 1997a, 107–8. It has also been argued, for English

towns, that transport costs were not a factor that inhibited urban growth (Rigby 1995, 148). A related matter, where archaeology could assist, is to determine how far rivers and creeks were navigable for boats of any size.

17. Astill 2000, 48–9.
18. E.g. Reynolds 1977, 54–5.
19. For an introduction to the main ideas about medieval town-planning in Britain and Gascony, see Beresford 1988; Platt 1976a, 38–44; papers in Barley 1976. For Wales, Soulsby 1983. For geographers' approaches, Dickinson 1961 is a classic text; see also Carter 1981.
20. Beresford 1988, 39–40, 550.
21. RCHMW 1960, 115–58; Soulsby 1983, 89–91; Beresford 1988, 42–5.
22. Britnell 2000, 316–17; Dyer 2000, 517–18.
23. Lauret *et al.* 1988.
24. Friedman 1988.
25. Nicholas 1997a, 97.
26. Slater 1980; Bassett 1982a on Lichfield, discussed further in Slater 1987.
27. Rogers 1969, 2; RCHME 1993, 3–4. For Leeds, Beresford 1988, 160–1.
28. Spearman 1988a, 1988b; for archaeological work in Perth, Bogdan and Wordsworth 1978, Holdsworth 1987; Yeoman 1995, 53–64.
29. Barley 1977; Clarke and Simms 1985; Brachmann and Herrmann 1991.
30. Beresford and St Joseph 1979, 245–6. For examples of excavation of a deserted Scottish town, Murray and Murray 1993 (Rattray, Aberdeenshire); for the deserted edge of a Welsh town, Murphy 1994 (Newport, Dyfed). A medieval farm has been excavated on the edge of medieval Usk (Courtney 1994).
31. RCHME 1972a, on the defences of York, is the best individual study of a British town's defences.
32. Bond 1987, with extensive bibliography.
33. Durham *et al.* 1983.
34. For Banbury, Harvey 1969; for Glasgow, Kellett 1969.
35. Soulsby 1983, 123, 152–4.
36. Frere *et al.* 1982.
37. Astill 2000, 47–8; Ayers 1993, 120.
38. Drage 1987.
39. Ellis 2000; Curnow and Thompson 1969.
40. Bassett 1982b.
41. Stamford: Mahany *et al.* 1982; Norwich: Ayers 1985, Atkin and Evans 2002; Winchester: Beaumont James 1997, 52–62. For further study of castles in both urban and rural landscapes, Creighton 2002.
42. Eddy and Petchey 1983, 39; Priddy 1983, 165.
43. Hassall 1976.
44. For a review of the light which castle sites throw on building techniques, military and household life, costume, pastimes and diet, and their urban functions, see Kenyon 1990.
45. Saunders 1980.
46. Williams 1977.
47. Verhulst 1999, 78.
48. Thompson 1986; for Cirencester, Wilkinson and McWhirr 1998.
49. Heers 1993, 166–7.
50. Morris 1989, 212–13.
51. Britnell 1996, 21–2.
52. Carelli 1999; compare work in Lille: Verhaeghe 1994, 167–8. Miller and Hatcher 1995, 155–76 and Blair 2000 for recent discussions of markets in medieval Britain.
53. An example of a well-developed market area, with whole blocks assigned to dif-

ferent trades (butchers, fishmongers, drapers, etc.) and a main square surrounded by covered galleries, was the Halles in Paris, in the twelfth century: Favier 1997a, 34–6. A more modest late thirteenth-century market building of stone in London was called Les Halles; the Halles in Bruges were begun in 1240.

54. Samuel 1989.
55. Hill 1948, 154, 170; Evans 1999.
56. Dyer 2000, 514; Campbell *et al.* 1993, 28 (London); Favier 1997a, 40 (Paris); Ewan 1990, 10. By the thirteenth century, Canterbury had separate markets dealing with wine (Wincheap), butter (Buttermarket), fish, timber, oats and salt (Urry 1967, 108–9).
57. Astill 1985; 2000.
58. Britnell 1981.
59. Bond 2001: for York, Raine 1955, 129–31.
60. There were several public installations for washing clothes along the Seine in medieval Paris (Favier 1997a, 28); these do not appear to have been found yet in British towns.
61. In this paragraph we mean by 'guildhall' the single town hall (Rathaus, Hotel de Ville). For examples of recording, Barron 1974 (London); Parker 1971, 143–5 (Lynn); for brief discussions, Girouard 1985, 51–4; Palliser *et al.* 2000, 176–7. The halls of craft guilds are briefly mentioned below in Chapter 5 on trade; and in so far as they, and fraternities which could also be called guilds, dispensed and arranged charity, in Chapter 6 on religion.
62. A good example of these themes explored by archaeological work is Qsar es-Seghir, Morocco (Redman 1986); for the archaeology of Muslim towns in general, Insoll 1999, especially Chapter 7.
63. Dean 2000, 5–56.
64. Dijon, Le Goff 1980, 390–1; Chew and Weinbaum 1970; Keene 1985b; i, 53.
65. Keene 1976.
66. Potters in Chichester: Schofield and Palliser 1981, 24; tenters in Bristol: *ibid.*, 11.
67. Stocker 1991; Gilmour and Stocker 1986.
68. Keene 1985b, i, 59–63; Cipolla 1981, 171–4; Britnell 2000, 327. A traditional view that in the thirteenth century fulling became a rural speciality, away from towns, is now disputed: Miller and Hatcher 1995, 110–11. By the middle of the thirteenth century mills were also producing paper in Spain and Italy: Gimpel 1992, 14.
69. Palmer 1980.
70. Hesnard *et al.* 1999; information from Myriame Morel-Deledalle.
71. London: Steedman *et al.* 1992; King's Lynn (Clarke 1973; 1981), Newcastle (O'Brien 1991; Fraser *et al.* 1995), Norwich (Ayers and Murphy 1983; Ayers 1988), Hull (Ayers 1979; 1981; Evans 1997). For general reviews and detailed reports of many excavations in Britain and Europe, Milne and Hobley 1981; Herteig 1985; Milne 1987; Good *et al.* 1991; for Scottish towns, also Ewan 1990, 6–7. For Ribe Kieffer-Olsen 1999.
72. Wallace 1981.
73. Milne and Milne 1982.
74. For correlation with documentary evidence, Dyson 1989; Horrox 1978; Dyson in Schofield and Dyson, in prep. D. H. Evans, from his experience in Hull, warns however that it may be over-optimistic to believe that finds in waterfront dumps are always closely dated. Rubbish was moved around the town and could accumulate material of a wide date range. Timbers in the revetments were often reused. We agree that the interpretation of these contexts has to be carefully argued.
75. Beaumont-Maillet 1997 is a guide to the surviving fragments of medieval Paris.
76. Krautheimer 1980. There does not appear to be a good guide to high medieval

Rome (1100–1500) in print in English.

77. Gem 1997; St Augustine's Abbey is a World Heritage Site.
78. Ayers 1985; 1988; 1993; 1994a; 1994b; *Current Archaeology*, 170 (Oct 2000); Atkin 1985; 1993 with bibliography for Norwich up to that date.
79. For studies of town fabric in England which show how features of medieval topography influenced the town in later centuries, and still do, see for instance Girouard 1990, Lloyd 1998.

3 Houses, properties and streets

1. Schofield *et al.* 1990.
2. Williams 1979; Perring 1981; Carver 1979.
3. Chew and Kellaway 1973; RCHME 1977, lii; Platt and Coleman-Smith 1975, 235; Carver 1980, 167.
4. Schofield 1987, 16, Fig. 3; Schofield *et al.* 1990, 153–9.
5. Schofield 1995, 28–34; Keene 1985b, 156, 169; Urry 1967.
6. Sarfatij 1990a, 190.
7. Barley 1986, 58–67; Armstrong *et al.* 1991; Jones *et al.* 1984; RCHME 1993. For French towns, Esquieu 1994; CNRS 1994.
8. Crummy 1981; Stephenson 1984–5; Urry 1967, 192–4, Maps 2/5 and 2/6; Price with Ponsford 1998, 45–52; Keene 1985b, i, 384–7.
9. Ayers 1988, 172–4; Clarke 1981, 132–3 and Figs 120–1; Schofield 1995, 27–31.
10. *Current Archaeology*, 170 (October 2000), 66; for Rouen, Esquieu and Pesez 1998, 207–9.
11. Flüeler and Flüeler 1992, 82 and for general survey of recent work in German and Swiss towns, pp. 225–87; Laleman and Raveschot 1994; Fehring 1991b, 204; Schneider 1992a; Verhaeghe 1994, 154–6.
12. Esquieu and Pesez 1998, 156–7; Garrigou Grandchamp *et al.* 1997, 189. Garrigou Grandchamp (1992, 113) makes the point however that in the first third of the twelfth century, whole quarters of Cluny were built in stone.
13. For Waterford, Hurley *et al.* 1997; for the London waterfront, Milne 1992. Work on the joints in excavated waterfront constructions dated by dendrochronology is now feeding into study of standing buildings (e.g. Walker 1999).
14. Pantin 1962–3.
15. For Edinburgh, Schofield 1975–6; for Scottish towns, Burton 1994, 243; Stevenson 1988a. For Barley Hall, York, Hall 2001.
16. For Elizabeth de Burgh, Ward 1994; for Battle Abbey, Searle and Ross 1967. For the monastic presence in Berwick, Stevenson 1988a.
17. Le Goff 1980. For excavation of a complex next to the royal palace in Paris, Van Ossel 1998.
18. For the buildings of Salisbury: RCHME 1980, 1993; for York, RCHME 1972b, 1975, 1981. For Treswell's surveys, Schofield 1987; 1995; 1997b. This London typology is discussed in relation to standing buildings in other towns in Grenville 1997.
19. Pantin 1947, 136–8; Portman 1966, 5, 25–6.
20. Horsman *et al.* 1988.
21. Biddle 1967; Williams 1979. Houses with clay walls, equated with the poor, have been excavated at Norwich (Atkin 1991), Beverley and Hull (Evans 2001b). Another group not to be forgotten are medieval squatters, those who build on the edges of towns, as in modern third-world cities: a colony of squatters could be

found outside the walls of Canterbury in the middle of the twelfth century (Urry 1967, 173–4).

22. Martin and Martin 1987, 16–17; Pantin 1962–3, 212–16. For the house at Goodramgate, York, Grenville 1997, 188–9. For the houses at Coventry, Phythian-Adams 1979, 34, after work by S. R. Jones and J. T. Smith.

23. Holdsworth 1987; Yeoman 1995, 53–64.

24. Clark 1984; for inns in Winchester, Keene 1985b, i, 274–7.

25. Salzman 1967, 432–4.

26. Munby 1992; 21 inns are known in Oxford by 1400. For an historical survey of inns in Winchester, Keene 1985b, i, 167–9 and gazetteer; for a ground plan of a London inn in 1610, Schofield 1995, 157–8 and fig. 61.

27. Short 1980; Salzman 1967, 446–8.

28. Atkin 1985.

29. Armstrong and Ayers 1987. For a recent survey of medieval houses in Hull from many excavations, Evans 2001b.

30. Daniels 1990.

31. Carver 1980, 155–220.

32. Evans and Carter 1985.

33. Horsman *et al.* 1988. For other examples, Eastgate Beverley, Evans and Tomlinson 1992; Norwich, Atkin and Evans 2002.

34. Schofield *et al.* 1990, 163–7.

35. For dendrochronology and houses, Pearson 1997; Roberts 2001. For dating beech and elm, Tyers 2001; for fir or pine, Groves 2000 (Britain) and Brisbane 1992, 70–1 (Novgorod).

36. J. Hillam in Brown (ed.) 1999, 139–50.

37. Crone 2000.

38. Lohrum 1992; Garrigou Grandchamp *et al.* 1997, 229–31.

39. At Nijmegen (Holland), a major archaeological study of the houses built between 1300 and 1500 relied upon a chronology which interwove historical evidence, stratigraphy, pottery types, and a classification system which recognized at least seven different brick sizes (Clevis 1989). In Siena, archaeologists have developed a brick typology of seven chronological groups from 1240 to beyond 1690, based on brick size: Parenti 1992.

40. For a survey of the archaeology of house construction in 49 medieval towns in fourteen European countries published as this book went to press, Gläser 2001a. On the Hanseatic house, see e.g. Hübler 1968 (the houses of Lübeck) and Büttner and Meissner 1983 (a Europe-wide survey from a German viewpoint). It should also be noted that the Hanseatic house around the Baltic is seen by some as a material expression of German colonial expansion in the medieval period; the conservation of its form through the period would therefore have been an intentional symbolic and political gesture: as it has become now.

41. Smith 1985; Emery 2000, 125–6.

42. Chew and Kellaway 1973.

43. For the improving technology of timber conversion and use, Milne 1992; Goodburn 1997. Höfler and Illi 1992 on medieval cesspits in Zürich. For jettied buildings after the fire of 1248 at Bergen, Reimers 2001.

44. Garrigou Grandchamp *et al.* 1997; Garrigou Grandchamp 1999; Flüeler and Flüeler 1992, 232–87; for thirteenth-century wall paintings discovered in Barcelona in 1998, Grau *et al.* 1999, 101–21. German towns have a series of studies called *Das Deutsche Bürgerhaus*, begun in 1959, with volumes on the standing houses in individual towns, notably Lübeck (Hübler 1968) and Regensburg (Strobel 1976); in some cases, standing only until World War II. For overall surveys of building recording in European countries, see Gläser 2001 for the Baltic

area; Carmiggelt *et al.* 1999 for the Netherlands; Esquieu and Pesez 1998 for France.

45. Alcock 1993; 1994. Inventories that can be associated with specific surviving buildings are occasionally but rarely identified from the middle of the sixteenth century.
46. Schofield 1995, 74–81; Parker 1971, 208; Brown 1999.
47. Platt and Coleman-Smith 1975, 72.
48. RCHME 1987, 215; Rapoport 1990 for wider discussion. For a catalogue of medieval furnishings, fittings and heating and lighting equipment, Egan 1998. These 1000 London objects were mainly from waterfront dumps, where they are out of original context; when furnishings are found *in situ*, no doubt this catalogue will be used. For a brief discussion of the likelihood of archaeologists' retrieving assemblages that accurately reflect individual households, in London or elsewhere, Egan 1998, 5–7.
49. Dodgshon 1987.
50. Schofield 1987; 1995.
51. Schofield 1987, 79–82.
52. Swanson 1999, 110.
53. Under the influence of the French scholar Ariès, it has for a long time been thought that medieval children were treated as small adults, a more modern attitude starting in the sixteenth and seventeenth centuries. This view is now rejected: Orme 2001. An archaeology of childhood has yet to be developed.
54. Phythian-Adams 1979, 80, 98, 238–42.
55. Thrupp 1948, 169–74; Power 1975; Goldberg 1992; Gilchrist 1994; Ward 1998. For Winchester as an example, Keene 1985b, i, 387–92.
56. Yentsch 1991 (reprinted in Preucel and Hodder 1996); criticized in Spencer-Wood 1999. A statement like 'starting in the sixteenth century, as cultural space was reorganised and pottery became more widely available, in addition to silver and pewter vessels, ceramic utensils also became an integral part of the symbolic inventory that surrounded the use of food in social display' (Yentsch 1991, 209) also needs further argument before it can be accepted, even for the sixteenth century.
57. Hillier and Hanson 1984. This pioneering but difficult work is concerned mainly with the analysis of modern space, to supply some theory to discuss what has gone wrong with contemporary design.

4 Crafts and industries

1. Two important surveys of English medieval industries are Swanson 1989; Blair and Ramsay 1991. The former explicitly sets out to complement the archaeological evidence with a primarily documentary study; the latter combines archaeological and documentary evidence. For Scotland, Ewan 1990; Spearman 1988b; for Europe generally, Pounds 1994, 283–342. For two surveys of archaeological material in German-speaking Europe, Flüeler and Flüeler 1992, 397–436; Fehring 1996, 66–71. The crafts of Novgorod are featured in Brisbane 1992.
2. For example, Rockingham Forest in Northamptonshire, where much evidence can be found for iron and charcoal industries, Foard 2001.
3. Foard 1991, 2001.
4. Beckmann 1974.
5. Salzman 1967; Parsons 1990, 1991.
6. Although this was not always the case: Dyer 1986.

7. Atkin 1983.
8. Webster and Cherry 1973, 162–3.
9. Stocker 1991; 1999; and see Chapter 6.
10. Pritchard 1991, 154–5, Fig. 3.38.
11. Simpson 1996.
12. Interestingly, a similar trade occurred in the Baltic Sea littoral, where honestones of a garnet mica schist occur instead of the Norwegian Rag hones. Why it should be that certain goods passed through the Ore Sund and others did not is unclear.
13. Dunning 1977, 326.
14. Pritchard 1991, 170–1, Fig. 3.53.
15. Baker *et al.* 1979, 46–50.
16. For iron working, Geddes 1991.
17. Evans with Davison 1985.
18. 250 kg of smithing debris was found in one small tenth- or eleventh-century sunken building in Cheapside, London: Hill and Woodger 1999, 37–8.
19. Charleston 1991 for a survey.
20. Biddle and Hunter 1990, 357–61: iii Group 3, durable blue window glass.
21. Atkin and Evans 2002. For clay as a building material see Atkin *et al.* 1985; Evans and Tomlinson 1992; Atkin 1991.
22. Woods 1989; Young and Vince in prep.
23. Dawson *et al.* 1972.
24. Pearce and Vince 1988.
25. Pers. comm. P. K. Madsen.
26. Miller *et al.* (1982), 32–3.
27. 43 out of 44 fourteenth-century coffins from the Austin Friary in Hull have been shown to be made of Baltic oak (pers comm D. H. Evans).
28. A solid wooden wheel, dated to the twelfth century by dendrochronology, has recently been excavated in Hereford. For a survey of woodworking, Munby 1991.
29. Evans 2001a. A large sheet of birch bark was also recovered from this excavation.
30. Hall and Kenward in prep. In particular the beetle *Trox scaber* appears to be highly correlated with occurrences of bark (see Fig. 7.5).
31. Jones *et al.* 1991.
32. Hall *et al.* 1984.
33. Hawthorne and Smith 1979, ch. 94.
34. Grew and de Neergaard 1988.
35. Higham 1989.
36. Ekwall 1960, 298–9.
37. Durham 1977.
38. This site is on the north-eastern fringe of the city in the valley of the River Foss. Hall *et al.* (2000). Technical Report: Environment and industry at Layerthorpe Bridge, York (site code YORYM 1996.345), Reports from the Environmental Archaeology Unit, York 2000/64.
39. Weinstock 2002.
40. O'Connor 1991, 259.
41. Jones 1983.
42. Work by Marianne Gechter and Sven Schütte in Cologne.
43. O'Connor 1991, 256.
44. For survey of the manufacture of objects in antler, bone and horn, MacGregor 1991.
45. Armitage 1982; Armitage 1989; Levitan 1985; Robertson 1989.
46. Walton 1991; Crowfoot *et al.* 1992, 15–25; for documentary survey, Miller and Hatcher 1995, 93–127.
47. Coppack 1986, 53.

48. Armstrong and Ayers 1987.
49. Margeson 1993.
50. Ponting 1957, 13. An early eighteenth-century example with wire bristles has been excavated at Gloucester: Goudge 1983, no. 47.
51. Pritchard 1984.
52. Walton 1992, 200.
53. Pritchard 1984; Crowfoot *et al.* 1992, 82–126.
54. Jones *et al.* 1991.
55. Hall and Kenward in prep.
56. Middleton 1984–5.
57. Waters 1912.
58. Eames 1980, i, 124–5.
59. Moorhouse 1983.
60. Herteig 1991.
61. Barclay *et al.* 1990.
62. Wilthew 1987.
63. Atkin and Evans 1984.
64. Harris 1985, 144
65. McNeil 1983.
66. Evans and Tomlinson 1992.
67. Allan 1984, 325; Heighway 1983; Henderson 1985.
68. Hall and Kenward in prep.
69. Stocker 1991.
70. West 1963.
71. Chitwood 1988; Hooper *et al.* 1989.
72. Pearce and Vince 1988.
73. Guy 1986.
74. By Dr G. MacDonnell.
75. Study by Jane Cowgill.
76. Keene 1985b, i, 278–335.
77. Nicholas 1987, 74–5.
78. Schofield *et al.* 1990, Vince 1991; for the slabs and brasses, Badham and Norris 1999.
79. Egan 1991; Ayers 1991.
80. Kelly 1983, 13–39.
81. Egan and Pritchard 1991, viii.
82. McCarthy and Brooks 1988, 79–80.
83. On the detection and definition of the medieval pin-making industry, see Caple 1991.
84. Biddle 1990, 70.
85. Grew and de Neergaard 1988.
86. Reaney 1967, 176–91. Occupations are sometimes explicitly mentioned in enrolled deeds and other records but is it rarely clear whether the land holder was carrying out his or her trade on that property or elsewhere. However, consistent patterns involving more than one family are probably a more reliable indicator. Names derived from occupations seem a valid method of analysis for the thirteenth and early fourteenth centuries: Keene 1985b; Miller and Hatcher 1995, 128–34.
87. Vince 1993.
88. Steane 2000.
89. Compare Pritchard 1991, 168–9.

5 Trade and commerce

1. For historians' discussions of medieval towns and trade in England, see Miller and Hatcher 1995; Swanson 1999, 32–43; Britnell 1996 and 2000; for general models of economic development, Hatcher and Bailey 2001; for Scotland, Ewan 1990, 64–91; continental Europe, Pounds 1994, 343–406; Verhulst 1999, Nicholas 1997a. For a regional study, that of the provision of grain to London about 1300 and the effect of the capital's needs on the agriculture of the surrounding ten counties, Campbell *et al.* 1993.
2. Clarke and Ambrosiani 1991, 176–8.
3. Carus-Wilson 1965.
4. Keene 1985b, 371–9.
5. Information kindly supplied in advance of publication by Dr P. Bischoff, University of Oklahoma.
6. Knight 1983.
7. Dunning 1959.
8. Analysis by John Cotter.
9. Kruse 1992.
10. Vince 1985, fig. 37.
11. Dolley 1975; Knight 1983.
12. Ulmschneider 2000.
13. Platts 1985, Appendix I.
14. Ewan 1990, 67.
15. For example, in the Assize of Bread and Ale of 1266 issued by Henry III: Skinner 1967, 92–3; Zupko 1968, 189.
16. Ward Perkins 1954, 171–4. The name 'steelyard' was originally that of the Hanse's London headquarters (a mis-translation of the Old High German name *stalhof*), and later became attached to similar commercial districts in other English towns and to the public weighing beams used at those places.
17. Cherry 1991.
18. Archibald 1991.
19. Forgeais 1866, 128–30.
20. E.g. in London: Keene 1990a.
21. Urry 1967, 107; Lyle 1994, 60–2.
22. Johnson and Vince 1992.
23. Clark 2000 surveys surviving shops and commercial halls from the late twelfth century to about 1550 in England, using 60 examples. He concludes that there may be more evidence of shops in standing buildings than seems to be the case. For shops and mercantile buildings in European cities, Girouard 1985, 18–31.
24. Giles 2000, a study based on scrutiny of three surviving late medieval halls in York. For the London livery company halls, Schofield 1995, 44–51 and gazetteer.
25. Hurst *et al.* 1986.
26. Gutiérrez 2000.
27. Hurst 1977; for wider study of lustrewares, Caiger-Smith 1985.
28. Allan 1984.
29. Vince and Jenner 1991.
30. Vince 1977.
31. Pearce and Vince 1988.
32. Pearce *et al.* 1985.
33. Barley 1936.
34. Armstrong 1977; Armstrong and Ayers 1987; Evans 1993.
35. Evans 1999.
36. Verhaeghe 1999.

37. In 1997, an international archaeological conference about medieval trade in northern Europe was held at Lübeck in Germany. Forty-one medieval towns and twelve countries were represented, from Ireland to Russia and from Sweden to Holland. The resulting volume of papers concluded that the archaeological study of medieval trade was difficult (Gläser 1999).

6 Religion in towns: churches, religious houses and cemeteries

1. Rodwell 1981, 105–29.
2. Morris 1996, xv; see now Blair and Pyrah 1996.
3. For some studies up to 1989, see Morris 1987; 1989, 172–5; Biddle and Keene 1976, 329–35.
4. Soulsby 1983, 45–6; Ewan 1990, 10–11.
5. Gilmour and Stocker 1986.
6. Schofield 1994a for London; Wilson and Mee 1998 for York.
7. Milne 1997, fig. 13.
8. Goldthwaite 1980, 12.
9. Schofield 1994a.
10. RCHME 1977, xlix, 24–5; Morris 1989, 367.
11. For examples of parish church excavations in Germany, Fehring 1996, 93–7; for Holland, Van Drunen 1983, Stoepker 1990. For a survey of medieval parish organization from Sweden to Italy, Kümin 1997.
12. Brown 1996; Peters 1996.
13. Blair and Blair 1991.
14. Morris (R.K.) 1992; 1996. On tooling, Stocker 1993; but *cf.* Alexander 1996; on the Yorkshire School, Morris 1989, 278–82, from work by L. Butler.
15. Stocker 1999.
16. Draper 1987; for interior fittings, Peters 1996.
17. For an example from a Saxon church, Rodwell 1976.
18. T. Ayers 2000.
19. For tiles, Axworthy Rutter 1990 (Chester).
20. Keene 1985b, i, 108–9; Rodwell 1981, 131–66; Barrow 1992; Rosser 1996; Daniell 1997, 116–74; for methods and research development in burial archaeology, Roberts *et al.* 1989.
21. White 1988. This brief survey does not include continental material: for one summary of work in churchyards in towns in southern Germany and Switzerland, Flüeler and Flüeler 1992, 477–93.
22. For Roman cemeteries, see e.g. Barber and Bowsher 2000. Norwich, Ayers 1985; Trowbridge, Graham and Davies 1993. Shoesmith 1980 is a similar study of an eighth- to twelfth-century cemetery at Castle Green, Hereford, but in this case the church was a Saxon minster with priests.
23. Rosser 1996; O'Brien and Roberts 1996; for Scotland, Ewan 1990, 11.
24. Morris 1987, 184–5.
25. Blair and Pyrah 1996.
26. Brown 1996, 64.
27. Biddle and Keene 1976, 334–5.
28. Spencer 1990; 1998.
29. Rosser 1984; Giles 2000.
30. Burton 1994.
31. Butler 1987; Palliser 1993.
32. Blair 1988; Fernie 2000 for an extensive survey of the architecture of the cathedrals and other Norman churches.

33. Urry 1967, 163–6; Keene 1985b, i, 51.
34. Tatton-Brown and Munby 1996 for general survey. For a study of a single cathedral, Maddison 2000; a geological study, Worssam 2000 on Rochester; excavation below the floor of Canterbury cathedral, Blockey *et al.* 1997.
35. Greene 1992; Steane 1985, 68–73; Coppack 1990. For French monasteries, Bouttier 1995.
36. Esquieu 1994; an example, Sapin 2000.
37. Huggins 1972. For a rural example with many potential parallels, the Outer Precinct of Tintern Abbey (Gwent) (Courtney 1989).
38. Schofield and Lea in prep.; RCHME 1980, 49; Ward 1990, 8.
39. Butler 1984; Dobson 1984.
40. Le Goff 1980, 236–7.
41. Ward 1990, 62–3.
42. Poulton and Woods 1984.
43. Lambrick and Woods 1976; Lambrick 1985; Daniels 1986, 271–2; Ward 1990, 125–6.
44. Mellor and Pearce 1981.
45. R. Gilchrist in Foreman 1996, 213–28.
46. Gilchrist 1992. Investigations of leper hospitals have taken place at Chichester (Magilton and Lee 1989) and High Wycombe (Farley and Manchester 1989).
47. Thomas *et al.* 1997.
48. Price with Ponsford 1998.
49. Swanson 1999, 3, 107–39.
50. We have not been able to summarize here work on Jewish religious sites or artefacts, but for certain or possible synagogues, Jewish buildings and tombstones, see for England, Pepper 1992, Roberts 1992, Alexander 1997; and for an excavated synagogue in Vienna, Helgert 1997. Work on towns in Islamic Spain has similarly been beyond our capacity for this edition.

7 *The environment of medieval towns*

1. Shackley 1981, Evans and O'Connor 1999.
2. Addyman 1982.
3. Brimblecombe 1982.
4. Steane 1985, 175.
5. Dyer 1989, 258–60.
6. Astill and Grant 1988, 232–3.
7. Boyd 1981.
8. Robinson in Lambrick and Woods 1976, 227–31; Maloney with de Moulins 1990.
9. Green 1982.
10. Carruthers 1997; Jones *et al.* 1991 and Davis 1997.
11. Jones *et al.* 1991.
12. Greig 1988, 125–7; Jones *et al.* 1991, 353.
13. Cobb 1990.
14. Greig 1982, 50–64.
15. For other British medieval examples see Scaife 1994 (Norwich) and note 24 below (Reading). An optimistic study of pollen in urban settings is Krzywinski *et al.* 1983 on medieval Bergen, Norway.
16. O. Rackham 1976, 69–95. For a general survey of the crafts using wood in the medieval period, Munby 1991.
17. E.g. O'Connor *et al.* 1984, 171.

18. Robinson in Palmer 1980, 199–206; Robinson and Wilson 1987, 63; for comment on urban insects, Kenward and Allison 1994.
19. Armitage 1985.
20. Armitage and West 1985.
21. J. Rackham 1982, 92.
22. Analyses by R. G. Scaife (pollen), W. J. Carruthers (plant remains), J. P. Coy (animal bone) and J. Winder (molluscs) in Hawkes and Fasham 1997.
23. Campbell *et al.* 1993.
24. For general introductions to animal bones, see Rackham 1994; O'Connor 2000; but both are largely concerned with methodological issues and pointing out interesting potential.
25. Noddle 1977.
26. The problems of arguing from bones to carcases, and from the sample to the animal population, are addressed in studies which put forward the various different methods of analysing bones: Chaplin 1971; Maltby 1979, 5–8; Scott 1991; Rackham 1994 compares four different methods of quantification.
27. Scott 1991.
28. O'Connor 1989.
29. Wilson 1989, 261–4.
30. Grant 1988, 166.
31. Coy 1982; Scott 1991, 222–3.
32. A. K. Jones and S. Scott in Atkin 1985, 223–8.
33. Rogerson 1976, 208–23.
34. Keene 1985b, i, 259.
35. Serjeantson and Waldron 1989, 3.
36. O'Connor 1982, 46–50.
37. Grant 1988, 153; Wilson 1989, 265–6; Wilson 1994.
38. Levitan 1989.
39. O'Connor 1993.
40. Berg 1987; Ijzereef 1989.
41. Fieldhouse 1986; Grant 1988, 178–82, where a high proportion of pig bones is thought to be a mark of status. For discussion of many aspects of food and feasting in the medieval period, Hammond 1993.
42. Marsh 1914.
43. Campbell *et al.* 1993.
44. Greig 1991; Wilson 1976; Harvey 1981; Kenward and Hall 1995; Hammond 1993; for two fifteenth-century cookery books, Austin 1888.
45. McKenna 1991, 215.
46. Galloway *et al.* 1996.
47. Waldron 1989; Mays 1997.
48. White 1988, 41.
49. Dawes and Magilton 1980, 58.
50. Thomas *et al.* 1997, Glass 2001.
51. Mays 1997; Cipolla 1981, 50–7. For 'urban' infections, see cautionary remarks in Manchester 1992.
52. Stirland 1985.
53. White 1988.
54. Dawes and Magilton 1980.
55. Stroud 1994a.
56. Lilley *et al.* 1994.
57. Stroud 1994b.
58. Jansen 1987.
59. McKenna 1987, 255–7; 1991, 214.

60. Ziegler 1971; the figure used here is from Hatcher 1977, 21–6.
61. Hawkins 1990.
62. Tanner and Everleth 1976, 146; Brothwell 1994.
63. Austin 1990.

8 Unfinished business

1. Roskams 2001.
2. Girouard 1990, 7–8.
3. For a start, Perring in prep. The major historical survey of regions in medieval Britain proposed and discussed in Palliser 2000, 541–737, should be tested archaeologically.
4. Braudel 1985a–c; for another approach, Abrams 1978.
5. Pevsner 1976.
6. Hilton 1982.
7. Archaeologists should look at the development of grounded theory in sociology: e.g. Strauss and Corbin 1998.
8. D. Evans reminds us (pers comm) that it would be much better to get a variety of sequences over the town, rather than look for them in the countryside.
9. Harris 1979.
10. Information from B. Sloane, Reading University.
11. Hilton 1990, 73. For a recent historical survey of small towns in medieval Britain, Dyer 2000.
12. P. Courtney in Jones 1998, 202–3, considering excavations in New Radnor (Powys).
13. Dalwood 2000 and pers. comm.
14. Although it is necessary to remain critical of both sources, it is unproductive to argue that medieval archaeology is subject to a tyranny of the written word (Champion 1990). No examples of the supposed tyranny are given. More refreshing is the idea that since documents are a form of material culture, then history is actually part of archaeology (Hodder 1986, 11).
15. E.g. Schama 1987, on Dutch culture in the seventeenth century, which was primarily urban.
16. Britnell 1996, 228.
17. At Chester, for instance, the existence and protection of the buildings on street frontages affect the amount of data available. From 1066 to about 1230 is a local Dark Age, darker than the two centuries before the Norman Conquest. Saxon buildings were spread throughout properties; Norman and later occupation concentrated on the street frontages, where it has remained since, partly inaccessible and partly destroyed. Norman material culture is also poor. For the period up to about 1230, Chester behaves like a small town (information from Simon Ward).
18. Godalming: Poulton 1998; Norwich: Ayers 1994a, ix.
19. Wright 1982; Swanson 1989, 174–5 and generally; Dyer 1989, 204–10; Dyer 1997.
20. Doubts are expressed about the period division of 1500 between 'medieval' and 'post-medieval' in Gaimster and Stamper 1997.
21. Hilton 1990; Rigby 1995; Swanson 1999 are proponents of this view.
22. Rosser 1984.
23. Keene 1979.
24. Brown 1997.
25. Weatherill 1996, 107.
26. Phythian-Adams 1979, 131–2; this example is Coventry in the 1520s.

27. McGuire and Paynter 1991, 1–13; for cultural hegemony, Beaudry *et al.* 1991. These theoretical developments are in north American historical archaeology, but there is no reason why they should not be tested in medieval European towns.
28. Sjoberg 1960; Cipolla 1981. Sjoberg specifically adds that the use of writing to aid memory and make contracts was crucial, and that writing or literacy (including the use of written numbers) was more widespread in towns. He is thinking about 'towns' since their formation in prehistory. For critical comment on Sjoberg, Hilton 1992, 7.
29. Weatherill 1993; 1996; Veblen 1899.
30. Hall 1998, 97.
31. Cobb 1990; Egan and Pritchard 1991. A surge in imports of household articles has also been noted at smaller towns around 1500: Phythian-Adams 1979, 286, n. 11.
32. Braudel 1985a–c; *cf.* Le Goff 1988 (a text originally of 1964).
33. Braudel 1985a, 479. It should be noted, however, that in the thirteenth century Western Europe was peripheral to larger world economies to the south and east, all the way to China; and that though Europe became a superior economy by the sixteenth century, in the thirteenth century it was less developed than the Middle East as regards business practices. At this time there were several connected world economic zones, and no leader (Abu-Lughod 1989).
34. Braudel 1985b, 579–80; 1985c, 22, 92. The Renaissance historian John Hale suggests that the idea of Europe as an entity, as opposed to 'Christendom', is largely a creation of the sixteenth century: Hale 1994, xix, 5–60. Here we are studying what led up to that crystallization. For the view that towns are better studied in their feudal setting, and not as special objects, Hilton 1992.
35. Lapidus 1984, Hourani 1991.
36. Insoll 1999; for an analysis of houses in Saudi Arabia which looks very familiar, Abu-Ghazzeh 1995.
37. Pickard 2001, 1–5.
38. This is the effect of medinas in many Arab cities; only the tourists shop there. It has also led to the appearance of fake historic medinas in other towns, for instance in Mali.
39. Pickard 2001, 51, 289.
40. A notable exception is a survey of Malta: according to Pace and Cutajar (2001, 213), the city of Mdina in Malta is a block of strata from the Bronze Age all the way up to the Baroque cathedral which forms the top layer.
41. Pickard 2001, 290.
42. Rogers and Power 2000, 1–8, 180, 232.

Appendix: bibliographical note

Within the confines of this fairly short survey of the archaeology of medieval towns (i.e. the period 1100–1500), we cannot do complete justice to the work of our many colleagues throughout Europe. Within each country, we have listed work on only a few representative towns, large and small; and they are summary or survey papers, not reports on individual sites. The works cited are largely archaeological, but we include documentary and topographical studies when they have taken account of archaeological work. Some of the national surveys are of the state of urban archaeology in the country, and while they are primarily about how archaeology is practised, they also have bibliographies of results.

Continental Europe

Archaeological surveys

Barley 1977; Dolgner and Roch 1990; Leech 1999; Vissak and Maësalu 1999; the series *Rotterdam Papers: A Contribution to Medieval Archaeology*, vols 1–10, Museum Boymanns van Beuningen, Rotterdam (1968–); and a series of thematic overviews of the towns in the Hanse world produced by archaeologists in Lübeck: Gläser 1997a, 1999, 2001a

Historical surveys

Pardo 1982; Jehel and Racinet 1986; Heers 1993; Braudel 1985a–c

Individual countries

Belgium

Verhulst 1999
Antwerp: Veeckman 1992; 1997; 1999; 2001; reports in *Berichten en Rapporten over het Antwerps Bodemonderzoek en Monumentenzorg (BRABOM)*, 1–3, 1996–9, Stad Antwerpen
Bruges: Vandenberghe 1983; De Witte 1997; 1999; Van Eenhooge 2001
Brussels region: Jurion-de Waha 1999

Czech Republic

Boháčová *et al.* 1999

Most: Klápšte and Velímský 1992
Prague: Huml 1990; Píša 1990; Richter 1991

Denmark

Liebgott 1999
Århus: Skov 1999, 2001
Copenhagen: Skaarup 1999
Ribe: Bencard 1981, 1984; Bencard *et al.* 1991; Madsen 1997, 1999; Kieffer-Olsen 1999, 2001
Svendborg: Jansen 1987, 1999

Estonia

Pärn and Tamm 1999; Pärn 2001
Tallinn (Reval): Pullat 1998
Tartu (Dorpat): Maësalu 1999, 2001; Vissak 1999

Finland

Turku: Hiekkanen 2001

France

Tours 1982; Garmy 1999
Caen: Collet *et al.* 1996; Marin and Levesque 2000
Marseilles: Hesnard *et al.* 1999; Bouiron 2001
Paris: Lombard-Jourdain 1985; Beaumont-Maillet 1997; Favier 1997a, 1997b; Van Ossel 1998
Saint-Denis: Wyss 1996

Germany

National and regional studies: Reinisch 1990; Brachmann and Herrmann 1991; Flüeler and Flüeler 1992; Fehring 1991b, 1996; Bräuning 1999; Oexle 1999
Bremen: Rech 1997, 2001
Brunswick: Rötting 1997, 2001
Duisburg: Gaimster 1988; Krause 1992, 1993; Bechert 2001
Einbeck: Heege 2001; Heege *et al.* 1998
Göttingen: Arndt 1997, 2001
Hamburg: Busch 1999, 2001
Kiel: Albrecht and Feiler 1996; Feiler 1999
Lübeck: Hansestadt Lübeck 1988; Fehring 1985, 1989, 1990; Gläser 1997b,

2001b; Mührenberg 1999. Excavations are published in a series of reports, *Lübecker Schriften zur Archäologie und Kulturgeschichte*. A synthesis of the first 25 years of investigations is Gläser *et al.* 1998

Lüneburg: Ring 1997, 1999, 2001; journal *Archäologie und Bauforschung in Lüneburg*

Rostock: Mulsow 1999, 2001

Schleswig: Vogel 1989

Soest: Melzer 1999; Thiemann 2001

Stade: Lüdecke 1997, 2001

Stralsund: Schneider 1997, 1999, 2001

Uelzen: Mahler 2001

Ulm: Oexle 1992b

Wismar: Hoppe 1999; a series of reports, *Wismarer Studien zur Archäologie und Geschichte*

Holland/Netherlands

Van Regteren Altena 1970; Sarfatij 1973, 1997a, 1997b, 1999a; Bartels 1998

Alkmaar: Alders *et al.* 1992; Cordfunke 1990

Amsterdam: Baart 1977, 1997, 2001

Deventer: Clevis and Kottmann 1989; Magdelijns *et al.* 1996; Spitzers 2001

Hasselt: Bartels *et al.* 1993

Kampen: Clevis and Smit 1990

Nijmegen: Thijssen 1991

s'Hertogenbosch: Boekwijt and Janssen 1997

Tiel and Dordrecht: Sarfatij 1999b

Zutphen: Groothedde *et al.* 1999; Groothedde 2001

Zwolle: De Vries 2001

Hungary

Gerevich 1990; Gerö 1990

Budapest: Gerevich 1971

Visegrád: Laszlovsky 1995

Ireland

Barry 1987; Hurley 1997; Manning 1999

Cork: Clearey *et al.* 1997; Hurley 1997, 1999, 2001

Dublin: Ó Ríordáin 1971; Wallace 1992; Duffy 2000

Waterford: Hurley *et al.* 1997; Hurley 2001

Italy

Gelichi 1997; Melli 1999; bibliography in De Minicis 1999

Cesena: Gelichi *et al.* 1999
Genoa: Melli 1996
Pavia: Hudson 1981
Pisa: Bruni *et al.* 2000
Rome: Paroli and Delogu 1993
Siena: Balestracci and Piccinni 1977

Latvia

Riga: Caune 1997, 2001
Vilnius: Kuncevičius 1997

Lithuania

Klaipeda: Žulkus 2001

Norway

Bergen: Herteig 1975, 1991; Øye 1997, 1999; Reimers 2001; a series of
    reports, *The Bryggen Papers*, three volumes 1984 to 1990; and a *Supple-
    mentary* series
Oslo: Shia 1989; Keller and Shia 1994; Molaug 1993, 1997, 1999, 2001
Trondheim: Long 1975

Poland

Elbląg: Nawrolska 1997, 1999, 2001
Gdańsk: Stankiewicz 1990; Paner 1997, 1999, 2001
Kolobrzeg: Rębkowski 2001
Szczecin: Cnotliwy 1997

Russia

Ladoga: Lebedev 1997
Moscow: Beliaev and Veksler 1996
Novgorod: Dejevsky 1977; Brisbane 1992; Rybina 1997, 1999; Sorokin 2001

Spain

Spanish Ministry of Culture 1999
Barcelona: Grau *et al.* 1999

Sweden

Hall 1990; Esgård *et al.* 1991
Lund: Carelli 1997, 1999, 2001; journal *Archaeologica Lundensia*
Malmö: Reisnert 2001
Sigtuna: Tesch 2001
Stockholm: Söderlund 1997, 1999, 2001
Uppsala: Anund 1997, 2001
Visby: Westholm 1997, 1999, 2001

Switzerland

Flüeler and Flüeler 1992
Geneva: Bonnet 1999
Konstanz: Oexle 1992a
Zürich: Hanser *et al.* 1983; Schneider 1992b

Ukraine

Kiev: Ioannisyan 1990

Bibliography

Abrams, P. (1978), 'Towns and economic growth: some theories and problems', in Abrams and Wrigley, 1–8.

Abrams, P. and Wrigley, E. A. (eds) (1978), *Towns in Societies: Essays in Economic History and Historical Sociology*. Cambridge University Press, Cambridge.

Abu-Ghazzeh, T. M. (1995), 'Domestic buildings and the use of space: Al-Alkhalaf fortified houses, Saudi Arabia,' *Vernacular Architecture*, 26, 1–17.

Abu-Lughod, J. L. (1989), *Before European Hegemony: The World System AD 1250–1350*. Oxford University Press, Oxford.

Addyman, P. V. A. (1982), 'The archaeologist's desiderata', in Hall and Kenward, 1–5.

Addyman, P. V. A. (1992), *York Archaeological Trust 21st Anniversary*. York Archaeol. Trust, York.

Addyman, P. V. A. and Black, V. (eds) (1984), *Archaeological Papers from York Presented to M. W. Barley*. York Archaeological. Trust, York.

Albrecht, U. and Feiler, A. (1996), *Stadtarchäologie in Kiel*. Neumünster.

Alcock, N. W. (1993), *People at Home: Living in a Warwickshire Village, 1500–1800*. Phillimore, Chichester.

Alcock, N. W. (1994), 'Physical space and social space: the interpretation of vernacular architecture', in Locock, 207–30.

Alders, G., Bitter, P., Bruin, J., Hildebrand, R. and Roedema, R. (1992), *Uit de Alkmaarse bodem: archeologische vondsten 1986–1992*. Alkmaar, Holland.

Aldsworth, F. and Freke, D. (1976), *Historic Towns in Sussex: An Archaeological Survey*. Institute of Archaeology, London.

Alexander, J. and Binski, P. (eds) (1987), *Age of Chivalry: Art in Plantagenet England 1200–1400*. Royal Academy of Arts, London.

Alexander, J. S. (1996), 'Masons' marks and stone bonding', in Tatton-Brown and Munby, 219–36.

Alexander, M. (1997), 'A possible synagogue in Guildford', in De Boe and Verhaeghe (1997a), 201–12.

Allan, J. P. (1984), *Medieval and Post-Medieval Finds from Exeter 1971–1980*. Exeter Archaeol. Reports 3, Exeter.

Andrews, D. and Mundy, C. (in prep.), 'Saffron Walden: the topography of the southern half of the town and the marketplace: excavations and watching briefs 1984–87', *Essex Archaeol. and Hist.*

Andrews, G. (1984), 'Archaeology in York: an assessment', in Addyman and Black, 173–208.

Anund, J. (1997), 'Urban archaeology in Uppsala', in Gläser 1997a, 403–18.

Anund, J. (2001), 'The curses and possibilities of wooden architecture: domestic buildings in medieval Uppsala', in Gläser 2001a, 635–57.

Archibald, M. M. (1991), 'Anglo-Saxon and Norman lead objects with official coin types', in Vince, 326–46.

Armitage, P. L. (1982), 'A system for ageing and sexing the horn cores of cattle from British post-medieval sites (17th to early 18th century) with special reference to unimproved British longhorn cattle', in B. Wilson, C. Grigson and S. Payne (eds), *Ageing and Sexing Animal Bones from Archaeological Sites*. Brit. Archaeol. Reports 109, 37–53.

Armitage, P. L. (1985), 'Small mammal faunas in later medieval towns', *Biologist*, 32(2), 65–71.

Armitage, P. L. (1989), 'The use of animal bones as a building material in post-medieval Britain', in D. Sergeantson and T. Waldron (eds), *Diet and Crafts in Towns*. Brit. Archaeol. Reports 199, 147–60.

Armitage, P. L. and West, B. (1985), 'Faunal evidence from a late medieval garden well of the Greyfriars, London', *Trans. London and Middlesex Archaeol. Soc.*, 36, 107–36.

Armstrong, P. (1977), *Excavations in Sewer Lane, Hull 1974*. Hull Old Town Report Series 1, East Riding Archaeologist 3.

Armstrong, P. and Ayers, B. (1987), *Excavations in High Street and Blackfriargate*. Hull Old Town Report Series 5, East Riding Archaeologist 8.

Armstrong, P., Tomlinson, D. and Evans, D. H. (1991), *Excavations at Lurk Lane Beverley 1979–82*. Sheffield Excavation Reports 1, University of Sheffield/Humberside Archaeological Unit.

Arndt, B. (1997), 'Die Hansestadt Göttingen', in Gläser 1997a, 149–60.

Arndt, B. (2001), 'Archäologische Aspekte zum Hausbau in Göttingen', in Gläser 2001a, 233–50.

Astill, G. G. (1978), *Historic Towns in Berkshire: An Archaeological Appraisal*. Berks. Archaeol. Committee Pubn 2.

Astill, G. G. (1985), 'Archaeology and the smaller medieval town', *Urban History Yearbook 1985*, 46–53.

Astill, G. G. (2000), 'General survey 600–1300', in Palliser, 27–49.

Astill, G. G. and Grant, A. (1988), *The Countryside of Medieval England*. Blackwell, Oxford.

Aston, M. and Leech, R. (eds) (1977), *Historic Towns in Somerset*, Committee for Rescue Archaeology in Avon, Gloucestershire and Somerset.

Atkin, M. (1983), 'The chalk tunnels of Norwich', *Norfolk Archaeol.*, 38, 313–20.

Atkin, M. (1985), 'Excavations on Alms Lane', in Atkin *et al.*, 144–260.

Atkin, M. (1991), 'Medieval clay-walled buildings in Norwich', *Norfolk Archaeol.*, 41, 171–85.

Atkin, M. (1993), 'The Norwich Survey 1971–1985: a retrospective view', in Gardiner, 127–43.

Atkin, M. and Evans, D. H. (1984), 'Population, profit and plague: the archaeological intepretation of buildings and land-use in Norwich', *Scottish Archaeol. Review*, 3/2, 92–103.

Atkin, M. and Evans, D. H. (2002), *Excavations in Norwich 1971–78. Part III*. East Anglian Archaeol. 100.

Atkin, M., Carter, A. and Evans, D. H. (1985), *Excavations in Norwich 1971–78, Part II*. East Anglian Archaeol. 26.

Austin, D. (1990), 'The "proper study" of medieval archaeology', in Austin and Alcock, 9–42.

Austin, D. and Alcock, L. (eds) (1990), *From the Baltic to the Black Sea*. Routledge, London.

Austin, T. (ed.) (1888), *Two Fifteenth Century Cookery Books*. Early English Text Soc. 91.

Axworthy Rutter, J. A. (1990), 'Appendix 1: Floor tile catalogue', in Ward, 229–79.

Ayers, B. (1979), *Excavations at Chapel Lane Staith, Hull, 1978*. East Riding Archaeol. 5.

Ayers, B. (1981), 'Hull', in Milne and Hobley, 126–9.

Ayers, B. (1985), *Excavations within the North-east Bailey of Norwich Castle, 1979*. East Anglian Archaeol. 28.

Ayers, B. (1988), *Excavations at St Martin-at-Palace Plain, Norwich, 1981*. East Anglian Archaeol. 37.

Ayers, B. (1991), 'From cloth to creel: riverside industries in Norwich', in Good *et al.*, 1–8.

Ayers, B. (1992), 'The influence of minor streams on urban development: Norwich, a case study', *Medieval Europe 1992: pre-printed papers 1, Urbanism*, York.

Ayers, B. (1993), 'The urbanisation of East Anglia: the Norwich perspective', in Gardiner, 117–26.

Ayers, B. (1994a), *Excavations at Fishergate, Norwich, 1985*. East Anglian Archaeol. 68.

Ayers, B. (1994b), *Norwich*. Batsford and English Heritage, London.

Ayers, B. (2001), 'Domestic architecture in Norwich from the 12th to the 17th century', in Gläser 2001a, 35–48.

Ayers, B. and Murphy, P. (1983), 'A waterfront excavation at Whitefriars Street car park, Norwich, 1979', *East Anglian Archaeol.* 17, 1–60.

Ayers, T. (ed.) (2000), *Salisbury Cathedral, the West Front: A History and Study in Conservation*. Phillimore, Chichester.

Baart, J. M. (1977), *Opgravingen in Amsterdam*. Haarlem.

Baart, J. M. (1997), 'Amsterdam', in Gläser 1997a, 87–94.

Baart, J. M. (2001), 'Medieval houses in Amsterdam', in Gläser 2001a, 159–74.

Badham, S. and Norris, M. (1999), *Early Incised Slabs and Brasses from the London Marblers*. Soc. of Antiquaries Research Committee Report 60, London.

Baker, D., Baker, E., Hassall, J. and Simco, A. (1979), *Excavations in Bedford 1967–1977*. Bedfordshire Archaeol. Journal 13.

Balestracci, D. and Piccinni, G. (1977), *Siena nel trecento: assetto urbano e strutture edilizie*. Edizioni Clusf, Florence.

Barber, B. and Bowsher, D. (2000), *The Eastern Cemetery of Roman London: Excavations 1983–1990*. Museum of London Archaeol. Service Monograph 4, London.

Barclay, K., Biddle, M. and Orton, C. (1990), 'The chronological and spatial distribution of the objects', in Biddle, 42–73.

Barker, P. (1968–9), *The Origins of Worcester*. Transactions Worcestershire Archaeol. Soc., 3rd series, 2.

Barley, M. (1936), 'Lincolnshire rivers in the Middle Ages', *Architectural and Archaeol. Soc. of the County of Lincoln*, 1, 1–21.

Barley, M. W. (ed.) (1976), *The Plans and Topography of Medieval Towns in England and Wales*. Council for British Archaeol. Report 14, London.

Barley, M. W. (ed.) (1977), *European Towns: Their Archaeology and Early History*. Academic Press, London.

Barley, M. W. (1986), *Houses and History*. Faber and Faber, London.

Barron, C. M. (1974), *The Medieval Guildhall of London*. London.

Barron, C. [M.] (2000), 'London 1300–1540', in Palliser, 395–440.

Barrow, J. (1992), 'Urban cemetery location in the high Middle Ages', in Bassett, 78–100.

Barrow, J. (2000), 'Churches, education and literacy in towns 600–1300', in Palliser, 127–52.

Barry, T. (1987), *The Archaeology of Medieval Ireland*. Methuen, London.

Bartels, M. H. (1998), *Steden in Scherven: archeologische vondsten uit beerputten als bron voor de materiële cultuur in Deventer, Dordrecht, Nijmegen en Tiel (1250–1900)*. Stichting Promotie Archeologie, Zwolle, Holland.

Bartels, M., Clevis, H. and Zeiler, F. D. (1993), *Van huisvuil en huizen in Hasselt: opgravingen aan het Burg Royerplein*. Stichting Archeologie Ijssel/Vechtstreek, Holland.

Bassett, S. R. (1982a), 'Medieval Lichfield: a topographical review', *Trans. S. Staffordshire Archaeol. Hist. Soc.*, 22, 93–121.

Bassett, S. R. (1982b), *Saffron Walden: Excavations and Research 1972–90*. Council for British Archaeol. Research Report 45, York.

Bassett, S. (ed.) (1992), *Death in Towns: Urban Responses to the Dying and the Dead, 100–1600*. Leicester University Press, London.

Beaudry, M. C., Cook, L. J. and Mrozowski, S. A. (1991), 'Artefacts and active voices: material culture as social discourse', in McGuire and Paynter, 150–91.

Beaumont James, T. (1997), *Winchester.* Batsford and English Heritage, London.

Beaumont-Maillet, L. (1997), *Guide du Paris médiéval*. Hazan, Paris.

Bechert, T. (2001), 'Mittelalterlicher Hausbau in Duisburg – eine erste Bilanz', in Gläser 2001a, 251–64.

Beckmann, B. (1974), 'The main types of the first four production periods of Siegburg pottery', in V. I. Evison, H. Hodges and J. G. Hurst (eds), *Medieval Pottery from Excavations: Studies Presented to Gerald Clough Dunning*. John Baker, London, 183–220.

Beliaev, L. and Veksler, A. G. (1996), 'The archaeology of medieval Moscow: recent explorations (1980s–1990s)', *Rossiiskaia Arkheologia (Russian Archaeology)*, 3, 106–33.

Beltrán de Heredia Bercero, J. (2001), *De Barcino a Barcinona (segles I–VII): Les restes arqueològiques de la plaça del Rei de Barcelona*. Museu d'Història de la Cuitat, Barcelona, Spain.

Bencard, M. (ed.) (1981), *Ribe Excavations 1970–76*. Vols. 1 & 4, Sydysk Universitetsforlag, Esbjerg, Denmark.

Bencard, M. (ed.) (1984), *Ribe Excavations 1970–76*. Vol. 2, Sydysk Universitetsforlag, Esbjerg, Denmark.

Bencard, M., Jørgensen, L. B. and Madsen, H. B. (eds) (1991), *Ribe Excavations 1970–76*. Vol. 3, Sydysk Universitetsforlag, Esbjerg, Denmark.

Beresford, M. W. (1988), *New Towns of the Middle Ages*. 2nd edn, Sutton, Gloucester.

Beresford, M. W. and St Joseph, J. K. S. (1979), *Medieval England: An Aerial Survey*. 2nd edn, Cambridge University Press, Cambridge.

Berg, D. S. (1987), 'The faunal remains', in Armstrong and Ayers, 245–52.

Biddle, M. (1967), 'Excavations at Winchester, 1967, sixth interim report', *Antiq. Journal*, 48, 250–85.

Biddle, M. (1974), 'The future of the urban past', in P. A. Rahtz (ed.), *Rescue Archaeology*. Penguin, Harmondsworth, 95–112.

Biddle, M. (1990), *Object and Economy in Medieval Winchester*. Winchester Studies 7.ii, Oxford University Press, Oxford.

Biddle, M. and Hudson, D. with Heighway, C. (1973), *The Future of London's Past*. Rescue, Worcester.

Biddle, M. and Hunter, J. (1990), 'Early medieval window glass', in Biddle, 350–86.

Biddle, M. and Keene, D. J. (1976), 'Winchester in the eleventh and twelfth centuries', in M. Biddle (ed.), *Winchester in the Early Middle Ages*. Winchester Studies 1, Oxford University Press, Oxford, 241–448.

Blair, C. and Blair, J. (1991), 'Copper alloys', in Blair and Ramsay, 81–106.

Blair, J. (1988), 'Minster churches in the landscape', in D. Hooke (ed.), *Anglo-Saxon Settlements*. Blackwell, Oxford, 35–58.

Blair, J. (2000), 'Small towns 600–1270', in Palliser, 245–70.

Blair, J. and Pyrah, C. (eds) (1996), *Church Archaeology: Research Directions for the Future*. Council for British Archaeol. Research Report 104, York.

Blair, J. and Ramsay, N. (eds) (1991), *English Medieval Industries*. Hambledon Press, London.

Blanchard, I. (1996), 'Lothian and beyond: the economy of the "English empire" of David I', in Britnell and Hatcher, 23–45.

Blatherwick, S. and Bluer, R. (in prep.), *The Medieval Great Houses of Southwark: The Rosary, Fastolf Place and Edward III's Residence at Rotherhithe*. Museum of London Archaeol. Service Monograph.

Blockley, K., Sparks, M. and Tatton-Brown, T. (1997), *Canterbury Cathedral Nave: Archaeology, History and Architecture*. The Archaeology of Canterbury new series I, Canterbury.

Boekwijt, H. W. and Janssen, H. L. (eds) (1997), *Bouwen & wonen: in de Schaduw van de Sint Jan*. Kroniek Bouwhistorisch en Archeologisch Onderzoek 's Hertogenbosch 2, 's Hertogenbosch, Holland.

Bogdan, N. Q. and Wordsworth, J. W. (1978), *The Medieval Excavation at the High Street, Perth, 1975–76: an Interim Report*. Perth High Street Archaeol. Committee.

Boháčová, I., Hrdlicka, L., Klápště, J., Dragoun, Z. and Procházka, R. (1999), 'Czech Republic (Bohemia and Moravia)', in Council of Europe (ed. Leech), 57–61.

Bolton, J. L. (1980), *The Medieval English Economy 1150–1500*. Dent, London.

Bond, C. J. (1987), 'Anglo-Saxon and medieval defences', in Schofield and Leech, 92–116.

Bond, J. (2001), 'Monastic water management in Great Britain: a review', in G. Keevill, M. Aston and T. Hall (eds), *Monastic Archaeology: Papers on the Study of Medieval Monasteries*. Oxbow Books, Oxford, 88–136.

Bonnet, C. (1999), 'Switzerland (Geneva)', in Council of Europe (ed. Leech), 209–16.

Boockmann, H. (1987), *Die Stadt im späten Mittelalter*. C. H. Beck, Munich.

Bouiron, M. (ed.) (2001), *Marseille, du Lacydon au faubourg Sainte-Catherine (Ve s. av. J-C – XVIIIe s.): les fouilles de la Place du Général-de-Gaulle*. Documents d'Archéologie Française 87, Editions de la Maison des Sciences de l'Homme, Paris.

Bouttier, M. (1995), *Monastères: Des Pierres pour la Prière*. REMPART, Paris.

Boyd, P. D. A. (1981), 'The palaeoecology of estuarine deposits associated with archaeological sites, with particular reference to the City of London', in D. Brothwell and G. Dimbleby (eds), *Environmental Aspects of Coasts and Islands*. British Archaeol. Reps. International Series 94, 87–8.

Brachmann, H. and Herrmann, J. (eds) (1991), *Frühgeschichte der europäischen Stadt*. Akademie Verlag, Berlin.

Bradley, J. (ed.) (1984), *Viking Dublin Exposed: The Wood Quay Saga*. O'Brien Press, Dublin.

Braudel, F. (1985a), *The Structures of Everyday Life*. Civilization and Capitalism 15th–18th Century vol. 1, Fontana, London.

Braudel, F. (1985b), *The Wheels of Commerce*. Civilization and Capitalism 15th–18th Century vol. 2, Fontana, London.

Braudel, F. (1985c), *The Perspective of the World*. Civilization and Capitalism 15th–18th Century vol. 3, Fontana, London.

Bräuning, A. (1999), 'Archäologischer Stadtkaster of Baden-Württemberg: problems, methods, first results and reactions', in Dennison, 107–19.

Brewer, J. and Porter, R. (eds) (1993), *Consumption and the World of Goods*. Routledge, London.

Brimblecombe, P. (1982), 'Early urban climate and atmosphere', in Hall and Kenward, 10–25.

Brisbane, M. (ed.) (1992), *The Archaeology of Novgorod, Russia*. Society of Medieval Archaeol. Monograph 13, Lincoln.

Brisbane, M. and Gaimster, D. (eds) (2001), *Novgorod: The Archaeology of a Medieval Russian City and Its Hinterland*. British Museum Occasional Paper 141, British Museum, London.

Britnell, R. H. (1981), 'The proliferation of markets and fairs in England before 1349', *Economic History Review*, 2nd ser. 34, 209–21.

Britnell, R. H. (1994), 'The Black Death in English towns', *Urban History*, 21, 195–210.

Britnell, R. H. (1996), *The Commercialisation of English Society 1000–1500*. 2nd edn, Manchester University Press, Manchester.

Britnell, R. H. (2000), 'The economy of British towns 1300–1540', in Palliser, 313–34.

Britnell, R. H. and Hatcher, J. (eds) (1996), *Progress and Problems in Medieval England*. Cambridge University Press, Cambridge.

Brogiolo, G. P. and Gelichi, S. (1998), *La città nell'alto medioevo italiano: archeologia e storia*. Laterza, Rome and Bari.

Brothwell, D. (1994), 'On the possibility of urban–rural contrasts in human population palaeobiology', in Hall and Kenward, 129–36.

Brown, A. (1996), 'Parish church building: the fabric', in Blair and Pyrah, 63–8.

Brown, A. (ed.) (1999), *The Rows of Chester: The Chester Rows Project*. English Heritage Archaeol. Report 16, London.

Brown, D. H. (1997), 'The social significance of imported medieval pottery', in C. G. Cumberpatch and P. W. Blinkhorn (eds), *Not So Much a Pot, More a Way of Life*. Oxbow Monograph 83, Oxbow, Oxford, 95–112.

Bruce-Mitford, R. (ed.) (1956), *Recent Archaeological Excavations in Britain*. Routledge and Kegan Paul, London.

Bruce-Mitford, R. (ed.) (1975), *Recent Archaeological Excavations in Europe*. Routledge and Kegan Paul, London.

Bruni, S., Abela, E. and Graziella, B. (eds) (2000), *Richerche di Archeologia Medievale a Pisa: 1, Piazza dei Cavalieri, la campagna di scavo*. All'Insegna del Giglio, Florence.

Bureš, M., Kašpar, V. and Vereka, P. (1997), 'The formation of the high medieval tenements along the Old Town Square in Prague', in De Boe and Verhaeghe 1997b.

Burton, J. (1994), *Monastic and Religious Orders in Britain, 1000–1300*. Cambridge University Press, Cambridge.

Busch, R. (1997), 'Stadtarchäologie in Hamburg', in Gläser 1997a, 171–80.

Busch, R. (1999), 'Handel im archäologischen Fundgut aus dem Mittelalter und der frühen Neuzeit', in Gläser, 201–6.

Busch, R. (2001), 'Die Entwicklung des Hausbaus in Hamburg aufgrund archäologische Quellen', in Gläser 2001a, 265–75.

Butler, L. (1976), 'The evolution of towns: planned towns after 1066', in Barley, 32–47.

Butler, L. (1984), 'The houses of the mendicant orders in Britain: recent archaeological work', in Addyman and Black, 123–36.

Butler, L. (1987), 'Medieval urban religious houses', in Schofield and Leech, 167–76.

Butlin, R. A. (1993), *Historical Geography: Through the Gates of Space and Time*. Arnold, London.

Büttner, H. and Meissner, G. (1983), *Town Houses of Europe*. Antique Collectors' Club, Edition Leipzig, Germany.

Caiger-Smith, A. (1985), *Lustre Pottery*, Herbert Press, London.

Campbell, B. M. S., Galloway, J. A., Keene, D. and Murphy, M. (1993), *A Medieval Capital and Its Grain Supply: Agrarian Production and Distribution in the London Region c 1300*. Historical Geography Research Paper series 30, Queen's University Belfast and Centre for Metropolitan History, University of London.

Campbell, J. (2000), 'Power and authority 600–1300', in Palliser, 51–78.

Campbell, M. (1991), 'Gold, silver and precious stones', in Blair and Ramsay, 107–66.

Caple, C. (1991), 'The detection and definition of an industry: the English medieval and post-medieval pin industry', *Archaeol. Journal*, 148, 241–55.

Carandini, A. (1991), *Storie dalla terra: Manuale di Scavo Archeologico*. Turin.

Carelli, P. (1997), 'The past and future of archaeology in Lund', in Gläser 1997a, 429–39.

Carelli, P. (1999), 'Exchange of commodities in medieval Lund – patterns of trade or consumption?', in Gläser, 469–92.

Carelli, P. (2001), 'Building practices and housing culture in medieval Lund: a brief survey', in Gläser 2001a, 659–75.

Carlin, M. (1998), 'Fast food and urban living standards in medieval England', in Carlin and Rosenthal, 27–52.

Carlin, M. and Rosenthal, J. T. (eds) (1998), *Food and Eating in Medieval Europe.* Hambledon, London.

Carmiggelt, A., Hoekstra, T. J., van Tierum, M. C. and de Vries, D. J. (eds) (1999), *Rotterdam Papers 10: A Contribution to Medieval and Post-medieval Archaeology and History of Building.* Rotterdam.

Carruthers, W. J. (1997), 'Plant remains', in Hawkes and Fasham, 78–97.

Carter, A. (1978), 'Sampling in a medieval town: the study of Norwich', in J. F. Cherry, C. Gamble and S. Shennan (eds), *Sampling in Contemporary British Archaeology.* Brit. Archaeol. Reports 50, 263–77.

Carter, H. (1981), *The Study of Urban Geography.* 3rd edn, Edward Arnold, London.

Carus-Wilson, E. M. (1965), 'The first half-century of the borough of Stratford-upon-Avon', *Economic History Review*, 18, repr. in Holt and Rosser 1990, 49–70.

Carver, M. O. H. (1978), 'Early Shrewsbury: an archaeological definition in 1975', *Trans. Shropshire Archaeol. Soc.*, 59, 225–63.

Carver, M. O. H. (1979), 'Three Saxo-Norman tenements in Durham City', *Medieval Archaeol.*, 23, 1–80.

Carver, M. O. H. (ed.) (1980), *Medieval Worcester: An Archaeological Framework.* Trans. Worcestershire Archaeol. Soc. 7.

Carver, M. O. H. (ed.) (1983), *Two Town Houses in Medieval Shrewsbury.* Trans. Shropshire Archaeol. Soc. 61.

Carver, M. O. H. (1987), 'The nature of urban deposits', in Schofield and Leech, 9–26.

Caune, A. (1997), 'Die Hauptergebnisse der Stadtkernforschungen in Riga in den Jahren 1838 bis 1995', in Gläser 1997a, 319–27.

Caune, A. (2001), 'Typen der Wohnhäuser Rigas im 12. bis 14. Jahrhundert aufgrund der archäologischen Ausgrabungen', in Gläser 2001a, 551–68.

Champion, T. C. (1990), 'Medieval archaeology and the tyranny of the historical record', in Austin and Alcock, 79–95.

Chaplin, R. (1971), *The Study of Animal Bones from Archaeological Sites.* Academic Press, London.

Charleston, R. J. (1991), 'Vessel glass', in Blair and Ramsay, 237–64.

Cherry, J. (1991), 'Steelyard weights', in Saunders and Saunders, 47–9.

Chew, H. M. and Kellaway, W. (eds) (1973), *London Assize of Nuisance 1301–1431.* London Record Soc. 10.

Chew, H. M. and Weinbaum, M. (eds) (1970), *The London Eyre of 1244.* London Record Soc. 6.

Chitwood, P. J. (1988), 'St Mark's Yard East', in *Archaeology in Lincolnshire 1987–8: Fourth Annual Report of the Trust for Lincolnshire Archaeology*, 24–6.

Cipolla, C. M. (ed.) (1981), *The Middle Ages.* Fontana Economic History of Europe 1, London.

Clark, D. (2000), 'The shop within? An analysis of the architectural evidence for medieval shops', *Architectural Hist.*, 43, 58–87.

Clark, J. (ed.) (1995), *The Medieval Horse and Its Equipment c 1150–c 1450.* Medieval Finds from Excavations in London 5, HMSO, London.

Clark, P. (1984), *The English Alehouse: A Social History 1200–1830.* Longman, London.

Clarke, D. (1968), *Analytical Archaeology.* Methuen, London.

Clarke, H. (1973), 'King's Lynn and east coast trade in the Middle Ages', in D. J. Blackman (ed.), *Marine Archaeology, Proceedings of the 23rd Symposium of Colston Research Society.* Bristol, 277–91.

Clarke, H. (1981), 'King's Lynn', in Milne and Hobley, 132–6.

Clarke, H. (1984), *The Archaeology of Medieval England.* British Museum Publications, London.

Clarke, H. and Ambrosiani, B. (1991), *Towns in the Viking Age*. London.

Clarke, H. and Carter, A. (1977), *Excavations in King's Lynn 1963–1970*. Soc. for Medieval Archaeol. Monograph 7.

Clarke, H. B. and Simms, A. (eds) (1985), *The Comparative History of Urban Origins in Non-Roman Europe*. Brit. Archaeol. Reports Int. Series 255.

Clearey, R. M., Hurley, M. F. and Shee Twohig, E. (eds) (1997), *Skiddy's Castle and Christ Church, Cork: Excavations 1974–77 by D C Twohig*. Cork Corporation.

Clevis, H. (1989), *Nijmegen: Investigations into the Historical Topography and Development of the Lower Town between 1300 and 1500*. ROB 37, 275–390.

Clevis, H. and Kottman, J. (1989), *Weggegooid en teruggevonden: aardewerk en glas uit Deventer vondstcomplexen 1375–1750*. Stichting Archeologie Ijssel/Vechtstreek, Holland.

Clevis, H. and Smit, M. (1990), *Verscholen in vuil: archeologische vondsten uit Kampen 1375–1925*. Stichting Archeologie Ijssel/Vechtstreek, Holland.

Cnotliwy, E. (1997), 'Stand, Aufgaben und Perspektiven der Archäologie in Stettin (Szczecin)', in Gläser 1997a, 267–76.

CNRS 1994: *Les chanoines dans la ville: Recherches sur la topographie des quartiers Canoniaux en France*. CNRS, Boccard, Paris.

Cobb, H. S. (ed.) (1990), *The Overseas Trade of London: Exchequer Accounts 1480–1*. London Record Soc. 27.

Collardelle, R. (1999), 'Saint-Laurent et le groupe épiscopale de Grenoble', in P. Baertschi (ed.), *Archéologie Médiévale dans l'Arc Alpin*. Patrimoine et architecture cahier nos. 6–7, Geneva, 18–26.

Collet, C., Leroux, P. and Marin, J.-Y. (1996), *Caen Cité Médiévale: Bilan d'Archéologie et d'Histoire*. Musée de Normandie, Caen.

Conheeney, J. (1997), 'The human bone', in Thomas *et al*. 218–30.

Conkey, M. W. and Spector, J. D. (1984), 'Archaeology and the study of gender', in M. B. Schiffer (ed.), *Advances in Archaeological Method and Theory*, 7, New York, 1–38.

Cook, G. H. (1947), *Mediaeval Chantries and Chantry Chapels*. Phoenix House, London.

Coppack, G. (1986), 'The excavation of an Outer Court building, perhaps the Woolhouse, at Fountains Abbey, North Yorkshire'. *Medieval Archaeol.*, 30, 46–87.

Coppack, G. (1990), *Abbeys and Priories*. Batsford and English Heritage, London.

Cordfunke, E. H. P. (1990), 'Thirty years of archaeological investigation in Alkmaar's town centre'. *Berichten ROB*, 40, 333–87.

Corfield, M., Hinton, P., Nixon, T. and Pollard, M. (eds) n.d. [1999], *Preserving Archaeological Remains in situ*. Museum of London Archaeol. Service and University of Bradford.

Council for British Archaeology (1987), *Recording Worked Stones: A Practical Guide*. Practical Handbooks in Archaeology 1, London.

Council of Europe (ed. R. Leech) (1999), *Report on the Situation of Urban Archaeology in Europe*. Council of Europe Publishing.

Courtney, P. (1989), 'Excavations in the Outer Precinct of Tintern Abbey', *Medieval Archaeol.*, 33, 99–143.

Courtney, P. (1994), *Medieval and Later Usk*. University of Wales Press, Cardiff.

Cowgill, J., de Neergaard, M. and Griffiths, N. (1987), *Knives and Scabbards*. Medieval Finds from Excavations in London 1, HMSO, London.

Coy, J. (1982), 'The role of wild vertebrate fauna in urban economies in Wessex', in Hall and Kenward, 107–16.

Creighton, O. (2002), *Castles and Landscapes*. Leicester University Press, London.

Crone, A. (2000), 'Native tree-ring chronologies from some Scottish medieval burghs', *Medieval Archaeol.*, 44, 201–16.

Crossley, D. W. (ed.) (1981), *Medieval Industry*. Council for British Archaeol. Research Report 40, London.

Crowfoot, E., Pritchard, F. and Staniland, K. (1992), *Textiles and Clothing c. 1150– c. 1450*. Medieval Finds from Excavations in London 4, HMSO, London.

Crummy, P. (1981), *Aspects of Anglo-Saxon and Norman Colchester*. Council for British Archaeol. Research Report 39, London.

Curnow, P. E. and Thompson, M. W. (1969), 'Excavations at Richard's Castle, Herefordshire, 1962–4', *Journal Brit. Archaeol. Ass.*, 3rd ser., 32, 105–27.

Dalwood, H. (2000), 'The archaeology of small towns in Worcestershire', *Trans. Worcestershire Archaeol. Soc.*, 3rd ser., 17, 215–21.

Daniell, C. (1997), *Death and Burial in Medieval England*. Routledge, London.

Daniels, R. (1986), 'The excavation of the church of the Franciscans, Hartlepool', *Archaeol. Journal*, 143, 260–304.

Daniels, R. (1990), 'The development of medieval Hartlepool: excavations at Church Close, 1984–5', *Archaeol. Journal*, 147, 337–410.

Davey, P. and Hodges, R. (eds) (1983), *Ceramics and Trade: The Production and Distribution of Later Medieval Pottery in North-west Europe*. University of Sheffield.

Davies, R. R. (1991), *The Age of Conquest: Wales 1063–1415*. Oxford University Press, Oxford.

Davis, A. (1990), 'Appendix 5: Plant remains from a medieval cesspit at Milk Street', in Schofield *et al.*, 231–2.

Davis, A. (1997), 'The plant remains', in Thomas *et al.*, 234–44.

Dawes, J. D. and Magilton, J. R. (1980), *The Cemetery of St Helen-on-the-Walls, Aldwark*. The Archaeology of York 12/1, York Archaeol. Trust, York.

Dawson, D. P., Jackson, R. G. and Ponsford, M. W. (1972), 'Medieval kiln wasters from St Peter's Church, Bristol', *Trans. of the Bristol and Gloucestershire Archaeol. Soc.*, 91, 1–9.

Dean, T. (2000), *The Towns of Italy in the Later Middle Ages*. Manchester University Press, Manchester.

De Boe, G. and Verhaeghe, F. (eds) (1997a), *Religion and Belief in Medieval Europe*. Papers of the Medieval Europe Brugge 1997 Conference, Vol. 4, Zellik, Brussels.

De Boe, G. and Verhaege, F. (1997b), *Urbanism*. Papers of the Medieval Europe Brugge 1997 Conference, Vol. 7, Zellik, Brussels.

De Groot, H. L. (1997), 'Utrecht: archaeology in transition?', in Gläser 1997a, 95–110.

Dejevsky, N. J. (1977), 'Novgorod: the origins of a Russian town', in Barley, 391–404.

De Minicis, E. (1999), *Temi e metodi di Archeologia Medievale*. Bonsignori Editore, Rome.

Demolon, P., Galinié, H. and Verhaeghe, F. (eds) (1994), *Archéologie des villes dans le Nord-Ouest de l'Europe (VIIe–XIIIe siècle)*. Douai, France.

Demolon, P. and Louis, E. (1994), 'Naissance d'une cité médiévale flamande: l'exemple de Douai', in Demolon *et al.*, 47–58.

Dennison, E. P. (ed.) (1999), *Conservation and Change in Historic Towns*. Council for British Archaeol. Research Report 122, York.

Dennison, E. P. and Simpson, G. G. (2000), 'Scotland', in Palliser, 715–37.

De Vries, D. J. (2001), 'The medieval district Voorstraat ("Front Street") in the town of Zwolle', in Gläser 2001a, 213–31.

De Witte, H. (ed.) (1991), *Die Brugse Burg*. VZW Archaeo-Brugge, Bruges, Belgium.

De Witte, H. (1997), 'State, tasks and outlook for archaeology in Brugge', in Gläser 1997a, 75–86.

De Witte, H. (1999), 'Archaeological indications for trade in Brugge from the 12th to the 17th centuries', in Gläser, 169–81.

Dickinson, R. E. (1961), *The West European City: A Geographical Interpretation*. 2nd edn, London.

Dobson, B. (1977), 'Urban decline in late medieval England', *Trans. Royal Hist. Soc.*, 27, 1–22.

Dobson, B. (1984), 'Mendicant ideal and practice in late medieval York', in Addyman and Black, 109–22.

Dodgshon, R. A. (1987), *The European Past: Social Evolution and Spatial Order.* Macmillan, London.

Dolgner, D. and Roch, I. (eds) (1990), *Stadtbaukunst im Mittelalter.* Verlag für Bauwesen, Berlin.

Dolley, M. (1975), 'The coins and jettons', in Platt and Coleman-Smith, ii, 315–31.

Drage, C. (1987), 'Urban castles', in Schofield and Leech, 117–32.

Draper, P. (1987), 'Architecture and liturgy', in Alexander and Binski, 83–91.

Duffy, S. (ed.) (2000), *Medieval Dublin I.* Four Courts Press, Dublin.

Dunning, G. C. (1959), 'Anglo-Saxon Pottery: A Symposium', *Medieval Archaeol.*, 3, 31–78.

Dunning, G. C. (1977), 'Mortars', in Clarke and Carter, 320–47.

Durham, B. (1977), 'Archaeological investigations in St Aldates, Oxford', *Oxoniensia*, 42, 83–203.

Durham, B., Halpin, C. and Palmer, N. (1983), 'Oxford's northern defences: archaeological studies 1971–1982', *Oxoniensia*, 48, 13–40.

Dyer, C. (1986), 'English peasant buildings in the later Middle Ages', *Medieval Archaeol.*, 30, 19–45.

Dyer, C. (1989), *Standards of Living in the Later Middle Ages.* Cambridge University Press, Cambridge.

Dyer, C. (1997), 'History and vernacular architecture', *Vernacular Architecture*, 28, 1–8.

Dyer, C. (2000), 'Small towns 1270–1540', in Palliser, 505–37.

Dyson, T. (1989), *The Medieval London Waterfront.* Annual Archaeology Lecture for 1987, Museum of London.

Eames, E. (1980), *Catalogue of Medieval Lead-glazed Earthenware Tiles in the Department of Medieval and Later Antiquities, British Museum.* British Museum, London.

Ebner, H. (1991), 'Die Frühgeschichte Wiens', in Brachmann and Herrmann, 60–7.

Eddy, M. R. and Petchey, M. R. (1983), *Historic Towns in Essex.* Essex County Council.

Edwards, J. F. and Hindle, B. P. (1991), 'The transportation system of medieval England and Wales', *Journal of Historical Geography*, 17, 123–34.

Egan, G. (1985–6), 'Finds recovery on riverside sites in the City of London', *Popular Archaeol.*, December 1985/January 1986, 42–50.

Egan, G. (1991), 'Industry and economics on the medieval and later London waterfront', in Good *et al.*, 9–18.

Egan, G. (1998), *The Medieval Household: Daily Living c. 1150–c. 1450.* Medieval Finds from Excavations in London 6, Stationery Office, London.

Egan, G. and Pritchard, F. (1991), *Dress Accessories.* Medieval Finds from Excavations in London 3, HMSO, London.

Ekwall, E. (1960), *The Concise Oxford Dictionary of English Place-names.* 4th edn, Oxford University Press, Oxford.

Ellis, P. (ed.) (2000), *Ludgershall Castle Wiltshire: A Report on the Excavations by Peter Addyman, 1964–1972.* Wiltshire Archaeol. and Natural Hist. Soc. Monograph Series 2, Devizes.

Emery, A. (2000), *Greater Medieval Houses of England and Wales 1300–1500: ii, East Anglia, Central England and Wales.* Cambridge University Press, Cambridge.

Ersgård, L., Holmstrom, M. and Lamm, K. (eds) (1991), *Rescue and Research: Reflections of Society in Sweden 700–1700 AD.* Riksantikvarieambetet, Stockholm.

Esquieu, Y. (1994), *Quartier Cathédrale: une cité dans la ville*. REMPART, Paris.

Esquieu, Y. and Pesez, J.-M. (eds) (1998), *Cent Maisons médiévales en France*. Monographie du Centre de Recherches Archéologiques 20, CNRS, Paris.

Evans, D. H. (ed.) (1993), *Excavations in Hull 1975–76*, Hull Old Town Report Series 2, East Riding Archaeol. 4.

Evans, D. H. (1997), 'Archaeology in Hull', in Gläser 1997a, 35–50.

Evans, D. H. (1999), 'The trade of Hull between 1200 and 1700', in Gläser, 59–97.

Evans, D. H. (2001a), '45–75 Gallowgate: medieval and post-medieval occupation within the Town Loch', in A. S. Cameron and J. A. Stones (eds), *Aberdeen: An In-depth View of the City's Past. Excavation at Seven Major Sites within the Medieval Burgh*. Society of Antiquaries of Scotland Monograph Series 19, Edinburgh, 83–115.

Evans, D. H. (2001b), 'Urban domestic architecture in the Lower Hull Valley in the medieval and early post-medieval periods', in Gläser 2001a, 49–76.

Evans, D. H. and Carter, A. (1985), 'Excavations on 31–51 Pottergate', in Atkin *et al.*, 9–86.

Evans, D. H. with Davison, A. (1985), 'Excavations in Botolph Street and St George's Street (sites 170N, 281N and 284N)', in Atkin *et al.*, 87–143.

Evans, D. H. and Tomlinson, D. G. (1992), *Excavations at 33–35 Eastgate, Beverley, 1983–86*. Sheffield Excavation Reports 3, Sheffield.

Evans, D. H., Murray, J. C. and Stones, J. A. (1987), *A Tale of Two Burghs: The Archaeology of Old and New Aberdeen*. Aberdeen Art Gallery and Museums, Aberdeen.

Evans, J. and O'Connor, T. (1999), *Environmental Archaeology: Principles and Methods*. Sutton, Stroud.

Ewan, E. (1990), *Townlife in Fourteenth-Century Scotland*. Edinburgh University Press, Edinburgh.

Eydmann, S. (1999), 'Scotland's historic towns: a conservation officer reflects', in Dennison, 196–205.

Farley, M. and Manchester, K. (1989), 'The cemetery of the leper hospital of St Margaret, High Wycombe, Buckinghamshire', *Medieval Archaeol.*, 33, 82–9.

Favier, J. (1997a), *Paris au XVe siècle*. 2nd edn, Nouvelle Histoire de Paris, Hachette, Paris.

Favier, J. (1997b), *Paris: deux mille ans d'histoire*. Fayard, Paris.

Fehring, G. P. (1985), 'The archaeology of early Lübeck: the relation between the Slavic and German settlement sites', in Clarke and Simms, 267–87.

Fehring, G. P. (1989), 'Archaeological evidence from Lübeck for changing material culture and socioeconomic conditions from the 13th to the 16th century', *Medieval Archaeol.*, 33, 60–81.

Fehring, G. P. (1990), 'Origins and development of Slavic and Germanic Lübeck', in Austin and Alcock, 251–66.

Fehring, G. P. (1991a), 'Lübeck und die hochmittelalterliche Gründungsstadt im einst slawischen Siedlungsraum: Vorraussetzungen, Entwicklungen und Strukturen', in Brachmann and Herrmann, 281–93.

Fehring, G. P. (1991b), *The Archaeology of Medieval Germany*. trans. R. Samson, Routledge, London.

Fehring, G. P. (1996), *Stadtarchäologie in Deutschland*. Archäologie in Deutschland Sonderheft, Theiss, Stuttgart.

Feiler, A. (1999), 'Archäologische Erkenntnisse zum Handel in der Frühen Stadt', in Gläser, 207–14.

Fernie, E. (2000), *The Architecture of Norman England*. Oxford University Press, Oxford.

Fieldhouse, P. (1986), *Food and Nutrition: Customs and Culture*. London.

Flüeler, M. and Flüeler, N. (eds) (1992), *Stadtluft, Hirsebrei und Bettelmönch: Die Stadt um 1300*. Theiss, Stuttgart.

Foard, G. (1991), 'The medieval pottery industry of Rockingham Forest, Northamptonshire', *Medieval Ceramics*, 15, 13–20.

Foard, G. (2001), 'Medieval woodland, agriculture and industry in Rockingham Forest, Northamptonshire', *Medieval Archaeol.*, 45, 41–95.

Foreman, M. (1996), *Further Excavations at the Dominican Priory, Beverley, 1986–1989*. Sheffield Excavation Reports 4, Sheffield Academic Press, Sheffield.

Forgeais, A. (1866), *Collection des plombes historiés trouvés dans la Seine*. 5th series, Paris.

Fraser, R., Jamfrey, C. and Vaughan, J. (1995), 'Excavation on the site of the Mansion House, Newcastle, 1990', *Archaeologia Aeliana*, 5th series, 22, 145–214.

Frere, S. S., Stow, S. and Bennett, P. (1982), *Excavations on the Roman and Medieval Defences of Canterbury*. Archaeology of Canterbury II, Canterbury Archaeological Trust, Canterbury.

Friedman, D. (1988), *Florentine New Towns: Urban Design in the Late Middle Ages*. MIT Press, Cambridge (MA) and London.

Friedrichs, C. R. (1995), *The Early Modern City 1450–1750*. Longman, London.

Gaimster, D. R. M. (1988), 'Pottery production in the Lower Rhineland: the Duisburg sequence ca. 1400–1800', in D. R. M. Gaimster, M. Redknap and H.-H. Wegner (eds), *Zur Keramik des Mittelalters und der beginnenden Neuzeit im Rheinland*. Brit. Archaeol. Reports International Ser. 440, Oxford, 151–71.

Gaimster, D. R. M. (1992), 'The publication of finds from medieval towns: Winchester reviewed', *Medieval Archaeol.*, 36, 309–14.

Gaimster, D. and Stamper, P. (eds) (1997), *The Age of Transition: The Archaeology of English Culture 1400 to 1600*. Society for Medieval Archaeol. Monograph 15, Oxbow Books, Oxford.

Galloway, J. (1998), 'Driven by drink? Ale consumption and the agrarian economy of the London region, c 1300–1400', in Carlin and Rosenthal, 87–100.

Galloway, J., Keene, D. and Murphy, M. (1996), 'Fuelling the city: production and distribution of firewood in the London region, 1290–1440', *Economic Hist. Review*, 49, 447–72.

Gardiner, J. (ed.) (1993), *Flatlands and Wetlands: Current Themes in East Anglian Archaeology*. East Anglian Archaeol. 50.

Garmy, P. (1999), 'France', in Council of Europe (ed. Leech), 91–102.

Garrigou Grandchamp, P. (1992), *Demeures médiévales: coeur de la cité*. REMPART, Paris.

Garrigou Grandchamp, P. (1999), 'Twelfth- and thirteenth-century domestic architecture north of the Loire: a summary of recent research', *Vernacular Architecture*, 30, 1–20.

Garrigou Grandchamp, P., Jones, M., Meirion-Jones, G. and Salvèque, J. D. (1997), *La Ville de Cluny et ses maisons, XIe–XVe siècles*. Picard, Paris.

Gauthiez, B. (1996), 'Rouen', in Pinol, 70–80.

Geddes, J. (1991), 'Iron', in Blair and Ramsay, 167–88.

Gelichi, S. (1997), *Introduzione all'archeologia medievale: Storia e ricerca in Italia*. Carocci, Rome.

Gelichi, S., Alberti, A. and Librenti, M. (1999), *Cesena: la memoria del passato*. All'insegna del Giglio, Florence, Italy.

Gem, R. (ed.) (1997), *St Augustine's Abbey Canterbury*. Batsford and English Heritage, London.

Gerevich, L. (1971), *The Art of Buda and Pest in the Middle Ages*. Akadémiai Kiadó, Budapest.

Gerevich, L. (ed.) (1990), *Towns in Medieval Hungary*. Social Science Monographs, Colorado Atlantic Research and Publications, Columbia University Press, Ohio.

Gero, J. M. and Conkey, M. W. (eds) (1991), *Engendering Archaeology: Women and Prehistory*. Blackwell, Oxford.

Gerö, L. (1990), 'Mittelalterliche Städte in Ungarn', in Dolgner and Roch, 92–6.

Gilchrist, R. (1992), 'Christian bodies and souls: the archaeology of life and death in later medieval hospitals', in Bassett, 101–18.

Gilchrist, R. (1994), *Gender and Material Culture: The Archaeology of Religious Women*. Routledge, London.

Gilchrist, R. (1999), *Gender and Archaeology: Contesting the Past*. Routledge, London.

Gilchrist, R. and Mytum, H. (eds) (1993), *Advances in Monastic Archaeology*. Brit. Archaeol. Report 227.

Giles, K. (1999), 'The "familiar" fraternity: the appropriation and consumption of medieval guildhalls in early modern York', in Tarlow and West, 87–102.

Giles, K. (2000), *An Archaeology of Social Identity*. Brit. Archaeol. Reports 315, Oxford.

Gilmour, B. J. and Stocker, D. A. (1986), *St Mark's Church and Cemetery*. The Archaeology of Lincoln XIII–1, Lincoln.

Gimpel, J. (1992), *The Medieval Machine*. 2nd edn, Pimlico, London.

Girouard, M. (1985), *Cities and People*. Yale University Press, New Haven and London.

Girouard, M. (1990), *The English Town*. Yale University Press, New Haven and London.

Gläser, M. (ed.) (1993), *Archäologie des Mittelalters und Bauforschung im Hanseraum*. Schriften des Kulturhistorischen Museums in Rostock, Rostock, Germany.

Gläser, M. (ed.) (1997a), *Lübecker Kolloquium zur Stadtarchäologie im Hanseraum I: Aufgaben und Perspektiven*. Lübeck, Germany.

Gläser, M. (1997b), 'Stand, Aufgaben und Perspektiven der Archäologie in Lübeck', in Gläser 1997a, 205–20.

Gläser, M. (ed.) (1999), *Lübecker Kolloquium zur Stadtarchäologie im Hanseraum II: Der Handel*. Lübeck, Germany.

Gläser, M. (ed.) (2001a), *Lübecker Kolloquium zur Stadtarchäologie im Hanseraum III: Der Hausbau*, Lübeck, Germany.

Gläser, M. (2001b), 'Archäologisch erfasste mittelalterliche Hausbauten in Lübeck', in Gläser, 277–305.

Gläser, M., Laggin, W. and Thoemmes, M. (eds) (1998), *25 Jahre Archäologie in Lübeck*. Lübecker Schriften zur Archäologie und Kulturgeschichte 17, Bonn, Germany.

Glass, N. (2001), 'Great excavations: a look at the excavation of a medieval hospital graveyard at Spitalfields', *The Lancet*, 357, 643–4 (24 February 2001).

Goldberg, P. J. P. (1992), *Women, Work and Life Cycle in a Medieval Economy: Women in York and Yorkshire, c 1300–1520*. Clarendon Press, Oxford.

Goldthwaite, R. (1980), *The Building of Renaissance Florence: An Economic and Social History*. Johns Hopkins University Press, Baltimore.

Good, G. L., Jones, R. H. and Ponsford, M. W. (eds) (1991), *Waterfront Archaeology: Proceedings of the Third International Conference, Bristol, 1988*. Council for British Archaeol. Research Report 74, York.

Goodburn, D. M. (1997), 'The production of timber for building in England before and after c 1180 AD', *Medieval Europe 1992, Pre-printed papers for York Conference 7, Technology*. Zellik, 155–61.

Goudge, C. E. (1983), 'The leather from 38–44 Eastgate Street', in C. M. Heighway (ed.), *The East and North Gates of Gloucester*. Western Archaeol. Trust Monograph 4, Bristol, 173–85.

Gould, J. (1976), *Lichfield: Archaeology and Development*. West Midlands Rescue Archaeol. Committee, Birmingham.

Graham, A. H. and Davies, S. M. (1993), *Excavations in Trowbridge, Wiltshire, 1977 and 1986–1988*. Wessex Archaeol. Report 2, Salisbury.

Grant, A. (1988), 'Animal resources', in Astill and Grant, 149–87.

Grant, L. (ed.) (1990), *Medieval Art, Architecture and Archaeology in London*. British Archaeol. Assoc. Conference Transactions for 1984.

Grau, R., Nicolau, A. and Sendra, E. (1999), *La Barcelona gòtica*. Museu d'Història de la Cuitat, Barcelona.

Green, F. J. (1982), 'Problems of interpreting differentially preserved plant remains from excavations of medieval urban sites', in Hall and Kenward, 40–6.

Greene, J. P. (1992), *Medieval Monasteries*. Leicester University Press, London.

Greig, J. (1982), 'The interpretation of pollen spectra from urban archaeological deposits', in Hall and Kenward, 47–65.

Greig, J. (1988), 'Plant resources', in Astill and Grant, 108–27.

Greig, J. (1991), 'The British Isles', in W. Van Zeist, K. Wasilikowa and K.-E. Behre (eds), *Progress in Old World Palaeoethnobotany*. Balkema, Rotterdam, 299–334.

Grenville, J. (1997), *Medieval Housing*. Leicester University Press, London.

Grenville, J. (2001), 'Out of the shunting yards – one academic's approach to recording small buildings', in Pearson and Meeson, 11–26.

Grew, F. and de Neergaard, M. (1988), *Shoes and Pattens*. Medieval Finds from Excavations in London 2, HMSO, London.

Griffiths, R. A. (2000), 'Wales and the Marches', in Palliser, 681–714.

Grimes, W. F. (1968), *The Excavation of Roman and Medieval London*. Routledge and Kegan Paul, London.

Groenman-van Waateringe, W. (1994), 'The menu of different classes in Dutch medieval society', in Hall and Kenward, 147–69.

Groothedde, M. (2001), 'Der Hausbau in Zutphen zwischen 850 und 1400', in Gläser 2001a, 175–95.

Groothedde, M., Hartmann, G. E., Hermann, M. R. and de Jonge, W. H. (1999), *De Sint-Walburgiskerk in Zutphen*, Walburg Pers, Zutphen, Holland.

Groves, C. (2000), 'Belarus to Bexley and beyond: dendrochronology and dendro-provenancing of conifer timber', *Vernacular Architecture*, 31, 50–66.

Gutiérrez, A. (2000), *Mediterranean Pottery in Wessex Households (13th to 17th Centuries)*. British Archaeol. Reports 306.

Guy, C. J. (1986), 'Excavations at Back Lane, Winchcombe, 1985', *Trans. of the Bristol and Gloucestershire Archaeol. Soc.*, 104, 214–20.

Habovstiak, A. (1991), 'Bratislava: Die Anfänge der heutigen Hauptstadt der Slowakei', in Brachmann and Herrmann, 159–65.

Hale, J. (1994), *The Civilization of Europe in the Renaissance*. Fontana, London.

Hall, A. R. and Kenward, H. K. (eds) (1982), *Environmental Archaeology in the Urban Context*. Council for British Archaeol. Research Report 43, London.

Hall, A. R. and Kenward, H. K. (eds) (1994), *Urban-Rural Connexions: Perspectives from Environmental Archaeology*. Symposia of the Association for Environmental Archaeol. 12, Oxbow Monograph 47, Oxbow Books, Oxford.

Hall, A. R. and Kenward, H. K. (in prep.), 'Can we identify biological indicator groups for craft, industry and other activities?', in *Proceedings of Assoc. of Environmental Archaeologists' Conference, Guildford, 2000*.

Hall, A. R., Tomlinson, P. R., Taylor, G. W. and Walton, P. (1984), 'Dyeplants from Viking York', *Antiquity*, 58, 58–60.

Hall, A., Kenward, H., Jaques, D. and Carrott, J. (2000), 'Technical Report: Environment and industry at Layerthorpe Bridge, York (site code YORYM 1996.345)', Reports from the Environmental Archaeology Unit York 2000/64, York.

Hall, D. (1999), 'Twenty-five years of urban archaeology in Scotland's medieval burghs', in Dennison, 69–76.

Hall, P. (1998), *Cities in Civilization*. Weidenfeld and Nicolson, London.

Hall, R. (1996), *York*. Batsford and English Heritage, London.

Hall, R. (1997), 'Archaeology in York', in Gläser 1997a, 51–65.

Hall, R. (2001), 'Secular buildings in medieval York', in Gläser 2001a, 77–99.

Hall, T. (1990), 'Die mittelalterliche Stadt in Mittelschweden', in Dolgner and Roch, 112–25.

Hammond, P. W. (1993), *Food and Feast in Medieval England*. Sutton, Stroud.

Hanawalt, B. (1986), *The Ties That Bound: Peasant Families in Medieval England*. Oxford University Press, Oxford.

Hanser, J., Mathis, A., Ruoff, U. and Schneider, J. (1983), *Das neue Bild des alten Zürich*. Zürich.

Hansestadt Lübeck: Amt für Vor- und Frühgeschichte der Hansestadt Lübeck (1988), *25 Jahre Archäologie in Lübeck*, Bonn.

Harbottle, B. and Clack, P. (1976), 'Newcastle-upon-Tyne: archaeology and development', in P. Clack and P. F. Gosling (eds), *Archaeology in the North*. Newcastle, 111–31.

Harden, G. (1978), *Medieval Boston and Its Archaeological Implications*. Lincolnshire Archaeological Unit.

Harris, C. J. (1985), 'An outline of ropemaking in Bergen', in Herteig, 144–50.

Harris, E. (1979), *Principles of Archaeological Stratigraphy*. Academic Press, London.

Harvey, J. (1981), *Medieval Gardens*. Batsford, London.

Harvey, P. D. A. (1969), 'Banbury', in M. D. Lobel (ed.), *Historic Towns [Atlas]*, 1. Oxford.

Hassall, J. (1979), 'The pottery', in Baker *et al.*, 147–240.

Hassall, T., Halpin, C. E. and Mellor, M. (1989), 'Excavations in St Ebbe's, Oxford, 1967–1976: Part I, Late Saxon and medieval domestic occupation and tenements, and the medieval Greyfriars', *Oxoniensia*, 54, 71–278.

Hassall, T. G. (1976), 'Excavations at Oxford Castle, 1965–73', *Oxoniensia*, 41, 232–308.

Hatcher, J. (1977), *Plague, Population and the English Economy 1348–1530*. Macmillan, London.

Hatcher, J. (1996), 'The great slump of the fifteenth century', in Britnell and Hatcher, 237–72.

Hatcher, J. and Bailey, M. (2001), *Modelling the Middle Ages: The History and Theory of England's Economic Development*. Oxford University Press, Oxford.

Hawkes, J. W. and Fasham, P. J. (1997), *Excavations on Reading Waterfront Sites, 1979–1988*. Wessex Archaeol. Report 5, Salisbury.

Hawkins, D. (1990), 'The Black Death and the new London cemeteries of 1348', *Antiquity*, 64, 637–42.

Hawthorne, J. G. and Smith, C. S. (eds) (1979), *Theophilus. On Divers Arts: The Foremost Medieval Treatise on Painting, Glassmaking and Metalwork*. Dover, New York.

Heege, A. (2001), 'Archäologische Befunde zum Hausbau in Einbeck (13. bis 16. Jahrhundert)', in Gläser 2001a, 307–27.

Heege, A., Heidrich, R., Kamphowe, T., Leers, K.-J., Paetzold, D., Schlütz, F., Schulze-Rehm, C. and Willerding, U. (1998), *Einbeck, Negenborner Weg Band I: Naturwissenschaftliche Studien zu einer Töpferei des 12. und frühen 13. Jahrhunderts in Niedersachsen. Keramiktechnologie, Paläoethnobotanik, Pollenanalyse, Archäozoologie*. Isensee Verlag Oldenburg, Germany.

Heers, J. (1993), *La Ville au Moyen Age*. Fayard, Paris.

Heighway, C. M. (1972), *The Erosion of History*. Council for British Archaeology, London.

Heighway, C. M. (1974), *Archaeology in Gloucester*. Gloucester City Museum, Gloucester.

Heighway, C. M. (1983), 'Tanner's Hall, Gloucester', *Trans. of the Bristol and Gloucestershire Archaeol. Soc.*, 101, 83–109.

Heighway, C. and Bryant, R. (1999), *The Golden Minster: The Anglo-Saxon Minster and Later Priory of St Oswald at Gloucester*. Council for British Archaeology. Research Report 117, York.

Helgert, H. (1997), 'Die spätmittelalterliche Synagoge in Wien (13.–15. Jahrhundert)', in De Boe and Verhaeghe (1997a), 185–99.

Henderson, C. G. (1985), 'Archaeological investigations at Alphington Street, St Thomas', in C. G. Henderson (ed.), *Archaeology in Exeter 1984/5*. Exeter City Council, Exeter, 1–14.

Herrmann, J. (1991), 'Siedlungsgeschichtliche Grundlagen und geschichtliche Voraussetzungen für die Entwicklung Berlins', in Brachmann and Herrmann, 7–18.

Herteig, A. E. (1975), 'The excavation of Bryggen, Bergen, Norway', in Bruce-Mitford, 65–89.

Herteig, A. E. (ed.) (1985), *Conference on Waterfront Archaeology in North European Towns No. 2, Bergen 1983*. Bergen, Norway.

Herteig, A. E. (1991), *The Buildings at Bryggen: Their Topographical and Chronological Development*. Bryggen Papers Main Series 3, pt 1 and 2, Bergen.

Hesnard, A., Moliner, M., Conche, F. and Bouiron, M. (1999), *Parcours de villes: Marseille, 10 ans d'archéologie, 2600 ans d'histoire*. Musées de Marseille, Marseilles.

Hewett, C. (1969), *The Development of Carpentry 1200–1700: An Essex Study*. David and Charles, Newton Abbott.

Hewett, C. (1980), *English Historic Carpentry*. Phillimore, Chichester.

Hibbert, A. B. (1978), 'The origins of the medieval town patriciate', in Abrams and Wrigley, 91–104.

Hiekkanen, M. (2001), 'Domestic building remains in Turku, Finland', in Gläser 2001a, 627–33.

Higham, M. C. (1989), 'Some evidence for twelfth- and thirteenth-century linen and woollen textile processing', *Medieval Archaeol.*, 33, 38–52.

Hill, D. (2001), 'Appendix 3: A short gazetteer of postulated continental wics', in Hill and Cowie, 104–10.

Hill, D. and Cowie, R. (eds) (2001), *Wics: The Early Mediaeval Trading Centres of Northern Europe*, Sheffield Academic Press, Sheffield.

Hill, J. W. F. (1948), *Medieval Lincoln*. Repr. 1990, Paul Watkins, Stamford.

Hill, J. and Woodger, A. (1999), *Excavations at 72–75 Cheapside, 83–93 Queen Street, City of London*, Archaeol. Studies Series 2, Museum of London Archaeol. Service, London.

Hillier, B. and Hanson, J. (1984), *The Social Logic of Space*. Cambridge University Press, Cambridge.

Hilton, R. H. (1982), 'Towns in English medieval society', in D. Reeder (ed.), *Urban History Yearbook: 1982*. Repr. in Holt and Rosser 1990, 19–28.

Hilton, R. H. (1984), 'Small town society in England before the Black Death', *Past and Present*, 105, repr. in Holt and Rosser 1990, 71–96.

Hilton, R. H. (1990), *Class Conflict and the Crisis of Feudalism*. Rev. edn, Verso, London.

Hilton, R. H. (1992), *English and French Towns in Feudal Society, Past and Present Publications*. Cambridge University Press, Cambridge.

Hindle, B. P. (1982), 'Roads and tracks', in L. Cantor (ed.), *The English Medieval Landscape*. Croom Helm, London, 193–218.

Hinton, D. A. (1990), *Archaeology, Economy and Society: England from the Fifth to the Fifteenth Century*. Seaby, London.

Hinton, D. A. (1999), ' "Closing" and the later Middle Ages', *Medieval Archaeol.*, 43, 172–82.

Hinton, D. A. (2000), 'The large towns 600–1300', in Palliser, 217–44.

Hodder, I. (1986), *Reading the Past: Current Approaches to Interpretation in Archaeology*. Cambridge University Press, Cambridge.

Hodges, R. (1982), *Dark Age Economics: The Origins of Towns and Trade AD 600–1000*. Academic Press, London.

Hodges, R. and Hobley, B. (eds) (1988), *The Rebirth of Towns in the West AD 700–1050*. Council for British Archaeol. Research Report 68, London.

Hodges, R. and Whitehouse, D. (1983), *Mohammed, Charlemagne and the Origins of Europe*. Duckworth, London.

Höfler, E. and Illi, M. (1992), 'Versorgung und Entsorgung der mittelalterlichen Stadt', in Flüeler and Flüeler, 351–64.

Hohenberg, P. M. and Lees, L. H. (1985), *The Making of Urban Europe 1000–1950*. Harvard University Press, London.

Holdsworth, P. (ed.) (1987), *Excavations in the Medieval Burgh of Perth 1979–1981*. Soc. of Antiquaries of Scotland Monograph 5.

Holt, R. (1985), 'Gloucester in the century after the Black Death', *Trans. of the Bristol and Gloucestershire Archaeol. Soc.*, 103, repr. in Holt and Rosser 1990, 141–59.

Holt, R. (1992), 'Mills in medieval England', in *Medieval Europe 1992: Pre-printed Papers 3, Technology and Innovation*, York, paper C2b.

Holt, R. and Rosser, G. (eds) (1990), *The Medieval Town: A Reader in English Urban History 1200–1540*. Longman, London.

Hooper, J., Wilmott, A. and Young, J. (1989), 'Pottery from St Marks East', *Archaeology in Lincolnshire 1987–1988*, Fourth Annual Report of the Trust for Lincs. Archaeol., 29–32.

Hoppe, K.-D. (1999), 'Wismar – handelspolitische Gründungsmotivation and spezialisierter Handel um 13. und 14. Jahrhundert', in Gläser, 215–24.

Horrox, R. (1978), *The Changing Plan of Hull 1290–1650*. Kingston upon Hull City Council, Kingston upon Hull.

Horsman, V., Milne, G. and Milne, C. (1988), *Aspects of Saxo-Norman London, I: Building and Street Development*. London and Middlesex Archaeol. Soc. Special Paper 11.

Hourani, A. (1991), *A History of the Arab Peoples*. Faber and Faber, London.

Hübler, H. (1968), *Das Bürgerhaus in Lübeck*. Das Deutsche Bürgerhaus 10, Wasmuth, Tübingen, Germany.

Hudson, P. (1981), *Archeologia urbana e programmazione della ricerca: l'esempio di Pavia*. All'insegna del Giglio, Florence, Italy.

Huggins, P. J. (1972), 'Monastic grange and outer close excavations, Waltham Abbey, Essex, 1970–72', *Essex Archaeol. and Hist.*, 4, 30–127.

Huggins, P. J. and Bascombe, K. (1992), 'Excavations at Waltham Abbey, Essex, 1985–1991: three pre-Conquest churches and Norman evidence', *Archaeol. Journal*, 149, 282–343.

Huml, V. (1990), 'Research in Prague: an historical and archaeological view of the development of Prague from the 9th century to the middle of the 14th century', in Austin and Alcock, 267–84.

Hurley, M. F. (1997), 'Tasks and outlook for archaeology in Irish towns especially Cork', in Gläser 1997a, 13–18.

Hurley, M. F. (1999), 'Archaeological evidence for trade in Cork from the 12th to the 17th centuries', in Gläser, 13–24.

Hurley, M. F. (2001), 'Domestic architecture in medieval Cork and Waterford (11th–17th century), in Gläser 2001a, 15–34.

Hurley, M. F., Scully, O. M. B. and McCutcheon, S. W. J. (1997), *Late Viking Age and Medieval Waterford: Excavations 1986–1992*. Waterford Corporation, Ireland.

Hurst, J. G. (1977), 'Spanish pottery imported into medieval Britain', *Medieval Archaeol.*, 21, 68–105.

Hurst, J. G., Neal, D. S. and Van Beuningen, H. J. E. (eds) (1986), *Pottery Produced and Traded in North-West Europe*. Rotterdam Papers VI, Rotterdam.

Ijzereef, F. G. (1989), 'Social differentiation from animal bone studies', in Serjeantson and Waldron, 41–54.

Insoll, T. (1999), *The Archaeology of Islam*. Blackwell, Oxford.

Ioannisyan, O. M. (1990), 'Archaeological evidence for the development and urbanisation of Kiev from the 8th to the 14th centuries', in Austin and Alcock, 285–312.

Jansen, H. M. (1987), 'Svendborg in the Middle Ages: an interdisciplinary investigation', *Journal of Danish Archaeol.*, 6, 198–219.

Jansen, H. M. (1999), 'Archaeological evidence for trade in Svendborg from the 12th to the 17th centuries', in Gläser, 571–84.

Jehel, G. and Racinet, P. (1996), *La Ville médiévale*. Armand Colin, Paris.

Johnson, C. and Vince, A. (1992), 'The South Bail Gates of Lincoln', *Lincolnshire Hist. and Archaeol.*, 27, 12–16.

Johnson, M. (1997), 'Vernacular architecture: the loss of innocence', *Vernacular Architecture*, 28, 13–19.

Jones, B. (1984), *Past Imperfect: The Story of Rescue Archaeology*. Heinemann, London.

Jones, G., Straker, V. and Davis, A. (1991), 'Early medieval plant use and ecology', in Vince, 347–85.

Jones, G. C. (1983), 'The medieval animal bones', in D. Allen and C. H. Dalwood, 'Iron Age occupation, a Middle Saxon cemetery, and twelfth to nineteenth-century occupation: excavations in George Street, Aylesbury, 1981', *Records of Bucks.*, 25, 31–44.

Jones, N. W. (1998), 'Excavations within the medieval walled town at New Radnor, Powys, 1991–92', *Archaeol. Journal*, 155, 134–206.

Jones, S., Major, K. and Varley, J. (1984), *The Survey of Ancient Houses in Lincoln: 1. Priorygate to Pottergate*. Lincoln Civic Trust.

Jope, E. M. (1952), 'Excavations in the city of Norwich: 1948', *Norfolk Archaeol.*, 30, 287–323.

Jurion-de Waha, F. (1999), 'Belgium (Brussels region)', in Council of Europe (ed. Leech), 31–40.

Keene, D. (1976), 'Suburban growth', in Barley, 71–82.

Keene, D. (1979), 'Medieval Winchester: its spatial organisation', in B. C. Burnham and J. Kingsbury (eds), *Space, Hierarchy and Society*. British Archaeol. Reports International Series 59, 149–59.

Keene, D. (1985a), *Cheapside before the Great Fire*. Economic and Social Research Council, London.

Keene, D. (1985b), *Survey of Medieval Winchester*. Winchester Studies 2, Oxford University Press, Oxford.

Keene, D. (1989), 'Medieval London and its region', *London Journal*, 14, 99–111.

Keene, D. (1990a), 'Shops and shopping in medieval London', in Grant, 29–46.

Keene, D. (1990b), 'The character and development of the Cheapside area', in Schofield et al., 178–93.

Keene, D. (1995), 'Small towns and the metropolis: the experience of medieval England', in *Peasants and Townsmen in Medieval Europe*. Belgisch Centrum Voor Landelijke Geschiedenis 114, Ghent, Belgium, 223–38.

Keene, D. (2000a), 'London from the post-Roman period to 1300', in Palliser, 187–216.

Keene, D. (2000b), 'The south-east of England', in Palliser, 545–82.

Keller, K.-F. and Shia, E. (1994), *The Medieval Town in Oslo*. Oslo, Norway.

Kellett, J. H. (1969), 'Glasgow', in M. D. Lobel (ed.), *Historic Towns [Atlas] 1*. Oxford.

Kelly, S. (1983), 'The economic topography and structure of Norwich in c. 1300', in U. M. Priestly (ed.), *Men of Property: An Analysis of the Norwich Enrolled Deeds 1285–1311*. Centre for East Anglian Studies, University of East Anglia, Norwich, 13–39.

Kenward, H. K. and Allison, E. (1994), 'Rural origins of the urban insect fauna', in Hall and Kenward, 55–78.

Kenward, H. K. and Hall, A. R. (1995), *Biological Evidence from Anglo-Scandinavian Deposits at 16–22 Coppergate*. The Archaeology of York 14/7, York Archaeol. Trust, York.

Kenyon, J. R. (1990), *Medieval Fortifications*. Leicester University Press, London.

Kermode, J. (2000), 'The greater towns', in Palliser, 441–65.

Kieffer-Olsen, J. (1999), 'Archaeological evidence for trade in Ribe from the 12th to the 17th centuries', in Gläser, 585–94.

Kieffer-Olsen, J. (2001), 'Domestic architecture in the town of Ribe', in Gläser 2001a, 811–18.

Klápště, J. and Velímský, T. (1992), 'The typological development of the town of Most, Bohemia', in *Medieval Europe 1992, Pre-printed Papers for York Conference, Vol. 1. Urbanism*, 197–206.

Knight, J. (1983), 'Montgomery: a castle of the Welsh March, 1223–1649', *Chateau Gaillard*, XI, 169–82.

Kowaleski, M. (2000), 'Port towns: England and Wales 1300–1540', in Palliser, 467–94.

Krause, G. (ed.) (1992), *Stadtarchäologie in Duisburg 1980–1990*. Duisburger Forschungen Band 38, Duisburg.

Krause, G. (1993), 'Duisburg: archäologisch-bauhistorische Beobachtungen zur frühen Duisburger Stadtbefestigung', in Gläser, 193–200.

Krautheimer, R. (1980), *Rome: Profile of a City, 312–1308*. Princeton.

Kruse, S. (1992), 'Late Saxon balances and weights', *Medieval Archaeol.*, 36, 67–95.

Krzywinski, K., Fjelldal, S. and Soltvedt, E.-C. (1983), 'Recent palaeoethnobotanical work at the medieval excavations at Bryggen, Bergen, Norway', in B. Proudfoot (ed.), *Site, Environment and Economy*. British Archaeol. Reports International Series 173, 145–69.

Kümin, B. A. (1997), 'The English parish in a European perspective', in K. L. French, G. G. Gibbs, G. G. and B. A. Kümin (eds), *The Parish in English Life, 1400–1600*. Manchester University Press, Manchester, 15–32.

Kuncevičius, A. (1997), 'Archaeology in Wilna (Vilnius): state, tasks and outlook', in Gläser 1997a, 313–17.

Laleman, M.-C. and Raveschot, P. (1994), 'Maisons patriciennes médiévales à Gand (Gent), Belgique', in Demolon *et al.*, 201–6.

Lambrick, G. (1985), 'Further excavations on the second site of the Dominican priory, Oxford', *Oxoniensia*, 50, 131–208.

Lambrick, G. and Woods, H. (1976), 'Excavations on the second site of the Dominican priory, Oxford', *Oxoniensia*, 41, 168–231.

Lapidus, I. M. (1984), *Muslim Cities in the Later Middle Ages*. Cambridge University Press, Cambridge.

Laszlovsky, J. (ed.) (1995), *Medieval Visegrád*. Institute of Archaeology, Eötvös Loránd University, Budapest.

Lauret, A., Malebranche, R. and Seraphin, G. (1988), *Bastides: villes nouvelles du Moyen Age*. Editions Milan, Toulouse.

Leach, P. (ed.) (1984), *The Archaeology of Taunton*. Western Archaeol. Trust Excavation Monograph 8, Gloucester.

Lebedev, G. (1997), 'Stand, Aufgaben und Perspektiven der Archäologie in Ladoga', in Gläser 1997a, 363–75.

Leech, R. H. (1999), 'The processional city: some issues for historical archaeology', in Tarlow and West, 19–34.

Le Goff, J. (ed.) (1980), *La Ville mediévale*. Histoire de la France urbaine 2, Seuil, Paris.

Le Goff, J. (1988), *Medieval Civilization*. Blackwell, Oxford.

Levitan, B. (1985), 'Early eighteenth-century horncores from Shooting Marsh Stile', in C. G. Henderson (ed.), *Archaeology in Exeter 1984/5*. Exeter City Council, 15–17.

Levitan, B. (1989), 'Bone analysis and urban economy: examples of selectivity and a case for comparison', in Serjeantson and Waldron, 161–88.

Leyser, H. (1995), *Medieval Women: A Social History of Women in England 450–1500*. Weidenfeld and Nicolson, London.

Liebgott, K.-N. (1999), 'Denmark', in Council of Europe (ed. Leech), 63–70.

Lilley, J. M., Stroud, G., Brothwell, D. R. and Williamson, M. H. (1994), *The Jewish Burial Ground at Jewbury*. The Archaeology of York 12/3, York Archaeol. Trust, York.

Lloyd, D. W. (1998), *The Making of English Towns*. Rev. ed, Gollancz, London.

Locock, M. (ed.) (1994), *Meaningful Architecture: Social Interpretations of Buildings*. Avebury, Aldershot.

Lohrum, B. (1992), 'Fachwerkbau', in Flüeler and Flüeler, 248–66.

Lombard-Jourdain, A. (1985), *Aux origines de Paris: la genèse de la Rive Droite jusqu'en 1223*. Editions du Centre Nationale de la Recherche Scientifique, Paris.

Long, C. D. (1975), 'Excavations in the medieval city of Trondheim, Norway', *Medieval Archaeol.*, 19, 1–32.

Lüdecke, T. (1997), 'Stadtarchäologie in Stade: Stand, Aufgaben und Prospektiven', in Gläser 1997a, 135–48.

Lüdecke, T. (2001), 'Der mittelalterliche Hausbau in Stade – Forschungsstand und Aufgaben', in Gläser 2001a, 329–43.

Lunde, O. (1985), 'Archaeology and the medieval towns of Norway', *Medieval Archaeol.*, 29, 120–35.

Lyle, M. (1994), *Canterbury*. Batsford and English Heritage, London.

Lynch, M., Spearman, M. and Stell, G. (1988), *The Scottish Medieval Town*. John Donald, Edinburgh.

Maalouf, A. (1984), *The Crusades through Arab Eyes*. Schocken Books, New York.

MacGregor, A. (1991), 'Antler, bone and horn', in Blair and Ramsay, 355–78.

Maddison, J. (2000), *Ely Cathedral: Design and Meaning*. Ely Cathedral Publications, Ely.

Madsen, H. J. (1997), 'Stadtarchäologie in Århus', in Gläser 1997a, 485–92.

Madsen, P. K. (1999), *Middelalderkeramik fra Ribe: byarkaeologiske undersøgelser 1980–87*. Den antikvariske Samlings skiftraekke bind 2, Jysk Arkaeologisk Selskab, Århus, Denmark.

Maësalu, A. (1999), 'Archäologische Erkenntnisse zum Handel in Tartu (Dorpat) vom 12. bis zum 17. Jahrhundert', in Gläser, 427–34.

Maësalu, A. (2001), 'Die Haustypen im hansezeitlichen Tartu (Dorpat)', in Gläser 2001a, 581–94.

Magdelijns, J. R. M., Nalis, H. J., Proos, R. H. P. and de Vries, D. J. (eds) (1996), *Het kapittel van Lebuinus in Deventer: nalatenschap van een immuniteit in bodem, bebouwing en beschrijving*. Arko Uitgeverij BV, Deventer, Holland.

Magilton, J. R. (1980), *The Church of St Helen-on-the-Walls, Aldwark*. The Archaeology of York 10/1, York Archaeol. Trust, York.

Magilton, J. and Lee, F. (1989), 'The leper hospital of St James and St Mary Magdalene, Chichester', in Roberts *et al.*, 249–66.

Mahany, C., Burchard, A. and Simpson, G. (1982), *Excavations in Stamford 1963–1969*. Soc. of Medieval Archaeol. Monograph 9.

Mahler, F. (2001), 'Mittelalterlicher Hausbau in Uelzen', in Gläser 2001a, 345–56.

Maloney, C. M. with de Moulins, D. (1990), *The Upper Walbrook Valley in the Early Roman Period*. Council for British Archaeol. Research Report 69, London.

Maltby, M. (1979), *Faunal Studies on Urban Sites: The Animal Bones from Exeter, 1971–75*. Exeter Archaeol. Report 2, University of Sheffield.

Manchester, K. (1992), 'The palaeopathology of urban infections', in Bassett, 8–14.

Manning, C. (1999), 'Ireland', in Council of Europe (ed. Leech), 123–32.

Margeson, S. (1993), *Norwich Households: Medieval and Post-medieval Finds from Norwich Survey Excavations 1971–78*. East Anglian Archaeol. 58.

Marin, J.-Y. and Levesque, J.-M. (2000), *Mémoires du Château de Caen*. Skira, Milan.

Marsh, B. (ed.) (1914), *Records of the Carpenters' Company, ii. Wardens' Accounts 1438–1516*. Privately printed, London.

Martin, D. and Martin, B. (1987), *A Selection of Dated Houses in Eastern Sussex 1400–1750, Rape of Hastings Architectural Survey: Historic Buildings in Eastern Sussex 4*. Hastings.

Mays, S. (1997), 'Life and death in a medieval village', in De Boe and Verhaeghe (1997a), 121–5.

McCarthy, M. R. and Brooks, C. (1988), *Medieval Pottery in Britain, AD 900–1600*. Leicester University Press, London.

McGuire, R. H. and Paynter, R. (eds) (1991), *The Archaeology of Inequality*. Blackwell, Oxford.

McKenna, W. J. B. (1987), 'The environmental evidence', in Armstrong and Ayers, 255–62.

McKenna, W. J. B. (1991), 'The plant, molluscan, insect and parasite remains', in Armstrong *et al.*, 209–15.

McNeil, R. (1983), 'Two twelfth-century Wich Houses in Nantwich, Cheshire', *Medieval Archaeol.*, 27, 40–88.

Melli, P. (ed.) (1996), *La città ritrovata: archeologia urbana a Genova 1984–1994*. Tormena Editore, Genoa.

Melli, P. (1999), 'Italy', in Council of Europe (ed. Leech), 133–42.

Mellor, J. E. and Pearce, T. (1981), *The Austin Friars, Leicester*. Council for British Archaeol. Research Report 35, London.

Melzer, W. (1999), 'Archäologische Erkenntnisse zu Handel und Handwerk im mittelalterlichen Soest', in Gläser, 245–62.

Michelmore, D. J. H. (1979), *A Current Bibliography of Vernacular Architecture 1970–76*. Vernacular Architecture Group.

Middleton, A. (1984–5), 'Examination of ash from the experimental firing group pottery bonfire held at Leicester in July 1984 and comparison with some archaeological ashes', *Bull. Experimental Firing Group*, 3, 19–24.

Miller, E. and Hatcher, J. (1995), *Medieval England: Towns, Commerce and Crafts, 1086–1348*. Longman, Harlow.

Miller, K., Robinson, J., English, B. and Hall, I. (1982), *Beverley: An Archaeological and Architectural Study*. RCHME Supplementary Series 4, HMSO, London.

Milne, G. (1987), 'Waterfront archaeology in British towns', in Schofield and Leech, 192–200.

Milne, G. (1992), *Timber Building Techniques in London c. 900–c. 1400*. London and Middlesex Archaeol. Soc. Special Paper 15.

Milne, G. (1997), *St Bride's Church London: Archaeological Research 1952–60 and 1992–5*. English Heritage Archaeol. Report 11.

Milne, G. and Hobley, B. (eds) (1981), *Waterfront Archaeology in Britain and Northern Europe*. Council for British Archaeol. Research Report 41, London.

Milne, G. and Milne, C. (1982), *Medieval Waterfront Development at Trig Lane, London*. London and Middlesex Archaeol. Soc. Special Paper 5.

Mitchiner, M. and Skinner, A. (1983), 'English tokens, c 1200–1425', *British Numismatic Journal*, 53, 29–77.

Molaug, P. B. (1993), 'Neue Ergebnisse zum mittelalterlichen Hafen Oslos', in Gläser, 243–50.

Molaug, P. B. (1997), 'Oslo', in Gläser 1997a, 455–66.

Molaug, P. B. (1999), 'Archaeological evidence for trade in Oslo from the 12th to the 17th century', in Gläser, 533–46.

Molaug, P. B. (2001), 'Medieval house building in Oslo', in Gläser 2001a, 765–82.

Moorhouse, S. (1983), 'The medieval pottery', in P. Mayes and L. A. S. Butler (eds), *Sandal Castle Excavations 1964–73*. Wakefield Historical Publications, Wakefield.

Morris, R. (1987), 'Parish churches', in Schofield and Leech, 177–91.

Morris, R. (1989), *Churches in the Landscape*. Dent, London.

Morris, R. (1996), 'Introduction', in Blair and Pyrah, xv–xvi.

Morris, R. K. (1992), 'An English glossary of medieval mouldings, with an introduction to mouldings c 1040–1240', *Architectural History*, 35, 1–17.

Morris, R. K. (1996), 'Mouldings in medieval cathedrals', in Tatton-Brown and Munby, 211–18.

Morriss, R. K. (2000), *The Archaeology of Buildings*. Tempus, Stroud.

Mugurēvičs, Ē. (1990), 'Interactions between indigenous and western cultures in Livonia in the 13th to 16th centuries', in Austin and Alcock, 168–78.

Mührenberg, D. (1999), 'Archäologische Erkenntnisse zum Handel in Lübeck vom 12 bis zum 17 Jahrhundert', in Gläser, 263–92.

Mulsow, R. (1999), 'Historische (und archäologische) Quellen zum Handel in Rostock', in Gläser, 293–305.

Mulsow, R. (2001), 'Archäologische Erkenntnisse zum mittelalterlichen Hausbau in Rostock', in Gläser 2001a, 357–76.

Munby, J. (1975), '126 High Street: the archaeology and history of an Oxford house', *Oxoniensia*, 40, 254–308.

Munby, J. (1978), 'J. C. Buckler, Tackley's Inn and three medieval houses in Oxford', *Oxoniensia*, 43, 123–69.

Munby, J. (1987), 'Medieval domestic buildings', in Schofield and Leech, 156–66.

Munby, J. (1991), 'Wood', in Blair and Ramsay, 379–406.

Munby, J. (1992), 'Zacharias's: a medieval Oxford inn at 26–8 Cornmarket', *Oxoniensia*, 57, 245–309.

Murphy, K. (1994), 'Excavations in three burgage plots in the medieval town of Newport, Dyfed, 1991', *Medieval Archaeol.*, 38, 55–82.

Murray, H. K. and Murray, J. C. (1993), 'Excavations at Rattray, Aberdeenshire: a Scottish deserted burgh', *Medieval Archaeol.*, 37, 109–218.

Nawrolska, G. (1997), 'Stand, Aufgaben und Perspektiven der Archäologie in Elbing (Elbląg)', in Gläser 1997a, 291–303.

Nawrolska, G. (1999), 'Archaeological evidence for trade in Elbląg from the 13th to the 17th centuries', in Gläser, 373–86.

Nawrolska, G. (2001), 'Domestic architecture in Elbląg', in Gläser 2001a, 473–89.

Nicholas, D. (1987), *The Metamorphosis of a City: Ghent in the Age of the Arteveldes, 1302–1390*. University of Nebraska Press, Lincoln Nebraska and London.

Nicholas, D. (1997a), *The Growth of the Medieval City from Late Antiquity to the Early Fourteenth Century*. Longman, Harlow.

Nicholas, D. (1997b), *The Later Medieval City 1300–1500*. Longman, Harlow.

Noddle, B. (1977), 'Mammal bone', in Clarke and Carter, 378–98.

Nydolf, N.-G., Runeby, C., Swanström, E. and Zerpe, L. (1991), 'Occupation layers as historical evidence for Visby', in Ersgård *et al.*, 98–121.

O'Brien, C. (1991), 'Newcastle upon Tyne and its North Sea trade', in Good *et al.*, 36–42.

O'Brien, E. and Roberts, C. (1996), 'Archaeological study of church cemeteries: past, present and future', in Blair and Pyrah, 159–81.

O'Connell, M. G. (1977), *Historic Towns in Surrey*. Surrey Archaeol. Soc. Research Vol. 5, Guildford.

O'Connor, T. P. (1982), *Animal Bones from Flaxengate, Lincoln, c. 870–1500*. The Archaeology of Lincoln XVIII–1, Lincoln.

O'Connor, T. P. (1983), 'Feeding Lincoln in the 11th century: a speculation', in M. Jones (ed.), *Integrating the Subsistence Economy*. Brit. Archaeol. Reports S181, 327–30.

O'Connor, T. P. (1989), 'Deciding priorities with urban bones: York as a case study', in Serjeantson and Waldron, 189–200.

O'Connor, T. P. (1991), *Bones from 46–54 Fishergate*. The Archaeology of York 15/4, York Archaeol. Trust, York.

O'Connor, T. P. (1993), 'Bone assemblages from monastic sites: many questions but few data', in Gilchrist and Mytum, 107–12.

O'Connor, T. (2000), *The Archaeology of Animal Bones*. Sutton, Stroud.

O'Connor, T., Hall, A. R., Jones, A. K. J. and Kenward, H. K. (1984), 'Ten years of environmental archaeology at York', in Addyman and Black, 166–72.

Oexle, J. (1992a), 'Konstanz', in Flüeler and Flüeler, 53–68.

Oexle, J. (1992b), 'Ulm', in Flüeler and Flüeler, 165–82.

Oexle, J. (1999), 'Germany', in Council of Europe (ed. Leech), 103–10.

Ó Ríordáin, A. B. (1971), 'Excavations at High Street and Winetavern Street, Dublin', *Medieval Archaeol.*, 15, 73–85.

Orme, N. (2001), *Medieval Children*. Yale University Press, New Haven and London.

Orton, C., Tyers, P. and Vince, A. (1993), *Pottery in Archaeology*. Cambridge University Press, Cambridge.

Oxley, J. (1999), 'The experience of York', in Dennison, 137–44.

Øye, I. (1997), 'State, tasks and outlook for archaeology in Bergen', in Gläser 1997a, 441–54.

Øye, I. (1999), 'Archaeological evidence for trade in Bergen from the 12th to the 17th century', in Gläser, 547–62.

Pace, A. and Cutajar, N. (2001), 'Historic centre management in Malta', in Pickard, 202–22.

Palliser, D. M. (1987), 'The medieval period', in Schofield and Leech, 54–68.

Palliser, D. M. (1993), 'The topography of monastic houses in Yorkshire towns', in Gilchrist and Mytum, 19–28.

Palliser, D. M. (ed.) (2000), *The Cambridge Urban History of Britain: 1, 600–1540*. Cambridge University Press, Cambridge.

Palliser, D. M., Slater, T. R. and Dennison, E. P. (2000), 'The topography of towns 600–1300', in Palliser, 153–86.

Palmer, N. (1980), 'A Beaker burial and medieval tenements in the Hamel, Oxford', *Oxoniensia*, 45, 124–225.

Paner, H. (1997), 'The archaeology of Danzig (Gdańsk)', in Gläser 1997a, 277–90.

Paner, H. (1999), 'Archaeological evidence for trade in Gdańsk from the 12th to the 17th centuries', in Gläser, 387–402.

Paner, H. (2001), '10th- to 17th-century domestic architecture in Gdańsk', in Gläser 2001a, 491–509.

Pantin, W. A. (1947), 'The development of domestic architecture in Oxford', *Antiq. Journal*, 27, 120–50.

Pantin, W. A. (1962–3), 'Medieval English town-house plans', *Medieval Archaeol.*, 6–7, 202–39.

Pardo, V. R. (1982), *Storia dell'urbanistica*. Laterza, Bari.

Parenti, R. (1992), 'Medieval bricks in Tuscany: use, size, bonding and decoration to develop a guide-fossil', in *Medieval Europe 1992: Pre-printed papers 3, Technology and Innovation*. York, paper C4d.

Parker, V. (1971), *The Making of King's Lynn*. Phillimore, Chichester.

Pärn, A. (1997), 'Die Lage der Stadtarchäologie in Estland: Der Stand der Forschungen und die bisherigen Ergebnisse', in Gläser 1997a, 329–42.

Pärn, A. (2001), 'Über die Hausbauentwicklung in Westestland im 13. bis 15. Jahrhundert', in Gläser, 595–604.

Pärn, A. and Tamm, J. (1999), 'Estonia', in Council of Europe (ed. Leech), 71–80.

Paroli, L. and Delogu, P. (eds) (1993), *La storia economica di Roma nell'alto Medioevo alle luce dei recenti scavi archeologici*. All'insegna del Giglio, Florence, Italy.

Parsons, D. (ed.) (1990), *Stone: Quarrying and Building in England AD 43–1525*. Phillimore, Chichester.

Parsons, D. (1991), 'Stone', in Blair and Ramsay, 1–28.

Pattison, I. R., Pattison, D. S. and Alcock, N. W. (1992), *A Bibliography of Vernacular Architecture: III, 1977–89*. Vernacular Architecture Group.

Pearce, J. E. and Vince, A. G. (1988), *A Dated Type-series of London Medieval Pottery: Part 4, Surrey Whitewares*. London Middlesex Archaeol. Soc. Special Paper 10.

Pearce, J. E., Vince, A. G. and Jenner, M. A. (1985), *A Dated Type-series of London Medieval Pottery: Part 2, London-type Ware*. London and Middlesex Archaeol. Soc. Special Paper 6.

Pearson, S. (1994), *The Medieval Houses of Kent: An Historical Analysis*. RCHM, Stationery Office, London.

Pearson, S. (1997), 'Tree-ring dating: a review', *Vernacular Architecture*, 28, 25–39.

Pearson, S. and Meeson, B. (eds) (2001), *Vernacular Buildings in a Changing World*. Council for British Archaeol. Research Report 126, York.

Penn, K. J. (1980), *Historic Towns in Dorset*. Dorset Natural Hist. and Archaeol. Soc. Monograph 1.

Pepper, G. (1992), 'An archaeology of the Jewry in medieval London', *London Archaeologist*, 7, 3–6.

Perring, D. (1981), *Early Medieval Occupation at Flaxengate Lincoln*. The Archaeology of Lincoln IX-1, Lincoln.

Perring, D. (ed.) (in prep.), *Town and Country in England: Frameworks for Archaeological Research*. Council for British Archaeology Research Report.

Peters, C. (1996), 'Interior and furnishings', in Blair and Pyrah, 68–75.

Pevsner, N. (1976), *A History of Building Types*. Repr. 1997, Thames and Hudson, London.

Phythian-Adams, C. (1979), *Desolation of a City: Coventry and the Urban Crisis of the Late Middle Ages*. Cambridge University Press, Cambridge.

Pickard, R. (ed.) (2001), *Management of Historic Centres*. Spon Press, London and New York.

Pinol, J.-L. (ed.) (1996), *Atlas historique des villes de France*. Hachette, Paris.

Pirenne, H. (1925), *Medieval Cities: Their Origins and the Revival of Trade*. English translation 1952, repr. 1974, Princeton University Press, Princeton.

Píša, V. (1990), 'Zur Entwicklung Prags im frühen Mittelalter', in Dolgner and Roch, 137–46.

Platt, C. (1973), *Medieval Southampton: The Port and Trading Community*. Routledge and Kegan Paul, London.

Platt, C. (1976a), *The English Medieval Town*. Secker and Warburg, London.

Platt, C. (1976b), 'The evolution of towns: natural growth', in Barley, 48–56.

Platt, C. (1978), *Medieval England: A Social History and Archaeology from the Conquest to 1600*. Routledge and Kegan Paul, London.

Platt, C. and Coleman-Smith, R. (1975), *Excavations in Medieval Southampton, 1953–69. 1, The Excavation Reports; 2, The Finds*. Leicester University Press, Leicester.

Platts, G. (1985), *Land and People in Medieval Lincolnshire*. History of Lincolnshire IV, Society for Lincolnshire Hist. and Archaeol., Lincoln.

Ponting, K. G. (1957), *A History of the West of England Cloth Industry*. Adams and Dark, Bath.

Portman, D. (1966), *Exeter Houses 1400–1700*. Phillimore, Chichester.

Postan, M. (1975), *The Medieval Economy and Society*. Penguin, Harmondsworth.

Poulton, R. (1998), 'Excavations at Mint Street, Godalming', in R. Poulton (ed.), *Archaeological Investigations of Historic Surrey Towns*. Surrey Archaeol. Collections 85, 177–86.

Poulton, R. and Woods, H. (1984), *Excavations on the Site of the Dominican Friary at Guildford in 1974 and 1978*. Surrey Archaeol. Soc. Research Vol. 9, Guildford.

Pounds, N. J. G. (1994), *An Economic History of Medieval Europe*. 2nd edn, Longman, London.

Power, E. (1975), *Medieval Women*. Cambridge University Press, Cambridge.

Prawer, J. (1972), *The Crusaders' Kingdom: European Colonialism in the Middle Ages*. Repr. 2001, Phoenix Press, London.

Preucel, R. W. and Hodder, I. (eds) (1996), *Contemporary Archaeology in Theory: A Reader*. Blackwell, Oxford.

Price, R. with Ponsford, M. (1998), *St Bartholomew's Hospital, Bristol: The Excavation of a Medieval Hospital 1976–8*; Council for British Archaeol. Research Report 110, York.

Priddy, D. (1983), 'Excavations in Essex 1982', *Essex Archaeol. and Hist.*, 15, 163–72.

Pringle, D. (2000), *Fortification and Settlement in Crusader Palestine*. Variorum Collected Studies Series CS675, Ashgate, Aldershot.

Pritchard, F. A. (1984), 'Late Saxon textiles from the City of London', *Medieval Archaeol*, 28, 46–76.

Pritchard, F. A. (1991), 'Small finds', in Vince, 120–278.

Pullat, E. (1998), *Brief History of Tallinn*. Estopol, Tallinn, Estonia.

Rackham, J. (1982), 'The smaller mammals in the urban environment: their recovery and interpretation from archaeological deposits', in Hall and Kenward, 86–93.

Rackham, J. (1994), *Animal Bones*. Interpreting the Past series, British Museum, London.

Rackham, O. (1976), *Trees and Woodland in the British Landscape*. Dent, London.

Raine, A. (1955), *Medieval York*. John Murray, London.

Rapoport, A. (1990), 'Systems of activities and systems of settings', in S. Kent (ed.), *Domestic Architecture and the Use of Space*. Cambridge University Press, Cambridge, 9–20.

RCHME: Royal Commission on Historical Monuments (England).

RCHMW: Royal Commission on Historical Monuments (Wales).

Reaney, P. H. (1967), *The Origin of English Surnames*. Routledge and Kegan Paul, London.

Rębkowski, M. (2001), 'Domestic architecture in medieval Kolobrzeg (13th–15th century)', in Gläser 2001a, 511–27.

Rech, M. (1997), 'Stand, Aufgaben und Perspektiven der Mittelalterarchäologie in Bremen', in Gläser 1997a, 123–34.

Rech, M. (2001), 'Zum Hausbau im mittelalterlichen Bremen', in Gläser 2001a, 377–85.

Redman, C. L. (1986), *Qsar es-Seghir: An Archaeological View of Medieval Life*. Academic Press, London.

Reimers, E. (2001), 'Medieval domestic architecture in Bergen: a sample of the archaeological material', in Gläser 2001a, 783–810.

Reinisch, U. (1990), 'Zur Grundrissentwicklung deutscher Planstädte im 12. und 13. Jahrhundert', in Dolgner and Roch, 126–36.

Reisnert, A. (2001), 'Houses and yards in Malmö during the medieval period and Renaissance', in Gläser 2001a, 677–701.

Reynolds, S. (1977), *An Introduction to the History of English Medieval Towns*. Clarendon Press, Oxford.

Richter, M. (1991), 'Zur ältesten Geschichte der Stadt Prag', in Brachmann and Herrmann, 174–9.

Rigby, S. H. (1995), *English Society in the Later Middle Ages: Class, Status and Gender*. Macmillan, London.

Riley-Smith, J. (1987), *The Crusades: A Short History*. Athlone Press, London.

Ring, E. (1997), 'Stadtarchäologie in Lüneburg: Resümee der ersten vier Jahre', in Gläser 1997a, 161–70.

Ring, E. (1999), 'Archäologische Belege für den Handel in Lüneburg', in Gläser, 323–30.

Ring, E. (2001), 'Bauen und Wohnen in Lüneburg vom 13. bis 16. Jahrhundert', in Gläser 2001a, 387–401.

ROB: Rijksdienst voor het Oudheidkundig Bodemonderzoek, Dutch State Archaeological Service.

Roberts, C. A., Lee, F. and Bintliff, J. (eds) (1989), *Burial Archaeology: Current Research, Methods and Developments*. British Archaeol. Reports 211, Oxford.

Roberts, E. (2001), 'The potential of tree-ring dating', in Pearson and Meeson, 111–21.

Roberts, M. (1992), 'A Northampton Jewish tombstone, c 1269 to 1290, recently rediscovered in Northampton Central Museum', *Medieval Archaeol.*, 36, 173–8.

Robertson, J. C. (1989), 'Counting London's horncores: sampling what?', *Post-Medieval Archaeol.*, 23, 1–10.

Robinson, M. (1976), 'The natural alluvium and dumped clay', in Lambrick and Woods, 227.

Robinson, M. (1980), 'Waterlogged plant and invertebrate evidence', in Palmer, 199–206.

Robinson, M. and Wilson, B. (1987), 'Survey of the environmental archaeology in the South Midlands', in H. C. M. Keeley (ed.), *Environmental Archaeology: A Regional Review*, 2, English Heritage Occasional Paper 1, 16–100.

Rodwell, K. (ed.) (1975), *Historic Towns in Oxfordshire: A Survey of the New County*. Oxford.

Rodwell, W. J. (1976), 'The archaeological investigation of Hadstock church, Essex: an interim report', *Antiq. Journal*, 56, 55–71.

Rodwell, W. J. (1981), *The Archaeology of the English Church*. Batsford, London.

Rogers, A. (1965), *The Making of Stamford*. Leicester, University Press.

Rogers, K. H. (1969), 'Salisbury', in M. D. Lobel (ed.), *Historic Towns [Atlas]*, 1, Oxford.

Rogers, R. and Power, A. (2000), *Cities for a Small Country*, Faber and Faber, London.

Rogerson, A. (1976), 'Excavations on Fuller's Hill, Great Yarmouth', *East Anglian Archaeol.*, 2, 131–246.

Roskams, S. (2001), *Excavation*. Cambridge University Press, Cambridge.

Rosser, G. (1984), 'The essence of medieval urban communities: the vill of Westminster, 1200–1540', in *Trans. Royal Historical Soc.*, 34, repr. in Holt and Rosser 1990, 216–37.

Rosser, G. (1996), 'Religious practice on the margins', in Blair and Pyrah, 75–84.

Rötting, H. (1997), *Stadtarchäologie in Braunschweig: Ein fachübergreifender Arbeitsbericht zu den Grabungen 1976–1992*. Forschungen der Denkmalpflege in Niedersachsen 3.

Rötting, H. (2001), 'Zu Hausbau und Grundstücksbebauung in der hochmittelalterlichen Altstadt von Braunschweig', in Gläser 2001a, 403–20.

RCHME: Royal Commission on Historical Monuments (England):
   (1972a), *City of York, ii: The Defences*. HMSO, London.

(1972b), *City of York, iii: South-west of the Ouse*. HMSO, London.

(1975), *City of York, iv: Outside the City Walls, East of the Ouse*. HMSO, London.

(1977), *The Town of Stamford*. HMSO, London.

(1980), *City of Salisbury, i. HMSO, London.*

(1981), *City of York, v: The Central Area*. HMSO, London.

(1987), *Houses of the North York Moors*. HMSO, London.

(1993), *Salisbury: The Houses in the Close*. HMSO, London.

RCHMW: Royal Commission on Historical Monuments (Wales) (1960), *Caernarvonshire*. 2 vols, HMSO, London.

Rybina, E. (1997), 'Stand, Aufgaben and Perspektiven der Archäologie in Novgorod', in Gläser 1997a, 351–62.

Rybina, E. A. (1999), 'Trade of Novgorod in the 10th–15th centuries established through archaeological data', in Gläser, 447–56.

Salter, H. E. (1960), *Survey of Oxford*. Oxford Historical Soc., ns 14 (and 20, 1969).

Salzman, L. F. (1923), *Medieval English Industries*. Clarendon Press, Oxford.

Salzman, L. F. (1964), *English Trade in the Middle Ages*. Fordes, London.

Salzman, L. F. (1967), *Building in England down to 1540*. Rev. edn, Oxford University Press, Oxford.

Samuel, M. W. (1989), 'The fifteenth-century garner at Leadenhall, London', *Antiq. Journal*, 59, 119–53.

Sapin, C. (2000), *Archéologie et architecture d'un site monastique: 10 ans de recherche à l'abbaye Saint-Germain d'Auxerre*. Centre d'Etudes médiévales d'Auxerre, Auxerre.

Sarfatij, H. (1973), 'Digging in Dutch towns: 25 years of research by the ROB in medieval town centres', *Berichten ROB*, 23, 367–420.

Sarfatij, H. (1990a), 'Dutch towns in the formative period (AD 1000–1400): the archaeology of settlement and building', in J. C. Besteman, J. M. Bos and H. A. Heidingam (eds), *Medieval Archaeology in the Netherlands*. Assen/Maastricht, 183–98.

Sarfatij, H. (ed.) (1990b), *Verborgen Steden: Stadsarcheologie in Nederland*. Meulenhof, Amsterdam.

Sarfatij, H. (1997a), 'Urban archaeology in the Netherlands', in W. J. H. Willems, H. Kars and D. P. Hallewas (eds), *Archaeological Heritage Management in the Netherlands*. ROB, Amersfoort, Holland.

Sarfatij, H. (1997b), 'Vier Städte in einem Projekt: Das Forschungsprojekt "Urbanisierung im Flussgebiet während des Mittelalters"', in Gläser 1997a, 111–21.

Sarfatij, H. (1999a), 'Netherlands', in Council of Europe (ed. Leech), 151–62.

Sarfatij, H. (1999b), 'Tiel und Dordrecht: Archäologie und Handel in zwei Städten im niederländischen Rheingebiet', in Gläser, 183–200.

Sarfatij, H. and Melli, P. (1999), 'Archaeology and the town', in Council of Europe (ed. Leech), 13–30.

Saunders, A. D. (1980), 'Lydford Castle, Devon', *Medieval Archaeol.*, 24, 123–86.

Saunders, P. and Saunders, E. (eds) (1991), *Salisbury and South-west Wiltshire Museum Medieval Catalogue Part 1*. Salisbury Museum, Salisbury.

Scaife, R. (1994), 'Pollen analysis', in Ayers, 50–4.

Schama, S. (1987), *The Embarrassment of Riches: An Interpretation of Dutch Culture in the Golden Age*. Repr. 1991, Fontana, London.

Schia, E. (1994), 'Urban Oslo and its relation to rural production in the hinterland – an archaeological view', in Hall and Kenward, 1–12.

Schiffer, M. B. (1987), *Formation Processes of the Archaeological Record*. University of Utah Press, Utah.

Schneider, J. E. (1992a), 'Der mittelalterliche Steinbau in Zürich', in Flüeler and Flüeler, 239–47.

Schneider, J. E. (1992b), 'Zürich', in Flüeler and Flüeler, 69–92.

Schneider, M. (1997), 'Stadtarchäologie in der Hansestadt Stralsund in den Jahren 1991 bis 1995', in Gläser 1997a, 237–44.

Schneider, M. (1999), 'Archäologische Erkenntnisse zum mittelalterliche Handel und Warenumschlag in Stralsund', in Gläser, 357–72.

Schneider, M. (2001), 'Der Hausbau in Stralsund nach archäologischen Befunden', in Gläser 2001a, 433–53.

Schofield, J. (1975–6), 'Excavations south of Edinburgh High Street, 1973–4', *Procs. of the Soc. of Antiq. of Scotland*, 107, 155–241.

Schofield, J. (ed.) (1987), *The London Surveys of Ralph Treswell*. London Topographical Soc. Publication 135, London.

Schofield, J. (1990), 'Medieval and Tudor domestic buildings in London', in Grant, 16–28.

Schofield, J. (1994a), 'Medieval and later towns', in B. Vyner (ed.), *Building on the Past*. Royal Archaeol. Institute, 195–214.

Schofield, J. (1994b), 'Saxon and medieval parish churches in the City of London: a review', *Trans. London Middlesex Archaeol. Soc.*, 45, 23–146.

Schofield, J. (1994c), 'Social perceptions of space in medieval and Tudor London houses', in Locock, 188–206.

Schofield, J. (1995), *Medieval London Houses*. Yale University Press, New Haven and London.

Schofield, J. (1997a), 'Archaeology in London', in Gläser 1997a, 19–30.

Schofield, J. (1997b), 'Urban housing in England 1400–1600', in Gaimster and Stamper, 127–44.

Schofield, J. (1999), *The Building of London from the Conquest to the Great Fire*. 3rd edn, Sutton, Stroud.

Schofield, J. and Dyson, T. (in prep.), *London Waterfront Tenements c. 1200–c. 1750*.

Schofield, J. and Lea, R. (in prep.), *Excavations at Holy Trinity Priory Aldgate, London*. Museum of London Archaeol. Service.

Schofield, J. and Leech, R. (eds) (1987), *Urban Archaeology in Britain*. Council for British Archaeol. Research Report 61, London.

Schofield, J. with Maloney, C. (eds) (1998), *Archaeology in the City of London 1907–91: A Guide to the Records of Excavations by the Museum of London*. Archaeol. Gazetteer Series 1, Museum of London.

Schofield, J. and Palliser, D. with Harding, C. (1981), *Recent Archaeological Research in English Towns*. Council for British Archaeol., London.

Schofield, J., Allen, P. and Taylor, C. (1990), 'Medieval buildings and property development in the area of Cheapside', *Trans. London and Middlesex Archaeol. Soc.*, 41, 39–238.

Schütte, S. (2000), 'Köln als Handelsplatz des Früh- und des Hochmittelalters', in A. Wieczorek and H.-M. Hinz (eds), *Europas Mitte um 1000*. Theiss, Stuttgart, i, 184–7.

Scott, S. (1991), 'The animal bones', in Armstrong *et al.*, 216–33.

Searle, E. and Ross, B. (1967), *Accounts of the Cellarers of Battle Abbey 1275–1513*. Sydney University Press, Australia.

Serjeantson, D. and Waldron, T. (eds) (1989), *Diet and Crafts in Towns: The Evidence of Animal Remains from the Roman to the Post-medieval Period*. Brit. Archaeol. Report 199.

Seyer, H. (1991), 'Die Entstehung von Berlin und Köln im Spiegel archäologischer Ausgrabungen', in Brachmann and Herrmann, 19–24.

Shackley, M. (1981), *Environmental Archaeology*. Allen and Unwin, London.

Shammas, C. (1993), 'Changes in English and Anglo-American consumption from 1550 to 1800', in Brewer and Porter, 177–205.

Shead, N. E (1988), 'Glasgow: an ecclesiastical burgh', in Lynch *et al.*, 116–32.

Shia, E. (1989), 'Urban Oslo: evolution from a royal stronghold and administrative centre', *Arkeologiske skrifter Historisk museum*, 5, Universitet I Bergen, Bergen, Norway, 51–72.

Shoesmith, R. (1980), *Excavations at Castle Green*. Hereford City Excavations 1, Council for British Archaeol. Research Report 36, London.

Short, P. (1980), 'The fourteenth-century rows of York', *Archaeol. Journal*, 137, 86–137.

Simpson, G. G. (ed.) (1972), *Scotland's Medieval Burghs: An Archaeological Heritage in Danger.*

Simpson, W. G. (1996), 'Master-builders: fresh research on cathedrals and other medieval buildings by the Historic Buildings Research Unit', *From River Trent to Raqqa: Nottingham University Archaeological Fieldwork in Britain, Europe and the Middle East, 1991–1995*. Nottingham Studies in Archaeology I, Nottingham, 87–92.

Sjoberg, G. (1960), *The Pre-industrial City*. Free Press of Glencoe, Illinois.

Skaarup, B. (1999), 'Archaeological evidence for trade from the 12th to the 17th centuries in Copenhagen', in Gläser, 595–602.

Skinner, A. (ed.) (1999), *Adam Smith, The Wealth of Nations, Books I–III*. Penguin, Harmondsworth.

Skinner, F. G. (1967), *Weights and Measures: Their Ancient Origins and Their Development in Great Britain up to A.D. 1855*. London.

Skov, H. (1999), 'Archaeological evidence for trade in Århus, Denmark, from the 10th to the 17th centuries', in Gläser, 603–12.

Skov, H. (2001), 'House types in Århus, Denmark, c 900–1600 AD', in Gläser 2001a, 819–32.

Slade, C. F. (1969), 'Reading', in M. D. Lobel (ed.), *Historic Towns [Atlas]*, 1, Oxford.

Slater, T. (1980), *The Analysis of Burgages in Medieval Towns*. University of Birmingham, Department of Geography, Working Paper 4, Birmingham.

Slater, T. R. (1987), 'Ideal and reality in English episcopal medieval town planning', *Trans. Inst. Brit. Geog.*, ns 12, 191–203.

Slater, T. R. (ed.) (2000), *Towns in Decline AD 100–1600*. Ashgate, Aldershot.

Slater, T. R. and Wilson, C. (1977), *Archaeology and Development in Stratford-upon-Avon*. University of Birmingham.

Smith, T. P. (1985), *The Medieval Brickmaking Industry in England 1400–1450*. Brit. Archaeol. Reports 138.

Söderlund, K. (1997), 'Archaeology in Stockholm', in Gläser 1997a, 419–28.

Söderlund, K. (1999), 'Trading City Stockholm – from the 13th to the 17th centuries, topography and catchment area', in Gläser, 505–12.

Söderlund, K. (2001), 'Domestic architecture in Stockholm', in Gläser 2001a, 703–21.

Sorokin, A. N. (2001), 'Domestic architecture in medieval Novgorod', in Gläser 2001a, 605–26.

Soulsby, I. (1983), *The Towns of Medieval Wales*. Phillimore, Chichester.

Spanish Ministry of Culture (1999), 'Spain', in Council of Europe (ed. Leech), 201–8.

Spearman, M. (1988a), 'The medieval townscape of Perth', in Lynch *et al.*, 42–59.

Spearman, M. (1988b), 'Workshops, materials and debris – evidence of early industries', in Lynch *et al.*, 134–47.

Spencer, B. (1990), *Pilgrim Souvenirs and Secular Badges*. Salisbury and South Wilts. Museum Medieval Catalogue, Part 2, Salisbury.

Spencer, B. (1998), *Pilgrim Souvenirs and Secular Badges*. Medieval finds from excavations in London 7, Stationery Office, London.

Spencer-Wood, S. M. (1999), 'Changing meanings of the domestic sphere', in P. M. Allison (ed.), *The Archaeology of Household Activities*. Routledge, London, 162–89.

Spitzers, T. A. (2001), 'Archaeological data on domestic architecture in Deventer from the 9th to the 15th centuries', in Gläser 2001a, 197–211.

Stalley, R. (1999), *Early Medieval Architecture*. Oxford History of Art, Oxford University Press, Oxford.

Stankiewicz, J. (1990), 'Ergebnisse der Stadtkernforschung in Danzig', in Dolgner and Roch, 147–55.

Staski, E. (ed.) (1987), *Living in Cities: Current Research in Urban Archaeology*. Society for Historical Archaeol. Special Publication Series 5.

Steane, J. M. (1985), *The Archaeology of Medieval England and Wales*. Croom Helm, Beckenham.

Steane, K. (2000), *The Archaeology of Wigford and the Brayford Pool*. Oxbow Books, Oxford.

Steedman, K., Dyson, T. and Schofield, J. (1992), *Aspects of Saxo-Norman London, 3: Billingsgate and the Bridgehead to 1200*. London and Middlesex Archaeol. Soc. Special Paper 14.

Stenning, D. F. and Andrews, D. (eds) (1998), *Regional Variation in Timber-framed Building in England and Wales down to 1550*. Essex County Council.

Stephenson, D. (1984–5), 'Colchester: a smaller medieval English jewry', *Essex Archaeology and Hist.*, 16, 48–52.

Stevenson, A. (1988a), 'The monastic presence: Berwick in the twelfth and thirteenth centuries', in Lynch *et al.*, 99–115.

Stevenson, A. (1988b), 'Trade with the South', in Lynch *et al.*, 180–206.

Stirland, A. (1985), 'The human bones', in Ayers, 49–58.

Stocker, D. A. (1990), 'Rubbish recycled: a study of the re-use of stone in Lincolnshire', in Parsons, 83–101.

Stocker, D. A. (1991), *St Mary's Guildhall, Lincoln*. The Archaeology of Lincoln 12/1, Lincoln.

Stocker, D. A. (1993), 'Recording worked stone', in Gilchrist and Mytum, 19–28.

Stocker, D. A. (1999), *The College of the Vicars Choral of York Minster at Bedern: Architectural Fragments*. The Archaeology of York 10/4, York Archaeol. Trust, York.

Stoepker, H. (1990), 'Church archaeology in the Netherlands: problems, prospects, proposals', in J. C. Bestman, J. M. Bos and A. Heidinga (eds), *Medieval Archaeology in the Netherlands: Studies Presented to H. H. van Regteren Altena*. Assen/Maastricht, 199–218.

Strauss, A. and Corbin, J. (1998), *Basics of Qualitative Research: Techniques and Procedures for Developing Grounded Theory*. 2nd edn, Sage Publications, London.

Strobel, R. (1976), *Das Bürgerhaus in Regensburg*. Das Deutsche Bürgerhaus 23, Wasmuth, Tübingen, Germany.

Stroud, G. (1994a), 'The Human Bones', in G. Stroud and R. L. Kemp, *Cemeteries of St Andrew, Fishergate*. The Archaeology of York 12/2, York Archaeol. Trust, York, 160–241.

Stroud, G. (1994b), 'The distinctiveness of the Jewbury population', in Lilley *et al.*, 523–6.

Swanson, H. (1989), *Medieval Artisans*. Blackwell, Oxford.

Swanson, H. (1999), *Medieval British Towns*. Macmillan, London.

Tanner, J. M. and Everleth, P. B. (1976), 'Urbanization and growth', in G. A. Harrison and J. B. Gibson (eds) *Man in Urban Environments*. Oxford University Press, Oxford, 144–66.

Tarlow, S. and West, S. (eds) (1999), *The Familiar Past? Archaeologies of Later Historical Britain*. Routledge, London.

Tatton-Brown, T. (1978), 'Canterbury', *Current Archaeol.*, 62, 78–82.

Tatton-Brown, T. (1990), 'Building stone in Canterbury, c. 1070–1525', in Parsons, 70–82.

Tatton-Brown, T. and Munby, J. (eds) (1996), *The Archaeology of Cathedrals*. Oxford Comm. for Archaeol. Monograph 42, Oxford.

Tesch, S. (2001), 'Houses, town yards and town planning in Late Viking and medieval Sigtuna', in Gläser 2001a, 723–41.

Thiemann, B. (2001), 'Bauformen des Hochmittelalters in Soest', in Gläser 2001a, 455–72.

Thijssen, J. (ed.) (1991), *Tot de Bodem uitgezocht: glas en ceramik uit een beerput van de 'Hof van Batenburg 'te Nijmegen, 1375–1850*. Stichting Stadsarcheologie Nijmegen, Holland.

Thomas, C., Sloane, B. and Phillpotts, C. (1997), *Excavations at the Priory and Hospital of St Mary Spital, London*. Museum of London Archaeol. Service Monograph 1.

Thompson, M. W. (1986), 'Associated monasteries and castles in the Middle Ages: a tentative list', *Archaeol. Journal*, 143, 305–21.

Thrupp, S. (1948), *The Merchant Class of Medieval London*. University of Michigan Press, Ann Arbor.

Tolley, T. (1991), 'Eleanor of Castile and the "Spanish" style in England', in M. Ormrod (ed.), *England in the Thirteenth Century*. Harlaxton Medieval Studies I, 167–92.

Tours 1982: Anon (1982), *Archéologie urbaine*. Proceedings of Conference at Tours (1980), Association pour les fouilles archéologiques nationales.

Tyers, I. (2001), 'Tree-ring analysis of the Roman and medieval timbers from medieval London Bridge and its environs', in Watson *et al.*, 180–9.

Ulmschneider, K. (2000), 'Settlement, economy and the "productive" site: Middle Anglo-Saxon Lincolnshire AD 650–780', *Medieval Archaeol.*, 44, 53–80.

Urry, W. (1967), *Canterbury under the Angevin Kings*. Athlone Press, University of London, London.

Vandenberghe, S. (ed.) (1983), *Het Hof van Watervliet in de Oude Burg te Brugge*. Bruges.

Van Drunen, A. H. (1983), 'De middeleeuwse kirken', in H. L. Janssen (ed.), *Van Bos tot Stadiopgravingen in 's Hertogenbosch*. Gemeinte 's Hertogenbosch, Holland, 89–100.

Van Eenhooge, D. (2001), 'The archaeological study of buildings and town history in Bruges: domestic architecture in the period 1200–1350', in Gläser 2001a, 121–41.

Van Ossel, P. (ed.) (1998), *Les Jardins du Carrousel (Paris)*. Documents d'Archéologie Française 73, Maison des Sciences de l'Homme, Paris.

Van Regteren Altena, H. H. (1970), 'The origin and development of Dutch towns', *World Archaeol.*, 2, 128–40.

Veblen, T. (1899), *The Theory of the Leisure Class*. Repr. 1994, Dover, New York.

Veeckman, J. (ed.) (1992), *Blik in de bodem: recent stadsarcheologisch onderzoek in Antwerpen*. Stad Antwerpen.

Veeckman, J. (1997), 'Urban archaeology in Antwerp (Belgium): results and prospects for the future', in Gläser 1997a, 67–74.

Veeckman, J. (1999), 'Trade in Antwerp from the 12th to the 17th centuries', in Gläser, 123–39.

Veeckman, J. (2001), 'Domestic architecture in High and Late Medieval Antwerp', in Gläser 2001a, 143–57.

Velay, P. (1991), 'Die Entstehung und die frühe Entwicklung der Stadt Paris', in Brachmann and Herrmann, 85–91.

Velay, P. (1992), *From Lutetia to Paris: The Island and the Two Banks*. CNRS, Paris.

Verhaeghe, F. (1991), 'Frühmittelalterliche Städte in Belgien: ein vorläufiger Überblick', in Brachmann and Herrmann, 97–115.

Verhaeghe, F. (1994), 'L'espace civil et la ville', in Demolon *et al.*, 145–90.

Verhaeghe, F. (1999), 'Trade in ceramics in the North Sea region, 12th to 15th centuries: a methodological problem and a few pointers', in Gläser, 139–68.

Verhulst, A. (1994), 'The origins and early development of medieval towns in northern Europe', *Economic History Review*, 47, 362–73.

Verhulst, A. (1999), *The Rise of Cities in North-West Europe*. Cambridge University Press, Cambridge.

Vince, A. G. (1977), 'The medieval and post-medieval ceramic industry of the Malvern region: the study of a ware and its distribution', in D. P. S. Peacock (ed.), *Pottery and Early Commerce*. Academic Press, London, 257–305.

Vince, A. G. (1984), 'The use of petrology in the study of medieval ceramics: case studies from Southern England', *Medieval Ceramics*, 8, 31–46.

Vince, A. G. (1985), 'Saxon and medieval pottery in London: a review', *Medieval Archaeol.*, 29, 25–93.

Vince, A. G. (ed.) (1991), *Aspects of Saxo-Norman London, 2: Finds and Environmental Evidence*. London and Middlesex Archaeol. Soc. Special Paper 12.

Vince, A. (1993), 'People and places: integrating documents and archaeology in Lincoln', in M. J. Jones (ed.), *Lincoln Archaeology 1992–1993, Annual Report of City of Lincoln Archaeology Unit 5*. Lincoln, 4–5.

Vince, A. (1997), 'Archaeology in Lincoln', in Gläser 1997a, 31–4.

Vince, A. and Jenner, A. (1991), 'The Saxon and early medieval pottery of London', in Vince, 19–119.

Vissak, R. (1999), 'The condition of archaeological research in Tartu after 20 years of rescue excavations', in Vissak and Mäesalu, 33–41.

Vissak, R. and Mäesalu, A. (eds) (1999), *The Medieval Town in the Baltic: Hanseatic History and Archaeology*, Tartu, Estonia.

Vogel, V. (1989), *Schleswig im Mittelalter: Archäologie einer Stadt*. Wachholtz Verlag, Neumünster.

Waldron, T. (1989), 'The effect of humanisation on health: the evidence from skeletal remains', in Serjeantson and Waldron, 55–76.

Walker, J. (1999), 'Late-twelfth and early-thirteenth-century aisled buildings: a comparison', *Vernacular Architecture*, 30, 21–53.

Wallace, P. (1981), 'Dublin's waterfront at Wood quay: 900–1317', in Milne and Hobley, 109–18.

Wallace, P. (1992), *The Viking Age Buildings of Dublin*. Royal Irish Academy, Dublin.

Walton, P. (1991), 'Textiles', in Blair and Ramsay, 319–54.

Walton, P. (1992), 'The dyes', in Crowfoot *et al.*, 199–201.

Ward, J. (1998), 'Townswomen and their households', in R. Britnell (ed.), *Daily Life in the Late Middle Ages*. Sutton, Stroud, 27–42.

Ward, J. C. (1994), 'Elizabeth de Burgh, Lady of Clare (d.1360)', in C. M. Barron and A. Sutton (eds), *Medieval London Widows 1300–1500*. Hambledon, London, 29–46.

Ward, S. W. (1990), *Excavations at Chester: The Lesser Medieval Religious Houses*. Grosvenor Museum Archaeol. Excavation and Survey Reports 6, Chester City Council, Chester.

Ward Perkins, J. B. (1954), *Medieval Catalogue*. London Museum Catalogues No. 7, London Museum, London.

Waters, W. B. (1912), *Church Bells of England*. London.

Watson, B., Brigham, T. and Dyson, T. (2001), *London Bridge: 2000 Years of a River Crossing*. Museum of London Archaeol. Service Monograph 8.

Weatherill, L. (1993), 'The meaning of consumer behaviour in late seventeenth- and early eighteenth-century England', in Brewer and Porter, 206–27.

Weatherill, L. (1996), *Consumer Behaviour and Material Culture in Britain, 1660–1760*. 2nd edn, Blackwell, Oxford.

Webster, L. and Cherry, J. (1973), 'Medieval Britain in 1973', *Medieval Archaeol.*, 17, 138–88.

Weinstock, J. (2002), 'The medieval and post-medieval bone remains from Heigham Street, Norwich', in Atkin and Evans 2002, 220–30.

West, S. E. (1963), Excavations at Cox Lane (1958) and at the Town Defences, Shire Hall Yard, Ipswich (1959). Proc. Suffolk Institute of Archaeology, 29.

Westholm, G. (1997), 'Visby: town history interpreted from archaeological results', in Gläser 1997a, 387–402.

Westholm, G. (1999), 'Gotland and Visby in the Hanseatic trade – preserved traces of times of prosperity', in Gläser, 513–32.

Westholm, G. (2001), 'Visby and Gotland: medieval building development', in Gläser 2001a, 743–63.

Westman, A. (ed.) (1994), Site Manual. Museum of London.

Wheeler, Sir M. (1954), Archaeology from the Earth. Penguin, Harmondsworth.

White, L. (jr) (1981), 'The expansion of technology 500–1500', in Cipolla, 143–74.

White, W. (1988), Skeletal Remains from the Cemetery of St Nicholas Shambles. London and Middlesex Archaeol. Soc. Special Paper 9.

Wilkinson, D. and McWhirr, A. (1998), Cirencester: Anglo-Saxon Church and Medieval Abbey. Cirencester Excavations IV, Cotswold Archaeol. Trust, Cirencester.

Williams, F. (1977), Excavations at Pleshey Castle. Council for Brit. Archaeol. Report 42, London.

Williams, J. H. (1979), St Peter's Street Northampton, Excavations 1973–76. Northampton.

Wilson, B. (1994), 'Mortality patterns, animal husbandry and marketing in and around medieval and post-medieval Oxford', in Hall and Kenward, 103–16.

Wilson, B. and Mee, F. (1998), The Medieval Parish Churches of York: The Pictorial Evidence. Archaeology of York Supplementary Series 1, York Archaeol. Trust, York.

Wilson, C. (1992), The Gothic Cathedral. Rev. edn, Thames and Hudson, London.

Wilson, C. A. (1976), Food and Drink in Britain. Penguin, Harmondsworth.

Wilson, R. (1989), 'The animal bones', in Hassall et al., 259–68.

Wilthew, P. (1987), 'Metallographic examination of medieval knives and shears', in Cowgill et al., 62–74.

Wood, J. (ed.) (1994), Buildings Archaeology: Applications in Practice. Oxbow Books, Oxford.

Wood, M. (1965), The English Medieval House. Dent, London.

Woods, A. (1989), 'Report on Silver Street shelly wares', in P. Miles, J. Young and J. Wacher (eds), A Late Saxon Kiln-site at Silver Street, Lincoln. The Archaeology of Lincoln 17/3.

Worssam, B. (2000), 'The building stones of Rochester Cathedral crypt', Archaeologia Cantiana, 120, 1–22.

Wright, S. M. (1982), 'Much Park Street, Coventry: the development of a medieval street, excavations 1970–74', Trans. Birmingham and Warwickshire Archaeol. Soc., 92, 1–132.

Wyss, M. (1996), Atlas Historique de Saint-Denis, des Origines au XVIIIe siècle. Documents d'Archéologie Française 59, Editions de la Maison des Sciences de L'Homme, Paris.

Yentsch, A. (1991), 'The symbolic divisions of pottery: sex-related attributes of English and Anglo-American household pots', in McGuire and Paynter, 192–230.

Yeoman, P. (1995), Medieval Scotland. Batsford and Historic Scotland.

Young, J. and Vince, A. (in prep.), Corpus of Anglo-Saxon and Medieval Pottery from Lincoln. Lincoln Archaeol. Studies 7, Oxbow Books, Oxford.

Ziegler, P. (1971), The Black Death. Collins, London.

Žulkus, V. (2001), 'Der Hausbau in Klaipeda', in Gläser 2001a, 529–49.

Zupko, R. E. (1968), A Dictionary of English Weights and Measures from Anglo-Saxon Times to the Nineteenth Century. University of Wisconsin Press, Madison.

Index